Divine Teaching:
An Introduction to
Christian Theology

Bruce McDuffee

Divine Teaching:
An Introduction to
Christian Theology

Mark A. McIntosh

Blackwell
Publishing

© 2008 by Mark A. McIntosh

BLACKWELL PUBLISHING
350 Main Street, Malden, MA 02148-5020, USA
9600 Garsington Road, Oxford OX4 2DQ, UK
550 Swanston Street, Carlton, Victoria 3053, Australia

The right of Mark A. McIntosh to be identified as the author of this work has been asserted
in accordance with the UK Copyright, Designs, and Patents Act 1988.

First published 2008 by Blackwell Publishing Ltd

1   2008

Library of Congress Cataloging-in-Publication Data

McIntosh, Mark Allen, 1960–
Divine teaching : an introduction to Christian theology / Mark A. McIntosh.
p. cm.—(Blackwell guides to theology)
Includes bibliographical references and index.
ISBN 978-1-4051-0270-4 (hardcover : alk. paper)—ISBN 978-1-4051-0271-1 (pbk. : alk.
paper)   1. Theology, Doctrinal.   2. Theology.   I. Title.   II. Title: Guide to Christian
theology.

BT15.M35 2008
230—dc22
2007019132

A catalogue record for this title is available from the British Library.

Set in 10 on 13 pt Galliard
by SNP Best-set Typesetter Ltd., Hong Kong
Printed and bound in Singapore
by Fabulous Printers Pte Ltd

The publisher's policy is to use permanent paper from mills that operate a sustainable forestry
policy, and which has been manufactured from pulp processed using acid-free and elementary
chlorine-free practices. Furthermore, the publisher ensures that the text paper and cover board
used have met acceptable environmental accreditation standards.

For further information on
Blackwell Publishing, visit our website at
www.blackwellpublishing.com

For all my students

Contents

Preface

To see whether this is a book that might be of any use to you, you could consider the following. Suppose you had become interested in learning all about a great author. Her works include plays and poems and novels, and you have spent time reading and thinking about many of them – although very often their strange beauty seems to hint at what always remains an elusive depth of meaning that you cannot quite fathom. In the course of your reading, however, you begin to find yourself oddly unsettled and moved by the author; you feel she gives voice to what seems both most wonderful and true about your own life, but also to what is most bitterly flawed or forever lost. You feel that you would somehow like to learn from her, not only about her work, but about everything. You actually try to find out how to reach her. What would it be like to try to learn from her?

The premise of this book is that the real teacher of Christian theology is, in the deepest sense, the author of everything that exists. To study theology would thus mean not only studying the works of this author but trying to imagine what it would be like to learn from the author directly. The author of all things, Christians believe, is God. And this presents us with remarkable opportunities and challenges – to put it mildly. After all, what might happen to would-be theologians who risk trying to learn about reality from God? Perhaps Christian theology might reasonably be expected to focus its energy, in the first instance, upon the seemingly prior question (at least, logically prior) of whether there *is* any such "author" from whom one could learn, either about the author or anything else.

Now let me say that I think this is a very reasonable and interesting question to try to answer, and there are good reasons for doing so. But not much of that project is going to get done in this book – at least not directly or as a foundation for everything else. You see, if you thought, as most Christians *have* thought over the centuries, that God is the best teacher of thinking about God (and everything else as it relates to God), then bracketing God off into a box labeled "hypothetical until proven otherwise" is going to make it difficult to sense the sheer vivacity, wonder, and insight that Christians have experienced in trying to learn from God.

And that would mean you would get only a "Christian theology" that is peculiarly lifeless, a pale polite murmur of its real boisterous self.

So my goal in this book is not so much to recount for you the long history of Christian theology or even to practice it right in front of you, but rather to guide you in trying it a little yourself. My aim is to give you a taste of what Christians think it is like to do theology, that is, to learn from God. In the long run, I expect, this may also give you a reasonable basis upon which to decide whether there *are* any good reasons for thinking that God does actually exist, and is worth listening to – or not. But for the sake of conveying *something* of why Christians do theology and what real point there might be to it, I shall have to leave to you the a posteriori judgment about God's existence and possible ability to communicate with creatures.

In the first three chapters, then, I try to describe what seems to happen to people who become theologians in this deep sense, that is, who learn about God in this very direct sort of way, and what that means for their thinking and talking about God. Then in the remainder of the book I set off into three vast dimensions of the strangely beautiful world of Christian belief that theology explores. Of course, this world is in fact the deep reality of our common universe, with its true spiritual structures and depths and colors and far horizons now made luminous with a new and revealing light. These three dimensions are the mystery of God's life, the mystery of creaturely life, and – as the crucial disclosure of both – the mystery of salvation. Moreover, in these chapters on salvation, God, and us, I organize our foray into three sections, each of which is designed to prepare you for the next. In keeping with the idea of this book as a sort of explorer's guidebook, I've called these sections "Orientation," "Landmarks," and "Pathfinding." In "Orientation" I will give you a basic sense of the big picture, what's at stake, and some of the chief questions. In "Landmarks" we take our bearings in a more advanced way by considering crucial figures in the history of Christian theology, writers whose perspectives have shaped the landscape for generations. Finally in "Pathfinding" we think our way out towards a few aspects of the subject that suggest paths heading forward, or particularly significant questions that face any further exploring.

At the risk of frightening you off, let me recall for you that Christian theology is not, in its most elemental form, a terribly tame and dutiful discipline; students of theology need to be intrepid and bold, even passionate. Near the end of the twentieth century, the Swiss Catholic Hans Urs von Balthasar once observed: "We need individuals who devote their lives to the glory of theology, that fierce fire burning in the dark night of adoration and obedience, whose abysses it illuminates" (1989: 160). And so I dedicate this book to all my students – past, present, and to come. As divine ideas come to life in their thoughts, my students have been teachers to me and I am most grateful to them all.

Especially I wish to thank all our wonderful graduate students in Loyola University's Department of Theology, particularly the remarkably wise, patient, and talented students whose research assistance has been invaluable to me over the years: thanks to all and especially to Derek Anderson, Denise Starkey, David Creech, Martin Cain, and Andrea Hollingsworth. And, as always, my deepest thanks to my colleagues at Loyola, the splendid team at Blackwell Publishing, and my dear family.

Mark A. McIntosh
June 2007

Part I
Becoming a Theologian

Chapter 1

How God Makes Theologians

Astonishment and Theological Virtue

Just about the worst thing that could happen to Christian theologians is for them to be taken too seriously. I don't mean to imply that I and my colleagues are all farcical figures, of course. Perhaps we could be compared to children wading in the sea: studiously cautious, not intending to get wet, but magnificently upended by the vast, joyful rolling of the tide. The tide pulling at theologians is God, trying to get us to float, even swim, or at least admit we have no business floundering along on two feet in such a current.

I picture theologians this way (myself included) because we are essentially hapless folk, ever prone to manage and clarify what remains, mercifully, beyond our grasp. The divine currents we paddle about in – grace, for example, or forgiveness, or resurrection – are, right down to their last filaments of eternal glory, entirely unaccountable to us, unexpected, and undeserved. The ordinary cycles of everyday life, by contrast, are conveniently predictable; they amble amiably along into the sleek charts and scholarly monographs in which we render them as subjects of study. Most of us contemporary theologians, soberly trained in the best scholarly methods, try our hardest to analyze the divine realities by dutifully herding them into the approved pens of dialectical arguments and critical studies. Yet when we open our mouths to discourse of deity, out come skirling parables, hopelessly impossible histories, and such reckless extravagances as the idea of a God who refuses to stay exclusively divine, and a savior who's such a miserable failure he cannot even save himself. As the Apostle Paul said, the whole thing seems comically weak and foolish by any human standard you like (1 Corinthians 1: 18–31).

Who can blame us if we theologians try to remain inconspicuous? The danger is that we will attempt to blend in all too well; we will master the academic and ecclesiastical arts so proficiently that people will not notice how outrageous is the subject of our work. We may even manage, perhaps without realizing it, to sub-stitute for the outlandishness of Christian faith, a gray orderliness in which nothing unexpected ever happens or ever could. But every once in a great while, theolo-gians of such good humor and humility come along that they are content to teach the truth about God precisely by *letting* the ludicrous inadequacies of their art appear in broad daylight. They let the divine truth shimmer gracefully in the soaking garments of their patiently constructed arguments, having walked through yet another doorway with grace like a pail of water perched comically above. That is my warning and my confession. We theologians cannot show you the *reality* of grace in a proper argument. We cannot explain it according to rational necessities. We can only gesture in what we believe is the right direction and hope our hand waving will entice you close enough to get splashed, indeed immersed, yourself.

This does not mean that the study of theology is a fruitless task. Like the study of poetry or music in a university setting, academic theology can accomplish any number of useful purposes. It should shed light on the history and forms of the-ologizing, on the ideas and imagery we try to compose with, on the nature and interrelationship of the thoughts of vast swathes of humankind. But at the end of the day these chores ought to leave one more sensitive to the truth and beauty that beckons ungraspably from within poetry or music or theology, not earnestly confident that one has wrestled reality to the ground. While writing one of the most voluminous efforts in theology in human history, the Swiss theologian Karl Barth (1886–1968) paused to remark:

> If anyone should *not* find himself astonished and filled with wonder when he becomes involved in one way or another with theology, he would be well advised to consider once more, from a certain remoteness and without prejudice, what is involved in this undertaking. The same holds true for any who should have accomplished the feat of *no longer* being astonished, instead of becoming continually *more* astonished all the time that he concerns himself with this subject. When he reconsiders the subject, however, such a man might find that astonishment wells up within him anew, or perhaps even for the first time. And this time such wonder might not desert him but might rather become increasingly powerful in him. That astonishment should remain or become wholly foreign to him is scarcely conceivable. But should that happen, both he and theology would fare better if he would devote his time to some other occupation. . . . If such astonishment is lacking, the whole enterprise of even the best theologian would canker at the roots. On the other hand, as long as even a poor theologian is capable of astonishment, he is not lost to the fulfillment of his task.[1]

As I have been suggesting, this recurring astonishment that theologians suffer has everything to do with the reality they seek to understand.

By now you may be sufficiently alarmed to suffer at least some mild wonderment yourself. You wanted an introduction to Christian theology, but so far you've been hearing about the peculiar fate of theologians. Indeed, as you probably noticed, I titled this crucial gateway chapter, "How God *Makes* Theologians." Why? What is it about theology that requires such attention to the impact its subject matter has upon its students? After all, studying the properties of chemical compounds doesn't turn you into the chemicals you are studying, nor do we imagine that such a metamorphosis would greatly assist the process of understanding. The trouble and astonishment of theology is that something like this does (or at least, potentially, can) happen in its case. A mysterious affinity kindles between theology's object and theologians. As this happens, theologians start to catch glimpses of reality, shimmering and beckoning far beyond the proper frames and disciplines of theology itself. Like children playing at the water's edge, theologians find themselves tugged by the tide and tumbled by waves that delight and lure them deeper. Of course, scholars in many disciplines find themselves enraptured by their objects of study. This certainly happens (or should happen!) in theology also, but I'm afraid there is something yet more unsettling going on.

Consider, by analogy, the difference between studying the chemical composition of a rock and studying the psychology of a human person. It's true that in both cases good scholars will grow fascinated by their objects of study, and devoted to the truth about them that they are seeking to discover and understand. Really great scholars might even speak about trying to learn from the rock or the human person, about letting the object of study become, in a sense, their teacher. But this is clearly going to be quite different in the two cases. The rock will speak only by means of an enigmatic silence, benign but undeniably stony. But the human person will be a much more active participant in the work: not simply filling out forms corresponding to the scholar's research template, but perhaps interrupting, correcting, transforming through conversation everything the scholar may have thought were the real data.

And what if the person you were studying had especially peculiar habits, like severe sleepwalking or refusing to talk with you except over gargantuan meals of fresh mussels in which you were required to partake? Pretty soon, if you really wanted to understand, you might begin to develop new habits yourself – allowing you to study your sleepwalking mussel-eater more adroitly and naturally. At first, you would tell yourself, I'm not really a nocturnal person and I don't really like mollusks of any kind whatsoever. Yet there you are, every evening, gorging with your research subject on mussels and trailing along a few hours later through the darkness on the nightly ramble. What has happened? You have become, at least for study purposes, a learner, an apprentice to the object of your study – who has in fact become your teacher. And for a while at least, you have acquired something of a new way of being, new habits of existence that fit you for your study encounters. We could call these new habits your sleepwalking mussel-eater research virtues; they are the dispositions that allow you a certain flourishing and even excellence as a student of sleepwalking mussel-eaters.

But now suppose that your research subject were even more peculiar still. Suppose that as you drew near, this person, astonishingly, told you the truth about *yourself*: both the truth you had been afraid to admit and a yet deeper truth you had never known but always longed to hear. Suppose this person was so available for you, so vulnerably honest and self-disclosing, and showed such fidelity towards your own work, that you began to develop a high degree of faith in the person's essential goodness and reliability. Over time, such a research subject might engender a fair portion of both humility and hope within you, a sense that your study would indeed take you somewhere wonderful and real. And suppose that over time you began to catch glimpses of your research subject helping others with such generosity and breathtaking selflessness that you began to be inspired yourself, feeling a kindred sort of love for people, and gradually finding yourself able to converse with your subject more freely, to understand more deeply, as you yourself began to sense something of this passion your subject had for others. In such a case, you would indeed be studying by a kind of apprenticeship, with your subject as your true teacher. Moreover, the research virtues that would have begun to grow in you – those habits equipping you to succeed in just being around and understanding this person – these virtues would have truly begun to transform you. *Faith, and hope, and love* taking root in you would point to a remarkable subject of study.

Thomas Aquinas (*c*.1225–74) calls such habits the "theological virtues," for they turn out to equip one to participate in a theological life, a life of *theo-logia*, of speech and meaning and truth about God and, astonishingly, *with* God (see Thomas Aquinas, *Summa Theologiae* I–II, question 62).These dispositions are the making of theologians; for they are the impact this subject (God) has upon those who draw near. As Thomas puts it, these theological virtues are the way God's life re-creates a human life as that human life partakes in God's life: "as kindled wood partakes of the nature of fire."[2]

So this is why it's worth talking a bit about what makes a theologian – because it offers us a glimpse of the "research subject" who makes such an impression on the theologian (indeed, a subject who is in the researcher like fire is in wood, according to Thomas Aquinas). We notice that, unlike having a rock or a sleep-walking mussel-eater as a research subject, the theologian is trying to engage with someone who seems to be supremely free, whose mystery is only available to the researcher by an act of free self-disclosure that is most likely to be visible in the peculiar influence it has upon the researcher. This subject is not like a lab specimen or even someone you can coax into the research program with the promise of a free meal. That's probably what makes theologians seem so hapless sometimes. The deepest truth of the one they seek to understand is only expressible, sometimes, in the transformations of their own lives.

Where do we get this idea that trying to understand God is going to have such a strange impact on people? From the same Paul the Apostle who said the truth of God seems foolish by human standards. Paul considers the variety of ways that early followers of Jesus express their common life, and he wonders about the leading impulses and gifts they each manifest. He thinks this gifted, transforming, communal life is in fact an ongoing organic expression of *Jesus'* continuing life in the world, constantly being brought to life by what Paul calls the Spirit. This means that the habits and virtues and gifts of the Christian community are in some mysterious way animated by the same Spirit who animated and directed Jesus. And guess what, in Paul's view, are the three most important of these communal habits of reflecting-Jesus-by-the-Spirit: the same three that Thomas calls the theological virtues. "And now faith, hope, and love abide, these three; and the greatest of these is love" (1 Corinthians 13: 13). What am I saying here?

I'm suggesting that (if we take Paul into account) we can be a good bit more precise about what happens to theologians, and why, and *how theologians are formed by their encounter with God.* For what Paul seems to be saying is that when you see these characteristics (faith, hope, and love) showing up in anybody – even a theologian – what you have going on is not just a little of the divine way of life impressing itself within the life of a human being. More than that, you have someone whose life has begun to partake of Christ's way of being in the world; what you have is someone whose way of thinking, and acting, and desiring is being inspired by the same Spirit who led Jesus towards the truth of himself and his relationship with one he called Abba. It is these three – the Spirit, Jesus, Abba – who seem to be the continually flowing source of Christian theology, and are the real teachers of theologians. In fact, we could even say that theology is constantly in danger of getting carried away – from a respectable discipline managed by theologians to a mysterious sharing in God's way of life, God's talk (*theo-logia*), God's knowing and loving of Godself. This would be theology in the most absolute and perfect sense.

Why do Christians think this?

Resurrection to Pentecost: Where Christian Theology Begins

Perhaps the simplest way to answer that question is to look at how early followers of Jesus tried to think about what had happened to them. We're looking for clues about what it's like to encounter God, and how that encounter might shape the way you think and feel about things (in analogy to how hanging around a sleep-walker mussel-eater might shape you). The New Testament portrays the disciples as not only routinely failing to understand Jesus but as frightened and disappointed to the point of abandoning him at the time of his crucifixion. Something which they came to describe as Jesus' resurrection began to change this, and began to form the disciples in a new way.

Let me introduce a brief primary source and commentary here, in order to reflect very directly on this transformation. Please believe me when I say that the most important thing I can offer you in this book is likely to be some exposure to these primary sources and some assistance in thinking through them. So don't skip this bit!

Roughly thirty years after Jesus' death and resurrection, Paul wrote a letter directed to the Jesus-following community in Rome. It gives an indispensable early glimpse of how the events surrounding Jesus were coming to inform the life of the community of his followers throughout the ancient Mediterranean world. My elucidation of the text is keyed by verse numbers to the original source. Most of what follows in this chapter will depend upon what we can notice here in thinking about these passages from the Letter to the Romans.

The Letter of Paul to the Romans, 6: 3–11

3 Do you not know that all of us who have been baptized into Christ Jesus were baptized into his death?

3–4 The early followers of Jesus adapted the ritual washing of baptism to become a sign of initiation into Jesus' own death and new life. Jesus' death is already understood as somehow *sharable*, an event or state of existence that remains open and available for those seeking it.

4 Therefore we have been buried with him by baptism into his death, so that, just as Christ was raised from the dead by the glory of the Father, so we too might walk in newness of life.

4 Paul understands Jesus to have been "raised" into a new state of aliveness, intense presence, and sheer vivacity by the Father; and he understands this to be an act of the Father's "glory," the shining forth of divine power in a manifest way. We might say that this power of the Father, when it appears *within* history, takes the form of the resurrection. In other words, the creative and giving life of the Father, shining forth within our world, looks like and indeed *is* a human being alive again entirely beyond the power of death. In other texts (e.g., 2 Cor. 5: 17) Paul describes this form of the Father's giving within our world as an event of new creation.

5 For if we have been united with him in a death like his, we will certainly be united with him in a resurrection like his. **6** We know that our old self was crucified with him so that the body of sin might be destroyed, and we might no longer be enslaved to sin.

5–6 Sharing in Jesus' death makes possible a sharing in this raising into a new life by the power of the Father. The crucial feature to note here is the way Paul envisions the death and resurrection of Christ as reaching into the lives of believers. Paul speaks of the "old self" as an identity we are forced into over time by sin (we might think of the ways in which we are sometimes forced into false positions by other people's expectations or peer pressure or our own poor judgments). This "old self" is for Paul not really the truth about us but rather a kind of lie we have been forced into accepting as the truth. Think, for example, of how the victims of racism are often forced to conceive of themselves in the demeaning and derogatory frame of mind used by the dominant groups. Paul believes that in accepting crucifixion, Jesus is able to enter these false or old selves, these sinful constructions of personal life, and let them be "destroyed."

Because of this, believers who "have been united with him in a death like his," that is, who have surrendered their old false selves completely, "will certainly be united with him in a resurrection like his."

7 For whoever has died is freed from sin.

7 In other words, a new identity, a new sense of self comes to be formed, and in Paul's view this is the beginning of a person's new life flowing no longer from the dominating and enslaving patterns of sin but from the liberating power of God.

8 But if we have died with Christ, we believe that we will also live with him.

8 Just as Jesus' dying is the power that puts the self enslaved by sin to death, so also Jesus' rising into new life is the power that generates a new self for believers.

9 We know that Christ, being raised from the dead, will never die again; death no longer has dominion over him.
10 The death he died, he died to sin, once for all; but the life he lives, he lives to God.

9–10 Paul conceives of what has happened to Jesus as an irreversible breakthrough into freedom ("death no longer has dominion over him"), and a transfer into a new and infinitely abundant source of life that is not in any way dominated by sin or death or fear or any of the things that control people. For Paul this new source of identity or personal existence is God; Jesus now "lives to God," meaning that Jesus' whole being now springs directly from God's infinite life and freedom as compared with the limited biological life (further weakened by sin) that normally sources one's existence.

11 So you also must consider yourselves dead to sin and alive to God in Christ Jesus.

11 Paul is convinced that this transfer of the source of one's existence from the dominating slavery of sin to the liberating freedom of God is now also happening to believers in Christ. This dying and rising is the impact that Jesus has on those who live in fidelity and companionship with him.

In this foundational passage, we have a preliminary sense of how early Christians understood their life to be shaped and formed, in a continually renewing way, by the events of Jesus' death and resurrection. Most of what would later come to be regarded as Christian theology springs from this ongoing transformation of the community. This is true in two senses: first, because the basic *beliefs* of the Christian community (which theology explores, seeking deeper understanding and coherence) all arise in various ways from this interaction of the community with Christ; and second, because the very *character* of the community in search of theological understanding is also continually shaped by the community's ongoing encounter with Christ. In fact it is this latter feature that gives rise to those chief characteristics or gifts (faith, hope, and love) that Paul highlights in his First Letter to the Corinthians and that Thomas Aquinas discusses as the "theological virtues."

I can give you a little better picture of this integrity between the community's beliefs and its character, and how they both spring from the community's encounter with God, by looking at another passage from the same Letter of Paul to the Romans.

Letter to the Romans 8: 9–11, 14–17

9 But you are not in the flesh; you are in the Spirit, since the Spirit of God dwells in you. Anyone who does not have the Spirit of Christ does not belong to him. 10 But if Christ is in you, though the body is dead because of sin, the Spirit is life because of righteousness. 11 If the Spirit of him who raised Jesus from the dead dwells in you, he who raised Christ from the dead will give life to your mortal bodies also through his Spirit that dwells in you.

9–10 To live "in the flesh" for Paul is to live according to the sources of the old self, namely, a ceaseless necessity and domination by the powers holding influence over one's life. To be affiliated with Christ, by contrast, means to be animated and enlivened by the same Spirit who animated him. Living as the followers of Christ comes to mean living from and with and for Christ, who dwells hiddenly (or mystically) within the patterns of the community's life together. In this sense the "body" may be passing away, living within the structures of the broken and sinful world, but the Spirit who enlivens Christ is now also the Spirit of Christ's community of followers.

11 Paul now refers also to "him to who raised Jesus from the dead." This is a crucial moment, for we have here (1) the One who by means of this Spirit raises Jesus from the dead, (2) Jesus who has died and is raised to new life, and (3) the Spirit who is the agent of this new life and freedom. In other words we have the Three who in later Christian reflection would be named the Holy Trinity of Father, Son, and Holy Spirit. Paul's point for the moment is simply that the very same one who raised Jesus will also pour out this life-giving Spirit within the community of Jesus. This is doubly remarkable, for it means not only that in some sense the community lives as Jesus lives – directly from the Spirit – within it and as its very head and heart; but it also means that the community stands in the same relationship to the Father as Jesus does. Both are raised by the very same Spirit from death to a new kind of life that reflects the glory of divine life within the world of time.

14 For all who are led by the Spirit of God are children of God.

14 Those who follow Jesus, who are "led by the Spirit of God," even as Jesus was so led in his earthly life, are also with Jesus "children of God." Note again the three-fold influence of God upon the community:

Jesus becomes the pattern and form of its life, the Spirit becomes the guiding inspiration and enlivening power, and in this way the community together discovers a new identity as "children of God."

15 For you did not receive a spirit of slavery to fall back into fear, but you have received a spirit of adoption. When we cry, "Abba! Father!" **16** it is that very Spirit bearing witness with our spirit that we are children of God,

15–16 This new relationship with the One who raised Jesus from the dead is underlined by Paul, precisely in terms of its formative impact upon the community. For the community's new identity, the new spirit that animates it is not "a spirit of slavery" leading "back into fear," but on the contrary "a spirit of adoption." In other words, the transformation from an old self driven by fear and necessity to a new self set free is a transformation bestowed through relationship with the very same One whom Jesus called "Abba." This new relationship seems to be opened up and made available to the community through Jesus; he cries out "Abba!" within and on behalf of the community, and so recovers for it this lost or broken relationship with the Creator and giver of all life.

17 and if children, then heirs, heirs of God and joint heirs with Christ – if, in fact, we suffer with him so that we may also be glorified with him.

17 The ability of the community to pray in and through Christ to the Father by the inward working of the Spirit is, says Paul, the witness to the community's new relationship to the Father. Sharing in Christ's suffering, as we saw above, sets believers free from their old selves controlled by sin and fear; and this opens up for them Jesus' own trusting relationship with the Father, so that they may come to be raised into that eternal life and thus "be glorified with him."

This passage from Romans 8 shows how utterly the ongoing life of the Christian community is (in Paul's view) a kind of living icon of divine activity in the world. The Church comes into being as that bit of the world within which God makes a finite, historical sign of what God is doing all the time and everywhere: forming the community into a new pattern of life (Christ-like), filling it with the Spirit of that life of new freedom and trust, and so drawing it into a new identity given through its new relationship with God as the outpouring Source or Father of all life.

Why is all this important for figuring out how theologians do their job? Because it shows how, exactly, we might notice God's teaching presence as the source of theology. And this for two reasons. First, because God is the acting agent who re-creates the new community and brings it to life with a new identity as God's beloved child; in other words, God is the acting agent continually evoking and provoking that new identity and *character*, that new way of being in the world. Second, God is equally the acting agent who inspires and incites the Church into some *teaching* about what is happening to it. And as Christians reflect on what happens to them – from the resurrection of Jesus to the giving of the Spirit at Pentecost – they notice a trinitarian pattern to their reflective life.

Let me put it this way:

1   Jesus' followers are shaped by him into a new form of life that shares his form of life; so also are their beliefs about what God is doing shaped and given a form in thought and word and eventually creed. Following Jesus, as opposed to following someone else, gives a very definite form to life and thought.

2   Jesus' followers are led by the Spirit into an ever deepening sense of new identity; this happens as they discover, through the Spirit, the meaning of Christ's relationship with the Father and their share in that relationship. So also are they led ever deeper into the truth and meaning of their beliefs about what God is doing.

3   Jesus' followers, formed in Christ and led by the Spirit, are continually faring into the presence of the Father who in Christ and through the Spirit raises them from death to life. So also they are journeying into that state of blessed intimacy with God when their faith and *beliefs* will come to an end, being consummated in the vision of God and perfect beatitude (faith will be superseded by sight, and belief by knowing).

What I have been suggesting here is that the character of Christian life and the beliefs of Christian faith are really two expressions of the same activity, namely, God's way of re-creating the world. One expression takes the form of practices of compassion and worship, and the other takes the form of beliefs, teachings, and a ceaseless quest of faith towards understanding. But both the practices of Christian life and the theory of Christian faith are human expressions of God acting within the lives and minds of the believing community. And both expressions have a markedly three-fold or trinitarian pattern. This means that theology itself, as the quest of faith for understanding, is really an expression of divine life at work re-creating the world in the little laboratory of the Church. We could think of this trinitarian life of God as the hidden spring of theology:

1   At the still center of every theological formulation, even the most cumbersome and abstruse, is really the formative and expressive power of Christ the *Word* provoking the church into reflective teaching.

2   At the yearning core of every theologian's search for understanding is the ceaseless striving of the *Spirit*, pulling the church into an ever deeper sharing in its new identity in Christ.

3   And at the unseen end of all theological endeavor is the ineffable reality of the *Father*, calling all things into the perfect fullness of their truth.

For many Christians across the centuries, this has meant that theology is really a form of prayer or communion with God, in which, ultimately, the thinking of the theologian about God comes to life as *God's presence* within the life of the theologian.

But Can You Study Theology without Having to Believe?

Does all this mean that everyone who studies theology needs to be a believer or lead a mystical life? The short answer is simply, "No" (though, if that should happen, you need not be alarmed). One can study the coherence and interrelationship of Christian ideas and even work out for oneself something of how they might shed light on many other topics, all without necessarily being a believer oneself. It would, on the other hand, be a most peculiar study of Christian theology which was quite unaware of what Christians themselves understood to be its hidden source of life.

By the time of early modernity, however, precisely this mystery of divine life had become a disputed question rather than a foundational axiom. So whereas earlier eras of theology had assumed the living priority of divine agency and teaching, this was very far from being a comfortable starting place for modern theology. This has led, I fear, to an unfortunate stiltedness and awkwardness when the subject of theology comes up in the academy, because the living spring of theology – in encounter with God – has had to be soberly left out of the discussion.[3] But we can, I think, make a useful and legitimate distinction between needing to believe in God in order to study theology (which I agree is not always necessary), and needing to understand that Christian communities themselves believe that *theology comes to birth because of their ongoing encounter with God*. The latter point is quite crucial, because without it our picture of theology would be gravely distorted.

One needs, in other words, to entertain the idea (which Christians believe) that Christian theology is an expression of an ongoing transformation of the world in encounter with God; otherwise one will not be studying Christian theology at all but only a boringly lifeless taxidermy of it in which nothing unexpected, gloriously unnecessary, or unbelievable can ever happen or be considered. And it is, Christians believe, precisely these sorts of wonder and astonishment that characterize the authentic impact of God on the world, and so on theology.

This is not such an odd assumption with which to engage in academic study. Many of us have accepted that we did not necessarily have to believe in this or that concept or theory in order to try to study its features and coherence, to understand its origins and its meaning for those who interpret the world by means of it. I do not necessarily have to believe in the truth of Marxism or even in the existence of quarks and gluons in order to study political philosophy or quantum physics. But I do have to be sufficiently attuned to what Marxists and quantum physicists think and say so that I can begin to understand their theories from the inside. The alternative would be simply to translate everything they say into my own terms and my own way of thinking about everything. But suppose it is precisely my own terms and my own way of thinking about everything that is incapable of conceiving the essential ideas of Marxists or quantum physicists? Nothing new or astonishing could ever really "get in."

I would be like a person who tries to understand Spanish by translating everything into English; I would never learn to think in Spanish or perceive reality in terms of Hispanic culture. I would have a kind of pale, insipid, Anglo version of what is in reality vibrant and vivacious. Furthermore, I would never have access to the particularly deft instrument that Hispanic culture could give me for exploring certain features of life. By analogy, theology (along with many other disciplines) serves as a particular kind of instrument, an apt conceptuality, for exploring various dimensions of life. And, clearly, assimilating theology's own mode of reflection to those of, say, cultural anthropology or philosophy or psychology, will only short-circuit theology's unique aptness for getting at truth in certain ways that other disciplines do not.

Perhaps I am needlessly belaboring this point. You may be perfectly happy exploring theology as an exotic realm of thought without feeling the least need to believe everything it has to say. If so, bravo for you; you are already going to find far more of interest than the sort of students who begin by asking theology not to talk about anything which they don't already know.

Perhaps you are wondering, on the other hand, whether I really mean to suggest that Christian theology is not in fact actually true or that having Christian faith makes very little difference to the theological endeavor. Let me try to take each of these concerns in turn. First, of course I think Christian theology is really true, indeed (speaking personally) I believe it bears within it a truth more truthful than anything else I can think of. But as I've been opining all along, this truth is not something I can just prove to you as an act of logical prestidigitation; it is a truth more like the truth you discover in getting to know someone with whom you've begun falling in love. Old marriage rites had the happy pair promising themselves to each other by saying, "I plight thee my troth," troth being the word (emerging from Old English) that meant truth precisely as pledged fidelity and loyalty.

The truth theology bears within itself is this kind of truth that discovers itself to people in a relationship with someone (God) who is faithful to them. This is a good example of how reducing Christian theology exclusively to the terms and concepts and logic of everything we already know is a disaster. Because if I try to translate theology this way into a series of truths that I can somehow prove to you according to all the things you already know, then theology's real truth – its truth as discovered through relationship with God – will become pristinely eclipsed by the smaller, tidier, and much more manageable kinds of truth that I can demonstrate. But of course, once again, we'd have arrived not at real Christian theology but a chilly simulacrum with not even a hint of the poignant depths and heart-stopping heights of the real thing. So somehow, good academic study of theology has to suggest the intelligibility and the truthfulness of Christian theology without constricting the full scope of those to an academician's ivory tower.

In an interesting lecture entitled "Theology in the university," the physicist and theologian John Polkinghorne remarks:

> Theology has a natural role in an age of science just because it shares with modern science this quest for intelligibility. A theological faculty is a necessary presence in a true university because the search for knowledge is incomplete if it does not include in its aim gaining knowledge of the Creator as well as gaining knowledge of creatures. The unity of knowledge is fractured if theology is excluded.[4]

So the common quest for the truth and intelligibility of existence, which academic disciplines are privileged to pursue, is not somehow politely put aside whenever theologians happen to swan into a classroom. Polkinghorne's point is that theology is deft at pursuing an aspect of reality that some other disciplines may not be; my point is congruent but slightly different, namely that theologians not only pursue a different aspect of reality, but that their exposure to this reality may, in important and useful ways, shape their personal capacities for knowing this dimension of reality. By contrast, as one theologian famously observed, one doesn't expect necessarily to become personally warmer by studying the laws of thermodynamics; whereas studying the object of theology may, if the theologian is honest and open, improve the level of communication and interaction with theology's object of study.

As to the question of faith and theology, I have to make a little confession: my personal hope is that everyone who studies Christian theology will in fact be given (should this be desired) the gift of faith. But, in the view of all this that I've been proposing, the gift of faith is entirely up to God anyway, and so neither here nor there for academic purposes. You may escape your study of theology perfectly unscathed by faith. In any case, for the purposes of *studying* Christian theology, it is adequate simply to notice and ponder the mysterious role that Christians believe God plays in shaping their life and thought. So, without insisting in the least that you, gentle readers, must all become theologians yourselves, let me sketch very briefly some turning points in a theological life. This should give us a final, further, sense of what Christians think happens to those whom God lures into encounter and how that gives rise to all the various ideas that Christians have.

Chapter 2

Strange Calling: Theologians as Adventurers, Pirates, Mystics, and Sages

Adventure: Continuing Conversion of the Theologian

In the middle of World War II in Europe, Simone Weil (1909–43) was writing about beauty and the order of the world. She was a brilliant adventurer, traveling *ad-venturam* (Latin for "towards the future"). And she was speaking of being lured by a reality more real than the shabby and brutal pseudo-reality that was consuming people all around her. In her view this devouring world leaks out from a strange dislocation of the world from truth, a dislocation that befalls us whenever individuals or nations or causes place themselves at the center of everything and try to make the rest revolve around themselves:

> We live in a world of unreality and dreams. To give up our imaginary position as the center, to renounce it, not only intellectually but in the imaginative part of our soul, that means to awaken to what is real and eternal, to see the true light and hear the true silence. A transformation then takes place at the very roots of our sensibility, in our immediate reception of sense impressions and psychological impressions.[1]

Weil was convinced that only if human beings were lured out of themselves would they make contact with the really real. Not that the human ego is unreal, but that its mapping of everything in terms of itself inevitably distorts reality, and diminishes it to the ego's grasp. But if the eye catches a glimpse of something immeasurably beautiful, something awesomely beyond any grasp, then humankind may become adventurous and escape the tidy prison of its small certainties. "A transformation then takes place at the very roots of our sensibility," says Weil; the very way such a person relates to the world becomes different, mysteriously lamed like Jacob after wrestling with the angel (see Genesis 32: 22ff.): less able to control, but more willing to receive beyond all expectations.

Another thinker, possibly the most influential theologian Christianity has ever known, noticed, like Weil, this curious link between egocentric possessiveness and narrowness of understanding. In his masterwork, *The Trinity*, Augustine of Hippo (354–430) describes the soul's anxiety to possess more and more for itself, as leading it, tragically, to perceive less and less of what is really there:

> The soul, loving its own power, slides away from the whole which is common to all into the part which is its own private property. By following God's directions and being perfectly governed by his laws it could enjoy the whole universe of creation; but by the apostasy of pride which is called the beginning of sin it strives to grab something more than the whole and to govern it by its own laws; and because there is nothing more than the whole it is thrust back into anxiety over a part, and so by being greedy for more it gets less. . . . It drags the deceptive semblances of bodily things inside, and plays about with them in idle meditation until it cannot even think of anything divine except as being such.[2]

Augustine's own personal series of often painful conversions left him acutely aware of the self's deceptive cunning and its tendency to cocoon itself within ego-gratifying fantasies of every kind. The result, says Augustine, is a barely noticeable shriveling of reality – even the reality of God – to the constraints of the mind's own concepts, imaginative constructs, and desires. The possibility that reality could be larger than this is conceivable to such a mind only as a threat.

Theology, in the deepest sense, is the complete reversal of this. Theology takes place when the theologian, lured by ungraspable truth, ceases to devour everything and is herself or himself "devoured," transformed by a reality too real to be, in Augustine's terms, dragged back into the mind's manipulations. In Simone Weil's view, theological formation is like an adventure into a labyrinth:

> The beauty of the world is the mouth of a labyrinth. The unwary individual who on entering takes a few steps is soon unable to find the opening. Worn out, with nothing to eat or drink, in the dark, separated from his dear ones, and from everything he loves and is accustomed to, he walks on without knowing anything or hoping anything, incapable even of discovering whether he is really going forward or merely turning round on the same spot. But this affliction is as nothing compared with the danger threatening him. For if he does not lose courage, if he goes on walking, it is absolutely certain that he will finally arrive at the center of the labyrinth. And there God is waiting to eat him. Later he will go out again, but he will be changed, he will have become different, after being eaten and digested by God. Afterward he will stay near the entrance so that he can gently push all those who come near into the opening.[3]

There are places and times in one's life, Weil seems to be saying, when we are lured beyond our customary view of the world. We become entranced by a poet, or a child we know approaches death, or we realize in the face of someone's forgiveness how much we have hurt him, or a vibration of iridescent green hummingbird hovers for a moment before our eyes – in such moments a journey may begin from which we will never come back as we used to be.

Christians believe that such a moment as this overtook Jesus' first followers shortly after his crucifixion. They wandered into a labyrinth, an empty tomb, and although they seemed simply to follow a trail of their own collapsing expectations, infidelities, and betrayals they were accosted instead by a love and forgiveness so intensely alive they could not believe it was the same one who had died until he showed them his hands and his side. They thought they were consuming his life, but the more he gave himself into their hands – "Take, eat; this is my body" (Matthew 26: 26) – the more they seemed to be taken into his life, taken up to become his Body. Theology in the truest sense begins with this adventure, this conversion or transformation towards a new way of experiencing and understand- ing reality. While we may very well study Christian theology without this having happened to us ourselves, we will never really see what theology is about until and unless we recognize that true theologians see everything from this new perspective, from this sharing in the dying and rising of Jesus.

Piracy: Thinking Analogically

Theology is this openness to a reality that gives itself away but remains ever won- drously ungraspable. It is a perspective increasingly free from the anxious need to fix everything within one's usual terms of control. And yet, urged along by a com- manding astonishment at the really real, theologians can't help behaving like pirates, at least linguistically and conceptually. It is not entirely their fault, remem- ber. Theologians have been lured by God to adventure out beyond the usual decent use of words, and they have been made divinely discontented with the common shrinking of reality into concepts that are too small. And so they barely pause before outrageously commandeering ordinary common words and ideas to express what really lies beyond them. "It is this piratical and savage behaviour of theologians towards words," remarks Herbert McCabe, that chiefly characterizes theological language. Why? Because there are no other words to use and the reality theologians are desperate to speak of is marvelously beyond the words they have. Theologians in general, says McCabe, have an interest

> in failure in that they have to be constantly aware of the inadequacy of the language they have to use. Our [normal decent use of] language does not encompass but simply strains towards the mystery that we encounter in Christ. . . . The theologian uses a word by stretching it to breaking point, and it is precisely as it breaks that the communication, if any, is achieved. He takes a perfectly good pagan word like "God" or "sacred" or "prayer" and twists it out of all recognition: and he does this not from verbal sadism but because there are not any other words to use.[4]

The problem for theology is that people will tend to tie up the words' meanings to their finite usage, whereas a theologian is keen to sail the words into an uncharted *surplus* of meaning.

And that's because theology is trying to talk about a reality that is not a force alongside us among all the other forces in the universe (only bigger, tougher, smarter, and invisible). So theology grabs hold of a language that is used for talking about things doing their thing in the universe. But theology is trying to talk about a reality who is absolutely and by definition *not* one of the things of the universe, or even the universe itself, but the reason *why* there is a universe rather than simply nothing. That is why theology becomes so joyfully abandoned whenever it can get its hands on a good metaphor (in which one reality is used to provoke our imaginative thought about another quite different from it) or a decent analogy. Take the use of the deliciously analogy-prone word "love."

Let's say I'm using it to talk about my gluttonous urge for ice cream: "I would love a chocolate malt." And then in total meltdown I cry out just two hours later, "I would really love a raspberry sundae with lots and lots of nuts on it." Now besides my personal gastronomic degradation what we have here is a case of univocal language ("uni-" as in one or single): language that conveys a single or nearly identical meaning in different cases. For although I might well be voicing a slightly different compulsion in the cases of the malt and the sundae, it is really all about the same urge for ice cream. The complete opposite of this use of language would be equivocal speech, in which I use the same word to say, equally, completely different things: as in "I love it when our dog chases rabbits" and "I love my wife." In this case we really have two utterly disparate cases, the first referring to my sadly fading hope for a few survivors from summer vegetable gardening and the second referring to my lifelong companion, best friend, and spouse.

Neither univocal nor equivocal language are much use (and are often dangerous) for theology. Univocal language would keep theology tied up at the mooring, able to explore nothing about a God who is not among the things of the universe. Equivocal language would give up exploring altogether, despairing of ever understanding anything truly about God. But Christian theology (for reasons we'll see in later chapters) has recourse to a middle way between these extremes of speech, and this is analogical language. While theories of analogy can become positively baroque in complexity, for our purposes the main idea is graspable in this example: "I love my children" and (analogically) "I love my wife." The word "love" does not name exactly the same (univocal) reality in both cases, for I love my wife and my children in different ways and with different sorts of feelings. Nevertheless, neither does the word "love" name a completely equivocal set of possibilities, for there is a real parallel between the two sorts of love. One kind of love can help you think about the other.

Our speech about God is almost entirely analogical. It is language we commandeer from ordinary speech and use to explore into a reality beyond our imagining. This means that while theologians know how to *use* the language, they don't know the whole of what it means when they use it to speak of God; they only know that it means more, not less and not the opposite, of what it usually means. (This is not completely idiotic; after all we often use things without knowing entirely how they work.) Perhaps the most famous discussion of this peculiar quality of theological language is offered by Thomas Aquinas. Interestingly, Thomas reflects on how we can talk about God right after an extended discussion of how we come to know God: by being taken more and more into God's own self-knowing (these are questions 12 and 13 of the *Summa Theologiae*, Part I). In the last chapter of this book, we will ponder this idea of the beatific vision; but for now it is already suggestive that Thomas has something up his sleeve. For he moves with suspicious alacrity from the first of the following points to the second: (1) that God turns out to be the very "thinking" by which humanity will come to think God, and, (2) that human language for "naming" God turns out to be a great deal more alive, more animated, than anyone anticipated (perhaps suggesting that God is the self-naming, self-disclosing activity which is the hidden source of human naming of God). It is as if the erstwhile theologian-pirates discover that the language-vessel they thought *they* had commandeered was in fact mysteriously *sent* by Someone to fetch them.

Look for a moment at these clues from *Summa Theologiae* I. 13, Thomas's section on theological language. He begins innocently enough, simply asking if we can use any words at all to refer to God. Yes, he says, we can, but we have to remember that we haven't a clue what God really is; our right to talk about God at all comes from the fact that God creates a universe that points to God: "We only know [God] from creatures; we think of him as their source, and then as surpassing them all and as lacking anything that is merely creaturely. It is the knowledge we have of creatures that enables us to use words to refer to God, so these words do not express the divine essence as it is in itself" (I. 13. 1). This means: (a) some of what we say about God will be merely analytic of this Creator/creature distinction, listing things that cannot be true of God if God is really the Creator and not one of the creatures (i.e., if God is the Creator of things that change and pass away, then God could not also be changing or liable to passing away, otherwise we would be looking for yet another God to keep things going), and (b) some of what we say about God will be merely analytic of God's role (as Creator) causing everything to exist moment by moment; so, e.g., "God is just" is a way of saying that God is the source and cause of all justice that ever exists in the universe. But Thomas is not satisfied with theological language as only (a) removing what doesn't belong to God and as merely (b) referring to God as cause of this or that.

Thomas sees that something more than these two uses of language is going on: " 'God is good' therefore does not [only] mean the same as 'God is the cause of goodness' or 'God is not evil'; it means that what we call 'goodness' in creatures pre-exists in God in a higher way. Thus God is not good because he causes goodness, but rather goodness flows from him because he is good" (I. 13. 2). Look at how your thinking has to be turned upside down, says Thomas to his theological students: you think about God in terms drawn from the world around you, fair enough, that's all we've got; yet *your* experience of these things doesn't define their meaning for God, but just the reverse! You can't just extrapolate upwards a bit, ratcheting up on the goodness meter to a higher pitch. We're talking about *the* Good: "God is not good because he causes goodness, but rather goodness flows from him because he is good." You thought you could climb aboard all these little goods and sail away into a pristine divine definition; but in fact, God sent these little goods to fetch you and carry you away into the infinite abyss of Goodness itself.

In other words, the meaning of such perfection-words as goodness, truth, unity, love, and so on, is really God's meaning in the first place. Human beings use these words to talk about the things they see, but it turns out that all along *God has been using the things humans see to talk to humans.* So, Thomas is saying, theologians have to let God's way of talking overtake and illuminate human talking; or, rather, they have to rediscover the deep dimension of all good things that has in fact been God-talk, theo-logy, all along.

All this leads to a hugely useful principle for theology. The human "mode of signifying" God, of talking about God, is of course always short of the reality, always pointing beyond itself precisely because it uses creatures to talk about the Creator. Yet there is a saving grace about this, says Thomas: for as long as theologians remember not to limit the perfections (goodness, life, etc.) to their usual creaturely meaning, God can let loose through those perfections an immeasurable superabundance of meaning, for the perfections really belong "primarily to God and only secondarily to others" and are "used more appropriately" of God (I. 13. 3).

Now put all this together with the fact that it follows a section on how human knowing of God turns out to be a partaking in God's own self-knowing, and see what you think. Far from being a long philosophical prolegomenon defining the rules for theology, I think Thomas is suggesting (in a fully theological fashion) how God sets up the possibility for theology to unfold: theology's ultimate destiny, he tells us, arises from God's beckoning of humanity towards the beatific vision, and theology is able to voyage in thought and word towards that end precisely because God has hidden a secret foretaste of that beatifying goal in every creaturely perfection. Perhaps, in Thomas's view, if theologians leave their words about God open to God's meaning, they will find their words and thoughts coming mysteriously to life, animated with the presence of the one who alone bestows the fullness of their meaning. Writing a little over a century prior to Thomas, the Cistercian theologian William of St Thierry (*c.*1085–1148) described this moment with considerable beauty:

> When the object of thought is God and the things which relate to God and the will reaches the stage at which it becomes love, the Holy Spirit, the Spirit of life, at once infuses himself by way of love and gives life to everything, lending his assistance in prayer, in meditation or in study to man's weakness. . . . The understanding of the one thinking becomes the contemplation of the one loving.[5]

And with this we have already reached the next stage in theology's voyage.[6]

Mystical Life: Interpreting Reality in Terms of God

What would this be like? Perhaps an analogy would be appropriate. Suppose that you are a character in a play, let's say a tragi-comedy. I don't mean you are an actor portraying one of the roles but simply yourself one of the characters in the world of the play. And you come to a crisis point, with everyone on the verge of taking revenge on everybody else for an endless string of wrongs. Just then another person appears and, wherever she moves among you, people stop quarreling. They seem less afraid of each other or of what will happen to them if they let go of the hatreds that have for so long defined them. Astonished, you ask her how this comes about. "I've been showing people how much they are loved and how much they have to live for," she says. But some of the people are angry at the disruption she causes in their usual patterns, and they do away with her. Later, however, you see her again, alive. "How can this be?" you ask. "I am the living voice of your author," she says, "the source of your life too; you cannot really silence me because I am echoing in every word and thought you have. Only you have been too frightened and angry to hear the voice clearly and so I am speaking to you directly, person to person."

Over time, as you listen to her, you begin to understand what it means that you too are a character with an author. The more attuned to the author's speaking you become, the more alive, the more "yourself" you come to feel as the purpose and truth of yourself grows more luminous within you. "Yes," says the woman, "it is just because you had all forgotten that you had an author, and could no longer sense the author's glad giving of everything to you, that you became fearful and envious, threatened and threatening to one another." Christians believe, analogously, that Jesus of Nazareth is the living voice in our world of the author of all life, speaking to humanity as a fellow human being.

Companionship with Christ, in this view, leads to the conversion of people towards the truth of the author's desire for them all. But just so far as the world has become deaf to the infinitely giving voice, the world has distorted people's characters so that they draw their identity not from the author's giving of them to themselves but from the fearful cycles of the world. (Think, for example, of how difficult it is for people who have grown up as children of alcoholics to discover the truth of themselves in adulthood.) This means that rediscovery of one's true identity, one's true character as beloved of the author of life, will entail a death. One will no longer draw a pseudo-life from the drives and urgencies of the world, but directly again from the living voice of the divine author of life. And this will be a resurrection: the true self appearing anew, intimately filled and brimming with the spirit or desire of the author. Theology does not simply think *about* these things, it has to think by *means* of them: with a theological mind that has died and is now alive in Christ, drawing its mode of reflection from Christ.

We can see this perspective in a very early (first-century) Christian text from the New Testament called the Letter to the Colossians. Possibly written by Paul while in prison, the Letter addresses a congregation in Colossae in Asia Minor, which seems not to have learned fully what is entailed in thinking by means of Christ's death and resurrection.

The Letter of Paul to the Colossians 2: 20–3: 4

2: 20 If with Christ you died to the elemental spirits of the universe, why do you live as if you still belonged to the world? Why do you submit to its regulations, **2: 21** "Do not handle, Do not taste, Do not touch"?

2: 22 All these regulations refer to things that perish with use; they are simply human teachings.

2: 23 These have indeed an appearance of wisdom in promoting self-imposed piety, humility, and severe treatment of the body, but they are of no value in checking self-indulgence. **3: 1** So if you have been raised with Christ, seek the things that are above, where Christ is, seated at the right hand of God.

2: 20–2 This section of the Letter begins by reminding the Colossians that, by sharing in Christ's death (see the commentary on Romans in chap. 1), they have ceased to be subject to the "elemental spirits," the drives and urgencies that dominate the normal way of life in the world. Suppose, for example, that you were once part of a clique or a group that affirmed its own identity by wearing certain kinds of clothing and looking down on certain other sorts of people. These habits were not simply what was cool for your group, they were "regulations" **2: 22** to which everyone had to "submit" or risk ostracism. But now suppose that your clique really hurts someone you care about very much; seeing what they did to your friend opens your eyes to how petty and spiteful and self-absorbed the clique is and you lose all faith in it. You could perhaps be said to "die" to it, for it no longer provides you with any sense of who you are or gives you life and energy. Paul is saying **2: 23** that while such "self-imposed" regulations seem sophisticated and may for a time even enforce particular behaviors, in the end "they are of no value in checking self-indulgence," because they simply trap people ever more deeply in an obsessive need to satisfy oneself over against everyone else – they are just one group's self-image in antagonism with all the other groups **3: 1** But, says Paul, you have died to this source of false-life and identity, and "you have been raised with Christ." Paul uses the spatial metaphor of heaven "above" (not among the old compulsions of the world) to encourage the Colossians to "seek the things . . . where Christ is," namely at the heart and living spring of all that is really real and alive ("at the right hand of God"). This means that their sense of identity, of being fully alive and loved, now flows again directly from the Giver of all life.

3: 2 Set your minds on the things that are above, not on things that are on earth,

3: 2 This translates fully into a new frame of mind, an outlook ceaselessly refreshed and resourced from the "things that are above" in the divine Source.

3: 3 for you have died, and your life is hidden with Christ in God.

3: 3 To an increasing extent, the true identity of the Colossians no longer exists in the world and cannot be known by the world, for their "life is hidden with Christ in God," the secret meaning and hope that burns within their every thought and deed is founded in their relationship with God.

3: 4 When Christ who is your life is revealed, then you also will be revealed with him in glory.

3: 4 The world will only fully understand the dead-and-risen Colossians when the dead-and-risen Christ "who is [the Colossians'] life is revealed," for then the inner principle and logic of all they do will be radiantly clear, shining unmistakably ("in glory") as the heart of the world's true destiny in God.

What we see in this early Christian text is a crucial distinction. It is not good enough for Christian thought (or theology) to teach about religious things or even to prescribe them; theology could do all this and still be thinking about them with a mind that has not yet been changed by Christ's dying and rising (I have suggested the kind of transformation this entails in the commentary on Colossians just above). It is not so much thinking *about* theological topics that really constitutes theology; for distinguishable from this is the *means by which* the theological mind reflects. And a truly theological mind, as we saw earlier in the chapter, is a mind that has begun to be shaped and attuned to God's way of thinking and loving. The work of theology certainly includes reflection on all the things that Christians believe God has been doing. But this reflection has, itself, to spring from a continual conversion, a continual sharing in this hearing of the living voice of the author of life. Otherwise, theologians will keep thinking like characters in a play who refuse to understand that they *are* characters in a play, and who for that reason cannot experience anything of the larger and infinitely beautiful vision of their author.

In other words, theologians themselves have to share in the mystical life, the life in which the hidden presence of God – as the voice speaking all things into existence – can be sensed and acknowledged in all things ("mystical" means hidden; it comes from the Greek verb *muō*, to close or shut). Notice that this does not mean things do not have their own reality; they are really there as mountains or dragonflies or football teams and they can be studied in terms of their geological formation or cultural significance or by means of any other disciplines that apply. But theology wants to consider all these things, indeed everything, precisely in terms of each thing's mystical identity as a character in the play of the universe, or, to use standard theological language, as a creature that is ceaselessly spoken by the Creator. As Thomas Aquinas puts it, everything is known in sacred teaching as it either is coming from God or returning to God: "In sacred science all things are treated of under the aspect of God; either because they are God Himself; or because they refer to God as their beginning and end" (*ST* I. 1. 7).

Early Christian thinkers believed that would-be theologians could and should prepare themselves for this mystical dimension of theology. The great teacher of new Christians, Origen of Alexandria (*c.*185–*c.*254) and another influential theorist of Christian spirituality, Evagrius of Pontus (346–99) both adapted a standard philosophical training pattern for Christian theological needs. In fact there was a common element shared by the pedagogy of early Christian theology and ancient philosophy: namely, the understanding that what is essential is the way of life and spiritual exercises by which a person grows and deepens in his or her character and becomes capable of more profound understanding. The specific teachings or doctrines of theology (or philosophy) are really not an independent expression of the theology/philosophy but are meant rather as a manual or guide to assist learners as they undertake a theological/philosophical life. The truth and understanding one seeks is found in the transforming practices of one's theological/philosophical life, not primarily in the written digest or reference work that summarizes them.[7]

The first step, in this view, would be for theologians-in-training to live into the continual conversion in which one moves (by means of Christ's dying and rising), from life dominated by fears, compulsions, and self-regarding desires to a life that draws its freedom and clarity from the living spring of God's free giving. Otherwise, says Origen, a person used to seeing everything as either threat or potential possession, will not know "how to hear love's language in purity and with chaste ears, and will twist the whole manner of his hearing of it away" from God's intention; everything will sound with only the petty, shrill clamor of one's cravings or fears rather than the deep resonance of the divine voice.[8]

As this moral and ascetical dimension of theology deepens, the theologian is enabled to consider everything from the freely giving perspective of the Creator; and from this perspective, the theologian is enabled to begin hearing the divine speaking in all things, which we humans encounter as the meaning or truth of each thing. We could say this is a new sensitivity to the inner logic of each thing; these early Christians called this the contemplation of nature, the hearing of the divine *Logos* (the word, truth, or meaning) who speaks through the inner *logoi* or rational principles of all things. At first, such a theologian would (in our era) simply hear these *logoi* as the chemical formulae of an item, or the DNA of a living cell, or the logical principles of an economic system. But a theologian who is trained to hear all the *createdness* of reality will also hear this chemical formula or DNA or logical principle as none other than the creaturely speaking of the divine *Logos*, the divine giving to each thing of its particular truth. As Andrew Louth puts it: the soul "begins by contemplating the natural order itself, then it rises beyond this and discerns the principles which lie behind it. Since the universe is created by the Word of God, this is to enter into the mind of the Word."[9] For Origen, this is like falling in love and beginning to recognize the signs or traces or voice of one's beloved in the world around one. The theologian comes "to ponder and consider the beauty and grace of all the things that have been created in the Word"; and seeing in them the continually giving life of their author, the theologian will be awake to "the grandeur of their brightness" and "will be kindled with the blessed fire of [God's] love."[10]

This natural contemplation (a kind of hearing the divine voice in everything) becomes a training, says Origen, for the ultimate form of contemplation, which Origen's successors called "theology": the more direct and immediate hearing of the divine speaking, *theo-logia*. As Origen hints, this ultimate form of theology is awakened and aroused by the divine loving at work within the theologian's own life, bringing the theologian to understand everything more and more from within the knowing and loving of all which is God's very life. In Evagrius' famous phrase: "If you are a theologian you truly pray. If you truly pray you are a theologian."[11] Communing with the divine *Logos*, apprentice theologians begin to notice the echo of this divine speaking in everything. And as this deeper recognition and understanding grows, they are enabled all the more to enter into this God-talk, theo-logy. It is as though the divine *Logos* speaking to theologians in and through all things is teaching them some of this divine language, allowing them to converse, to pray, to see the universe itself as *logikos*, structured with meaning and truth.

What Origen and Evagrius are describing, I think, is the moment when theologians realize that the concept (*logos*) by means of which they are thinking is becoming transparent and open and available to the divine "thought" (*Logos*). Or put another way, the light by which they have begun to see everything begins to be identifiable as God's own radiance; they cannot look at this light directly for it is too bright, but they can begin to see everything by means of it, as it illuminates everything. Perhaps this sounds outlandish; but there are many everyday parallels. For example, I enjoy going to the art museum even though I know very little about art. When I look at the paintings and reflect on them, my mind does so by means of a few, fuzzy, and imperfectly formed ideas. As a consequence, while I may enjoy the paintings at a very basic level, I have to admit that there is a lot "in" them that I don't really "see." Of course I literally see the same pigments on canvas that everyone else sees (I'm not color-blind), but often I have a feeling of mingled yearning and frustration, sensing I'm missing something. Suppose, however, that on one occasion I could visit the museum with an art historian who is herself also an artist. For a few bright hours, she shares her way of thinking about painting with me, and my mind comes to life with a whole new set of concepts, ideas, ways of looking and feeling about art; and, more to the point, I could *see* things I had never seen before. Even though I still wouldn't fully understand everything my guide taught me, my mind would begin to come alive, to think, by means of her thinking, and to see things by means of those ideas that I couldn't really perceive or understand before.

Now my strong hunch is that this is exactly analogous to the kind of theological formation of mind we've been discussing throughout this chapter. The divine artist, who knows the hidden principles of beauty by which all things exist, begins to share this way of "thinking" with apprentice theologians. Gradually their minds become animated and awakened by this way of thinking, and they begin to think about everything they see by means of these ideas. But of course, in God's case, the "ideas" we're talking about are really themselves simply God (for God's "ideas" are nothing less than God in the eternal act of knowing all things). Thus God becomes, so to speak, the living structure of a theologian's thinking, present as the very knowing and loving by which the theologian understands reality. As I suggested above, for Thomas Aquinas (and for most of the Christian tradition) the ultimate form of this kind of seeing-by-means-of-the-divine-ideas is the vision of God that blesses (beatifies) all who gaze within the divine life.

Herbert McCabe summarizes Thomas's view:

> When, in beatitude, [a person] understands the essence of God, the mind is not realized by a form [an idea or concept] which is a likeness of God, but by God himself. God will not simply be an object of our minds, but *the actual life by which our minds are what they will have become.*[12]

Of course this is the ultimate state of theology, a state of sharing in God's own "ideas" that, Christians believe, only the blessed in heaven now enjoy. Yet my whole point in this section has been that apart from some preliminary form of this thinking-by-means-of-God's-thinking even now, theologians will tend to think about things with minds that are still closed to the fullness of reality. They may think about very religious things but fail to think by means of God's own thinking. Conversely, theology (in this view of it that I'm proposing), might think about things that seem far beyond the limits of "religious" things, yet think about such things precisely by means of God's thinking.

Every theologian needs to be open to the possibility of continual conversion to the ever greater mystery of God. And all who really want to study theology, while not perhaps needing to become mystics themselves, will best understand theology if they can sense what Christians experience as the tide of mystical life flowing towards God. William of St Thierry notes that, every once in a while, people are "shown a certain light of God's countenance," so that what they are "allowed to glimpse for a passing moment may set the soul on fire with longing for full possession of eternal light, the inheritance of full vision of God."[13]

Wisdom: Thinking by Means of God's Thoughts

I have been arguing that true theologians cannot be simply content, in any old frame of mind, to study particularly religious topics. That would not be theology;

after all, religious phenomena can be studied very perceptively by psychology, political theory, philosophy, sociology, neurobiology, among many others, and indeed by a special discipline invented in modernity just for studying religious phenomena, which is called religious studies. One could, analogously, study paintings in a museum by analyzing the chemical composition of the paint, studying the economic systems in which artists functioned, considering the historical developments in theories of representation, examining the psychological profiles of the artists as well perhaps as their brain chemistry while painting, and so on. Good art historians would likely draw on a number of these disciplines in focusing on their particular subject matter of art, just as good scholars of religious studies draw together in a constructive and critical way the insights of many disciplines as applicable to their particular subject field of religious phenomena.

Theology, however, does not really have a particular subject field. What differentiates it is rather that, as we have seen in the previous section, it inquires by means of divine teaching; it inquires regarding anything and everything by holding whatever it considers up into the divine light. If we went back to our analogy with studying art, theology would be a discipline that attempts to get the artists' own thinking on everything out on the table and then to see how the artists' ideas and feelings about things might illuminate not just paintings but anything at all from landscapes to the aesthetic structures of scientific equations. Theology is trying to think about everything and anything with the *divine* artist's ideas about things singing in the mind. Most of what I'm laboring to say here is probably more simply captured by the distinction between the material and the formal. The material subject of theology (i.e., the things it thinks about) might well include world hunger or economic justice or architecture as well as various Christian doctrines or practices. Any or all of these subjects could be the matter of reflection for theology or for a number of other disciplines. What makes Christian theology *theology* is not so much its matter as its form, the mode by which it reflects, namely the forms of thought we have been analogically calling the divine ideas.

I have been pointing to the beatific vision as the ultimate state of this vision of everything as God envisions it, with God as the means of envisioning. But this side of the vision of God, Christians believe that knowing things by faith is a kind of provisional sharing in that divine knowing of everything which is the consummate theological life (rather like my provisional sharing in my artist guide's understanding). Faith, says Thomas, allows the believer to sense the truth of things, "not due to what is seen by the believer but to what is seen by him who is believed" (*ST* I. 12. 13). Faith is a provisional sharing, says Thomas in "what is seen by him [i.e., God] who is believed." So faith is the means of divine teaching that allows theologians, even prior to the beatific vision, to begin to see things as God does, to understand things by means of God's ideas about them.[14]

Thinking about anything by means of God's thinking perhaps seems a tall claim. But in a sense this is always happening in every sort of thinking. Every time we see the truth of something, understand it, recognize that it is this and not that –

any and all of these things are only possible because there are certain fundamental structures (logical and moral) that both the universe and our minds seem to share. There is a difference, for example, between what is true and what is not. Or, a slightly different point, if something is "p" it cannot also at the same time be "not p." Christians believe that these sorts of truthful structures inhere in the universe (and in that dimension of the universe we think of as our minds) *because* God is truth and creates a universe that mirrors in its rational structures the divine truthfulness. That's why I claim that every time we come to truth about things we are, in a sense, already thinking by means of God's thoughts; for it is by God thinking all things (things as "thingks"!) according to the divine truthfulness that all things exist at all. Christians believe that we are able to think whatever we do think because there is a "think-able," or logical, framework to reality (we do not encounter everything as sheer nonsense), and this intelligible dimension to everything flows within everything from the divine speaking of God.

Christians also believe that God is not only flowing thinkable reality to us at every moment, but also attempting to draw us into the intelligibility of all things, eventually even to lure us into the full vision of their truth as it exists eternally in the mind of God. What would it mean for this divine teaching or sharing of ideas to transfigure the way theologians think about things? Of course I've been portraying this in the astonishing terms more nearly suitable to what Christians think of as the life of the world to come. But even in the limited sharing of God's thoughts possible in this world, there is the phenomenon usually called "wisdom." This is a particular form of knowledge in which a wise person, a sage, is so imbued with the principles of a certain matter that she seems almost intuitively to understand how to get at the particular truth in any given case. For example, say she is an exemplary teacher and walks into a highly disturbed classroom. Not having been there before, she hasn't seen with her own two eyes exactly what has been going on there. But after observing and talking with the students and teacher for awhile, she notices all kinds of things that other people would miss; she uses her deep knowledge of the *principles* of teaching and learning to "see" into the truth of the case. How is Christian theology like this?

Christians believe that God, in many and various ways, has been able to share with humanity some of the fundamental principles or ideas God has – including, especially, Jesus as the incarnation of the eternal Idea or Word in which everything is "thought" by God. Christian theology attempts to clarify what God's teaching is, what the divine ideas are, and then tries to use them to think with – as the principles of wisdom by means of which to understand things. Of course, as Thomas points out, this possibility may be somewhat constrained by the personal qualities of the theologian: "A [person] of sharp intelligence who grasps a principle can see at once what is implied in it, whereas a duller [person] has to have each conclusion explained" (*ST* I. 12. 8) (one senses Thomas was speaking as a veteran teacher here). Thus the goal would be to become so intuitively formed by the divine teaching that one is able in a new way to see its implications, i.e., what light it sheds, in any given circumstances. Theologians as sages are not simply learning to think about especially religious things, but are, rather, seeking to become accustomed to the divine principles and teaching at the heart of everything.

There is no guarantee, of course, that would-be theologians who risk the adventure of thinking into the deep truth of reality will ever become sufficiently enthused to take up piracy, nor that such theological pirates will discover that their words and ideas have in fact become disconcertingly and secretly inhabited by an original speaker quite beyond themselves. Nor, finally, is there any guarantee that, having grown at least haltingly conversant in the divine ideas, they will see clearly enough how the implications of God's thoughts might be discerned in everything. Christian theology is, as I warned you at the outset, never really in the hands of the theologians at all. But we can at least study what mysteries they encounter and what happens to them along the way.

Chapter 3

Divine Teaching and Christian Beliefs

If a close personal friend came and told you something she was very sure about but that you couldn't verify for yourself, would you believe her? Most of us might say, well, it depends on what sort of thing our friend was so sure about. The more unusual our friend's claim, the more we might have qualms. In that case, we might find ourselves suspending judgment until we could check things out for ourselves. Or, we might find that our trust in our friend, our confidence in her, and the strength of our friendship all dispose us to take what she says as true even though we don't know about it ourselves. In other words, we would "take on faith" what she proposes as true but beyond our certain knowledge at present. Now suppose the friend is God.

Faith has two aspects: the teachings of faith that a community accepts (the beliefs the community holds as true), and the faith *by* which a community believes (the act or virtue of believing). In this chapter I want to develop our account from the previous chapter of the act or virtue of faith. I also want to build up a more definite sense of how the beliefs or teachings (doctrines) of Christian faith actually work, how they can hold or mediate truth even when we cannot have present certain knowledge of that truth just by ourselves. We'll see (1) that the beliefs of Christian faith serve as a kind of training or apprenticeship while human understanding of God is growing, (2) that they are pedagogical tools in the hands of the master teacher, namely God, (3) that they therefore have a most peculiar quality of working in the mind like the ideas of a more informed teacher or friend – ideas that one doesn't yet completely grasp but which nonetheless begin (as one "tries them on") to make sense of things, and (4) that while one might attempt to demonstrate the intelligibility of these beliefs (i.e., show that they're not nonsensical), they are not primarily intended as a means to prove the truth of faith to a rational certainty but rather as a means for sharing more and more in the life of God. This last point is particularly significant, because it warns us that while we may show the coherence of theology within the limits of human rationality, we will badly misunderstand the real goal of theology if we come to a halt there.

Theology's Weakness and Wisdom's Parting Gift

In the first two chapters, we have been identifying what it is that shapes and forms the theological endeavor. This has led us to notice two peculiar facts, peculiar at least in terms of our usual notions of academic disciplines. First, we've seen that Christian theology is trying to learn about a subject, God, who is, to put it mildly, far more involved in the whole process than any other conceivable research subject could ever be – and involved in ways that will likely expose the theologian to some risk of personal change as a result. Second, if regular exposure to this research subject is to yield any actual growth in understanding, it will entail the development of research skills that are particularly well-suited to interaction with this particular subject (i.e., God). These settled dispositions that suit theologians for an ever deepening understanding of God are, we saw, called the theological virtues. Of the three – faith, hope, and love – only love will remain at work in the life of the world to come. This is because, Christians believe, in the vision of God, human beings will no longer need to have faith, for they will see face to face (they believe) that truth which they have longed to understand. Nor will they need to hope, for they shall taste in abundance that goodness which (they believe) has been the flowing source of all motion toward the good in this mortal life. The continuing role of love in the life of the world to come is something that will become clearer in later chapters.

In Chapter 2 we saw more particularly how these theological virtues might unfold themselves in certain callings, habits, and skills that especially mark the life of the theologian: risking reality beyond the neatly knowable (adventure), thinking into the unthinkable by way of analogy (piracy), transformational attending to the hidden presence of God (mystical life), and discerning the truth of everything by means of God's ideas about it (wisdom). But, you may still wonder, why exactly are these strange skills needed? Let me state the problem in the form of three fundamental points:

1   Christians believe that because God is the Creator of everything that exists, God cannot be *one of* those things; God is, rather, the reason why there is anything at all rather than simply nothing.
2   But all human language and ideas derive from our dealings with precisely those things that do exist; our language is very naturally conditioned by creatureliness.
3   Therefore whatever we say or think about God is going to be either
    (a)   an inadequate concept that we foolishly mistake for the reality, and so a form of idolatry, or
    (b)   an inadequate concept that we humbly employ as a pointer towards the divine reality, one which infinitely exceeds the grasp of our language, and is thus a form of analogy.

So the four strange skills we discussed in the previous chapter are needed as a kind of constant practice of the humility and wonder needed to think theologically rather than idolatrously, to think about God in ways that allow God to determine the meaning of our speech rather than to make that determination ourselves. By now it should be abundantly clear, as I tried to warn you at the beginning of this book, how weak and hapless a thing theology really is in and of itself – apart, that is, from its divine source. And here will come the first critical test for a would-be theologian. For the pressure of wanting to have something under our control, something that we can really say for ourselves – and feel as though we know what we're talking about – this pressure is going to entice would-be theologians into taking matters into their own hands. They may, of course, become straightforward, uncritical idolaters, setting up concepts like golden calves; but this happens only rarely. More commonly, and more insidiously, would-be theologians may accept the limitedness of human speech about God, but then, and perhaps without quite realizing it, they may turn that limitation into an impermeable barrier against God's suasions.

This would be a considerable problem, for (as we saw in the previous chapter) the limitations of human speech about God are not necessarily barriers at all, but may become – by their very inadequacy – signs pointing beyond themselves into the really real. Human words about God may become vessels provided by God and carrying the theologian from the shoreline of human meanings out into the apparently unreachable depths of divine meaning.

That is why I have been emphasizing humility and wisdom for theology; the humility needed to accept the weakness of our position, and the wisdom needed to learn from God. For Christian theology is not a mere acquisition of religious information nor an arid critiquing of pious postulations, it is (as I argued at the end of Chapter 2) an apprenticeship to divine wisdom. And since Wisdom is known to be a lavish party-giver (see Proverbs 8 and 9), it seems fair to beg from her one last gift before we set off in exploration of particular Christian beliefs. At the very least this might mean a growing ease and adroitness in seeing the whole in all the parts of theology, and a mature ability to see how the beliefs of Christian faith cohere and order one's knowledge of reality. But there is yet a greater parting gift we should seek from Lady Wisdom, and just to awaken in you some sense of expectation, consider these lines ascribed to King Solomon the Wise:

> Wisdom is radiant and unfading, and she is easily discerned by those who love her, and is found by those who seek her. She hastens to make herself known to those who desire her. . . . To fix one's thought on her is perfect understanding . . . she goes about seeking those worthy of her, and she graciously appears to them in their paths, and meets them in every thought. (The Wisdom of Solomon 6: 12–16)

Here we see not only that wisdom is friendly and gracious to those who desire to learn, but also that wisdom "appears to them in their paths, and meets them in every thought." This suggests that wisdom is not only a high and ineffably beautiful reality, but may also become, self-givingly, a luminous presence within the very thoughts and struggling words of the theologian. Wisdom's radiance may become the light by means of which human speech about God is transfigured into God's speech. How could this be?

Christians believe this happens most fully and definitively in that speech event they call the Incarnation of the Word. In this view, Jesus of Nazareth comes into history as the very human expression of divine meaning, or, as John's Gospel puts it, as the Word made flesh. It will be worthwhile pausing here for a moment and making sure of our ground. I'm suggesting that there is a direct analogy (and more) between the event of Christ and the human effort to talk intelligently about God. How so? Because in both the case of Jesus' humanity and the case of human theology, what is human is taken up to become a form of divine speech; that is the miracle, the secret majesty, which alone makes any sense at all of theology's existence. Of course this seems odd and rare, but there are ordinary parallels: you use the word "pain" to describe an unpleasant sensation, but a French-speaker might "incarnate" another meaning of his own (bread, of course) in the same word. Jesus of Nazareth, as a historical human being, bears all the meaning and significance that any human has; Christians believe that by means of this very human meaning – not in spite of it or alongside it but by means of it – God's eternal meaning has been expressed in our world. In an analogous way, human words and thoughts and beliefs about God, Christians believe, can be taken up by God and employed as a way of drawing human understanding beyond itself, into a meaning it could never have fathomed.

In fact, we have to go farther, for these two phenomena – God's Word speaking humanly, Jesus, and God speaking by means of human God-talk (theo-logy) – are not only related analogically. It is only because of how God takes human life into God in Jesus, Christians believe, that human speech about God (theology) can come to be a mode of divine speaking. Jesus might well have been seen and known as all other humans are, but for him to be heard and recognized as God's speaking would require that the same act by which Jesus exists should become graciously present in those who know him truly. Karl Barth puts it this way:

> Recognition of this man [Jesus] can obviously take place only as a new act of cognition, i.e., as one which shares in the newness of His being. . . . In the power and mercy of the same divine act of majesty which is the ground of His being the man Jesus speaks for Himself, expounds Himself and gives Himself to be known. . . . This means that in and with His self-disclosure He induces and initiates the human seeing and interpreting which attaches itself to the divine act of majesty in and by which He has His being, following and accompanying it, repeating the being which He has on this basis, and therefore become and being a relevant human seeing and interpreting.[1]

Perhaps we could think about it this way: some people clearly met Jesus and simply kept on going; but others, often against their expectations and in spite of their inclinations, found themselves caught up, encountering in him such mercy and truth, goodness and authority, that they were drawn to accompany him and be taught by him. As this happened, they found that what he said and did was often inexplicable to them, until in a strange way Jesus seemed to create, to speak into existence the very meaning of his words and deeds within their own hearts. In the Gospel of John, Jesus speaks of this experience as being taught by the Holy Spirit; the Father, he says, will pour out the Spirit of sonship within the disciples, and "when the Spirit of truth comes, he will guide you into all the truth. . . . He will take what is mine and declare it to you" (John 16: 13–14). Barth is saying that the very same Spirit by which the Word comes to be conceived in Mary, in our humanity, brings about an accompanying self-disclosure of the Word within human understanding. In other words, our unfolding understanding of God can only have any real basis in us insofar as it is an unfolding within us of God's own self-under-standing, and this, Christians refer to as Jesus, present in the power of the Spirit. This is the faith by which the Church believes what God is teaching.

Sacred Teaching: The Nature and Function of Christian Beliefs

In saying that theology is a kind of wisdom, I am saying that it is possible for God to befriend the human mind well enough for human thinking, so to speak, to lean on the divine mind. In the previous chapter I spoke of this by a simple analogy: going around a museum with my own uninformed ideas about paintings in con-trast to going around the same museum "leaning on" (informed by) the insights of a true artist. In the latter case I begin to see and understand significant dimen-sions of the art that were really there before, but which my uninformed mind could neither perceive nor comprehend. This is what theology would describe as faith leading to wisdom. First of all there is the act of faith, the faith *by which* I believe; this is the trust in my friend which my friend has engendered in me, and in its highest state this is the theological virtue of faith. It allows me confidently to lay hold on ideas and perceptions and insights that I myself did not originate and probably do not, at least to start with, understand very well. Second, there are my friend's ideas and insights themselves, and these correspond to the truths of faith, the faith *in which* I believe, the teachings, doctrines, or articles of faith. These are truths that I begin to use like lenses for viewing reality with new depth and clarity. As this happens, as I become more skilled in thinking with these ideas of my friend's, and they become more and more the animating dynamics of my own thinking, I would be moving towards theological wisdom.

Consider another analogy. Suppose you were a student in the beginning of term, visiting the room of a new acquaintance. As you look round, you sense a great many things, from desk supplies to personal objects to posters to shoes and (already!) dustballs under the bed. You know these things might tell you some-thing about your new acquaintance but at the moment they are mostly mute, just a jumble of impressions not pointing much farther than to the bare fact that there is indeed a person living in this dorm room. Now suppose that much later in the term this person has become a good friend to you, and you visit her room again. Because of your friendship with her, you see everything in the room differently. You no longer look at things and speculate from them about their owner; instead you begin now by knowing your friend's personality and character, and these aspects of her life lead you into a deeper understanding of all the things in her room: the photo on her computer desktop is a snap of the place in the mountains her family visited the summer before her father died, the shoes under her bed are her favorite running shoes that she wore in her best races the year before university, even the dustballs in the corner now seem less like signs of indolence than the inevitable result of her hours in the library and helping out at the homeless shelter. We might compare the first perspective (examining things and speculating about the person) to the approach of philosophy of religion or religious studies, and the second perspective (seeing everything with the knowledge of your friend) to the approach of theology.

Just as you might get to know a person and so see things from her point of view, Christians believe that God has also conveyed a sense of the divine character in certain paradigmatic events such as the liberation of Israel from slavery and the life, death, and resurrection of Jesus. The Christian community's shorthand for this revelation of God takes the form of a network of beliefs, the articles of faith, by means of which Christians seek to think about everything from God's point of view. Taken together, the Church's communal life, reading of scripture, patterns of worship and service all comprise this activity of sacred teaching, or being taught by God – the medium within which God's meaning becomes illuminatingly present through the words and actions and thoughts of human beings.

What's the point of all this? Well, if you thought that the beliefs or doctrines we are trying to think about in theology were simply erudite bits of argumenta-tion, then you might well be tempted, at times, to set them aside as so much pedantry not worth the toll they've taken over the centuries. Or, if you were of an entrepreneurial frame of mind, you might think that you could convert them entirely into a domesticated human system. But if you thought that the doctrines of Christian theology were in fact human communal expressions of divine teach-ing, you might pause in wonder over the mystery beckoning to you within each article of faith. You might pause to reflect that you were not simply having a few interesting ideas but rather that the ideas might be having you! Not having you in the sense of "having you on," fooling you, but having you in the sense of holding you, considering you, bringing you into a new place of being. For so, Christians believe, they are. The ideas in their primordial form are God's "ideas" of Godself and of all that is as it participates in God's gift of existence, the ideas by which God brings every creature into existence. Christian doctrine is the distilled human form in which the most fundamental principles of God's ideas – fundamental in the sense of being the explanatory foundation of everything else –

become available as teaching for the human family. Thinking theologically, in other words, might be said to be an undergoing of the divine, an allowing of one's own thinking to be addressed and re-schematized by the divine thinking.

We saw in Chapter 2 how this theme unfolded in early Christian thinkers: the divine knowing and speaking, the *Logos*, echoes as the creative ground in every creature, thus providing a knowable rationale or idea according to which every creature exists. When human thinking apprehends this thinkable or intelligible dimension of anything, it is in effect brushing gently into an encounter with the divine idea by which the creature is. Theological ideas of the type we call properly Christian beliefs or doctrines are those ideas that, Christians think, explain every-thing else precisely because they express most fundamentally the divine character and purpose and plan according to which the whole of reality lives and moves and has its being.

Let's try an example: how does the belief that God is Trinity illuminate Christian thinking about all the creatures? Thomas Aquinas argues that God reveals the mystery that God is Trinity because, for one thing, we wouldn't otherwise be able to understand creation itself. This "was necessary," he writes, "for the right idea of creation" because

> the fact of saying that God made all things by His Word excludes the error of those who say that God produced things by necessity. [And] when we say that in Him there is a procession of love [the Holy Spirit], we show that God produced creatures not because He needed them, nor because of any extrinsic reason, but on account of the love of His own goodness.[2]

Knowing that God the Father creates in and through God the Word and Spirit suggests, in Thomas's view, that God acts by a free intelligence and decisive purpose rather than according to some cosmic necessity. How does this affect our understanding of creation? It means that freedom is the very ground of every creature; everything exists not because it "has" to be, but rather because it is a freely made choice of God's. And not only that, adds Thomas, this production of the creatures in time is also the result of the eternal event of loving in God, the procession of the Holy Spirit; thus each creature is in its own way an epiphany of divine joy and delight, and no matter what may befall each creature, it can be fairly said to be loved into existence and to live from a continual act of divine cherishing.

We can perhaps see the significance of this if we revert for a moment to our visit-to-a-friend's-room analogy. I said there that theology is not primarily like a process of reasoning from what one sees in the room to knowledge of the person who lives there, but rather that it works the other way around: your friendship with the person enables you to see into the meaning and truth of the items in the room. So as we have just seen with Thomas, the friendly teaching of God about God's trinitarian life enables one to see into the meaning and truth of the creatures in the "room" of God's universe. Of course, for God to teach humans by sharing

God's own knowledge of God's life would require one to have friendship with and trust in God, and this is what the *act* of faith implies. The *beliefs* of faith, which a believer holds in virtue of this act of loving trust, are the initial glimmerings within the confines of human thought of the infinite truth of God's own reality. What God, the saints, and angels all behold clearly, earthly believers can partake according to the limitations of our present state of being. The whole point of this chapter, in fact, has been to clarify this feature of Christian theology, namely that the limitedness of human understanding is nonetheless open to God's self-communication. The fact of human noetic limitedness would only deter us if we thought theology were primarily about arriving at a graspable, provable certainty of our own. But, as we've seen, Christian theology is much more like a process of apprenticeship in which the one learning has to accept at first certain teachings that one cannot quite grasp, but which are, nevertheless, the fundamental ideas one needs to move towards real understanding.

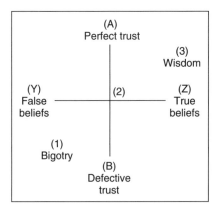

For those of you who are helped by visual descriptions, it might be useful to pause for a moment and use the accompanying figure to make what we're talking about a little clearer. The vertical axis (A) to (B) represents the act of faith or loving trust, the virtue of faith by which one believes. The horizontal axis (Y) to (Z) represents the teachings of faith, the doctrines of faith in which one believes. The consensus of Christian thinking is that these two dimensions of faith are in a directly proportional relationship. This means that as one's loving and trusting relationship with God grows and deepens in a healthy way, one's apprehension of the beliefs of faith likewise grows and becomes more profound and a source of insight about reality (moving from point 1 to 2 to 3); and this is because it is precisely, Christians think, one's friendship with God that makes possible a glimpse (even in this world) of the full reality of God's life which is only knowable in the life to come. Likewise, Christians think, if one's beliefs about God are genuinely pointing to the divine life, they will the more easily point you in the right direction for a deepening relationship with God. Conversely, if one's relationship with God has become defective (perhaps one has stopped trying to pray) or degenerated into a form of idolatry (perhaps one has become unconsciously enslaved to a god of physical perfection or demon of self-despising), then one's understanding of the beliefs of faith correspondingly becomes attenuated, one-sided, and distorted (moving from point 3 down to point 1). And likewise, if one's beliefs about God are not very adequate (say you were taught, for example, that God had abandoned this universe to evil forces), then those inadequate beliefs are the less capable of pointing you towards a relationship with the true and living God – and may in fact make you prey to forms of fanaticism, bigotry, or superstition.

So Christians believe that authentic faith moves one towards human flourishing and, not coincidentally, towards ever deeper engagement with reality. Along these lines, Thomas Aquinas makes the rather astonishing proposal that what God knows about Godself and everything else can, by faith, come to be the basis for human reasoning about things:

> We cannot perfectly possess this [divine] way of knowing in the present life, but there arises here and now in us a certain sharing in, and a likeness to, the divine knowledge, to the extent that through the faith implanted in us we firmly grasp the primary Truth itself for its own sake. And as God, by the very fact that he knows himself, knows all other things as well in his way, namely by simple intuition without any reasoning process, so may we, from the things we accept by faith in our firm grasping of the primary Truth, come to know other things in our way, namely by drawing conclusions from principles.[3]

Thomas is saying here that just as a good physicist, knowing the fundamental principles of, say, quantum mechanics, is able to interpret the data of an experiment and draw conclusions about it, so a theologian holding the beliefs of Christian faith, as fundamental principles, is able by means of them to interpret the data of reality and move to a deeper understanding of things.

Yet as much as Thomas shows us this capacity of basic Christian beliefs to shed light on reality, we have to keep reminding ourselves that this is only possible given faith's highly unusual characteristic: instead of being a knowledge of basic principles that we can grasp for ourselves, it remains "in the present life" (as Thomas puts it just above) a "certain sharing in, and a likeness to, the divine knowledge." And no matter how accommodatingly God shares the divine knowledge with human knowers, God's knowledge (by virtue of its infinity), is always going to remain for humans in this life a kind of darkness. Even through the self-disclosure of God in grace and revelation, says Thomas, God "joins us to him as to an unknown."[4] The faith that believers put in Christian beliefs, which theology seeks to understand, "is not due to what is seen by the believer but to what is seen by him who is believed."[5] It is because of what God "sees" so to speak, that believers have something worth believing and the grace to believe it. So we have to say that while this may seem like a handicap for theology, and indeed would be if we were working in a discipline circumscribable by human understanding, it turns out instead to be the sign of an unimaginable benefit. For the very reason theology suffers this lack of full comprehension is because it is swimming in a reality of such limitless, transcendent, eternally resourceful, endlessly giving goodness.

Visions of the Whole: Origen, Aquinas, and Barth

We've been considering how the basic beliefs or principles of theology, as taught by God, build up in the mind a skill at seeing everything in terms of God. Now we want to ask how the unfolding of that skill or know-how, as a kind of theological wisdom, could lead to an integrated picture of the whole. After all, theology like any discipline can easily fall into thickets of ever narrower minutia. The special danger of this for theology is that it may lure theologians into a cozy domesticity within their own little parochial patches of thicket. This may tempt them to think that they rather than God are now in charge of the matter of their study, that it is all simply a business of very clever intellectual gymnastics of which they are the masters; worse yet, losing sight of the whole may tend to dampen the theologian's much-needed enthusiasm for those refreshing and broadening journeys onwards towards the far horizons of the divine plan – without which theology grows stale and mechanical, partial, provincial, and one-sided.

So before going any further, it will be helpful to catch at least a fleeting glimpse of how some master theologians envision the whole coherent sweep of Christian beliefs. To do this I will compare (in a grossly oversimplified form) the theologies of Origen of Alexandria, Thomas Aquinas, and Karl Barth, focusing simply on the respective ordering they give to Christian beliefs.[6] By risking these visions of the whole, I hope our later chapters on particular doctrinal themes will be less liable to suffer as a result of their necessary, but artificial, isolation from the integrity and full-bodiedness of Christian theology taken as a whole. In the near vicinity here, I offer a crude parallel column outline of what are beyond question three of Christianity's greatest sustained theological interpretations: Origen's *On First Principles* (*c*.220–30), Thomas Aquinas's *Summa Theologiae* (1266–73), and Karl Barth's *Church Dogmatics* (1936–69). As you cast your eyes over these schemes, remember that my paltry phrases represent many thousands of words and hundreds of pages and years of devoted effort on the part of these three theologians. You could also begin to ask yourself the crucial question at this point: What might be the overarching principles that have guided these theologians in envisioning their accounts of Christian faith, in seeing the whole, and how might these principles have influenced the shape or structure of their accounts? I will outline these three visions of the whole according to the standard divisions of their texts, with painful compression needed to permit at least some comparisons.

Origen of Alexandria	Thomas Aquinas	Karl Barth
I. The Heavenly World	Part One: God and the	I. The Word of God
Preface: *The First Principles*	Procession of the	I/1: *Prolegomenon on*
of Christian Teaching	Creatures from God	*Theology. Revelation as*
1. The Father	1. Sacred Teaching	*the Act of God the*
2. Christ	2–11. The Existence	*Trinity.*
3. The Holy Spirit	and Unknown Nature	1. The Word of God
4. Falling Away	of God	and Dogmatics
5. Rational Natures	12–13. Knowing and	2. The Revelation of
6. Consummation	Naming God from	God: Triune God,
7. The Heavens	What God is Not	Incarnation,
8. The Angels	14–18. God's Knowing	Outpouring of Holy
	19–26. God's Loving	Spirit
II. The Material Cosmos	and Acting	I/2: *The Word*
1. The World	27–43. God's Trinitarian	*Provides Witnesses*
2. Bodies	Life	3. Holy Scripture
3. Beginning of the World	44–9. God as Creator	4. Church Teaching
4. One God of Old and	50–74. Angels and the	in Proclamation and
New Covenants	Cosmos	Theology
5. God both Just and	75–102. Human Being	
Good	and Knowing: the Image	II. The Doctrine of
6. The Incarnation	of God	God
7. One and Same Spirit in	103–19. Divine Order	II/1: *God Wills to Be*
Moses, Prophets, and	and the Life of the World	*Known in God's Reality*
Apostles		5. Knowledge of God
8. The Soul		6. The Reality of God
9. Motion of Rational	Part Two: The Journey	who Loves in
Creatures in the World	of the Creatures to God	Freedom: the Divine
10. Resurrection and	Section I of Part II:	Perfections
Punishment	*Human Destiny and the*	II/2: *God Elects All*
11. The Promises of the	*Structures of Human Life*	*in Christ*
Life to Come	1–5. Beatitude as the	7. The Election of
	Goal	Grace
III. Human Destiny and	6–21. Human Action	8. The Command of
Duty: The Cosmic Moral	and Moral Life	God
Struggle	22–48. Feelings	III. The Doctrine of
1. Freedom of the Will	49–70. Shaping Human	Creation
2. Demons at War with	Action: Virtues, Gifts of	
Humanity, Attempt to	the Spirit, Gospel	III/1: *The Work of*
Prevent Communion with	Blessings	*Creation*
God	71–89. Sin	9. The Story of
3. Wisdom and Spiritual	90–105. Law	Creation and God's
Influences on Humanity	106–14. Grace	Covenant

4. Interior Conflicts: Will, Soul, Flesh
5. Destiny of Creation
6. Consummation of all Things in God

IV. Interpreting the Living Word: the First Principles of Christian Teaching
1. Inspiration of Scripture
2. How to Interpret the Word
3. Wisdom in Interpretation: the Spiritual Meaning of the Word
4. Summary of the First Principles

Section II of Part II: *Living Towards God*
1–46. The Theological Virtues of Faith, Hope, and Love
47–170. The Moral Virtues and the Social World
171–189. Special Vocations

Part Three: Christ as the Way to God
1–6. The Incarnation
7–26. The Grace and Mediation of Christ
27–30. The Virgin Mary
31–45. The Life of Christ
46–52. The Passion
53–9. The Resurrection
60–5. Continuing the Incarnation: Sacramental Life in Christ
66–90. Baptism, Confirmation, Eucharist, Penance
[Thomas died before he could conclude Part Three as he intended, with sections on the consummation of all things in the general resurrection and vision of God.]

III/2: *The Creature*
10. Human Being as God's Covenant Partner, Soul and Body, Existence in Time
III/3: *God with the Creatures*
11. God's Providence, Nothingness, Angels and Demons
III/4: *The Command of God the Creator*
12. Freedom for God, for Humanity, for Life; Freedom within Limitation and Calling

IV. The Doctrine of Reconciliation
IV/1: *The Self-Humbling of God in Christ*
13. Survey of Soteriology
14. Jesus Christ, The Lord as Servant: Obedience of the Son, Pride and Justification of Humans, Holy Spirit and Faith
IV/2: *The Exaltation of Humanity in Christ*
15. Jesus Christ, The Servant as Lord: Raising of Humanity to Fellowship with God, Sloth and Sanctification of Humans, Holy Spirit and Love

IV/3: *Jesus Christ as
the True Witness and
Light of Life*
16. Jesus as Victor:
Mediatorship of Christ,
Falsehood and
Vocation of Humans,
Holy Spirit and Hope
IV/4: *Fragment on
Baptism*
[Barth died before
completing his
intended Part V, on
the Final Redemption
or Eschatology.]

As we look through these columns (and I beg you to go back and forth and up
and down these columns for a while, and then go and look at the volumes themselves in your library), we can notice some basic points of commonality. For
example, all three theologians:

1   begin with some reflection on the nature of theology,
2   structure their theological visions as a journey from God to creation and then
     from this world into more perfect relationship with God,
3   discuss the Trinity near the beginning,
4   place significant emphasis on God's providential role throughout the duration
     of creaturely existence,
5   understand the life of this world as in some ways a struggle to move towards
     closer relationship with other creatures and with God, and interpret this
     struggle in both spiritual and moral terms,
6   see the death and resurrection of Jesus and the outpouring of the Holy Spirit
     as the absolute turning point in the creation's long pilgrimage away from and
     then towards God
7   have sections on angels!

So what are the basic beliefs that have guided these theologians in structuring
things as they have?
   I think we want to note first of all how each theologian traces out a version of the
fundamental biblical story of the universe: creation, fall, the calling of Israel, descent
into slavery, liberation, difficulties in communal life, the teaching of prophets, the
coming of the Christ, the death and resurrection of Christ, the outpouring of the
Holy Spirit and formation of a new community, and finally the vision of perfect

blessedness in the New Jerusalem. It is this vast sweep and stunning reversal, this secret working of divine initiative even through the most desolate human struggles, this cosmic beauty and strangeness of the biblical world-story that breathes throughout these theologians' work like a divine wind. None of them would say that their theology is the *meaning* of the biblical story, rather they would each say that the scriptures retain an irreducible depth of mystery, a hidden threshold into the divine self-communication which theology is meant to assist one in more deeply understanding – and, ultimately, in encountering transformingly for oneself.

We may also learn something by considering the different modes in which each theologian pours out his reflections. We can trace these differences directly to the fundamental principles of each theologian, and from there we can see how these principles characteristically shape each theologian's entire project. Why bother with such an effort in theological aesthetics? Well, besides the fact that it's a pretty good way to learn some basic theological ideas and to learn some basic facts about three central Christian theologians, it is also crucial practice for anyone who wants to learn how to think theologically. By that I do not mean simply how to think about a lot of theological ideas, but how to think through theological ideas and, most importantly, by means of them.

Consider a brief example. Suppose it was your fundamental theological principle that the realm of the divine was chiefly marked by contentious rivalries among a range of deities, their jealous patronage and partisanship among human beings, and an inscrutable and implacable fate that seemed fully capable of incinerating anyone's notion of justice to smoldering ash. Perhaps this sounds a daunting prospect, and yet it pretty well describes the theology of the *Iliad* and the *Odyssey*. What sorts of things would you notice about the world if these were your illuminating principles? Perhaps the driving necessities of survival would frame your vision, so that the good would equate to whatever permitted another day of existence for oneself and one's own – and did not arouse the lethal rivalry of the gods against one. It would be hard, with such a fundamental principle as one's guide, to perceive much point in sheer, unmerited goodness in the world, or for self-giving humility as its sign. As Paul the Apostle commented with reference to the crucifixion of Christ, such a life and such a death – far from appearing as the mysterious work of divine mercy and forgiveness – to the eyes of the Greeks could seem like nothing but the most senseless and utter folly (1 Corinthians 1: 23).

So what illuminates the theological visions of Origen, Thomas, and Barth, and what do they see because of this? I would describe the parallel yet idiomatic emphases in each like this:

- Origen envisions the whole in terms of a primeval fracture in the creatures' contemplative presence to God, their subsequent fall into this world – a world prepared by God for their re-education and healing – and their cosmic spiritual struggle to return to full communion with God.
- Thomas envisions the whole in terms of the eternally ecstatic knowing and loving that mark God's life as Trinity, and the unfolding of that eternal act of

existence into a gift of creaturely existence, which bears within itself the ever-present calling of grace towards perfect sharing in God's knowing and loving.

- Barth envisions the whole in terms of God's eternal election never to be God without humanity and, through Jesus Christ, to bring into existence a faithful covenant partner whose obedience wins for the creation, even in the midst of the world's pride, sloth, and mendacity, the promise of genuine fellowship with God.

Having a sense of these fundamental beliefs helps us to understand some of each theologian's most characteristic decisions. For example, Barth famously locates the doctrine of election – the teaching that God elects or desires humanity for relationship with God – within the doctrine of God (see his Part II, chapter 7 in the outline above). Where else might he have put it? He could have placed it within the doctrines of salvation or of the Church, with the implication that salvation and the community of believers are only for the "elect" and therefore not for everyone. This would also imply that God's choosing to be in relationship with humankind is a consequence of something else more fundamental to God, perhaps (as in the great Reformed theologian John Calvin) a consequence of God's eternal intention to manifest the divine glory and power – even, if necessary, by saving some human beings and allowing some to perish forever. By contrast, Barth's option to locate God's decision (never to be without humanity) within the very doctrine of God is a direct consequence of his most basic theological principle: we know everything we can ever know about God only through the event of God in Christ reconciling the world to himself. Barth, working with this fundamental principle as his lens for envisioning the whole, sees that we have to assume there must be some eternal feature of God's very own act of existence that unfolds in our world as the events concerning Jesus of Nazareth.

So before you move on from this section, you may like to look back at the parallel outlines of these three theologians. Use my brief statements of their fundamental principles and see what you can notice about the structures of their respective works. Given, for example, Origen's emphasis on the return and consummation of the universe in God, why do you think he has concluded *On First Principles* with a book on the interpretation of scripture? What is it about the process of biblical study and interpretation that might be related to the return of creation to God? (See Chapter 7 on creation and revelation for a possible answer.) Or for another theological exercise, consider the oft-repeated claim or criticism that Thomas seems to bracket all discussion of Christ till the end of the *Summa*. Is this quite right? If you bear in mind my brief statement of Thomas's fundamental principle, namely that everything flows from and returns to the trinitarian act of God's existence, what might you notice about Thomas's structure? How might the eternal processions of the Word and Spirit, which reach their most incarnate historical form in the event of Christ, be at work in the unfolding of creation and in the very structures of the human person? (See Chapter 6 on the Trinity for further thoughts on this question.)

How Not to Believe: The Dangers of Fantasy and Fanaticism

We still need to inquire about what might be termed a "critical" moment for theology: How do we know when the beliefs of faith, or their theological articulations, are being misconstrued or distorted? By now two points should be especially clear: first, doctrines are not ends in themselves, but second, they can only function as intended if the apprentice is genuinely open to the teaching of the divine teacher. If this second point is not the case, then the doctrine is liable to become the toy of the apprentice and get used in all manner of unfortunate ways, usually issuing in a painful sense of disillusionment with religious beliefs in general or a lethal metamorphosing of beliefs into a narrow dogmatism. If, for example, you insisted on grasping Christian beliefs as simple reports about things (perhaps, seemingly, inaccurate and pre-scientific reports), you would be oblivious to the crucial momentum within Christian beliefs, the tide of divine grace pulling the believer, by means of the beliefs, into an understanding of reality from God's point of view. The creed, argues Thomas, "touches on the things of which there is faith," but the "act of the believer does *not reach its end* in a statement, but in the thing: we do not form statements except so that we may have apprehension of things through them."[7] In other words, the realities of faith that theology is trying to understand are not enclosed within the words of the faith; the words are the necessary yet never sufficient conditions for being moved towards the infinite truth of God.

In effect, Thomas is saying, don't be surprised: if you turn beliefs into idols, you will find them disappointing! If you insist on arresting your gaze at our everyday meaning of the words themselves, that will necessarily prevent you from being taught by *means* of the words how to encounter the reality beyond, to which they point. They are meant to function more like icons: always pointing beyond themselves, bringing one into an encounter with reality. Or again, carrying around a foreign language textbook is not meant to take the place of finally being able to encounter the reality of another culture yourself; and yet you need to practice the vocabulary and the principles of grammar if you are going to enjoy coherent conversation with that other culture. In the case of theology, this other culture is, Christians believe, the blessed society of saints and angels in communion with God.

The goal of Christian beliefs, then, is a goal infinitely beyond the limits of the human creature's natural capacities. This goal, Christians believe, is the eternal vision of God. But if both that vision and the understanding that would facilitate the human pilgrimage towards it are beyond human capacities, how can beliefs be of any use? Thomas proposes this solution:

> The last blessedness of human being lies in a certain supernatural vision of God. To which vision humanity cannot attain except in the way of one who learns from God as teacher, according to John 6, "Whoever listens to the Father and learns comes to

me" [John 6: 45]. But this kind of learning does not make a human being participant all at once, but successively, as is the way of human nature. It follows that every such learner must believe, so that they might come to complete knowledge. . . . Hence in order that humankind come to the complete vision of blessedness it is required beforehand that one believe God, just as a student must believe a master who teaches him.[8]

Although the goal of eternal blessedness is beyond humankind's natural capacities, God offers to teach humanity in a way that educates it into sharing God's own life. But because human beings can only learn things (let alone divine life) little by little, it will be necessary for humankind to take a good number of these teachings on faith to begin with – just as a student trying to learn something at university has to start with what a professor is teaching in order to get anywhere in that subject. This means that the element of trust involved is only a liability if you insisted on thinking that Christian beliefs were primarily human possessions one ought to be able to control and use at will. But if you saw Thomas's point just above, then the element of faith (as virtue) in learning from Christian beliefs would not be a liability but simply the joyful risk one would necessarily take in being taught by God. So we don't want to meet the need for a critical moment in theology by ruling out from the start the very openness to divine agency that gives it its vivacity and surprising beauty.

And yet how does this very transcendent orientation of theology toward the ungraspable keep its feet on solid ground if it is always supposed to be sailing off into the unknown? Won't that very tendency incline theology towards self-deluding superstition, credulousness, and fantasy on the one hand, or arrogant bigotry and fanaticism on the other? Can authentic Christian faith really steer towards a golden mean between these two extremes? One answer to these questions, what I'll call the characteristically modern answer, overcomes theology's apparent liabilities by making some other standard, external to theology and common to most people (say, human reason, or perhaps science, or, maybe, the basic assumptions of the age), the measure and criterion of theology's health.

Perhaps the single clearest and most influential argument of this sort (repeated countless times by later thinkers in varying forms) was offered by the British empiricist philosopher John Locke (1632–1704). In his great work, *An Essay Concerning Human Understanding* (1690), Locke repeatedly warns against the stubbornness and obduracy of zealots who refuse to test their supposed inspirations and beliefs at the bar of reason. Having an enthusiastic conviction that something is a matter of faith does not, in fact, ensure that it is so, says Locke: "the strength of our persuasions is no evidence at all of their own rectitude: crooked things may be as stiff and inflexible as straight: and men may be as positive and peremptory in error as in truth."[9] Locke proposes to distinguish more clearly between faith and reason, and accepts entirely, he says, that there are some beliefs of faith quite above reason's natural way of arriving at knowledge. But in order to verify that these beliefs are genuinely of faith – given by God in revelation and not by the excited deliverances of our own feelings – we need to determine by reason that these beliefs are genuinely given by God. In this famous passage, Locke makes his crucial distinction between subjecting to reason the beliefs themselves and subjecting to reason the assumption that the beliefs come from God:

> God when he makes the prophet does not unmake the man. He leaves all his faculties in their natural state, to enable him to judge of his inspirations, whether they be of divine original or no. When he illuminates the mind with supernatural light, he does not extinguish that which is natural. If he [God] would have us assent to the truth of any proposition, he either evidences that truth by the usual methods of natural reason, or else makes it known to be a truth, which he would have us assent to, by his authority, and convinces us that it is from him, by some marks which reason cannot be mistaken in. *Reason* must be our last judge and guide in everything. I do not mean, that we must consult reason, and examine whether a proposition revealed from God can be made out by natural principles, and if it cannot, that then we may reject it: but consult it we must, and by it examine, whether it be a *revelation* from God or no: and if *reason* finds it to be revealed from God, *reason* then declares for it, as much as for any other truth, and makes it one of her dictates.[10]

So Locke here appears to say that if something is really a legitimate belief of religious faith, there ought to be something about it that makes it reasonable to suppose that it is in fact a matter of faith, given by God in revelation. This seems fairly benign, even obvious; he even explicitly says that he does not mean that reason should predetermine the content of the belief, but only judge the authenticity of its delivery and apprehension.

This criterion would seem on first glance to have at least two advantages: first, it tethers theology to a real standard that almost everyone can observe and so enhances the legitimacy of theology's claims, when these claims can be seen to have a justifiable basis; but it also, second, appeals to something more universal; after all, human reason is common to both believers and unbelievers and indeed to believers in different religions. And this use of reason to verify beliefs should make theology more clearly a public claim and not merely an alienating in-group code only available for those who've already made it into the charmed circle of belief. I wonder, however, whether you may have noticed some problems with this answer. For example, even though Locke may say that reason judges of a belief's legitimacy by markers external to the belief itself (e.g., its arrival was perhaps attended by miracles), this slopes down in a quickly slippery fashion to judgments about the belief itself; for how could reason assent to beliefs as truly coming from God if the contents of those beliefs seem alien to our natural knowledge? As Hume would later point out, it seems contrary to reason that miracles should occur, in which case, how can one verify the divine origins of beliefs supposedly warranted by miraculous origins? Locke suggests that we can distinguish between beliefs that transcend reason (possibly acceptable) and those that simply contradict our reason (unacceptable), but how realistic and practicable a distinction would this be? Suppose we "know" that it is impossible for the dead to rise from the grave, then on Locke's view (and no matter how he may try to avoid the implication) it would be against reason that God should act in a way (i.e., raising Jesus from the dead) that so clearly contradicts our reasonable knowledge. As Locke himself puts it:

> Faith can never convince us of anything, that contradicts our knowledge. Because though *faith* be founded on the testimony of God (who cannot lie) revealing any proposition to us; yet we cannot have an assurance of the truth of its being a divine revelation, greater than our own knowledge. Since the whole strength of the certainty depends upon our knowledge, that God revealed it, which in this case, where the proposition supposed revealed contradicts our knowledge or reason, will always have this objection hanging to it, viz. that we cannot tell how to conceive that to come from God, the bountiful author of our being, which if received for true, must overturn all the principles and foundations of knowledge he has given us.[11]

Notice in this passage how quickly the supposedly formal criterion – reasonable evidence that a belief comes from God – slips into becoming a criterion touching directly upon the material content of the belief. But what if the whole point of revelation were to liberate human reason from pseudo-knowledge that had come in various times and places to dominate human thinking? In racist cultures, for example, it is "common knowledge" that people of color are inferior to whites and that their own incorrigible laziness is the real reason for their poverty. Presumably, in such a case, a belief that teaches adherents to see all persons as equally beloved creatures and children of the Creator would have to be ruled inadmissible and not authentically stemming from divine revelation because it would indeed "overturn" (as Locke puts it) the "foundations of knowledge" that such a culture holds to be self-evidently the case.[12]

So who gets to decide what counts as "reasonable"? And how do we know that what is supposedly a "universal" common ground is not in fact just the in-group code of cultural assumptions for some other dominant group? One of the most significant and enduring observations of both liberation and feminist theologians in our own era has been the awareness that every theology has *some* context – some social, political, economic, or cultural horizon from which it emerges. So might there be another way to appreciate modernity's call for rationality and universal accessibility in theology without handing it over to a misleading, if not deforming, insistence upon a supposedly universal reason? I think there is, and that, paradoxically, the best chance of meeting these modern concerns is by taking yet more seriously the very thing modernity may have most profoundly overlooked about theology. In its anxiety to achieve rational certainty and universality, modernity often assumed that the most reliable guarantor of these goals is humanity itself. But now suppose, as Christian theology has done through almost the entirety of its history, that the real guarantor of truth's universality is God, and that God achieves this goal on humanity's behalf, and, furthermore, that God accomplishes this precisely by drawing humanity beyond its own (often self-serving, sometimes mendacious, always limited) views of reality into an encounter with God's own view of reality.

Modernity has felt understandably uncomfortable with this approach to theology for the very reason that such an activity of divine teaching would seem, as Locke pointed out, to be subject to no critical or evaluative awareness at all. Thus we are back at our earlier questions: How do believers know that what they take on faith, as a facet of divine teaching, will not lead them into mere fantasy or fanaticism? I readily agree that this is a perfectly reasonable question, and yet if we answer it in a way that closes the door to divine agency in theology we turn theology into the dry taxidermied specimen I warned about in Chapter 1. We would have "rescued" theology by ensuring that nothing really new could ever be heard within it, nothing beyond the limits of human reason or imagination or self-interest. Instead, as Rowan Williams argues, "Language about God is kept honest in the degree to which it turns on itself in the name of God, and so surrenders itself to God: it is in this way that it becomes possible to see how it is still *God* that is being spoken of. . . . Speaking of God is speaking to God and opening our speech to God's."[13]

Moreover, as I've been hinting, apart from this we would fail to realize the one most profoundly critical principle already present within theology: if theology is really allowed to be an event of divine teaching, and believers are really encouraged thereby to move through beliefs into an actual encounter with the one whose conversation the beliefs of faith teach one to share, then this encounter will leave some observable traces within the lives of believers. In other words, if it is really God that theology is trying to understand, and it is really God who is inciting the search, then we should be able to recognize something good and perhaps even something holy developing in the character of those who are being genuinely and authentically theological. What I'm suggesting, then, is a test for theological legitimacy and integrity that does not predetermine the forms of thought in which theologians venture out, but rather examines the kind of persons their theological journeys make of them.

This doubtless seems an odd sort of criterion to us, and yet that may be due to modernity's severing of the integrity between theory and practice. For the ancient and medieval worlds, the journey towards wisdom or contemplation was no abstract, notional affair that could be measured purely in intellectual terms; rather it was a way of life, a pattern of existence under the steady shaping motion of one's encounter with the really real, and it was both made possible and measured in its authenticity by one's practice. By the later Middle Ages the pursuit of knowledge had come to be understood purely in terms of a theoretical discourse rather than, or alongside of, a discipline or training; this severing of theory and practice made it inevitable that modernity would assume that knowing could be measured in purely conceptual terms alone. By contrast, as one historian puts it, the goal of ancient philosophy was "not to develop a discourse as an end in itself but to act upon souls"; even the conceptual teaching of a philosophical school was not to communicate to them [inquirers and disciples] some ready-made knowledge but to *form* them. In other words, the goal was to learn a type of know-how; to develop a *habitus*, or new capacity to judge and to *transform* – that is, to change people's way of living and of seeing the world.[14]

So if we consider Christian theology in parallel with this, then the chief critical measure of its health and legitimacy would be found not first of all in the domain of rational argument but in the domain of its moral and spiritual influence within the lives of believers. After all, if it is really God that theology is trying to attend to, then insisting that theology's ideas be immediately graspable within the common range of what we already know will irretrievably foreclose the possibility of encountering something genuinely beyond our preconceptions. Yet this need not mean, as Locke thought, that there is no critical moment for theology; for it is still possible to assess someone's ideas at second hand, so to speak, by noticing what impact they have on the person's life. We often, for example, get to know people whose expertise in a particular field of knowledge far exceeds our own, and yet we don't immediately rule their knowledge out of bounds and insist that it must be circumscribed within the limits of our own understanding. Instead, we often find ourselves getting a sense of the people themselves and noting whether their ideas seem to cohere into a life of compassion or of selfishness, of integrity or of duplicity, of self-worth or self-denigration, of patience and hospitality or of intolerance and xenophobia.

One of the most extended modern reflections on these matters comes from the British theologian John Henry Newman (1801–90). In his *University Sermons* delivered between 1826 and 1843, Newman addressed precisely the difficulty that faith faces in the modern era: when people rightly raise critical concerns about faith degenerating into fantasy or fanaticism, the classic modern solution has been to subject faith's claims to the test of universal human rationality. But so often what results, claims Newman, is a cold assortment of rational propositions that were never the original ground of anyone's belief, would never draw anyone into belief, and commonly reduce the teachings of belief to a banal series of platitudes whose triviality is only exceeded by their obviousness. In Newman's view, this is the sadly predictable result of asking people to explain within purely logical terms what only really lives for them in the whole fabric of their lives as thinking, feeling, moral, and spiritual beings. This very interrelatedness of faith, its quality of being so interwoven with the very structure of a person's character, makes the rational articulation of the deep grounds of one's faith quite difficult. In this passage, Newman likens the person of faith to a person of some long-standing virtue or character trait who is asked to explain in purely rational terms the warrants for his or her beliefs.

The gifted individual . . . will of all men be least able (as such) to defend his own views, inasmuch as he takes no external survey of himself. Things which are the most familiar to us, and easy in practice, require the most study, and give the most trouble in explaining. . . . The longer one has persevered in the practice of virtue, the less likely is he to recollect how he began it; what were his difficulties on starting and how surmounted; by what process one truth led to another; the less likely to elicit justly the real reasons latent in his mind for particular observances or opinions. He holds the whole assemblage of moral notions almost as so many collateral and self-evident facts. Hence it is that some of the most deeply-exercised and variously gifted Christians, when they proceed to write or speak upon Religion, either fail altogether, or cannot be understood except on an attentive study; and after all, perhaps, are illogical and unsystematic, assuming what their readers require proved, and seeming to mistake connexion or antecedence for causation, probability for evidence. And over such as these it is, that the minute intellect of inferior men has its moment of triumph.[15]

Newman points to the double-edged liability and opportunity of religious belief as inhering deeply in the whole of a person's life: it is just this quality that, on the one hand, makes it difficult to explain in merely rational terms (for how can you explain the shaping pressure of infinite truth upon the whole life-experience of someone?), and yet, on the other hand, this very multidimensional quality to belief is precisely what makes it possible to evaluate the legitimacy of beliefs. It does this, not by reducing them to pale rational abstractions, but by attending to the way in which they animate and shape the character and life of the person who holds those beliefs.

Thus, over almost the entire course of these fifteen addresses, Newman distills a critical process for assessing theological beliefs. We should expect that those whose beliefs carry them into encounters with the reality of God will manifest signs that they are animated by love and humility in their bearing: "Faith leads the mind to communion with the invisible God."[16] By contrast, those whose beliefs seem trapped within their own anxieties, self-gratifying fantasies, or a hardened insistence on being right, will tend to manifest signs of superstition or bigotry. "The safeguard of Faith is a right state of heart. This it is that gives it birth; it also disciplines it. This is what protects it from bigotry, credulity, and fanaticism."[17] In Newman's view, it is the personal relationship between believers and the one in whom they believe that is the ground of their faith, and by the same token this very personal relationship shapes the character of believers in notable ways. Their fidelity, obedience, and trust in one who is holy and loving engenders in their ways of life an echoing holiness and love; and, argues Newman, if it is authentic this will work against the self-enclosing tendencies of human existence. "Holiness, dutifulness, or love, however we word it, and not Reason, is the eye of faith, the discriminating principle which keeps it from fastening on unworthy objects, and degenerating into enthusiasm or superstition."[18] A "right religious Faith," says Newman, is "instinct with Love towards God and towards man," and so whether this love is evident in a life springing from this faith must be the crucial test: "Love towards man will make it [faith] shrink from cruelty; love towards God from false worship. . . . I say the principle of Love, acting not by way of inquiry or argument, but spontaneously and as an instinct will cause the mind to recoil from cruelty, impurity, and assumption of divine power" to itself.[19]

Just as Newman sees positive signs by which to discern healthy faith, so he also develops negative criteria for identifying a form of faith that is not truly conducting one into a deeper relationship with the living God. We've already seen the implicit hints that a tendency towards cruelty and a mock-divine self-importance are likely marks of an unhealthy faith. The central idea for Newman here is, again, relationship: apart from the stretching, life-giving growth that authentic, faithful relationship with God makes possible, the human person hardens into a self-concerned caricature of itself, falling into an unattractive narrowmindedness that insists on the conformity of all ideas to its own. Whereas a faithful believer is trying to understand the faith well enough, though "with a confession of ignorance," to grow in her or his personal life with God, a bigot is particularly interested in instructing and directing the conduct and beliefs of others:

> Men of narrow minds, far from confessing ignorance and maintaining Truth mainly as a duty, profess . . . to understand the subjects which they take up and the principles which they apply to them. They do not see difficulties. They consider that they hold their doctrines, whatever they are, at least as much upon Reason as upon faith; and they expect to be able to argue others into a belief of them, and are impatient when they cannot. They consider that the premises with which they start just prove the conclusions which they draw, and nothing else. They think that their own views are exactly fitted to solve all the facts which are to be accounted for. . . . They conceive that they profess just *the* truth which makes all things easy. They have their one idea or their favorite notion, which occurs to them on every occasion. They have their one or two topics, which they are continually obtruding, with a sort of pedantry, being unable to discuss, in a natural unconstrained way, or to let their thoughts take their course, in the confidence that they will come safe home at the last.[20]

Newman's acidly comical description suggests personal acquaintance with such types of persons – as well, perhaps, as the recognition, which we surely all share, of an uncomfortable (and not quite escapable) sense of describing oneself. Perhaps the chief symptom noted here is a kind of hectoring sureness, laboring uneasily with an unconscious feeling that everything must be kept in order just so, lest the whole edifice of faith begin to totter.

The correlate of this is impatience with others and with multiple perspectives; this seems to argue a weakened trust in God to bring things to fruition as God wills. "Narrow minds have no power of throwing themselves into the minds of others. They have stiffened in one position, as limbs of the body subjected to confinement . . . They have already parceled out to their own satisfaction the whole world of knowledge; they have drawn their lines, and formed their classes."[21] Underlying Newman's critique, I believe, is his conviction that when believers (and theologians) have ceased to seek out the spiritual companionship of God, when their minds are no longer nourished by the infinite abundance and generosity of God, then they are far more likely to be taken over and captivated by their own anxieties and prejudices. In other words, if the act of faith (as trust and friendship with God) has become vitiated, then the beliefs of faith (as doctrines or teachings) are likely to grow lifeless or eccentric, enforced with a mechanical rigor or idiosyncrasy – or perhaps corroded from within so that they become hollow shells, false and disillusioning in a time of trial. Conversely, if the beliefs of faith are themselves faulty or idolatrous, then they are likely to lead believers not into authentic communion with the living God but into debilitating servitude to a demanding idol, which may often be a cultural or psychological impulse of almost addictive power.

Newman's descriptions of the effects of healthy as opposed to unhealthy faith make at least a good start on a critical moment for theology. Rather than simply ignoring the need for such a perspective, he accepts it. Yet he argues against constraining doctrines to a supposedly common reason that would likely prohibit, even before its inception, the journey of faith into an ever deeper understanding of God's own ideas. Instead, he proposes a recovery of the ancient sense that beliefs, even when they exceed our understanding, can be measured in a practical sense by the shaping effect they have on the lives and consciousness of a believing community and its members.

Now it is time to turn, with this in mind, to some of the particular beliefs of the Christian community over time. While most of our energy will be devoted to understanding the beliefs of faith in and of themselves, it will be salutary to recall, as Newman has shown us, that a healthy act of faith is always the precondition for believing with honesty, generosity, and an authentic desire to grow theologically.

Part II

Theology's Search for Understanding

Chapter 4

Salvation: The Foundation of Christian Theology

ORIENTATION

Why Start with Salvation?

Of all the paths theology could take into the heart of Christian belief, you might wonder why I propose we start with salvation. Let's think about where else we might begin, and how we could decide. Why not begin with the beginning, with creation? We could, but then why not get back "before" time and start at the real beginning with the very *being* of God? But how could we say anything about God apart from the ways human beings have come to know God? What's happening here? Why are we having a problem deciding where to begin? Here's a useful distinction that might clarify how we can begin to think about beginning!

- On the one hand there is the *order of being*, in which God comes before everything,
- on the other hand, there is the *order of knowing*, that is, the order in which we come to know things . . .
- and within the order of knowing, we can order things according to the order of *historical encounter* (the order in which we happen historically to encounter things),
- or we can order things according to the *order of understanding*, that is, the sequence in which persons come logically to apprehend things.

If we were just trying to think about items we meet in everyday experience, say, pencils or postage stamps, it probably would not make much difference where we began. But when we're trying to think about a reality, God, far beyond our ordinary experience, then (as we decided in earlier chapters) we might want to be cautious about allowing the order of our knowing or experience to frame the discussion – lest we unconsciously shrink reality to fit our normal grasp. Suppose, for example, you grew up in a culture that prized warfare and violent conquest; it would be only natural to conceive of ultimate reality as an absolute power that necessarily exercises itself by the overwhelming subjugation of every other being. By contrast, Christians believe they have been encountered by an absolute reality, God, whose "power" seems to be expressed most characteristically, in our world, through humility and self-giving. Furthermore, they think this precisely because they have let their order of knowing be shaped by the order of being, of reality, as they believe that reality has met them in the life, death, and resurrection of Jesus. This definitive encounter of our world by God in Christ is what Christians refer to as salvation.

Or, consider another example. Near the very beginning of the *Summa Theologiae*, Thomas Aquinas puts our order of knowing into a healthy and eye-opening encounter with the order of being. What do you in fact know?, asks Thomas. Well, we know that there are things that exist, that have *being*. If we want to think about God, starting with what we know, then we would have to say that "God" is whatever or whoever it is that causes there to be anything at all, rather than simply nothing. The upshot of this is that our knowing gets confronted by a reality of being whose very definition most marvelously exceeds the grasp of our knowing. Why? Because our knowing is always knowing according to our experience of creatures and, by definition, God is not one of those. So why does Thomas begin with this strange exercise? It has sometimes been thought that Thomas is here (*ST* I. 2. 3) offering a series of proofs for the existence of God, and that he is confirming our reason, our order of knowing, as the correct starting point in theology; that he is leading it as far as it can go before he has to turn more directly to faith and what we can only know by revelation. I think this is not quite accurate.

It is true that Thomas is exercising our knowing here, but I think what he is really aiming at is not so much a proof of anything as a healthy theological exercise in humility; this is the humility that arises when our knowing begins to sense how far beyond its grasp is the reality that confronts it.[1] Recall that in Thomas's view, the first of the gifts of the Holy Spirit (which dispose us to cooperate with God's teaching us) is awe or fear of the Lord: the overwhelming sense of God's infinite reality and beauty and mystery, and with that sense should come an ease in making oneself more available to God. Thus Thomas begins by conducting us to the humility that arises in us when we consider the difference between creatures and Creator. Whatever we know ourselves to mean by the word "God" we cannot mean something like one of the things that exist only bigger and more powerful, like Zeus, or cleverer, like Athena. That would mean that this deity is simply another one of the things that exist and not the reason *why* there are things. Thomas has led our knowing out to its very edge, and then given it the blessed reminder that it exists and knows at all because it is being called into existence moment by moment by God.

So are we just back to our original question, why begin with salvation? Not quite. Thomas's starting point has clarified things by showing us (1) that our knowing may well be where we have to begin (since it is after all we who are trying to understand things), but that (2) our knowing will know best when it is brought out beyond itself into an unknowing, an encounter with the ultimate, infinitely giving reality of God. In this way the order of knowing is illuminated and liberated by the order of divine being, and thus our knowing is opened up to God, in whom knowing and being are one eternal act.

Now let me make a somewhat odd suggestion. Christians believe that the place where our way of knowing and God's way of being most intimately encounter one another, so that our knowing is transformed, is in Jesus by the Holy Spirit. This is so, first, in the sense that our human way of knowing is, in Christ, taken up into a particular divine way of being, and second, in the sense that as people encounter Jesus in various ways, their forms of knowing are transformed. You could even say that their knowing undergoes, through their encounter with him, a death and resurrection. Thus the knowing that is theology comes into being through the event that Christians call salvation.

Salvation as the Basis for Christian Theology

Whatever we mean by "salvation," and we have barely begun to define it, let's consider for a moment how it functions as the source and structure of Christian theology. The idea would be to bracket for the time being what we may think we already know about God or the world and see what it would be like to understand everything from the standpoint of what Christians experience as salvation by Christ in the Holy Spirit. This seems to be what happened to early followers of Jesus: they experienced him as the explanation or the means for understanding everything else. They contrasted their own new, weak, even childlike, understanding in Christ with the apparently firm grasp of other modes of understanding:

> Jews demand signs and Greeks desire wisdom, but we proclaim Christ crucified, a stumbling block to Jews and foolishness to Gentiles, but to those who are the called, both Jews and Greeks, Christ the power of God and the wisdom of God. For God's foolishness is wiser than human wisdom, and God's weakness is stronger than human strength. (1 Corinthians 1: 22–5)

Paul, writing to a congregation of both Jewish and Gentile followers of Jesus, reminds them of their most characteristic and traditional modes of knowledge.[2] For Jews this would mean the great and overwhelming historical signs of God's saving power such as the liberation of Israel from Egypt and the return from exile in Babylon. Note that Paul is not suggesting that there is *no* sign, no power, but that its mode of appearing, "Christ crucified," has to become the new way of understanding God and God's work. Similarly, the Gentile hearers are warned that they have to let their understanding of what really is wisdom be re-modeled by what God is doing in Christ.

It is crucial to realize how utterly unconvincing this would have seemed: the cultural bias of the Gentile world toward success and glorious reputation and high status would have found a humiliated and crucified criminal an impossible, utterly foolish, basis from which to understand reality. One historian comments that the "preaching of the crucified Messiah must have seemed aesthetically and ethically repulsive" to Gentile contemporaries who found it "a dark or even mad superstition."[3] For Jews, to associate God and God's plan with such an odious death would seem blasphemous, and indeed the very death itself was accounted by some as a punishment for Jesus' own blasphemies against the truth of God (see Deuteronomy 21: 23 and Galatians 3: 13). So when Paul pushes this line of argument, he is forcing these early followers of Jesus to confront something they would rather have avoided, namely, the fact that their adherence to Christ crucified could never conceivably be the result of their own predispositions or insights or profound understanding – for all of that would have led them very quickly *away* from Christ crucified. This suggests that the saving power of Christ is not a limited reality, encapsulated within the historical past, but reaches out to call and claim "both Jews and Greeks" by saving also their understanding, by transforming their vision of reality. Paul certainly counted it as central to his message about the crucified Messiah that it would re-schematize and renew the minds of those who were called by God to receive it: "Do not be conformed to this world, but be transformed by the renewing of your minds, so that you may discern what is the will of God – what is good and acceptable and perfect" (Romans 12: 2).

This sense that salvation in Christ becomes the key for reinterpreting everything is omnipresent in early Christian thought. "All things have been handed over to me by my Father," says Jesus in Matthew's Gospel, "and no one knows the Son except the Father, and no one knows the Father except the Son and anyone to whom the Son chooses to reveal him" (11: 27). As we will see, this mutual knowing of the Father and the Son is the very "place" into which Jesus' saving work seems to bring people, and here we can see already that this mutual knowing of the Father and the Son is the basis for understanding everything else. Similarly in Luke's Gospel, the crucified and risen Jesus begins a process of opening the understanding of his followers. In the story of two disciples walking sadly and numbly away from the crucifixion (24: 13–35), Jesus accompanies them although they are not yet able to recognize his presence. Significantly, Jesus seems to move them toward a recognition of himself beside them precisely as he opens their eyes to the ways in which the Hebrew scriptures speak of himself, and then as he re-enacts for them the Last Supper in which he had fed them in advance with the meaning of his death on the cross. Thus in this whole episode Jesus is revealed, as the crucified and risen one, to be the living and self-interpreting Word of God.

Upon later reflection, the two disciples who experienced this self-interpretation of Jesus describe it as an ardent, fiery awakening of their consciousness: "Were not our hearts burning within us while he was talking to us on the road, while he was opening the scriptures to us?" (Luke 24: 32). This is especially significant since the burning, fiery quality points towards the tongues of fire that mark the outpouring of the Holy Spirit upon the disciples at Pentecost (Acts 2). It seems that just as the saving presence of Jesus is the condition for the possibility of the disciples encountering the real meaning and truth of things, so the inspiration of the Holy Spirit is the necessary condition for the disciples coming to hear and understand and speak rightly of what Christ puts before them. And indeed in John's Gospel Jesus says repeatedly to the disciples that the Spirit will be the one to "remind you of all that I have said to you" (14: 25, 16: 12ff.), and will "take what is mine and declare it to you. All that the Father has is mine. For this reason I said that he [the Spirit of truth] will take what is mine and declare it to you" (16: 14–15).

Why is all this important? Because it takes us right back to our initial question in a fundamentally new way: how do we know anything in Christianity? We know the beliefs of faith, Christians think, through God's saving work in Christ and the Spirit. But recall how, when we began this section, we saw how tempting it would be to think that there might be preconditions for faith, conditions determined by our prior knowledge, or by the various psychological and cultural factors that shape our knowing, or more radically yet, on the basis of the very structures and categories of human consciousness itself. Does this mean, if all these features of our experience are made subject to a transformation through the event of salvation, that we are not really talking about human knowing at all when it comes to faith, that we have surreptitiously substituted a supposed "believing mind" for a human mind and that the believing mind is simply "free" from the very nature and reality of what it means to be a thinking human being?

Not at all. First of all, notice how slippery this problem really is. The critical questions just above, while perfectly reasonable, are very far from neutral. If you look at them again, you can see they already presuppose a pretty definite knowledge of "what it means to be a thinking human being." So they are saying, in effect, look here, Christian faith, it is all very well thinking x, y, or z just so long as thinking those things is actually possible within the framework of normal human knowing.[4] But it is precisely the framework of "normal human knowing" that we are wondering if we really know as well as we think we do! What the early followers of Jesus seem to have been saying is that they did *not* know what it means to know and understand reality until the event of salvation overtook them. Consider a feeble analogy. Suppose you had fallen from an airplane as an infant, been rendered blind by your injuries, and then were raised by a pack of gruffly affectionate wolves. You might get along reasonably well, but you would be entirely unaware that there was a dimension such as sight that you lacked. You would not really even know the full scope of your human nature, unless someone came along who could enter into your wolf-life sufficiently (a) for you to learn from her a way of communicating, and (b) for her to help you understand that you were blind – and you could not even really understand the full meaning of *that* until you could also be healed, until you had been enabled to "see" what seeing is like and how much more there was to reality than you had thought.

This is not so very far from what early followers of Jesus seem to have felt had happened to them as a result of their encounter with Christ. Someone whom they could not entirely understand came to be with them. Over time they seemed to pick up from him a way of being and acting and communicating that began to change their perspectives about things; in particular they sensed a depth opening up around and within themselves, a presence of deeper awareness and communion with reality that Jesus called the Spirit and which seemed to fill their hearts with Jesus' own way of being and communicating with the one he called "Abba" or Father. Watching him going out in the early mornings to pray, and then coming back to them; going out into the wilderness, and then returning; going out into the roaring hostility and anger of the crowd, out into death, and then coming back to them again – they felt as though Jesus were opening up a unknown dimension, tracing out a space, and revealing within the very depths of reality a pattern they had not sensed before, a pattern of intelligent, life-giving, loving generosity. After his death and resurrection and the coming of the Spirit, it was if their eyes were opened to see all the ways he had been leading them into this hidden dimension of reality, this living presence of God. But for reasons they could not initially fathom, it seemed to take Jesus' complete entrusting of himself on the cross to the one he called Father, and the Father's response in raising Jesus from the dead, and the outpouring of Jesus' communion with the Father into the lives of Jesus' followers by the giving of the Holy Spirit – it seemed to take all of that before they were healed enough to see that they had been blind.

This brief and fragmentary description of salvation should at least make clear how entirely this would mean not the undermining or replacement of our human nature and human knowing but rather its healing and liberation. It was from this standpoint, then, that early Christians began to sense that Jesus had been, somehow, the very point of God's plan all along, and that everything has been "in accordance with the eternal purpose that he [God] has carried out in Christ Jesus" (Ephesians 3: 11). Indeed the very coming of everything into being seems itself to be marked by the involvement of Christ: there is, Paul writes to the Corinthians, "one God, the Father, from whom are all things and for whom we exist, and one Lord, Jesus Christ, through whom are all things and through whom we exist" (1 Corinthians 8: 6). Note here the prepositions: the Father is the one "from whom" and "for whom" all things exist, their source and goal; and it is "through" Christ that all things are and exist, so that Christ is described as the way, the means, by which the Father's giving of existence is accomplished. In other words, the earthly events of Jesus' life, death, resurrection, and the outpouring of the Holy Spirit are experienced as the unfolding in our world of an eternal and universal divine plan and activity. It would be like coming to the turning point in a story where you suddenly realize what everything has really meant, and even having a sense that this is what it has all been "for," that everything is only fully explicable in terms of this event.

This would mean that humankind not only didn't know the truth of its own humanity until Jesus brought it to life by bringing it into communion with God, but that humans didn't really even know what the creation itself meant, or who God is. It is not a question of being exclusive or dismissive of other points of view;

rather, the early Christian writings suggest an overwhelming sense that the process of salvation in Christ and the Spirit has radically changed the perception of Jesus' followers. The simple logic, later articulated by Athanasius of Alexandria (*c*.296–373), goes something like this: (1) what happened to the world in the event of Christ is an infinite, transcendent act only comparable to the act of creation itself, (2) only God can truly create reality, therefore the event of Christ is in fact an act of God, for as Paul had said, salvation is the advent of a new creation. Perhaps the most concentrated and compact expression of this growing sense that the act of salvation is the revelation of the ultimate truth about everything comes in this passage from the Letter to the Colossians. I can best explain what I mean if you will switch back and forth below, reading a verse or two of the text, and then turning to my running commentary.

Letter to the Colossians 1: 13–20

13 He has rescued us from the power of darkness and transferred us into the kingdom of his beloved Son, **14** in whom we have redemption, the forgiveness of sins.

13–14 We start with the event of salvation, which both here and at the end of the passage frames, reveals, and interprets the eternal creative purposes of God. Notice the language here of rescue, of redemption or liberation from enslavement, from the "power of darkness" into the "kingdom of his beloved Son." The key is the movement from one state of evil or nonexistence into a state ordered by the Son's relationship with the Father, a state of sharing in the Son's being as beloved and therefore a state marked by the releasing of sins.

15 He is the image [*eikōn*] of the invisible God, the firstborn of all creation; **16** for in him all things in heaven and on earth were created, things visible and invisible, whether thrones or dominions or rulers or powers – all things have been created through him and for him. **17** He himself is before all things, and in him all things hold together.

15–16 Jesus' identity as God's beloved is something only revealed by the resurrection, but thus revealed it displays two aspects: he is the icon, the visible sign of God's reality which is beyond all visibility, but also, this very iconic or representational quality is made manifest not only in Jesus' earthly life, death, and resurrection; but the resurrection also reveals him as the agent of God's *creating* event of infinite life-giving from the very beginning. Everything that exists, even the most exalted realities of the world as we know it and of the hidden spiritual world, receives its existence in, through, and for Christ.

17 This means that things only "hold together" or have coherence and integrity as they unfold and take part in God's eternal purpose being worked out through Christ.

18 He is the head of the body, the church; he is the beginning, the firstborn from the dead, so that he might come to have first place in everything. **19** For in him all the fullness of God was pleased to dwell, **20** and through him God was pleased to reconcile to himself all things, whether on earth or in heaven, by making peace through the blood of his cross.

18 This inner meaning and interrelationship of everything in Jesus manifests itself by taking an iconic form within the world, namely the inner meaning and interrelationship of members of Christ's body, the Church: creatures whose identity is constituted and revealed precisely through their sharing in his life beyond the power of death. **19–20** Again, we note how the reflections on creation in Christ are embraced at the end within reflections on salvation in Christ. Here the world's dividedness and lack of integrity are now revealed as in fact the results of all things' estrangement from God. Since, as we saw in 16 and 17 above, things only cohere or have real existence through their sharing in the Son's relationship with God and so in the divine purpose, apart from that all things would be falling away into a region of darkness and enmity. But the eternal creative purpose of God for all things is renewed and accomplished as he reconciles all things back to himself in Christ. Christ's blood shed on the cross is likened to the blood of a sacrifice that marks the re-establishing of people's relationship to God: the relationship of peace, the relationship of God's beloved with God.

We can identify at least four instances of "iconic" logic here, in which the events of salvation serve as the image or icon of that which is beyond our sight:

- The foundational icon: Christ as image or icon of the invisible God.
- Christ's self-giving on the cross as the icon of an eternal divine self-giving in creation.
- Christ's relationship with the Father as the icon of humanity's relationship with God.
- The re-integrated, coherently meaningful, and peaceful life of Christ's body, the Church – in virtue of the Church's salvation or new creation in Christ – as the icon of the integrated, coherently meaningful, and peaceful life the creatures were intended to share with God in virtue of their original creation in Christ.

So in each case, salvation makes possible (like an icon) an authentic encounter with the reality beyond our present imagining.

Bearing all this in mind, we might want to try our hand at a theological understanding that begins from the doctrine of salvation. For example, how might this alter our understanding of human being? Consider how we might have thought that our ordinary, often painfully broken or diminished experience of human life is simply "the way things are." But if we start from the reality of salvation, it would mean that the most troubling aspects of human existence (the very things we see Christ encountering and overcoming) would now be seen not as things we must simply accept but as dimensions of existence that are in the process of being trans-formed, as things that are *not* the ultimate truth of human existence at all. Starting from salvation would also mean, positively, that God may be in the process of calling humanity out beyond the seeming limits of what we thought was human life but which may be only the provisional form of human existence. Hence, for example, we find the idea developing in at least one early Christian community that humanity has been brought, through Christ and the Spirit, into a new way of relating to God, a way of existing that has begun to take effect now but whose ultimate pattern is bounded only by God's own pattern of existence: "Beloved, we are God's children now; what we will be has not yet been revealed. What we do know is this: when he is revealed, we will be like him, for we will see him as he is" (1 John 3: 2).

Similarly, if we were to develop our theological understanding from salvation outwards, we would need to allow many of our ideas – about God, about the defini-tion of sin, about the goal of creation, and so on – to be reconfigured. This is not simply a theoretical point. It is the reason, in fact, behind the great yet beneficial struggle that Christian theology underwent before and after the Council of Nicaea in 325: as we will see, the reality of what God had accomplished in Christ and the Spirit was gradually transforming the very idea of God towards the idea of God as Trinity. Just for the moment, we merely want to be clear about this fundamental shift in knowing that lies at the foundation of Christian theology: the act of salva-tion becomes the lens by which everything else is perceived and understood.

Identifying Different Approaches to the Mystery of Salvation

The wide range of emphases and approaches to salvation over the course of Chris-tian history testifies to its depth and mysteriousness. In this section it will be helpful to provide some very preliminary sense of this range of thought. Every discourse about salvation, known as soteriology (from the Greek term for savior, *sōtēr*), has to answer four fundamental questions:

- What are the saved being saved *from*?
- What are they being saved *for*?
- What is the *means* by which salvation is accomplished?
- How wide is the *scope* of salvation?

If you can get clarity about those four questions when you are reading the great primary sources, you will have a firm basis for going deeper. We can probably also map possible responses to these questions so that almost every approach to salvation could be placed somewhere on the axes described in the accompanying figure.

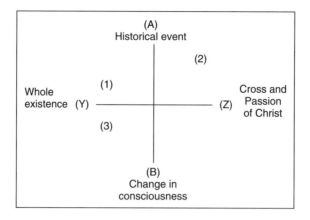

Axis A–B marks the polarity between those theories (A) that understand salvation primarily in terms of an actual turning point in the history of the world or an objective change in the status of the saved (perhaps apart from whether they are able to realize or cooperate with this), as contrasted with those soteriologies (B) that emphasize a more subjective shift in humanity's own consciousness and self-understanding; while this may be occasioned by an account of some event in the past, salvation per se can, in this view, only be a present existential event in the person being saved. Axis Y–Z marks the polarity between those soteriologies (Y) that emphasize, as the chief means of salvation, the Incarnation of the eternal Word itself, or the whole life, death, resurrection of Jesus and outpouring of the Holy Spirit, in contrast with those soteriologies (Z) that understand salvation as accomplished more exclusively by means of Jesus' suffering and death on the cross. As a crude practice exercise, we might very roughly pinpoint Origen (*c.*185–*c.*254) at (1), Calvin (1509–64) at (2), and Elizabeth Johnson (contemporary with this book) at (3); we can see why if we state their basic responses to our four fundamental questions, as laid out in the table.

This should give you a preliminary sense of the shape of the landscape ahead of us (its contours or polarities) and the sorts of questions one needs to ask (from, for, means, scope) in finding one's way through theological reflection on salvation. Now let's briefly consider some sense of the range of metaphors or underlying conceptual domains. For convenience, I have identified these as medical, legal, cosmic-historical, military-political, sacrificial, and mystical (see accompanying table); and of course we always need to bear in mind that most often any given writer will interweave two or more of these modes of thought; indeed too narrow a dependence on only one seems almost inevitably to signal distortion or exaggeration. The seminal significance of these fundamental metaphors cannot be overemphasized, and warrants me in exploring them a bit; I want in each case to give you a taste of how pungent and flavorsome they each are so that you can recognize them at work in the later developments of soteriology. Because I intend to examine the interaction of these conceptualities in a variety

How three theologians treat salvation

	Origen (1)	*Calvin (2)*	*Johnson (3)*
Saved from?	distraction from God, enslavement to evil	eternal damnation, the wrath of God justly due to disobedient creatures	structures of political, economic, cultural, and sexual oppression
Saved for?	return to communion with and joyful contemplation of God	enjoyment of intended covenant status with God, as sign of God's power and glory	full flourishing of all, especially the marginalized, through communion with all and with God
By what means?	union of our humanity with the eternal Word, enjoying unbroken vision of the Father, and so re-educating humankind	the sufferings and death of Christ on the cross bear the punishment and penalty of our sins	Jesus' solidarity with the oppressed and his refusal to use power release a new way of being in the world with each other
Scope?	probably universal; the hoped-for return of the whole creation to God	limited to the elect	available to all who are drawn to enter the communion of mutual solidarity

of theologians later on, for the moment I will simply exemplify each mode with biblical sources.

Medical. It might be argued that healing is the most central image of salvation in the Bible. The Greek terms associated with salvation "related generally to rescue from misfortune of all kinds: shipwreck, the ravages of a journey, enemies in times of conflict, and so on. By far, however, the most common usage of these terms in the larger Greco-Roman world was medical. 'To save' was 'to heal.'"[5] In order to interpret this mode of reflection correctly, we have to recall that in the ancient world, healing was rarely conceived in narrowly biological and individualist senses: healing is a process of restoring harmony for the whole of a person's existence including, especially, restoring the person to integrity within the community.

In the Old Testament, we can see this communal sense of healing as salvific in Exodus: after the whole story of Israel's liberation from slavery has been recounted, and the people are being led into the wilderness toward freedom, God declares "I am the LORD who heals you" (Exodus 15: 26). The prophet Jeremiah cries out, "Heal me, O LORD, and I shall be healed; save me, and I shall be saved" (17: 14). And of course, healing figures prominently throughout Jesus' ministry. Most

Conceptual domains for salvation

Medical: God heals everything through Christ.

Legal: Christ bears all punishment for sins.

Cosmic-historical: Christ re-enacts human history correctly, reinitiating the human race.

Military-political: Christ conquers evil and liberates those it holds in captivity.

Sacrificial: As the full and final sacrifice, Christ restores full communion with God.

Mystical: By his Incarnation, death, and resurrection, Christ unites humanity to God.

---

significantly, he regularly connects his authority to heal and his authority to forgive sins (e.g., Matthew 9: 2–8). Early followers of Jesus understood his healing power as a direct expression of his divine commission and indeed as a sign of the advent of God's healing and salvific reordering of human affairs (e.g., Matthew 12: 24–33; Mark 2: 22–30). In this mode of reflection, the emphasis is nicely balanced between the act of God and the transforming realization of that divine act within the lives of the healed. In other words, the healing or medical metaphor inherently holds together dimensions of salvation that some other metaphors tend to emphasize at the expense of one another.

Legal. In this conceptuality the notions of offense and punishment, disobedience and consequent penalty, are brought to the fore. Salvation is understood in a variety of ways within this mode of thought. It can be understood as a bearing of punishment by a savior so that the penalty does not fall upon those being saved. Something like this seems to be at work in texts that were hugely influential in the early Christian era, namely the Suffering Servant songs in the Book of the Prophet Isaiah (42: 1–9; 49: 1–6; 50: 4–11; 52: 13–53: 12). In these texts, which early Christians interpreted as speaking of Jesus, the sufferer is seen as undergoing a punishment in place of those who deserve punishment but are unable or unwilling to suffer it themselves. Note the intermingling in this passage of legal language about suffering a punishment for wrongdoing with the language of healing, indicating that the bearing of suffering on behalf of another makes possible the healing or salvation of the other:

> Surely he has borne our infirmities
> and carried our diseases;
> yet we accounted him stricken,
> struck down by God, and afflicted.
> But he was wounded for our transgressions,
> crushed for our iniquities;
> upon him was the punishment that

made us whole,
and by his bruises we are healed . . .
For he was cut off from the land of the living,
stricken for the transgression of my people. (Isaiah 53: 4–5, 8)

Early Christians, commenting on these texts, came to think of Jesus' suffering and death as a vicarious sharing in human sin or alienation from God; on the basis of the resurrection, Christians understood Jesus' suffering as truly life-giving to others: "For our sake [God] made [Jesus] to be sin who knew no sin, so that in him we might become the righteousness of God" (2 Corinthians 5: 21); or again, Christ "himself bore our sins in his body on the cross, so that, free from sins, we might live for righteousness" (1 Peter 2: 24). Note in these texts, first, the idea of Jesus' solidarity with sinners in entering into their broken state of existence, and, second, the very definite momentum in both texts towards a new state of life and being righteous, that is, being in accord with God.

The question that will engage Christian theology from that moment onwards is "How?" How is it that Jesus' suffering and death achieves this new life and righteousness for others? The passages from Isaiah seem to suggest that such suffering is accepted by God as a bearing of the penalty that ought to fall upon sinners by virtue of their sin. The crucial idea here is that the "punishment" or inevitable result of sinning is deeper and deeper separation from God, a living death and a deathly counterfeit of true life. As we will see, later eras of Christian theology sometimes literalized the metaphors, so that God is understood as demanding that a punishment be suffered as the necessary precondition for forgiving sinners. In these readings, the passion and death of Christ are interpreted as making satisfaction, in effect recompensing God for the offenses committed by sinners against divine justice.

The imagery can also, however, be read somewhat less literally; in this interpretation the "bearing of a punishment" would be taken as figurative language that seeks to express Jesus' utmost loving solidarity with those who are separated from God. In this reading, the resurrection becomes the crucial sign that God accepts Christ's loving obedience to the law, in solidarity with those who are not obedient, and so, *because* of Christ's solidarity with sinners, God accepts them also into forgiveness and new life. In this very acceptance, made known by the resurrection of Jesus, early Christians came to see that the whole of Christ's work had itself been from the first an expression within the world of God's loving desire to overcome the death imposed by sin and raise humanity to life with God: "God, who is rich in mercy, out of the great love with which he loved us even when we were dead through our trespasses, made us alive together with Christ – by grace you have been saved – and raised us up with him and seated us with him in the heavenly places in Christ Jesus" (Ephesians 2: 4–6). It is worth noting that in this reading of the legal metaphors, what is saving is not so much the suffering and death of Jesus in and of itself, but rather Jesus' utter attachment of himself to the suffering depths of the human condition; thus his death would be the sign of his saving refusal to forsake humanity in its need. Furthermore, the judgment or verdict that God then passes upon humanity in Christ would not be his death upon the cross (as a penal substitution for humanity's rightful punishment by death); but rather God's verdict would be the resurrection of Jesus from the dead, by which Jesus' loving solidarity with the human family is vindicated and revealed as the true and rightful sign of God's inexhaustible love for the creation.

Cosmic-historical. This complex of metaphors draws its power from the whole sweep of the biblical narrative: creation, fall, calling of Israel, covenants, disobedience, slavery in Egypt, deliverance, disobedience, exile, longing for the rebuilding of Jerusalem. The Gospel of Matthew recounts the story of Jesus as embracing many elements of Israel's life story, complete with a sojourn into Egypt, a return to Israel, and a divine teaching from the mountain. The later Pauline literature interprets this long history in cosmic terms as the unfolding of God's eternal plan of salvation, the secret meaning of which is revealed in Christ. The Letter to the Ephesians speaks of this as the "mystery of Christ" and as "the plan of the mystery hidden for ages in God who created all things," a plan whose unfolding in history "was in accordance with the eternal purpose that he has carried out in Christ Jesus" (Ephesians 3: 4, 9, 11). The idea is that the story of the human race was meant to find its turning point in the story of Israel, but the whole story has grown distorted by human disobedience, so that the divine purpose and meaning in events and the calling of humanity has grown obscure and lost to human comprehension.

Into this narrative, the original divine meaning or rationale (*Logos* in Greek) has now appeared, coming to exist within the very humanity that can no longer perceive or comprehend God's Word which is in reality the truth and meaning of their own existence. In the sublime Prologue to the Gospel according to John, this eternal Word is described as the one through whom all things came into being, and as now coming into the world "yet the world did not know him": "But to all who received him, who believed in his name, he gave power to become children of God" (John 1: 10, 12). The original "children of God" were Adam and Eve and the Gospel of John might be read as, in part, as an early Christian commentary on Genesis, with the story of Jesus serving as the revelation and restoration of God's primordial meaning (*logos*) for all things. Through his seven signs and discourses, the Word incarnate unlocks the original divine purpose within creation, and sets humanity itself back in motion towards its true identity as "children of God."

Paul had already interpreted the story of Jesus as a summing up in one human being of the whole human story begun in Adam; but whereas with Adam the human story had gone badly off course through human disobedience to God, Christ reverses the whole sequence and initiates a fresh beginning, a new creation, for the human journey.

> Just as one man's trespass led to condemnation for all, so one man's act of righteousness leads to justification for all. For just as by the one man's disobedience the many

were made sinners, so by the one man's obedience the many will be made righteous. (Romans 5: 18–19)

In this cosmic-historical perspective, salvation is achieved by the whole incarnate life, death, and resurrection of Jesus, yet a special prominence is accorded to the complete fidelity and obedience of Jesus, exemplified by his acceptance of the cross. The idea is that in all the places, both small and great, where humankind has turned away from God – preferring a way that is really no way at all but rather death – Jesus enters in, and there in all of those places, in the most intense and fully realized way, he chooses to hear and respond faithfully to the divine calling for humanity. Why is this saving? Because in this view, by his obedience Jesus not only re-establishes the roots of humanity's life in relationship with God, but by calling to his side a community of disciples he brings into the world a new beginning for the human race, a gathering in which the world's practices of disobedience may become transformed by the Spirit into the practices of Jesus' obedience.

Military-political. With this metaphorical field, we can begin by thinking of Israel's experience of having been rescued from slavery by God and claimed as God's own people from alien forces. This fundamental ground of Israel's existence suggested at least two lines of metaphorical development. First, God is sometimes likened to a victorious warrior who conquers and holds in derision the forces who would overmaster and enthrall the children of God:

> The LORD is with me like a dread warrior;
> therefore my persecutors will stumble,
> and they will not prevail.
> They will be greatly shamed,
> for they will not succeed.
> Their eternal dishonor
> will never be forgotten.
> O LORD of hosts [armies], you test the righteous,
> you see the heart and the mind;
> let me see your retribution upon them,
> for to you have I committed my cause.
> Sing to the LORD;
> praise the LORD!
> For he has delivered the life of the needy
> from the hands of evildoers. (Jeremiah 20: 11–13)

The yearning and gratitude of this imagery is immediately evident and speaks of its power to evoke Israel's faith and hope in God. In a tumultuous and perilous region of the world, beset by many opposing nations, the sense of God's protection of the people was also a readily available metaphor for God's overwhelming salvation from sin, evil, and death itself.

A second and closely allied development was the image of God as liberator, vindicator, and redeemer from bondage of every kind, including malicious and mendacious treatment at the hands of one's persecutors. This biblical language rarely goes into a detailed or literal analysis of who is holding one in oppression and what price God must pay for one's ransoming, though responses to these questions will emerge in sometimes surprisingly flamboyant detail during the patristic era of theology. A typical Old Testament instance arises in the austerely beautiful cry of Job, nettled by his "friends" and seemingly abandoned by God for transgressions that Job claims he has not in fact committed. "How long will you torment me, and break me in pieces with words?" Job asks his comforters; and yet he is convinced that the truth of his innocence, of his care for the poor, and of his genuine love for God will finally be declared by one who will come to vindicate him, even perhaps after he has departed this life:

> I know that my Redeemer lives,
> and that at the last he will stand upon the earth;
> and after my skin has been thus destroyed,
> then in my flesh I shall see God,
> whom I shall see on my side,
> and my eyes shall behold, and not another.
> My heart faints within me! (Job 19: 25–7)

Remember that Job's dreadful plight has been brought upon him by the Accuser, Satan, who insinuates that Job only really loves God because he has received favor from the Lord. So, by laying waste to all of Job's joys and even his sense of his own identity, Satan thinks he can bring Job to the point of cursing God and betraying him. Yet it is precisely Job's trust in a redeemer, someone who can vindicate the truth of his life and set him free at last from the prison of lies and despair into which he has fallen, that sustains him. He speaks of it as a virtual resurrection, a truthful knowing that brings him to life again in the presence of the one who knows him.

The theme of Jesus as the redeemer who will vindicate his people against the lies and deceptions of Satan emerges prominently in the Gospel of John. There Jesus declares that following him will undo the spell of illusion and deceit that has mesmerized people: "Jesus said to the Jews who had believed in him, 'If you continue in my word, you are truly my disciples; and you will know the truth, and the truth will make you free'" (John 8: 31–2). John contrasts this liberating truth with the enslavement of false belief; he understands Jesus to be restoring humanity to its truthful identity as God's beloved children and so freeing them from falling under the murderous and deceitful manipulation of a false parent, the devil. John portrays Jesus speaking openly of the ominous antagonism towards him breeding at the devil's behest in the hearts of those who, at the end of this very scene, will pick up stones to throw at him: "You are from your father the devil, and you choose to do your father's desires. He was a murderer from the beginning and does not stand in the truth, because there is no truth in him. When he lies, he speaks according to his own nature, for he is a liar and the father of lies" (John

8: 44). In this conception, redemption is fundamentally an act of rescuing people from mortally destructive illusions and fears that dominate and oppress them.

Throughout the other gospels too, Jesus is often portrayed in conflict with malign spiritual forces which brutalize and enslave the people. The temptations in the wilderness highlight this conflict at the beginning of Jesus' ministry. Luke in particular sees the climactic struggle of Christ's passion and death as perhaps the covertly manipulated work of the evil one who, after failing to seduce Jesus in the wilderness "departed from him until an opportune time" (Luke 4: 13). Perhaps the most arresting description of Jesus' saving activity in terms of the defeat of the devil and rescue of his people comes in the Letter to the Hebrews: "Since therefore the children share flesh and blood, he [Jesus] himself likewise shared the same things, so that through death he might destroy the one who has the power of death, that is, the devil and free those who all their lives were held in slavery by the fear of death" (Hebrews 2: 14–16). Here we see Jesus as clearly entering deeply into the human condition in order to pry loose the powerful grip that the devil has gained upon people by menacing them with death. Later theologians will interpret Jesus' death as itself the price of our redemption, the fee paid to set us free from slavery to this fallen and hence dying form of life. But again, it may be more fruitful not to literalize the metaphor too drastically: Jesus' death is the "price" of humanity's life, but that may be understood as the unlimited and unstinting extent of his work to reach into humanity's plight and deliver it from its jailor. The fact that Jesus accomplishes this by trusting the true God even into the jaws of death – thus unmasking its mendacious assertion of authority over humanity – need not imply that God has literally to "pay off" the devil to redeem humanity.

Sacrificial. This range of metaphors has perhaps the widest and deepest roots in scripture. The fall away from direct communion with God in the Garden of Eden necessitates the rise of sacrifice, a religious mediation process in which people's relationship with God can, as it were, be marked out by ritual and practice, and so restored. The whole sacrificial system, the actual function and legitimacy of which is often critiqued within the Old Testament itself, speaks of the deep urging and longing of the people for a renewed relationship with God. The Old Testament often portrays God as working to transform completely the inevitable mental habits that sacrificial systems seem to have engendered in the ancient Mediterranean world. In Genesis, the dark and desperate urge to offer up anything to placate a powerful deity is suddenly interrupted: God does *not* require the sacrifice of Abraham's beloved child in order for Abraham's relationship with God to be fostered.

> He bound his son Isaac, and laid him on the altar, on top of the wood. Then Abraham reached out his hand and took the knife to kill his son. But the angel of the LORD called to him from heaven, and said, "Abraham, Abraham!" And he said, "Here I am." He said, "Do not lay your hand on the boy or do anything to him; for now I

know that you fear God, since you have not withheld your son, your only son, from me." And Abraham looked up and saw a ram, caught in a thicket by its horns. Abraham went and took the ram and offered it up as burnt offering instead of his son. So Abraham called that place "The LORD will provide"; as it is said to this day, "On the mount of the LORD it shall be provided." (Genesis 22: 9–14)

Early Christian writers sometimes interpreted Golgotha, the site of Jesus' crucifixion, as the same mount where God provides.

The Old Testament critique of sacrifice emphasized that such offerings were not something God needs, not something humanity has to offer in order to propitiate God, but rather that such offerings are provided *by* God. It is God who graciously gives the bounty, the means by which the people may make a sign for themselves of the communion God offers them and of their thankful participation in it:

I will not accept a bull from your house, or goats from your folds. For every wild animal of the forest is mine, the cattle on a thousand hills. . . . Do I eat the flesh of bulls or drink the blood of goats? Offer to God a sacrifice of thanksgiving, and pay your vows to the Most High. (Psalm 50: 9–10, 13–14)

Similarly, the prophets remind God's people that the deepest means of communion with God is not the slaying of animals or vegetable offerings but a pattern of humble love that walks in fidelity with God: "I desire steadfast love and not sacrifice, the knowledge of God rather than burnt offerings" (Hosea 6: 6).

All these themes are developed in the New Testament interpretation of Jesus. Most famously perhaps, John's Gospel portrays Jesus as the sacrificial Passover lamb whose death at the very time of the slaying of the lambs in Jerusalem (19: 14) accomplishes the salvation of his people. The Book of Revelation envisions this theme in cosmic terms, glimpsing at the heart of heaven the sacrificial Lamb upon the very throne of divine sovereignty (22: 1), thus making clear the victory and acceptability of Christ's self-offering, and, most importantly, suggesting to later writers the idea of an eternal self-giving as the very rhythm of divine life. This Lamb which has been slain frees people for life with God, leads them as their shepherd and becomes the very light by which they see (see John 10 and 12 for links to Jesus as shepherd and light of the world). It is important to see that in this conceptuality, Christ is not simply the sacrificial victim who makes possible communion with God but is seen as the eternal outflowing into our world of God's communion-bestowing life. Thus Christ's life, death, and resurrection become the earthly form of this eternal offer of communion. Within the conditions of a broken world, the event of communion takes the form of sacrifice offered in the temple and finally on the altar of the cross; but within the infinite graciousness of heaven, God and the Lamb take the place of the temple as the locus of sacrifice (21: 22), suggesting that the true heavenly reality to which earthly sacrifice corresponds is in fact the eternally flowing life of divine self-sharing. In this view, then, we can see an opening toward later soteriological ideas in which salvation is understood as nothing less than an embracing of our violent earthly patterns of relationship within the infinitely peaceful self-giving relations of God the Trinity. Sacrifice is revealed as the ambivalent earthly expression of the eternal divine self-giving which is the very life of God, a life of infinite trinitarian communion.

Perhaps the apex of this conceptuality comes in the Letter to the Hebrews. There Jesus is interpreted not only as the sacrifice being offered but as the true High Priest who, because he is unblemished by sin, can authentically make the perfect offering, an offering so fulfilling and complete that it brings all need for sacrifice to an end. Indeed, says Hebrews, "Christ did not enter a sanctuary made by human hands, a mere copy of the true one, but he entered into heaven itself, now to appear in the presence of God on our behalf. . . . He has appeared once for all at the end of the age to remove sin by the sacrifice of himself" (9: 24, 26). In this view, the life of self-giving and obedience, and above all the death upon the cross, are interpreted as a priestly action within our world; but because they are offered by one who is "the reflection of God's glory and the exact imprint (character) of God's very being" (Hebrews 1: 3), the offering is understood as having cosmic and eternal significance, an offering made within heaven itself and opening the way to heaven for others. Especially in later eastern Christian soteriology, the self-offering made by Christ on the cross is understood as consummated and accepted by the Father in the resurrection; thus the whole paschal mystery of Jesus' passing over from death to life may be seen as saving because it re-establishes within the human situation the channel of communion between humanity and God.

Mystical. Our final range of metaphors follows on closely from the previous, though it focuses less on the sacrificial means for establishing and re-establishing communion and more directly on the phenomenon of communion itself, made possible by the hidden (or mystical) presence of God with humanity and the exaltation of humanity into the mystical (or heavenly) presence of God. In Israel's wilderness journey out of Egypt, God is present not only via the guiding pillar of cloud and fire or the overwhelming voice on Mount Sinai. In massively gorgeous detail (see Exodus 25–30, for example), God teaches Israel how to embody a mysterious ark and tent of meeting where the divine presence may sojourn within the life of the people. God promises to hallow this means of encounter and the saving significance of the divine presence is highlighted:

> I will consecrate the tent of meeting and the altar; Aaron also and his sons will I consecrate, to serve me as priests. I will dwell among the Israelites, and I will be their God. And they shall know that I am the LORD their God who brought them out of the land of Egypt that I might dwell among them. (Exodus 29: 44–6)

The last phrase even suggests that the liberation from Egypt is itself merely a preparation for this indwelling of the people by God in order to effect their growth in holiness and likeness to the divine life.

The same theme is at work in the stories of David's yearning to build a temple in which the ark and God's presence might have a fitting site fixed at the heart of the people of God in the land. David's desires reach fruition through the work of his son Solomon, who erects a lavish and intricately designed temple of vast splendor as a site of communion for the people with God and as a dwelling place for the divine "name." After years of toil, Solomon offers a deeply moving prayer to God, beseeching that whenever the people cry out in distress and need in this temple, whenever they seek forgiveness there for their sins, or even if they are far away and yet turn to face this temple, that God would hear their entreaties. Solomon cries out:

> But will God indeed dwell on the earth? Even the heaven and highest heaven cannot contain you, much less this house that I have built! Regard your servant's prayer and his plea, O LORD my God, heeding the cry and the prayer that your servant prays to you today; that your eyes may be open night and day toward this house, the place of which you said, "My name shall be there." (1 Kings 8: 27–9)

> When Solomon had ended his prayer, fire came down from heaven and consumed the burnt offering and the sacrifices; and the glory of the LORD filled the temple. The priests could not enter the house of the LORD, because the glory of the LORD filled the LORD's house. When all the people of Israel saw the fire come down and the glory of the LORD on the temple, they bowed down on the pavement with their faces to the ground, and worshiped and gave thanks to the LORD. (2 Chronicles 7: 1–3)

For the biblical writers, the beauty and intensity of these passages express something of the profound longing for God's saving presence that years of following God through the wilderness had awakened in Israel. The almost inconceivable majesty of the divine glory – so filling the temple that not even the priests could get to their work – is always both dangerous and wonderful for the people: dangerous, in that ages of routinized ritual could dull the people's awareness of the radical holiness in their midst, desensitizing them to their calling as a priestly people whose way of life should signal the radiant holiness of God to all the nations (a charge often leveled against the temple and its servants by the prophets); wonderful, in that it permitted an ever deeper exploration of life lived intimately within the very presence of God (a theme lovingly expressed in many of the psalms and also perhaps in the Song of Songs).

As a range of metaphors for salvation in Christ, these themes reach their fullest expression in John's Gospel, where Jesus himself is described as the incarnate presence of the divine glory living or "tenting" (John 1: 14) in humanity's midst, and Christ's body is described as the new temple (2: 19ff.) wherein many will be called to worship God in spirit and in truth (4: 23ff.). In the Farewell Discourses of John 13–17, the evangelist portrays Jesus as, in effect opening up this space of prayer and worship to the disciples by drawing them intimately within his own relationship to the Father and the Spirit. In these remarkable chapters, of inexpressible significance for Christian theology and the life of faith, humankind is invited to abide in Christ and so to pass over into the very heart of God. In a quite different way from Solomon, and yet not without strangely transformed echoes of his prayer, Jesus asks on behalf of all who follow him:

> Father, I desire that those also, whom you have given me, may be with me where I am, to see my glory, which you have given me because you loved me before the foundation of the world. Righteous Father, the world does not know you, but I know you; and these know that you have sent me. I made your name known to them, and I will make it known, so that the love with which you have loved me may be in them, and I in them. (John 17: 24–6)

Jesus makes the "name" of the Father known to his disciples, that is, he initiates them into the new personal relationship with the one who sent him, and makes possible an outpouring of their mutual love, the Holy Spirit, the Comforter, into the lives of the disciples. This is already to suggest that salvation is accomplished by virtue of the Incarnation in and of itself, and yet John's Gospel clearly interprets Jesus' self-giving on the cross as the consummation of his calling and mission to incarnate the Word, the message of the Father's true identity as love, within the broken structures of the world humanity has made.

In a somewhat different way, Paul also considers the means by which salvation works itself out through one's being "in Christ," through a profound offer of Jesus to make his life and death the means of sharing also in the Father's raising him to new life. This participation in Christ's dying and rising achieves a relinquishment of the old self enslaved to sin and the creation of a new self-in-Christ: "I have been crucified with Christ; and it is no longer I who live, but it is Christ who lives in me. And the life I now live in the flesh I live by faith in the Son of God who, loved me and gave himself for me" (Galatians 2: 19–20). For Paul as for John's Gospel, salvation is objectively accomplished in Christ; the world has been transformed, and yet both texts balance this with a portrayal of the real response Christ's work brings to fruition in his followers. In other words, to "live by faith in the Son of God" is only possible because God has indeed sent his Son who has in fact passed through death to resurrection life, and yet these very acts of God in Christ awaken and call forth a faith that opens one's life to the new creation that Christ makes possible.

As a final note before we explore some of the crucial landmarks in the development of soteriology, you might like to go back to the two axes and the four questions I offered above as constitutive features of almost any soteriology. Now that you've seen the considerable range of metaphors for thinking about salvation, where would you place each conceptual domain on our axes, and how do you think each would answer the four questions?

As a further assistance in reading the primary sources, here are some common soteriological terms that one is likely to encounter, as seen within four of the more dominant metaphorical frameworks that we have considered:

Legal	Military-political	Sacrificial	Mystical
Satisfaction: to recompense an injured party	*Redemption*: to win release, usually from slavery	*Atonement*: literally from at-one-ment, to make one again, usually by offering some compensation	*Adoption*: to accept someone as one's own beloved
Justification: to make right again one's legal or moral standing	*Deliverance*: to rescue or liberate one from peril	*Reconciliation*: to achieve a renewed accord between those divided	*Participation in God*: to share in the life of God
Penal substitution: to substitute for another in paying a penalty	*Ransom*: to pay for one's release from unlawful captivity	*Sanctification*: to make holy	*Deification*: to be raised into God's life yet still being a creature

Chapter 5

Salvation: Meeting Heaven Face to Face

Hell received a body, and encountered God;
it received mortal dust, and met Heaven face to face.
    (from an Eastern Orthodox sermon for the Great Vigil of Easter)

In the previous chapter, we began our exploration of soteriology by noting, first, its foundational quality for thinking about any and all things in Christian theology, and then by some initial surveying of the landscape. Now we continue to head more deeply into the matter, first noting some crucial landmark formulations of the doctrine in Ireneaus, Augustine, and Anselm, and then venturing to mark out a possible way forward in our own time.

LANDMARKS

As you are doubtless aware, there are already many fine histories of Christian theology available. In what follows I am not trying to duplicate them, but to explore the kinds of theological decisions some of these theologians have made, and to ask what we can learn from them about how to do theology. So in this section I offer a brief inquiry into some landmark thinkers, whose ideas have come to inform the very shape of this theological landscape. We might consider how, in their differing circumstances, they were each thinking about the human condition and the divine initiative by means of the metaphorical complexes sketched in the previous chapter. These served them as basic principles and modes of thought for conceiving things theologically. How do these figures pioneer toward a deeper theological understanding by means of these sorts of basic principles of faith?

Irenaeus: Salvation and New Creation

A native of Asia Minor who settled in Gaul, Irenaeus (*c*.130–*c*.200) was crucial to early Christianity's struggle to retain its roots in the faith of Israel, its embrace of the creation as good and capable of growth toward God, and its confidence in the common public teaching of the believing community rather than an esoteric *gnosis* (advanced spiritual knowledge) of the enlightened elite. As Christianity struggled to find a place among the many exotic cults of the Roman world, it was probably only natural that within it a variety of masters of "secret knowledge" should find a foothold. Irenaeus describes the various gnostic tendencies as incorporating lush accounts of multiple realms of spiritual beings, mixed with a fatalism, dualism, and a world-denying disgust with the material world. Irenaeus argued against the gnostics' denigration of the Old Testament and creation in his greatest work, the massive *Against Heresies*, and attempted to clarify the precise grounds for believing that the Creator of the world is good and is one and the same God as the Redeemer of the world.[1]

The gnostics could point to the obvious facts of death, decay, and degradation in the world, and they offered initiates a complex range of secret teachings about divine beings in conflict with one another as the explanation for the world's plight. Jesus was interpreted as the purely spiritual emissary of the distant high God, who came to provide the esoteric wisdom (gnosis) which would be, for those who received it, a way of enlightenment and escape from this material world. In many of the gnostic accounts, Jesus did not actually die on the cross but only feigned suffering and death as a ruse against the malign powers seeking to entrap humanity within this world.

Against all this Irenaeus clearly would have to choose his theological ground carefully. You might ask yourself: Where would *you* begin? Since so much of the gnostics' accounts of salvation turned on the acquisition of secret knowledge, it might seem a winning tack to wean away from their more extreme views by starting out with those elements in Christianity that would have a ready appeal to them. In fact, however, Irenaeus begins with what seems to him the very heart of Christianity, and reveals there – in the very place most distasteful to the gnostics – the most unimaginable mercy and grace. He begins from the fact that Jesus of Nazareth was a real, physical, material human being who truly suffered and died like other mortals.

So Irenaeus is directing our attention to three crucial questions that he thinks we ought to ponder:

- How and why can God exist not only "spiritually" and transcendently but also within the very structures of human existence?
- How and why can Jesus be said to "save" humanity, not *in spite of* his authentic humanity with all its attendant vulnerabilities, but *because of* his true humanity?
- How and why does Jesus' death play a role in salvation?

In many ways, the powerful impression of Irenaeus' answers has enduringly shaped Christianity's self-understanding. In the context of the Greco-Roman world of late antiquity, it would have been easy for Christianity to mutate into a kind of gnosis, with Jesus as a wisdom teacher whose cryptic parables and freedom from material concerns could have enabled countless personal quests of self-discovery and enlightenment – while downplaying the vulgar aspect of his death and the crude "mythology" of a divine being pretending to be a human for a brief appearance among his devotees. Perhaps this tendency is a perennial temptation for Christianity. But Irenaeus offers a crucial lesson: go to the hard and least accessible elements of faith and you may discover there the crucial gifts, precisely because they are least accessible, least domesticated, and least affirming of what "everyone knows" about reality.

Let's take Irenaeus' questions in order. How and why can God be humanly incarnate? The underlying question here is, how can the created order really be apt for intimacy with God? Isn't being a creature precisely what humanity needs to be saved from? So at least the gnostics suggested. Far from acceding to the gnostic view that humanity is separated from God by a vertiginous variety of intermediate beings, Irenaeus emphasizes unabashedly the intimate role of God in the creation of the whole human being. In fact, one of the most important lessons he teaches theology is how to understand the relationship between creation and salvation. For Irenaeus, salvation is fundamentally the recovery, renewal, and discovery of what the true glory and potential of creation might be. His most fundamental theological axiom is that we can learn how to understand ourselves as creatures by trying to understand what God has done for us in salvation.

In tracing Irenaeus' logic, therefore, it will seem that we are moving backwards, from salvation to creation. His point, as we'll see, is twofold: first, we don't really know what we have the possibility of being as human creatures, because this potential has been squandered and distorted; second, as we begin to catch a glimpse (in Christ) of what true humanity might really be like, we will then be able to understand that what God is doing for us in salvation is nothing less than the recovery of our own true human possibility, the re-creation of the human existence we were meant to grow into and enjoy. "Man is a mixed organization of soul and flesh, who was formed after the likeness of God, and moulded by His hands, that is, by the Son and the Holy Spirit, to whom also He said, 'Let Us make man.'"[2] Irenaeus is saying here that the Christ who saves humanity is the same person, the Son, who with the Spirit accomplished the creation of humankind in the first place. Irenaeus sees human existence in developmental terms: being a creature is not bad, it is rather to be capable of and in need of growth. His playful way of speaking about this is to adapt the poetic language of Genesis 1: 26: "Then God said, 'Let us make humankind in our image, according to our likeness.'"

Irenaeus, thinking about the roles of the Son and the Spirit in salvation, and believing that only God could re-create what God created to begin with, reads the plural pronoun "our" in this passage as the Father speaking to the Son and Spirit, his "hands" reaching forth in love to pour out his infinite life. Furthermore,

Irenaeus uses the poetic parallel – image and likeness – as a way of distinguishing the developmental stages of human life: that is, moving from the basic state of image to the deeper relationship of spiritual likeness to God. Humans, says Irenaeus, are created by the eternal Son of God, who is the archetypal Image or Icon of God; and so to exist at all is to be *in* the image of God. We could say that this image-echoing quality is part of the deep structure of human existence; human beings have been created in the image of the Son, who is directly the image of the Father. Thus being fully human would mean growing up into one's true identity as the beloved children of the Father, whom the Father knows and recognizes, so to speak, because humans exist in the image, in the pattern of relationship to the Father we call sonship. But this image could remain only vestigial and undeveloped, or even worse, under the wrong influence it could grow into a deformed and distorted version, and that would mean growing away from one's own true identity as a child of God. So what is needed is to make healthy growth from image to "likeness," that is, to nearer relationship with God marked by moral and spiritual vibrancy. In Irenaeus' view, the agent of this spiritual and moral growth is the Holy Spirit. Apart from this growth, human existence remains at a very rudimentary and immature level:

> If the Spirit be wanting to the soul, he who is such is indeed of an animal nature [i.e., having a soul], and being left carnal, shall be an imperfect being, possessing indeed the image in his formation, but not receiving the similitude [likeness] through the Spirit; and thus is this being imperfect. (V. vi. 1)

Let's pause to think for a moment about the human being Irenaeus is describing here. To be human is to be a dynamic reality, in motion from mere existence toward a fuller state. The condition for existing at all is existing in the image of the Son, which means that the condition for existing is being made for sharing in the Son's "imaging" relationship with the Father. The energy or momentum that vitalizes this basic human state of being, and assists it in moving toward perfect likeness, is the Spirit. In summary, to be human is to be moving toward an ever deeper participation in the life of God the Trinity. It is important to note that this dynamic human existence is not "spiritual" if that is understood in the gnostics' sense as meaning something opposed to the material. The authentically spiritual dimension of human life, says Irenaeus, is what people have who share in the Spirit's dynamic movement of ever deeper intimacy, and they do this "because they partake of the Spirit, and not because their flesh has been stripped off and taken away" (V. vi. 1). This means, as Irenaeus' humorous tweaking of the gnostics suggests, that being human very normally and authentically includes both a spiritual dimension and a physical bodily dimension; and these are no more in mutual conflict than the Son and the Spirit are in conflict.

It might seem obvious to connect the spiritual dimension of being human with the divine Spirit, but why, you might ask, does Irenaeus associate the bodily physical dimension of human life with the image or Son? I think this is because the Son is the dimension of God that expresses, images, verbalizes, and, in Christ, embodies, the Father's meaning. So, for example, the fact that human beings are not amorphous blobs but have a definite form or shape means that they can be expressive and communicative. For Irenaeus this is not solely a physical quality but a physical quality that serves many other dimensions: for the fact that humans can spend their lives in definite acts and ways of life means that these patterns of life can express moral and spiritual qualities. Human beings can image into the world, by their way of life, the goodness and holiness from which the universe springs, indeed that is their particular calling. And it is that imaging quality, grounded in their physical being but reaching up into spiritual significance, that Irenaeus associates with their creation in the image, or Son, of God.

Do we seem to be a long way from thinking about salvation? Not so far as you might think! Remember that Irenaeus' understanding of human existence actually starts from what he has noticed about the Son and the Spirit at work in humanity's salvation. Jesus expresses or images the truth of the Father for humanity; the Spirit energizes Jesus on his mission to be the perfect expression of the Father, and brings to fulfillment the radiance of this image by raising him from death itself – shining with the living light of an infinite love that knows no boundaries, not even death. Working backward in his mind, Irenaeus then asks what equivalent role the Son and the Spirit would play in the bringing of each human being into existence. Answer: humanity is created in the image of God and moved by the Spirit to ever greater likeness to God (fullness of intimacy with God through greater holiness). The fact that this path from image to likeness moves, in Irenaeus' prototype (the life of Jesus) from life through death to resurrection, should alert us to the awesome trajectory humankind is called to follow.

We can now answer the first question: how can God exist humanly? Humankind has been created in the image of God and for ever greater relationship with God. In a sense, we could say, humankind has a trinitarian dynamic as the deep structure of its very existence, so it is already deeply oriented toward the pattern of God's trinitarian life. And, conversely, the Son and the Spirit have already been bringing about human being as image and likeness to God. This means that for the Son and the Spirit to accomplish the embodiment of that pattern in a particular human life, the life of Christ, is for the Son and Spirit a particular case of their normal ways of acting. For humanity, it is the fulfillment and consummation of its very being: imaging brought to the very fullest likeness.

And that takes us to our second and third questions: how can Jesus' human existence be the means of salvation, and in particular, what role can the deepest extent of his human weakness, his suffering and death, play in the process? Irenaeus develops a central concept in answer to these questions and it works like a magic key unlocking the most stubborn doors. In Greek the term is *anakephalaiosis*, literally re-heading or more broadly, recapitulating, summing up. The life, death, and resurrection of Jesus, as the work of the Son and Spirit who brought humanity to existence from the first, is the recapitulating, the summing up, of human existence. It is the gathering of humanity's fractured and distorted ways of existing back into the true image it was created to express; and it is the perfecting of that image through every trial that evil can throw at it, until it comes by the Spirit's power to a perfect likeness in the resurrection of Christ from the dead. Drawing very closely on the theme of Christ as the new Adam, a new beginning of the human race (found in Romans 5 and 1 Corinthians 15: 47), Irenaeus again and again describes Jesus as entering profoundly into every dimension of fallen human existence. When the eternal Son, says Irenaeus,

> became incarnate, and was made man, he commenced afresh the long line of human beings, and furnished us, in a brief, comprehensive manner, with salvation; so that what we had lost in Adam – namely, to be according to the image and likeness of God – that we might recover in Christ Jesus. (III. xviii. 1)

Irenaeus argues that the archetypal image, the Son, comes to exist within the human condition, and thereby, filled with the power of the Spirit, "he commenced afresh" the whole human journey, re-making it from within, so to speak. In Irenaeus' view, it is highly significant that Jesus lived through something corresponding to each age of a human life (33 years was pretty old in the ancient world), concluding with the last step of mortal existence: "He therefore passed through every age, becoming an infant for infants, thus sanctifying those who are of this age," and so on until "at last he came on to death itself" (II. xxii. 4). Each period of human life has its own difficulties and temptations, and says Irenaeus, Jesus enters into each of those in order to renew in every corner of human life the possibility of genuine growth toward God.

How does Jesus accomplish this transformation from within? Remember that, in Irenaeus' view, we only know what real human life should be like by looking at Jesus. What we see there, he says, is a perfect imaging of the Father's goodness and mercy, an obedience and trust that characterize one who is truly the beloved child of God. Not surprisingly then, says Irenaeus, when we look at fallen human existence what we see is a perpetual slavery to temptation, to mistrust of God; and because humanity is made for communion with God, this turn away from God has dire consequences. It subjects humanity to a downward spiral of lies, fear, and violence; essentially, humankind is trying, delusionally, to live against the whole structure of its very nature. Here Irenaeus weaves together the cosmic-historical metaphors that are his basic framework (the new Adam, re-creation of human life) with a dramatic use the military-political metaphors.

Irenaeus describes how the rebel angel, Satan, having rejected God's authority himself, has taunted and tantalized humankind into mistrusting God also (as the Genesis 3 story depicts), and finally into choosing willfully to disobey God. But, as I've just pointed out, because humanity is created *for* God, this turn away *from* God has the hideous effect (as Satan well knows, having already learned it the hard way himself) of subjecting humanity to an alien law of fear – which Satan then uses to terrorize and enslave humanity. In effect, the rebel angel has now bred in human hearts a niggling resentment and envy of God, so that the law of God (which was meant to guide humanity into holiness and deeper relationship with God) has come, under the devil's tutelage, to seem to human beings like a frightful burden designed to afflict humanity and keep it from its rightful progress in life. What Jesus does is to defeat the devil, not by playing around with his own weapons of fear and lies and power, but simply by delighting utterly in the law of God, serving the Father in loving obedience, and so revealing the truth at last – both about God and about Satan. When Jesus refused the temptations in the wilderness, says Irenaeus, Jesus showed that the law of the Lord is good and trustworthy; it truly offers the way to God and sets humanity free from a false way:

> Who, then, is this Lord God to whom Christ bears witness, whom no man shall tempt, whom all should worship, and serve Him alone? It is, beyond all manner of doubt, that God who gave the law. . . . By the words of the law the Lord showed that the law does indeed declare the Word of God from the Father; and the apostate angel of God is destroyed by its voice, being exposed in his true colors, and vanquished by the Son of Man keeping the commandment of God. For as in the beginning he enticed man to transgress his Maker's law, and thereby got him into his own power; yet his power consists in transgression and apostasy, and with these he bound man. (V. xxi. 3)

Humanity fell into the slavery of sin by a vicious cycle of mistrust and disobedience, leading to yet deeper fear, antagonism, and even more hardened and habitual disobedience. But, says Irenaeus, the nasty little secret of this vicious cycle that Satan goads humanity to spin so toilsomely upon is this: "his power consists in transgression and apostasy, and with these he bound man" and so whenever the prisoners get the courage and strength to revolt and turn to God in trust, their chains turn out to be mere illusions, poisonous enchantments that have no more power to bind than the lies by which sin coaxed the prisoners into donning them so foolishly in the first place.

So by recapitulating or summing up in himself the whole journey of humanity, both across time and in each individual's life, Jesus is able to act in obedience in all the places where humanity has been disobedient, to trust God wherever humanity has turned away, and so to deprive sin of its binding grip upon human existence. In effect, Jesus' passion and death are the paradigm elements of this reversal of humanity's condition: Jesus does away with the effects of "that disobedience of man which had taken place at the beginning by occasion of a tree" (the tree of the knowledge of good and evil), and he does this most fittingly "through that obedience" which he made perfect "upon the tree" of the cross (V. xvi. 3). Because Jesus is the eternal Son incarnate in whose image humanity is made, what is achieved in his life, death, and resurrection is not only a sign for humanity (that it can be free), but an actual transforming of humanity's conditions, a new beginning for the human journey. And the goal of this liberation is, as we noted above, a maturing and deepening of the human relationship with God: the journey from image to likeness. About this Irenaeus employs language drawn from the mystical family of metaphors, even speaking of humanity's intended "promotion into God":

> For it was for this end that the Word of God was made man, and he who was the Son of God became the Son of Man, that man, having been taken into the Word, and receiving the adoption, might become the Son of God. For by no other means could we have attained to incorruptibility and immortality, unless we had been united to incorruptibility and immortality. But how could we be joined to incorruptibility and immortality, unless, first, incorruptibility and immortality had become that which we also are, so that the corruptible might be swallowed up by incorruptibility, and the mortal by immortality, that we might receive the adoption of sons? (III. xix. 1)

Thus, for Irenaeus, the assumption of our human condition into union with the eternal Son was not merely for the purposes of freeing humanity from sin's addiction and fear, but for the sake of recuperating the human calling towards ever greater intimacy with God.

Over the vast sweep of Irenaeus' theology, he employs many other images and metaphors for thinking about salvation; but it would be fair to say that he generally interprets them in light of God's renovation of creation in Christ and the Spirit. As we should expect, many of his themes found a variety of different expressions in later patristic thought. Athanasius of Alexandria (*c.*296–*c.*373), for example, would develop very powerfully the theme of the Word appearing within the human situation to re-create it from within. Gregory of Nyssa (*c.*330–*c.*95) develops further the theme of the devil's insatiable need for rule, having turned away from the vision of God's unstinting goodness and fallen into envy.

Brief Interlude: A Crucial Difficulty in Soteriology

Now we have to pause for a moment and consider an abiding conundrum in soteriology. There seems to be a kind of tug-of-war between two different organizing principles at work when people try to think about salvation. On one hand, we have an emphasis on the overarching plan of God to renew the creation and re-establish humanity's calling towards deeper relationship with God. On the other hand, we have necessary attention to the impediments, such as humanity's fall away from God and enslavement to sin, death, and the devil. In early writers like Irenaeus these fundamental tendencies work together in a creative tension, but other writers often seem to find themselves pulling for one "side" against the other. When this happens, we can get some theologians emphasizing the transformation of human consciousness and its elevation into communion with God, almost as though the roadblocks to this were merely matters of trying a little harder to be good and paying closer attention to God. But, of course, it is precisely humanity's inability to do this that Christ's crucifixion makes so agonizingly apparent.

On the other side, perhaps especially in theology as it develops in the West, we can get a pretty tight focus on the negative side of salvation as punishment for sin or as an overwhelming and seemingly impossible need to compensate God for the world's evil. It is almost as though we already knew and understood everything about sin and Jesus is simply necessary to come along and perform the heavy lifting that we're not quite up to. Do you see the danger here? In my view this one-sided fascination with "the problem" obscures from sight the overarching divine plan to love creation into communion, and so ever more narrowly focuses humanity's attention upon itself instead of God. Whenever this happens, there is a danger of misconstruing the problem in the first place. As I suggested in the first part of this chapter, we often cannot adequately see creation's true potential or true problem until we see what *God* has been doing about both. The true dimensions, in other words, of humanity's potential and its problems are only made apparent when we can see the sorts of measures God takes to deal with them. Before we go on to consider a crucial landmark in particularly western soteriology, it will be helpful to note, at least in passing, one of the most creative efforts to keep the two emphases – God's love and humanity's fault – from being separated from each other.

Augustine and God's Justice

Augustine of Hippo (354–430) addresses a theme in western soteriology that emerges into later prominence, namely, the idea that Christ's death is somehow necessary to appease God's wrath at sinful humanity. Because this idea barely figures in Irenaeus, and is important to later developments, it will be useful to note the great African theologian's response. Augustine is commenting on Romans 5: 8–9 where Paul says: "God proves his love for us in that while we still were sinners Christ died for us. Much more surely then, now that we have been justified by his blood, will we be saved through him from the wrath of God." What can this mean? Can it really be the case, asks Augustine incredulously, that God was so angry he could only be appeased if Jesus were tortured and put to death?

> Is it really the case that when God the Father was angry with us he saw the death of his Son on our behalf, and was reconciled to us? Does this mean then that his Son was already so reconciled to us that he was even prepared to die for us, while the Father was still so angry with us that unless the Son died for us he would not be reconciled to us? . . . Would the Father have not spared his own Son but handed him over for us, if he had not already been reconciled? . . . I observe that the Father loved us not merely before the Son died for us, but before he founded the world.[3]

Augustine is perturbed that anyone might take Paul in an overly literalistic way and so misunderstand salvation, mistaking it for the sort of appeasement of wrathful deities common to many ancient religions but, in his view, entirely untrue to Christianity. Augustine is surely correct. In fact, I would argue that this is exactly the kind of view of salvation – appeasement of the gods – that natural human religious tendencies will almost certainly advance: if theology does not start from what God does in Christ, then it will have to start from what it normally sees of the natural order of things in the world, i.e., the weak have to appease the strong, because they certainly cannot win a fight against them. The danger is that this underlying, background assumption, which may be the way the world generally works in its fallen state, will entirely shape the logical framework within which theology tries to think. And this will mean, just as Augustine warns, that we will end up interpreting Jesus very much as a pagan sacrifice to the gods. So let's see Augustine's remedy, which I think we can trace in four steps.

(1) As we saw in the quotation just above, Augustine argues that Paul's language creates a healthy cognitive dissonance in us: God loves us and sends the Son, God is reconciled to us by the Son's death; holding these two together ought to pry us loose from thinking about Jesus' death in pagan terms as appeasing God. So what is Jesus' death? It is an extension into our fallen world of God's eternal love for humanity "from before he founded the world" and desire for humanity's flourishing. This means that we cannot simply keep on reading biblical language about God's wrath and Jesus' sacrifice for sins according to the old natural, pagan models. "Wrath" has to be understood in terms of God's eternal love made concrete for humanity in Christ. So we need a new interpretation.

(2) Augustine goes on to say that, with reference to God, language of "wrath" must not be likened to human anger, "an emotional disturbance," but is rather the tranquil unfolding of God's own plan for the universe, which we call justice (XIII. 5. 21). Furthermore, in Augustine's view, what holds humanity back from fellowship with God is not God's anger or some divine demand for humanity to compensate God for having been sinful. Rather, the problem is that humanity has fallen more and more into the clutches of its own lust for power and domination; and this domination by the desire for domination is aptly spoken of as the devil's dominion:

> The essential flaw of the devil's perversion made him a lover of power and a deserter and assailant of justice, which means that men imitate him all the more thoroughly the more they neglect or even detest justice and studiously devote themselves to power, rejoicing at the possession of it or inflamed with the desire for it. (XIII. 4. 17)

Augustine is describing a fearful game of power: the "zero-sum" conviction that if someone else has power then I correspondingly have less. The more humanity is dominated by this satanic vision of reality, the more it is entrapped by it in a single-minded pursuit of power. Any act of humility or unselfish generosity seems increasingly foolish and inimical to one's own flourishing. Not surprisingly, in such a mentality, God would begin to look increasingly like a god: jealous, envious of humanity's possible advances as threats to divine power, demanding appeasement in order to withhold cosmic violence, and so on. In response to all this, Augustine argues, God has to set humanity free from this satanic grip and to heal humanity's consciousness.

(3) God might, of course, have simply wiped away the grip of sin by an omnipotent divine fiat; but, says Augustine, this would have been to win on the devil's own terms. A divine victory by power play would only leave the lingering suspicion in humanity's mind that perhaps Satan's murmurings were right after all: God has silenced the devil, but does indeed operate by an invincible power that brooks no opposition. It is far more efficacious for God to liberate humanity by an act of justice.

> So it pleased God to deliver man from the devil's authority by beating him at the justice game, not the power game, so that men too might imitate Christ by seeking to beat the devil at the justice game, not the power game. Not that power is to be shunned as something bad, but that the right order must be preserved which puts justice first. (XIII. 4. 17)

We'll see in (4) just below how this "justice game" works, but for the moment note how Augustine limns God's desire to win and woo humanity back into a healthy mindset, to open up the possibility of humanity fulfilling its vocation to share in the life of divine wisdom and justice. Because humanity had "proudly longed to be God," its addiction to power subjected it to the very quintessence of injustice, the devil; and so God sets humanity free as Irenaeus had argued, by entering and reversing the whole process. Humanity proudly wants to be God, but God humbly consents to join humanity (XIII. 5. 23). And thus "once we had been brought in this way to believe how much God loved us and to hope at last for what we had despaired of," God is able freely to "confer his gifts on us with a quite uncalled-for generosity, without any good deserts of ours, indeed with our ill will our only preparation" (XIII. 4. 13). The great and painful irony of sin, suggests Augustine, is that it frantically attempts to seize in its grip – and so misses – the very thing (living like God) that God most longs to pour out unstintingly with utter freedom and entirely unmerited generosity.

(4) But we come back to our original question: why exactly does Jesus have to die, given that it is not necessary to appease divine wrath? Later theologians, par-ticularly Peter Abelard (1079–1142), will find entirely unacceptable the references of Augustine and other patristic authors to God's defeat of the devil by Christ's death, or to God's winning the release of humanity by means of Christ's death. Anselm of Canterbury, as we'll see just below, proposes to leave the devil out of the discussion and interpret the problem entirely in terms of God, humanity, and

justice. Abelard will take another tack and propose that Christ's death achieves salvation, not by any effect it has on either the devil's power over humanity or on God's wrath against humanity; rather, Christ's death achieves its goal by showing us how much God truly loves us, thus leading us to repentance and new life with God. This, it seems to me, does pick up Augustine's point in (3) above, but I do think it misses the final crucial insight Augustine offers.

Humanity, in Augustine's view, cannot simply see things differently: it is truly under a fearful domination by the forces of envy and violence. One would think that world events in the twentieth and twenty-first centuries would be grim but sufficient evidence of this. Whether it is so incorrigibly naive and mythological to speak, like Augustine, of these dominating structures in personified terms, as the devil, is at least arguable. But it certainly does prevent theology from complicitly turning a blind eye to the structures of violence that do indeed seem to dominate humanity – very often, it seems, against our best intentions. Thus Augustine thinks that humanity, even given the most wondrously loving example imaginable of self-sacrificing love, will keep on falling back into a cycle of violence, acquisition of power, more violence as revenge for earlier violence, and so on – straight to hell. Just as Irenaeus had argued that Christ needs to recapitulate the whole human journey in order to enact loving trust and obedience wherever humanity had acted by fear and disobedience, so Augustine thinks that God can only truly save us by entering into the structures of power that dominate the human situation and dismantling them. In Christ, God accepts this. In a way, Augustine argues, it is a kind of justice that humanity should be so subjected to power, in the sense that insofar as one makes power one's absolute goal, it does tend to subject one to itself. But God in Christ enters this human situation, and ultimately this eventuates in his condemnation and death by the powers of the age. But Satan's power is derived entirely from human sinning; that is the basis of evil's grip. In Jesus' case, the malignant envy that has perverted justice in the name of power is unmasked and undone, for it ends up condemning one who is in fact innocent and over whom it has no rightful power or authority at all. Augustine puts it this way:

> The devil was holding on to our sins, and using them to keep us deservedly fixed in death. He [Christ] who had none of his own discharged them, and was undeservedly led away by the other [the devil] to death. Such was the value of that blood, that he who killed Christ even with a momentary death he did not owe would no longer have the right to hold anyone who had put on Christ. (XIII. 5. 21)

As I said, later theologians would be uncomfortable with the idea here that the devil could either have any legitimate rights to dominate sinners or that God would permit any illegitimate domination of sinners by the devil. Still, I think Augustine's insight stands, namely that humanity is in fact dominated, and given this, mere gesturing in the direction of a good example will not accomplish much. In Augustine's view, salvation is not reducible to imitating Christ's example, rather it is possible to imitate Christ and so act differently in the world, precisely because the grip of fearful envy and violence has in Jesus' death and resurrection been pried loose from human life.

Anselm and the Divine Order

Anselm of Canterbury (*c*.1033–*c*.1109), though a faithful reader of Augustine, was not altogether satisfied with his account of salvation. Both saints see God in Christ acting by means of Jesus' innocent death to free humanity from the effects of sin. For Augustine these effects, as we have seen, are suffered, above all, in humanity's subjection to an ever deepening addiction to sin, namely fear and violence. But for Anselm this seemed too much to subject humanity to a power alien to God, and thus in a strange way to diminish divine authority and rule over the universe. Augustine, of course, would reply that it is precisely God's authority that arranges a universe with real justice inherent in its fabric, so that to seek power before justice is, naturally, to fall away from the freedom of justice into a fearful and slavish pursuit of power for its own sake. Anselm, by contrast, wants to bring the whole discussion of justice and obedience into an immediate polarity between the creature and the Creator. I may as well announce my fear about this at the outset: I wonder whether, with his concern that humanity must repay to God the debt it owes, Anselm does not seem to you to risk moving towards the very same anxious zero-sum understanding of reality that Augustine was trying to help us see as, itself, a demonic temptation? That is too strong, perhaps; see what you think.

At the core of Anselm's thought on salvation is this basic line of thought: by sinning, humanity has robbed God of the complete devotion due him; only a human being can fittingly recompense God for what humanity has defaulted upon; but only God-become-human has the capacity to make such an offering of sufficient worth. It has become a commonplace to suggest a background to Anselm's *Why God Became Man* (*c*.1100) in feudal notions of service owed to a lord by a subordinate. So great, however, is the archbishop's achievement in this work that it would be most unfortunate to slight it on the excuse that his presuppositions no longer appeal to us. I am not, myself, entirely convinced in any case that social hierarchy plays so significant a role in framing the archbishop's thought, especially when we consider the great deal of trouble he had in his relations with the English crown.

To understand Anselm's notion of what humanity owes to God, we probably need look no farther than his own spiritual wisdom as an abbot and teacher of the religious life. At the heart of this would have been his sense of a profound, fundamental orientation of the whole person to God. This idea springs from the nature of a vowed life, a religious life in which one's fidelity and love for God are given concrete embodiment in one's vows of obedience according to a monastic rule. This complete availability for God is meant to be the presupposition of one's every thought and deed, not one particular obligation among the others. In Anselm's dialogue between himself (A) and his younger monk Boso (B), the argument is as follows:

A. If an angel or a man always rendered to God what is due to him, he would never sin.
B. I cannot contradict you.
A. Thus, to sin is the same thing as not to render his due to God.
B. What is the debt which we owe to God?
A. Every inclination of the rational creature ought to be subject to the will of God.
B. Nothing could be truer.
A. This is the debt which angels and men owe to God. No one who pays it sins; everyone who does not pay it sins. This is the justice or rectitude of the will, which makes men just or upright in heart, that is in will. This is the sole and entire honor which we owe to God, and God requires of us. . . . One who does not render this honor to God takes away from God what belongs to him, and dishonors God, and to do this is to sin. Moreover, as long as he does not repay what he has stolen, he remains at fault. And it is not enough merely to return what was taken away; in view of the insult committed, he must give back more than he took away. . . . It is not enough for someone who violates another's honor to restore the honor, unless he makes some kind of restitution that will please him who was dishonored, according to the extent of the injury and dishonor. . . . So, then, everyone who sins must repay to God the honor that he has taken away, and this is the satisfaction that every sinner ought to make to God.[4]

We ought not to take Anselm's references to "honor" here as mere personal respect or high opinion, as though he imagined God to be a mortal ruler avid for acclaim. Rather, Anselm is thinking here of the kind of honor that serves a societal function in maintaining order and right relations rather than permitting a collapse of society into self-will and chaos.[5] We can see hints of this concern in the archbishop's numerous references to the beauty of the divine plan, the ordering of the cosmos, and the role of the divine will in bringing all things to their appointed and unique perfections. Nor does Anselm at all envision God as either needing human fealty or losing anything whatsoever should it not be forthcoming; for God "himself is honor incorruptible and absolutely unchangeable" (I. 15). *The problem is with the impact that disobedience to God has on the universe itself.* Here Anselm agrees strongly with Augustine that rational creatures are created for communion with God, and if they pull themselves away from this orientation, then they increasingly find themselves not merely pursuing lesser goods and goals but enslaved to them.

> When [a rational creature] wills what it ought to will, it honors God – not because it bestows something on him, but because it willingly submits itself to God's will and direction, and keeps its own place in the universe of things, and maintains the beauty of that same universe, as far as in it lies. But when it does not will as it ought, it dishonors God . . . [and] disturbs the order and beauty of the universe. (I. 15)

So we can see here that when Anselm speaks of sinners needing to pay God the debt they owe, we need to interpret this entirely in terms of God's intention to restore sinful creatures to their proper place and vocation in fostering the "order and beauty of the universe" (as Anselm puts it) – and not as though sinners were being required to give God something needed or insisted upon by God for God's own sake.

Anselm famously goes on to prove by most fitting reasons that the one act of sufficient merit which humanity can offer for this restoration of universal order is the death of the God-man, Jesus, who offers himself in a life and death of perfect obedience to God. In a sense we can see another parallel with Augustine here: for the bishop of Hippo, Jesus' self-giving death is an act of justice, not the arbitrary assertion of an overmastering divine power; and for the archbishop of Canterbury, Jesus' self-giving death is also in service to the restoration of cosmic justice. But here the parallel abruptly ends, and it will be crucial to see exactly how. Perhaps we can put it like this: the fundamental logic of Augustine's position suggests that Jesus' death is not a good thing just *as* a death per se, indeed as a death it is the brutal and vicious act of humanity enthralled to violence; rather, the good for humanity lies in Jesus' willingness to find human beings there in subjection to evil, and to accept subjection to this state for the sake of accompanying fallen humanity and liberating it from its captivity to corrupted power. In Anselm, however, the death of Jesus has now come to be of value in and of itself, indeed its infinite value – precisely as an act of suffering and death – is the very offering required for the restoration of justice and harmony within the universe.

> B. You have proved most straightforwardly that the life of this Man was so sublime, so precious, that it can suffice to pay what is owing for the sins of the whole world, and infinitely more. It now remains, therefore, to show how it is paid to God for the sins of men.
> A. If he let himself be killed for the sake of justice, did he not give his life for the honor of God? . . . No man besides him ever gave to God, by dying, what he was not necessarily going to lose at some time, or paid what he did not owe. But this Man freely offered to the Father what he would never have lost by necessity, and paid to sinners what he did not owe for himself. (II. 18)

What Christ would not necessarily lose was his life, because in Anselm's view, human mortality is the result of sin and Christ was sinless. Thus his offering of his life on the cross is a perfectly unlimited offering, not a sort of early return of what everyone has to surrender in any case. Likewise, Christ freely paid a recompense, which he did not owe, for the sins of the world and because *he* did not owe it, its merit is poured out for all who do owe but cannot pay what is required.

In the centuries that followed, many other approaches to salvation emerged, but the fundamental logic of Anselm's position echoed ever more significantly. In the teaching of John Calvin (as I mentioned earlier in this chapter), we meet again the idea of Christ's death as a transaction between humanity and God that is necessary for the restoration of humanity's relationship with God. In Calvin, however, Anselm's emphasis on an infinite act of justice capable of restoring the order of the universe is interpreted quite differently as an act of suffering capable of substituting for the punishment God would otherwise need to inflict upon sinners. In the next sections of this chapter we will reconsider the question of Christ's suffering and death, clarifying how best to understand its relationship to the salvation of the world.

PATHFINDING

The time has come at last to venture out into the territory we have been survey-ing. We need to identify and mark out constructive ways forward, given the par-ticular contours and landmarks we've already noted as shaping the landscape of soteriology. I'm going to think out loud with you about two central matters in the doctrine of salvation: (1) as promised, and as a bridge from the previous section, we'll start with the significance of Jesus' passion and death; (2) this should lead us to consider some constructive approaches to the mystery of salvation that take greater account of Christ's resurrection and glorification.

On the Death of Christ: Orthodox, Feminist, and Girardian Concerns

I begin by noting the insightful concerns of three very different theological schools: Eastern Orthodox theology, feminist theology, and the mimetic theory associated with the work of René Girard. As we go along, consider where you think these three sorts of critique might intersect and whether that might perhaps suggest a fruitful way forward.

For many decades now, Eastern Orthodox theologians have raised very critical voices regarding what they see as western Christianity's far too exclusive focus in soteriology on the suffering and death of Jesus. In an essay originally published in 1947, the great Russian Orthodox theologian Vladimir Lossky critiqued the tendencies he felt had grown, very perniciously, from Anselm's *Why God Became Man*, the chief problem being the development of soteriology in isolation from the other central mysteries of the faith. God as seen strictly through the eyes of original sin now can only be understood as "infinitely offended," and humanity is crushed by "the impossible demands of vindictive justice." And what of other central Christian beliefs?

> What becomes of the dispensation of the Holy Spirit here? His part is reduced to that of an auxiliary, an assistant in redemption, causing us to receive Christ's expiating

merit. The final goal of our union with God is, if not excluded altogether, at least shut out from our sight by the stern vault of a theological conception built on the ideas of original guilt and its reparation. The price of our redemption having been paid in the death of Christ, the resurrection and ascension are only a glorious happy end of His work, a kind of apotheosis without direct relationship to our human destiny. This redemptionist theology, placing all the emphasis on the passion, seems to take no interest in the triumph of Christ over death. The very work of the Christ-Redeemer, to which this theology is confined, seems to be truncated, impoverished, reduced to a change of the divine attitude toward fallen men, unrelated to the nature of humanity.[6]

Whether this is quite a fair construal of Archbishop Anselm's teaching is perhaps a matter for some debate, but in any case we can see very clearly what concerns Lossky. I think this might be put in three points. (1) A formal concern: the mystery of salvation ought to be the heart of theology through which all the other mysteries of Christian faith circulate, reveal themselves, and lead outward into every dimension of belief; but with the penal substitution or satisfaction theory, Lossky says, all the other mysteries of faith are shrunken, collapsed, or divided from their organic interrelationship. This would seem to be evidence that we have an unhealthy theological approach at work. (2) A first material concern: by placing all the emphasis in soteriology on the death of Christ as a satisfaction for sin, we are unable to conceive of the resurrection or the role of God the Holy Spirit as organically crucial to salvation; again, this suggests an inadequate soteriology, if such significant elements cannot be accommodated by it. (3) A second material concern: because the dominant western soteriology focuses so narrowly on an external change in humanity's standing with God, it seems unable to embrace any real change in the structures of human existence itself, in the very being of the human and its relationship to life and death.

Bearing these concerns in mind, what points of contact might there be, if any, with contemporary feminist accounts of salvation? As do the Orthodox, feminist thinkers warn us of the damaging effects of certain soteriologies on both our understanding of God and our understandings of human life. At its worst, these thinkers note, a focus on Jesus' suffering and violent death as redemptive just in and of themselves (apart from a larger vision of Jesus' social contexts and motivations) can damagingly sacralize violence, legitimize many forms of victimization, and inculcate a self-annihilating consciousness that is especially dangerous for those who are already in minority or marginalized groups. As Elizabeth Johnson writes:

Feminist theology repudiates an interpretation of the death of Jesus as required by God in repayment for sin. Such a view today is virtually inseparable from an underlying image of God as an angry, bloodthirsty, violent, and sadistic father, reflecting the very worst kind of male behavior. Rather, Jesus' death was an act of violence brought about by threatened human men, as sin, and therefore against the will of a gracious God. It occurred historically in consequence of Jesus' fidelity to the deepest truth he knew, expressed in his message and behavior. . . . Challenging the validity of powerful relations normed by dominance and submission, his liberating life bore the signature of his death; in that sense, suffering was most probable. What comes clear in the event, however, is not Jesus' necessary passive victimization divinely decreed as a penalty for sin, but rather a dialectic of disaster and powerful human love through which the gracious God of Jesus enters into solidarity with all those who suffer and are lost.[7]

We can see here a strong parallel with Lossky's concern about the effect of penal notions of salvation upon our understanding of God. At the fore in Johnson's critique, however, is the new note of urgency raised by feminist and liberationist theological concerns for the victimization of the vulnerable. This yields two important criteria in evaluating notions of salvation: (1) Do they imply that God demands or employs violence in effecting the saving divine will? (2) Do they model for imitation a passive victimization as intrinsically salvific, holy, or the means of life for others?

It would be a painful irony if an understanding of salvation tended toward complicity with the very patterns of oppression and violence that Christianity believes Jesus overcame. Darby Kathleen Ray points out that, unintentionally, some Christian teachings on atonement have fostered environments in which abuse is left uncondemned, oppressive structures are left unchallenged because they are simply seen as opportunities for self-sacrifice, and consequently victims' belief in the fundamental blessedness of life are crushed.

> Taken together, the salvific values of suffering, self-sacrifice, and obedience are too easily distorted into a theological tool of subjugation. Removed from a context that values and attempts to safeguard the health and fulfillment of all beings, these values can be emphasized to a pathological degree, contributing to the suffering and exploitation of the vulnerable and hence demeaning the humanity of oppressor and oppressed alike.[8]

What exactly, then, are we looking for in a healthy soteriology? As Kathryn Tanner observes in her own lucid exposition of soteriology, what we want is to see how Jesus' death is "the effect of his saving us and not the very means or mechanism by which Jesus saves."[9] Understanding this would help to recover an awareness of the salvific significance of the entirety of Jesus' presence in the world, including as Lossky reminds us, the coordinate role of the Holy Spirit by whose power the Word can be spoken into our world and spoken with the full liveliness of God's own vivacity even across the boundary of death itself. If, as Johnson suggested in the passage above, Jesus' death is understood as the result of his saving solidarity with humankind, then his suffering and death are not the "goal" of his life but consequences – perhaps savingly significant ones – of the larger saving plan of God. This also means that we would, following Augustine, be trying to understand the divine plan as a refusal to play by the power and violence game that so hypnotizes the world. Perhaps this happens (as Ray suggests in her re-imagining of patristic themes), when through the life and death of Christ "God has acted not only to reveal the true nature of evil but also to decenter and delegitimate its authority by luring it into exposing its own moral bankruptcy and thus defeating itself, hence opening up the possibility for human beings to escape enslavement to evil."[10]

That brings us very close indeed to the insights of mimetic theory, which was developed (in the latter half of the twentieth century) by the literary scholar René Girard and the theologians who have elucidated the significance for Christian theology of this approach.[11] Girard had noted that violence in human relations often springs from imitation (mimesis), which has degenerated into envy and rivalry. As desiring, loving beings, humans are deeply formed in our desiring by the desires of those around us (as advertisers know all too well). But when what we desire is a finite good, and those desiring it are close to one another, envy and increasingly dangerous rivalry ensue. This breaks out into a violence that has, in the right circumstances, the curious capacity to quieten down, for a while, the impulse to violence; in time, human cultures can grow more and more dependent on these violent purgings and the role of victim becomes increasingly significant. The victim of the violence, the scapegoat upon whom all the blame and rage is heaped, even comes to be perceived as a divine gift, a religious sacrifice; and in time, religion turns into a vast systemically functioning mechanism for controlling and managing deep cultural urges to violence by means of ritualized, sacralized violence. But this system only manages to keep the deep frustration and envy at a slightly contained simmer without being able to set anyone free from it. Meanwhile the culture continues to be electrified by a profoundly zero-sum, rivalrous, violent momentum in which blame and anger are unconsciously poured out, especially on the weak, the different, and the marginalized.

I know this may seem like a rather towering scheme, but its explanatory power is quite remarkable, especially when in dialogue with the biblical texts. Now think of Jesus, challenging the dominance-submission social order, embracing outcasts, and declaring the absolutely unbounded, gratuitous, universal favor of God. If you are one of his followers and he is put to death, you would very likely have begun to accept the authority's view that in executing Jesus, God's will was being done. But if Jesus is not bound by death, if he returns to you – dead yet more alive than ever – and instead of continuing the cycle of violence by seeking revenge, he pours out forgiveness and shares his new life with you, then, as James Alison has so well remarked,

> the whole system of thought which had led to his execution is called into question. In the first place it means that Jesus had been right in the testimony which he had given about God: God is indeed like the one who Jesus had described and that means that God is not like Jesus' adversaries had claimed him to be. So the reasons given for doing away with Jesus were not reasons, but part of a sinful human mechanism for getting rid of people, which has nothing to do with God. . . . Jesus' resurrection . . . revealed the whole mechanism by which innocent victims are created by

people who think that by creating such victims they are working God's most holy will.[12]

Alison has already begun to show us a particularly lucid way of recovering the soteriological significance of the resurrection, and we will turn directly to that in the final section, just below. But for the moment note how closely this perspective tracks with the observations we've gathered from Orthodox and feminist thought: the violent suffering and death of Jesus are *not* the means God has decreed for saving humankind.

But what of the satisfaction God requires to atone for the limitless offense of human sinning? The assumption had been that if God simply remitted sins without recompense this would suggest that justice is unreal in the universe, that God does not take it seriously. But mimetic theory prompts us to ask, why is something required to "make up" for what sin has done? This perspective seems to emerge suspiciously from a zero-sum, finite vision of the good, in which if you have a certain good then I or somebody else must have been deprived of it. But according to a venerable Christian axiom, anything that God "has," God is. In other words, while we may speak of God's goodness, or justice, or truth, we conceive these as attributes that God somehow "possesses" to the fullest degree; but in fact, Christians believe, God doesn't need to "hang on" to anything, there is nothing lacking to God (God is already the perfect act of every excellence), for these attributes are really aspects of God's own reality. Thus it would be more accurate, though perhaps less immediately apparent to us, to say that God *is* Goodness itself, or Justice itself, etc. And if God is Justice, and God is infinite, then God does not need or require any "making up" for our shortfalls in being just.

Furthermore, there is no cosmic law of justice that God must somehow bother about enforcing by means of wringing compensation from the suffering of Jesus, because God's own act of existence as God is already an infinite act of justice itself. As the Jesuit theologian Raymund Schwager points out,

> The parables of the prodigal son (Luke 15: 11–32) and the merciless creditor (Matthew 18: 23–35) make it clear that God forgives without demanding satisfaction and payment in return. He demands only that we forgive others as unconditionally as we are granted unconditional mercy. . . . If Jesus demands of human beings a limitless forgiveness, then the Father whom he makes known must be even more willing to do so. For according to the Sermon on the Mount, it is the tax collectors and the heathens who love and do good only to those from whom they expect the same (Matt. 5: 43–7). The idea of a god who demands satisfaction is thus of heathen origin. . . . The God of Jesus Christ is exactly the opposite of violence. He does not seek a quid pro quo. He does not demand an eye for an eye.[13]

If that is the case, and the killing of Jesus has nothing to do with God's intentions, then is his death in effect incidental to salvation? How can we make any soteriological sense of it at all? To do so, I believe, we need to recall Lossky's admonition: we need to contemplate the death of Jesus in the light of his resurrection.

Salvation and the Paschal Mystery

Perhaps we can put the question this way: is there an interpretation of Jesus' death that sees its significance for salvation, but does not: (1) isolate his death from the rest of what Christians believe, (2) reduce the import of his death to a form of satisfaction for a divine demand, or (3) legitimize passive suffering or violence as inherently necessary, praiseworthy, or divinely sanctioned? I think there is, and it flows, not surprisingly, from the manner in which Jesus' followers themselves interpreted his death as a "paschal mystery," an intensificaton (even fulfillment) of the Passover. (The term "paschal" derives from the Greek transliteration of the Hebrew *pesach*, Passover.) The transition marked by the Jewish feast of Passover is the transition from the slavery to freedom, from the death of separation from God to the new life of covenant relationship with God. In the time of Jesus, the commemoration of the redemption from Egypt also came to be associated with three other redemptive moments: the creation of the world, the binding (or "sacrifice") of Isaac, and the expected coming of the Messiah.[14] The paschal lamb, whose blood was shed for those being redeemed from slavery (Exodus 12: 21ff.), was prefigured in the moment when another took the place of Isaac so that he would go free. And on either side of these two redemptive moments were the beginning and the end: the calling of this world into existence out of nothingness, and the coming of the Messiah to bring about the new creation of God's final sovereignty and justice. In this many-layered context, Paul reminds the Corinthians that they should prepare themselves, and ready their lives for God's redeeming act, "for our paschal lamb, Christ, has been sacrificed" (1 Corinthians 5: 7).

The Passover signifies not only leaving the old life of slavery behind, but represents nothing less than liberation, a freeing into the new life of covenant. Moreover it conceives God's calling into being of a new people for himself as a new creation, echoing the original creation, and as a foreshadowing of the consummate moment of God's calling: the calling into existence of God's chosen and anointed one, the Christ, the beloved, who would bring creation to its fulfillment in God. Thus we have loss of old life (death) and birth of new life (resurrection), and this passing over is understood as the turning point in God's creative giving of existence and calling of creation into ever more intimate friendship. We would seem to be justified, at the least, in interpreting Jesus' death and resurrection together, allowing the light of the resurrection to unveil the meaning of the passion and death. At the risk of over-schematizing things, could we say that the paschal mystery embodies and makes visible the conflict between the world as we have structured it and the abiding creativity of God? In what follows, I want to propose that we can inquire into this paschal mystery in three dimensions of its transforming or saving power: (1) in terms of the world of human interactions, (2) in terms of the wider creation or cosmos, and (3) in the widest terms of all, that is, the infinitely relational life of God the Trinity. At each level, or dimension, the dying and rising of Jesus leads into a deeper vision of God's abiding generosity and giving life.

The social dimension

First, then, what light does the resurrection throw on the significance of Jesus' death in the domain of human affairs? We saw above James Alison's point in this regard: the fact that Jesus' followers are encountered by him as dead yet risen suggested to them that God certainly did not leave or abandon him, as the religious and political authorities said that God had done. Furthermore, Jesus returns with life and power and authority, not for revenge, but to forgive and transform the lives of his followers; this casts a harshly revealing light on the machinations of those who had condemned him. The powerful and the power structures are revealed not as soberly and sagely upholding God's law and public order by silencing a dangerous blasphemer, but rather as utterly blind to the innocence of their victim. Jesus' suffering, read in the light of God's raising him from the dead, unmasks and de-legitimizes the structures that govern worldly order. As Alison puts it so clearly, "the resurrection of the victim made possible a certain intelligence, a certain perspective on things, which Jesus had had before his death and which began to possess the apostolic group after the resurrection."[15]

What does this "intelligence of the victim" make possible in the minds of the apostles? We have a pretty clear sense, I think, from the fact that in the accounts of their early preaching, they stress in unmistakable terms the difference between human agency and God's role in the events of the paschal mystery. Eight times in the Book of Acts, the apostles speak of Jesus as the one "whom you crucified, whom God raised from the dead" (Acts 4: 10; see also 2: 23–4, 32, 36; 3: 15; 5: 30; 10: 39–40; 13: 28–31). At one point, Peter says, "you killed the Author of Life, whom God raised from the dead" (Acts 3: 15). Jesus is already experienced as authoring and re-sourcing life, as the re-creator of what it means to be human with other human beings, and the resentment and aversion towards this on the part of the powers is unmasked by the Father's embrace and vindication of Jesus in raising him from the dead. Herbert McCabe observes: "The fact that to be human means to be crucified is not something that the Father has directly planned but what we have arranged. We have made a world in which there is no way of being human that does not involve suffering."[16]

This perspective, or intelligence of the victim, has permeated global culture in ways we might not necessarily recognize, in part because we now take it for granted. But it is worth considering that the ancient world, by and large, apart from Israel, identified the weak and vulnerable with divine disfavor and rejected status, whose lowliness was profoundly to be avoided without sympathy. By contrast Israel lived from the experience of being called by God into freedom and covenant *not* because it was a great nation or "worthy" of God's love but purely by God's grace for the small and the helpless. Against that background, early Christians began to perceive the possibility that God in fact did not condemn and reject the weak and vulnerable Jesus, whom the powerful had said was worthy of condemnation. And that would mean that the assumed divine or sacred legitimation of the ruling powers would become more and more questionable, and their ruling order would be more and more exposed as built upon violence – economic, military, cultural, and sexual – against those with less power than themselves.

In this sphere of social and political interactions, then, perhaps we could envision the saving work of Jesus as undoing the controlling and dominating forces of fear. Jesus' suffering and death are not victimizing but rather, set in motion the liberation of victims. His suffering unmasks a hidden truth about them, and about those who would like to condemn them and use their victimizing to sustain their own grasp on power. In fact we could read the Gospel of John's use of legal and trial imagery (see, e.g., John 5, 12, 18–19) as evidence of this: John exposes the profound irony that the world which blindly insists it is putting Jesus on trial and judging him is in fact, by that very act, putting itself on public trial and unveiling the judgment against itself. If Jesus had remained silenced, then the power within human affairs that works to create a false peace would have remained masked and hidden. But by his life Jesus forces this power into the open, and his death made a public spectacle of its malignant capacities. The resurrection unveils the infinitely greater capacity of divine goodness, subverting all human power plays, and wooing humanity towards a pattern of relationships not founded on fear and envy but resourced by the endless generosity of God.

The cosmic dimension

This brings us directly to the second vantage point, the place of the whole cosmos in the unfolding of salvation. The power structure of this world depends on the poisonous economy of scarcity in which my well-being is seen as necessarily in rivalry with the well-being of others. The ultimate authority in this regime, not surprisingly, is grounded in what it sees as the ultimate deprivation of well-being, death itself. And death is the totem, the bogey, that reminds its suppliants constantly, as a dark shadow falling across every moment, that there will never be "enough," there will never be a plenitude that can fully insulate me from the final deprivation; and this means that whatever there is for me now is itself already dying away, slipping from my grasp, falling to another, and so must be supplemented more and more at any cost. The being of things is attenuated and emaciated from within. The resurrection of Jesus, as I suggested just above, works to unmask the deadly grip of this mentality upon human culture. But it also begins to raise questions about death itself and about its pretensions to absolute dominion as the enforcer of the regime of scarcity, rivalry, and deprivation. As Paul writes, "We know that Christ, being raised from the dead, will never die again, death no longer has dominion over him" (Romans 6: 9). What would this mean about the being of things? Is the wellspring of their very existence permanently choked off, or does the prying loose of death's dominion also affect the very being of creatures themselves?

The resurrection of Jesus reveals a creaturely existence, his own, now fully and immediately and uninterruptably alive with the everlasting vivacity of God. The flowing generosity of God is displayed in the resurrection in ways that echo and lend a new and beautiful resonance to all the scenes of abundance-out-of-scarcity in Jesus' ministry: the miraculous feedings so lovingly and numerously recounted (and like the bread, multiplied) in the gospels; the fading away of nuptial joy lavishly reversed by means of water-into-wine in Jesus' first "sign" in John 2; the broken-down bodies, and lives, and hopes mysteriously healed, forgiven, made overflowing with new hope; the strange parables of loss miraculously recuperated into more-than-equivalent delight, and of small insignificant seeds growing into unimaginable, barn-bursting yields of grain. John surely hears the secret interpretive key that leads into the very source of all this flowing abundance:

> The hour has come for the Son of Man to be glorified. Very truly, I tell you, unless a grain of wheat falls into the earth and dies, it remains just a single grain; but if it dies, it bears much fruit. Those who love their life lose it, and those who hate their life in this world will keep it for eternal life. (John 12: 23–5)

The resurrection of Jesus reveals that his surrendering of life "in this world" opens the hidden dimension within all life, the doorway through which floods the unmediated existence, life, and glory of the divine Giver of life. How and why can this be so?

The first and most obvious point is simply that, in virtue of the resurrection, the crucified Jesus is able to teach his followers that death is not the end: Christ's loving relationship with the Father has reopened creaturely existence – even across the barrier of death itself – to direct communion with God's everlasting abundance. As that conviction grows, Christians believe, the life of faith takes hold and makes possible a transformation in everything as it is taken up into a paschal life (a crucified-yet-risen life) set free from the fear and tyranny of death. Christians believe that the celebration of the Eucharist enacts this paschal transformation of creation in a paradigmatic way. Yet this still leaves unanswered the question of how Jesus' death and resurrection could achieve a reopening, within the very being of creatures, to the abundance of God which is their source. We may find help by recalling Irenaeus from earlier in this chapter: following John, he proposed that creatures come to exist in and through the Son, the beloved Child of God, and, therefore that a filial pattern of imaging the Father is intrinsic to the very structure of creaturely existence ("filial" as in having the relation of a daughter or son to a parent). But if the creatures renounce their own deep structure, if they refuse or no longer remember how to express the divine generosity in their lives, then they would, so to speak, begin to wither, to atrophy; their very hold on their own existence would grow tenuous, frantic, and fearful. But if the archetype, the Image in whom we are created, enacts the imaging afresh within the very structures of creaturely existence, then the way would be open again: the creaturely imaging of the Father's loving would begin to brighten into radiance and light, and the creation-in-Christ would live anew from the outpouring of God's own life.

But what exactly do I mean when I say that in his life, death, and resurrection, Jesus "enacts the imaging afresh," so that creaturely life in Christ transforms the alienation of existence back again into a channel for communion with God? In his earthly life, Jesus seems to possess nothing and yet to enrich everything: receiving everything from God as a gift received without anxiety, he restores to it its unique way of expressing the divine abundance from which it springs. This is paradigmatically represented in the gospel stories of his feeding the multitudes, healing the sick, and raising the dead. And yet even this reopening of creation to the free flowing of its source derives ultimately from the paschal mystery. For the renunciations by which Jesus refuses to dominate the creation as merely his own possession all spring from the deep personal stance that identifies him: his characteristic motivation, present in all his thoughts and words and deeds, is in everything to seek and serve the glory of God. This reaches its consummation in his passion and death. And it's worth noting that in Christ this is no passive victimization, but an active, consciously chosen decision to be in everything the servant of communion with God.

We must see how, in this way, Jesus restores the self-communication of God flowing inexhaustibly within creation as the very ground of its being. The result of human refusal of communion – refusal of the creatures as gift and the toxic domination of them as possession – is the attenuation and distortion of the very patterns by which created being is itself. And the necessary end of that is death. Creation becomes subjected to the law of its own biological limitation as though that – rather than communion with God – were the only real orientation and finality of its existence. If this seems overly dramatic, consider an analogy to this idea of creatures as fundamentally created for communion. Think of your own experience of throwing a party: you work to prepare refreshments that you hope will be an important element in the conviviality and common happiness of people who by means of your gifts become, at least briefly, sharers in life together. But what if the guests turned out to be rather savage and grossly self-centered, squabbling over the food and drink and wolfing it down by themselves as if it existed for no other purpose than their own bodily needs. Soon everything in your household (especially all the refreshments!) would be depleted and picked over, and worst of all, the whole point of them would be entirely lost and debased. Of course, you are not exactly the very source and ground of your party appetizers' existence (though you may have worked hard to make them out of suitable ingredients); so in a sense, while your refreshments' meaning and beauty would be sorely degraded by your thuggish guests, they could not begin to shrivel in their very being. But God's giving of the creatures to one another as gifts to be mutually shared and cherished is indeed the very ground of their existence, and to abuse that purpose is in effect to abandon the deep calling of every being by abasing it to one's own aggrandizement.

I think we could find support for this view in Athanasius of Alexandria (*c.*296–*c.*373), who analyzes creaturely existence as poised between its calling towards interaction and communion with God, and, on the other hand, its origin as having been called by God out of nothing into existence. Human beings, "having turned from the contemplation of God to evil of their own devising, had come inevitably under the law of death," because "as they had at the beginning come into being out of non-existence, so were they now on the way to returning, through corruption, to non-existence again. The presence and love of the Word called them into being; inevitably, therefore, when they lost the knowledge of God, they lost existence with it."[17] Athanasius' point here is that humankind, and through it, the rest of creation, can be turned in one of two directions: if turned towards communion with God (which is the very basis and goal of its existence), then creation becomes the more vivacious, communicative, sharable, and living, for it is being awakened and drawn towards its very consummation in fellowship with God; but if humankind turns away from God, subjecting itself and the other creatures to the bare laws of biological necessity and living for no more than its own ends, then humanity no longer attends to the deep delightful current of divine communion flowing through it and drawing it into communion. Thus humanity itself becomes nothing more than the nearly mechanical pulsing of a biological organism, inevitably governed by the most basic privations, instincts, and mortality as with any organism.

Athanasius goes on to observe that the very Word by whom the creatures are called into existence steps lovingly into their perishing and faltering existence to rescue them. "Pitying our race, moved with compassion for our limitation, unable to endure that death should have the mastery," the Word assumes our failing existence into union with his own" (§8). In this way, the Incarnate Word, Jesus, is able to take our perishing existence, our subjection to biological mortality and the grievous fear that sin had unleashed, and to make of these very dire consequences the fullest act of his loving desire to serve in every way the One who sent him. In other words, where humanity, dominated by fear of death and deprivation, clings to its life – even to the extent of crushing the life out of others, if need be, to preserve itself – by contrast Jesus makes of his life an offering of love to his friends, even to his enemies, and so to God. In this way he subverts the evil in death and makes of even it a way of communion with God. In Athanasius' view, Christ "waited for death in order to make an end of it, and hastened to accomplish it as an offering on behalf of all" (§22). In this way, Jesus converts the most desperate deprivation and finitude, with which sin had infected creation, into a means of solidarity with others and an inextinguishable desire to receive everything from God and restore everything to God.

Christians believe that this cosmic dimension of salvation begins to work itself out within the creation, in ways beyond our present imagining. In Paul's words, the transformation of humanity in Christ seems to be part of a yet wider and deeper yearning within all creatures: "the creation waits with eager longing for the revealing of the children of God," for there is "hope that the creation itself will be set free from its bondage to decay and will obtain the freedom of the glory of the children of God" (Romans 8: 20–1). Something of this recovered freedom of the "children of God" may be slightly observable even now, in two ways that directly involve humans. First, if in Christ I see that death is not the end, I may be released from the illusory "necessity" of using the creation and seeking to possess it, dominate it, because I'm afraid I will not get enough; thus I can release all creatures (myself included) to their true filial calling as children of God, living gifts to be given and received, shared in love, earthly signs of the heavenly banquet of God's abundance. Second, as this happens, I begin to cherish in each creature its own peculiarly treasurable echoing of the Word through whom and for whom it is made. In this way the creation itself is assisted in its passover from a constricted perishing "life" to its primordial filial identity, flowing from the imperishable spring of divine life, and growing towards the richly ecstatic existence of divine communion.

Creation, through the paschal mystery, is in the process of being born as a new creation-in-communion. Or as Paul says, "we know that the whole creation has been groaning in labor pains until now; and not only the creation, but we ourselves, who have the first fruits of the Spirit, groan inwardly while we wait for adoption" (Romans 8: 22–3). This mystery of "adoption," or the recovery of the creatures' filial identity (as children of God), seems to be closely connected with Jesus' willingness to make from constricted and perishing creaturely existence an offering to the Father. I argued above that it was precisely Jesus' ability to do this, most completely by means of his own mortality on the cross, that broke through the barriers of sin and death and "reopened" creaturely existence to its infinitely giving source in God. But how does this readiness on Jesus' part relate to Jesus' identity as the Son of God and to the filial identity of creaturely existence?

The trinitarian dimension

For the answer, we turn to the third vantage point for pondering salvation: sharing in the life of the Trinity. Divine abundance and inexhaustible giving have been the common threads weaving through our exploration of the paschal mystery, in both its socio-political and its cosmic aspects. What is the infinite giving of God that pours out into visibility in Jesus? I don't mean, in the first place, the giving that Jesus makes possible, or even the gift from God to us that Christians believe Jesus is. I think we would want to understand these sorts of giving (or grace) as themselves the outflow of a yet more fundamental outpouring of divine self-sharing. We said we would try to reason from the resurrection to the meaning of the whole paschal mystery, so what is it that the resurrection reveals about Jesus and divine giving? The French biblical scholar F. X. Durrwell put it very luminously:

Christ always preserved something of the child's attitude towards the Father. He spoke of "his" Father; he spoke of his power with a son's pride: "That which the Father hath given me . . . no one can snatch out of the hand of my Father" (John 10: 29). He showed utter confidence in him: "Father . . . I knew that thou hearest me always" (John 11: 42). On the Cross his tone is one of sorrowful surprise: "Why hast thou forsaken me?" (Matt. 27: 46). With his last breath, most filial of all, he puts his life into his Father's hands. He never ceased to be God's Son, and in the early Church he was lovingly called [in the New Testament Greek] *pais Theou*, a name combining a reminder of the Servant of Yahweh with an affectionate allusion to the Child of God.

Then the Father took him to himself, and introducing him totally into the secret of his divine being, into that embrace which confers sonship, he abolished in him the "condition of a slave" [Philippians 2: 5ff.] and brought his whole, once mortal, humanity into the eternal origins of his life of sonship, into the instant of divine generation. He generated him as Son of God in his entire being, saying in the act of glorifying him: "Thou art my Son, this day have I begotten thee" (Acts 13: 33).[18]

The resurrection of Jesus is the consummate moment in Jesus' filial relationship with God. It is the moment when Jesus most completely and perfectly receives the gift of his own identity and existence from the Father. As we have already noted (and will see more clearly in the next chapter), Christians believe that they have been drawn by their discipleship in Jesus into a sharing, a participation, in his relationship with the one he called Father. From that vantage point, Christians have come to believe that this relationship of sonship is the very heart of Jesus' identity and mission and existence. In other words, Jesus is the expression in our world of the eternal sonship, the Word of this abiding relational life that constitutes God's life. God's everlasting yearning to communicate and share divine life with another is an eternal event of self-sharing (there couldn't be a "time" when God was somehow withholding this gift), and the theological expression for this eternal sharing of divine life with another is the eternal begetting of the Son by the Father. When this eternal self-sharing of the Father, this everlasting generosity, comes to be incarnate in our world, what you get is the historical human being, Jesus of Nazareth. But to receive and consciously embrace the fullness of so infinite a gift could not happen for Jesus all at once.

What Durrwell, rather dramatically, proposes is that we recognize the historical, developmental reality of Jesus as a human being. In other words, for Jesus to receive the full gift of his identity as God's beloved child, to live into it completely, would take time. For anyone to perceive and recognize and actualize the deep gifts of her own personhood takes time and often considerable struggle. Over time, you may sense many possible ways of being the person you truly are, of unfolding the deep desire and potential of your identity. Sometimes you have to relinquish less authentically fulfilling ways of being true to yourself, which is certainly a painful and perplexing aspect of human growth. Moreover, we often are not perfectly clear about what we are doing, or that the course of our life is in harmony with the deep calling and truth of ourselves. And if the deep calling of our identity were to embody the gift of eternal sonship, to express the everlasting Word of the Father's love within the constraints of the human condition – this certainly would be a momentous journey. Durrwell's point is that the resurrection of Jesus is the reflection into our world of the Father's embrace of Jesus, of his eternal joy and delight in Jesus' authentic and true-hearted realization of his sonship. We might consider this by an analogy: our experiences of sensing the "rightness" of our path in life. For the most part we have to come to this sense of fitness or rightness in what we are doing by ourselves; but there are occasions when someone who knows you and loves you can say, "Yes! I am so happy for you; what you are doing is really 'you,' really the thing that seems to bring you to life and give you peace." The resurrection is the Father saying to Jesus, within the visibility of time, "Yes, this is really you, and this really brings you to life."

Now, if we think about the resurrection this way, what would that bring to light about Jesus' passion and death? Most fundamentally, it would show us that no matter what the powers of this world may have intended, Jesus is able to make his best of their worst. It also shows us that far from demanding something from us or Jesus, God (as we've been suggesting all along) seeks to give to us something imperishably wonderful: a fulfilling sharing in Jesus' filial relationship with the Father. But how can Jesus hold together human antagonism towards God, and God's love for humanity, by means of his filial life? Precisely by transmuting the first into a means for receiving the second. Let me explain. While the gospels depict Jesus as very humanly struggling with the fear and brutal suffering that are meted out to him, his early followers also sensed his awareness that this might be the likely outcome of his life (see Mark 10: 33). In John, Jesus is clearly understood as fashioning, by means of his death, the fulfillment of his life:

> For this reason the Father loves me, because I lay down my life in order to take it up again. No one takes it from me, but I lay it down of my own accord, and I have power to take it up again. I have received this command from my Father. (John 10: 17–18)

What is this "command" from the Father but for Jesus to receive and to realize the gift of his own life and identity as the Beloved Child of the Father? As we noted above, to receive so overwhelming a gift would be most difficult, and it might well require Jesus "to lay down [his] life in order to take it up again," that is, to relinquish every limited and finite expression of his identity in order to take up more and more the infinite intimacy of filial life.

We recall how often Jesus' contemporaries, even his own disciples, misunderstood his calling and identity, attempting to fit him into their own visions of what he should be, even at one point intending to "take him by force to make him king" (John 6: 15). Jesus has always to withdraw, to lay down these would-be lives that are proffered to him, just as in the temptation in the wilderness he chooses to refuse the distorted realizations of his identity held out to him by Satan. But perhaps the most difficult renunciations would be those entailed by his maturing sense of his own calling and identity, of how best to embody the gift of filiation, the loving expression of the Father's desire for fellowship. Perhaps he must often have felt joy in bringing about a certain level of understanding among his disciples or consciousness among the people, only to have these achievements shattered many times over. And with each apparent failure, there would be required a deep personal relinquishment, and a growing openness to the unknown "more" that the Father would bring about.

The Letter to the Hebrews emphasizes this very human process of discovery and growth on Jesus' part, struggling through his obedience to the Father's will to receive and embody the fullness of filiation, of being God's beloved to the very roots and in every different and difficult situation: "Although he was a Son, he learned obedience through what he suffered; and having been made perfect, he became the source of eternal salvation for all who obey him" (Hebrews 5: 8–9). Here it is important to recollect the underlying meaning of obedience, deriving from its Latin sources: *ob-*, a prefix meaning to, towards, or on account of, and *audire*, meaning to hear; obedience is thus a way of being that's profoundly marked by hearing, understanding, perceiving. We might think by analogy of someone's struggle, even suffering, in the effort to hear and respond to a particular calling in life; this would be an example of the kind of obedience Jesus learned: a growing attentiveness and availability to the true depths, perhaps largely unforeseen, of the possibilities inherent in his identity as God's beloved. Perhaps we have known persons who struggled in an analogous way to hear and respond to a profound gift in music or dance or poetry or athletics: the costliness to them as persons may be nearly unbearable at times, yet they long for the pure and excellent fulfilling of their callings with every fiber of their beings. The sacrifices they make of themselves are not self-diminishing but are in the service of the deepest truth of their own identity.

The beauty and achievement that such gifted persons bring into being are tangible rewards and confirmations of their callings. But what confirmations might human beings in general have of their universal calling? Christians believe that every human being is called into existence with a fundamental or universal calling to enter fully into the life of a child of God. As we have seen over the course of these two chapters on salvation, the distortion of this calling, and the degenerating ability to respond to it, are at the center of most notions of sin. So vast and great is the gift, so unimaginable is the calling to be a beloved child of God within the very intimacy of God's eternal Beloved, that humanity is easily deluded into pursuing something lesser – until idolatry begins to dominate the human person. The downward spiral we have traced already: as less of the divine goodness is contemplated, humanity becomes the more desperate to possess anything, and the tighter the grip the narrower the grasp, so that in time one labors harder and harder in thrall to a demonic and punishing scarcity.

Into this state Jesus comes, refusing to settle for the small completions and successes of the world. The Holy Spirit, poured out within Christ at his baptism, vivified in his life the passionate and infinite longing for the authentic holiness of the Father. But how tempting it would be to do the good that he *could* accomplish and to stay there; the pain would come from the sense that the gift he had to embody was ever greater still. Again, if you think of the deepest, truest calling of your life, how often an authentic availability to that requires a painful relinquishment of the self you think that you have achieved. The American theologian Daniel Day Williams remarks:

> So long as we aim at the maintenance of this present self, as we now conceive it, we cannot enter the larger selfhood which is pressing for life. This natural resistance of the self to becoming is not in itself sin. It is a self-protective device of the human spirit; but when it becomes an invitation to use our freedom against the risk of becoming it is temptation to sin. The meaning of sin is usually not that we try to make ourselves the centre of everything. That may happen, but it is a monstrous perversion. We are usually more subtle. We make our present state of selfhood the meaning of existence, and thus refuse the deeper meaning which lies within and beyond this present. When that refusal becomes refusal to trust in the giver of life and the greater community he is creating it is sin.[19]

In the case of Jesus, I am suggesting, the "larger selfhood" is the full filial relationship with the Father, poured out within humanity; for this, Christians believe, is the deep calling and identity of his own being, and for this he came to see that he would have to relinquish every worldly achievement.

I think it is probably good for us to ponder how very bitter this renunciation likely would have been for Jesus. In a sense, he had probably come to terms with the fact that he would be put out of the way; his death as an end to *himself* seems to have been the least of his concerns. Instead the gospels all depict his last hours as filled with efforts to prepare his followers, to shape their understandings in advance of whatever became of him. And yet, as the betrayals and abandonments began, he had to make the final renunciation: he had to make even of his death and the destruction of everything he had worked for an act of availability to the larger purposes of God. Herbert McCabe puts this with painful clarity:

> On the cross Jesus finally abandons himself to the Father. His life work has ended in failure. . . . The whole attempt to form a little community of friends based on himself, and, through him, the Father's love, one in which people could relate to each other in love and mutual forgiveness instead of domination and submission, has been a complete failure. . . . He accepts his failure and refuses to compromise his mission by using the weapons of the world against the world. It is his Father's mission and it is for the Father to bring his own purposes out of Jesus' failure. Jesus knows he is not going to live to establish the Kingdom. He did not transform the world; the colonial society went on as before; the same kinds of bitterness and meanness and hatreds went on as before. In death on the cross he handed over all the meaning of his human life to the Father; this is his prayer. The Father has not accomplished his will through any success of Jesus; Jesus is left with nothing but his love and his obedience, and this is the prayer to the Father to work through his failure. And, of

course, the answer to the prayer is the resurrection, when the Father through the dead but risen Christ *does* accomplish his loving will for human creatures.[20]

Perhaps we could say that this way of looking at salvation makes clear its ultimate point, namely the recovery of humanity's relationship to the Father. On the cross, Jesus is able to use even humanity's separation from God as a means of entrusting humanity back again into that filial relationship whose infinite intimacy was beyond any human achieving. This infinite sharing in God's life comes to be understood by Christians as God the Holy Spirit: "Through the risen Christ the Spirit is poured out upon all men, or, to put it another way, the relationship between Jesus and the Father, between the Son and the Father, is extended to all men."[21] And so from the experience of salvation, Christians have come to think of God as a Trinity of infinitely generous self-sharing life – as we see in the next chapter.

Chapter 6

Divine Life: Trinity, Incarnation, and the Breathing of the Spirit

ORIENTATION

Sheer Bliss: Why God Reveals Divine Life to be the Trinity

What is at stake in thinking God to be, as Christians claim, the Trinity: one God in three Persons? A short answer might be: what's at stake is not how creatures think about God, but how God thinks about them. But how *does* God think about them? The final section of the previous chapter introduced this discussion: there we saw that in the event of salvation God might be said to offer what Christians believe to be the most definitive divine "thinking" about creatures – by knowing and loving them in Christ and the Spirit. And, indeed, as early Christians deepened their ongoing encounter with Christ and the Spirit, they sensed that what had happened to the world could only be the work of God directly: that Jesus and the Spirit must somehow be divine, God at work in their midst: "in Christ, God was reconciling the world to himself" (2 Corinthians 5: 19).

Thus two impressions began to grow within the mind of early Christian communities. First, whatever had overtaken them in Jesus and the outpouring of the Spirit seemed to them to be truly saving, salvific, but in a way they could only liken to creation or re-creation (2 Corinthians 5: 17) – such that only God, as the Creator, could accomplish. This naturally inspired in them a desire to move more deeply into the presence of the God who encountered them in Christ and the Holy Spirit. This divine presence they identified as none other than the very same God who had led Israel out of Egypt and led a universe out of nothingness into being. The second impression arose from the fact that their communal practicing of this presence of Word and Spirit seemed always to lead them into a yet deeper and deeper intimacy with God. It was as if they were somehow always invited "farther in" to an infinitely flowing meaning and generosity that had already begun to transform their lives. As Christians shared in Jesus' relation to the Father in their Spirit, they began to sense that the impact of all this on their own lives was only the beginning, and that they were in fact being fitted and made apt for another kind of life altogether – a life that seemed strangely fulfilling to them and yet was no longer *their* life only but God's life in them. An early Christian seer tried to put into words what this would be like, when God would simply be the life of the whole people: "I saw no temple in the city, for its temple is the Lord God the Almighty and the Lamb. And the city has no need of sun or moon to shine on it, for the glory of God is its light, and its lamp is the Lamb" (Revelation 21: 22–3). Another early writer went so far as to say that believers were being invited to "become participants of the divine nature" (2 Peter 1: 4).

Paul, writing in the first decades of the Christian era, already emphasized this mysterious transformation and indwelling of Christians as they share in Jesus' death. In his view, their old identity is set behind them and they share in a new resurrection identity in Christ, an identity breathed within them by his Spirit:

> If the Spirit of him who raised Jesus from the dead dwells in you, he who raised Christ from the dead will give life to your mortal bodies also through his Spirit that dwells in you. . . . When we cry, "Abba! Father!" it is that very Spirit bearing witness with our spirit that we are children of God, and if children, then heirs, heirs of God and joint heirs with Christ – if, in fact, we suffer with him so that we may also be glorified with him. (Romans 8: 11, 15–17)

Sharing in Jesus' death and being raised to new life in the Spirit – whatever else this might mean, for Paul it clearly meant a journey into a new standing before God. Being raised in Christ to stand before the Father seemed to mean a new status, not only as creatures but as beloved children, heirs entitled to stand in a new way before the One whom Jesus had called "Abba." In other words, early Christians were being led to discover not only the possibility of a new standing with God but of a new "place" to stand within God: a way in which, by the power of the Spirit, one could stand in the "place" of the beloved Son, Jesus, and in him and through him and with him, face toward the Father. Jesus seemed to have won the right to pour out within the lives of his friends the very Spirit of his relationship with the Father, and so bring them into that place where he had always known himself to be loved eternally: "As you, Father, are in me and I in you, may they also be in us. . . . Father, I desire that these also, whom you have given me, may be with me where I am, to see my glory, which you have given me because you loved me before the foundation of the world" (John 17: 21, 24). Speaking of this chapter in John, Michael Ramsey remarks:

> Jesus speaks to the Father as the Father's eternal Son, and yet He speaks from the midst of a historical crisis of human flesh and blood. The prayer thus belongs both to the timeless converse of the Father and the Son, and to the conflict in time wherein the Son embraces the Father's will.[1]

The point I am making is that Jesus addresses the Father from the midst of humanity, and thereby holds open to view a new vision of God "from the inside," as it were: of God as an event of relations between Jesus and the One he called Father in their Spirit.

Herbert McCabe expresses very well this mysterious sense of Christ opening for humanity a new way of being in relation to God, and, indeed, of coming to know and love God by entering into God's knowing and loving of Godself:

> If [Jesus] had wanted something less than the kingdom, if he had been a lesser man, a man not obsessed by love he might have settled for less and achieved it by his own personality, intelligence and skill. But he wanted that all men should be as possessed by love as he was, he wanted that they should be divine, and this could only come as gift. Crucifixion and resurrection, the prayer of Christ and the response of the Father are the archetype and source of all our prayer. . . . But the crucifixion, the total self-abandonment of Jesus to the Father is not just a prayer that Jesus offered, a thing he happened to do. What the Church came to realize is that it was the revelation of *who* Jesus is. . . . The deepest reality of Jesus is simply to be *of* the Father. . . . He is not first of all an individual person who then prays to the Father, his prayer to the Father is what constitutes him as who he is. He is not just one who prays, not even one who prays best, he is sheer prayer. In other words the crucifixion/resurrection of Jesus is simply the showing forth, the visibility in human terms, in human history, of the relationship to the Father which constitutes the person who is Jesus. The prayer of Jesus which is his crucifixion, his absolute renunciation of himself in love to the Father, is the eternal relationship of Father and Son made available as part of our history.[2]

Over time, then, an overwhelming and soul-shaking question arose for Jesus' followers: could our experience of salvation, of being known and loved in Christ and the Spirit, be telling us not just of God knowing and loving *us* in our time and world, but of how God is in Godself, of God's knowing and loving in eternity? In other words, if early Christians came to experience Christ and the Spirit as in some sense divine, what could that mean about God?

Here is what's at stake with the doctrine of the Trinity: an infinite interplay of relational life into which a whole universe is created and called to share. As Nicholas Lash observes, "We *have* relationships, God *is* the relations that he has . . . God, we might say, is relationship without remainder."[3] Maybe that's why God, as Christians think, has been trying to teach intelligent creatures how to relate to God precisely as the Trinity – namely, because of the sheer bliss of God's own life of relational joy. In other words, if Christians are right about all this, then God is trying to teach the universe how to know and love God because this is a crucial stage in the creatures' homeward journey into that infinitely knowing and loving existence that is the Trinity. This trinitarian life was, as McCabe puts it above, woven into the fabric of our world in Jesus and the Spirit, not simply as a new self-disclosure on God's part, but in order to draw the world more and more within the patterns of the divine life.

Why am I bothering about all this? Why not just get on with "explaining the Trinity," as countless decent textbooks carry on with in a suitably studious manner? Because, as I've been suggesting throughout this book, the only one who can really teach anyone theology in the deepest sense is God. And thus the question arises, how and why might God want to teach humans (angels too, presumably, though that would be much easier) to envision God in this particular way, i.e., as Trinity? Perhaps the best answer for now is simply the one we saw in John's Gospel above: because Jesus wants his friends to be where he is in the love of the Father. If that's the case, then, God is teaching the world to know and love God as Trinity precisely because this "teaching" is actually a transforming. By unveiling the mystery of the trinitarian life, Christians believe, God is preparing the world to be taken up into God's own beatific life of knowing and loving, of being Father, and Word, and Spirit.

So while we may, quite properly, want to learn something about the Trinity in academic terms, we'll need to bear in mind that, in the view of Christians, this very process of our thinking as it is drawn forth by our desire to know something – especially when that "something" is God – is itself a particularly resonant echoing within us of the Trinity's own eternal event of knowing and loving. Indeed Thomas Aquinas thought that, in certain circumstances, this kind of thinking might turn out to be none other than the mystical presence of the eternal Word and Spirit within the thinking human being, such that the event of knowing might "break forth into the affection of love" who is the Holy Spirit (*ST* I. 43. 5). But then, I've already warned you that God teaches like that. In any event, this should make clear that no account of the Trinity can be at all on the right track unless it consistently shows how Christian reflection on the *doctrine* of the Trinity leads believers more deeply into the living *mystery* of the Trinity.

Forgiveness and Abundance: Origins of Trinitarian Awareness

Perhaps the most direct way to talk about this is to consider how early Christians thought about their new life in Christ through the Spirit, about the new identity that seemed to unfold within them. For the Christian vision of the divine Trinity relates intrinsically to a vision of human identity that has been set free from cultural and biological impulses to fear, envy, and violence. Early Christians describe this as a "new creation" of human being (see 2 Corinthians 5: 17), springing from something utterly mysterious taking place in an interplay between Jesus, the One he calls Abba, and the Spirit, an interaction definitively expressed in Jesus' death and resurrection. This new creation takes the form of a new birth, a new identity, which is marked above all by sharing in Jesus' relation with the Father by means of his Spirit at work in the believers. Paul puts this most clearly in Galatians 4: 4–7:

When the fullness of time had come, God sent his Son, born of a woman, born under the law, in order to redeem those who were under the law, so that we might receive adoption as children. And because you are children, God has sent the Spirit of his Son into our hearts, crying, "Abba! Father!" So you are no longer a slave but a child, and if a child then also an heir of God through Christ.

What was this experience of "adoption" like? It seems to have been based on meeting the crucified but risen Jesus, being healed by his power to forgive, and thereby, through his Spirit, being enabled to enter into a new relationship with God.

In other words, Jesus' followers describe themselves as shaped and given identity by their encounters with this same Jesus whom they had abandoned to death, and whom they experienced as now alive and bearing toward them neither a will to revenge, nor recrimination, but peace. They describe the crucified Jesus who meets them as repeatedly saying things like "Greetings! . . . Do not be afraid" (Matthew 28: 9–10), or "Peace be with you" (John 20: 19, 26). They report these experiences as taking a particular form: an offer of new friendship and affiliation, a peace-bestowing presence of the crucified Jesus that seems intended to move the disciples beyond their fears and probable sense of anger, guilt, and grief. We can gauge the power that these experiences of the risen Jesus had for his followers because we can see how they shaped for them a powerful new sense of their own identity.

One good place to consider this is with the story of Stephen, the first martyr, looking up into heaven at the moment of his death (Acts 6 and 7). The Gospel of Luke and the Book of Acts, written as a two-volume work, clearly portray Stephen as not only a witness to Jesus (martyr comes from the Greek word *martureō*, to bear witness) but as finding a new identity by sharing in Jesus' identity. Stephen is described (Acts 6: 8ff.) as "full of grace and power," as doing "great wonders and signs among the people," and as having prophesied against the Temple, all clearly echoing Luke's account of Jesus (see, e.g., Luke 4 and 19). Most importantly, at the time of his death Stephen is shown as radiating two crucial features of Jesus' own way of being: first, Stephen like Jesus commends his spirit into the hands of the One he trusts; and second, Stephen like Jesus prays forgiveness for those who persecute him:

Jesus:	Stephen:
"Father, into your hands I commend my spirit" (Luke 23: 46)	"Lord Jesus, receive my spirit" (Acts 7: 59)
"Father, forgive them; for they do not know what they are doing" (Luke 23: 34)	"Lord, do not hold this sin against them" (Acts 7: 60)

What do we learn from these passages? Clearly the early followers of Jesus wished to show how Jesus' way of being could draw them within itself, so that *their* lives might each radiate his life in their own ways. And what they reflect is something of Jesus' strange freedom to entrust himself to the One he called Father, and (perhaps as a result of this freedom) a conviction of that divine Other's merciful and generously forgiving nature. It is this relationship, this entrusting of oneself to the divine Other, that seems to enable Jesus and his followers to live beyond the bitter constraints of fear and a need for revenge on their persecutors. In other words, it sets flowing within them and their community a new experience of abundance, of giving joy, of there being somehow "enough," such that one could trust this overruling goodness of God as the deepest truth of every situation.

In fact the Book of Acts portrays Stephen's final words of peace-bestowing forgiveness as pouring forth directly from his visionary participation in Jesus' relationship with God: "Filled with the Holy Spirit, [Stephen] gazed into heaven and saw the glory of God and Jesus standing at the right hand of God. 'Look,' he said, 'I see the heavens opened and the Son of Man standing at the right hand of God!'" (Acts 7: 55–6). The most obvious biblical allusions here are to the unsealing of the mysteries of God's hidden plan for the redemption of the world in the Old Testament Book of Daniel. In that book, during a time of terrible persecution for the people of God, Daniel is granted a vision of "one like a son of man" being received into the glory and power of God (Daniel 7). This human one, representing the persecuted people, is revealed by the vision *not* to be rejected and in the wrong (as the worldly powers declare) but is instead shown to be honored and accepted into the very presence of God.

As we saw Paul declaring in Romans 8 and Galatians 4, there is a strong sense here of a "place" being unveiled, a place in which humanity can stand before God. And this means the growing sense that there must be something like a place "before the face of the other" *in* God, a way in which there is in God something like an eternal making-place-for-the-other and an embracing of the other, an opening to the other and a cherishing of the other. And the abundance and graciousness of this trinitarian making-space-for-the-other is what begins to inhabit Jesus' followers, such as Stephen, empowering them to live for others rather than against them or in fear of them, just as God, as Trinity, exists as an eternal event of being "for the other": Father for Son for Father through the Spirit. So something secret is being communicated here, something inconceivably holy that is also at the same time the transcending of all natural expectations. Stephen catches a glimpse of this same mystery revealed in its consummate moment, when the persecuted victim Jesus is revealed not in fact to be just another failed, blasphemous, malcontent whom the powerful have appropriately silenced, but as someone alive in the presence of God, unaccountably and everlastingly precious to God. And it is Stephen's visionary sharing, "filled with the Holy Spirit," in this relationship of Jesus with the One who welcomes him, that sets free within Stephen a radical self-sharing and merciful generosity towards those who are about to stone him to death.

I've been suggesting here that far from being an obscure piece of metaphysical speculation, the Christian vision of God as Trinity emerges organically from early Christians' experience of their own transformation by means of relationship, through Jesus, in the Spirit, with the Father. We might usefully pause here and simply ask ourselves: what can we notice as the most striking characteristic of Jesus' way of being, a characteristic that seems to flow, to be sharable, capable of drawing Stephen and thousands of others like him into Christ? Is it mercy, forgiveness? Certainly it takes those forms because it is, like many things, most clearly revealed in its most extreme, even desperate, forms: in this case in the inconceivable for-giveness and peace-giving of a victim to those who persecute him. But this itself flows from the yet more inconceivable revelation that the victim is in fact not cursed and abandoned by God but rather is beloved by God, given a "place" to stand before God by a love stronger than death itself. Could this unbroken rela-tion of love, revealed in the world by the resurrection of Christ, be the wellspring of mercy and forgiveness? The crucified-yet-risen presence of an unfathomably peaceful mercy impressed itself upon early Christians, leading them to wonder about the source of this abundance within the life of God.

The Life of the Incarnate Word and the Power of the Spirit

Christian reflection on the Trinity may not reach full doctrinal formulation until the fourth century, but I'm suggesting that it is already intrinsic to the earliest encounters with Jesus, both in his earthly ministry and as crucified yet risen. It makes itself known as a strangely attractive power of self-sharing and giving life. Think for a moment of how prominently the theme of this mysterious abundance features in the New Testament. It appears in some fashion in almost all the para-bles: seeds grow into unfathomable plenty or size, fish are caught to net-bursting astonishment, the lost and the broken-down are ecstatically recovered and received home. Jesus' imagination seems radically alive to this abundance beyond all expec-tation, this grace. Think too of his actions as signs of the same imagination at work: welcoming outcasts with an inexplicable mercy, feeding the hungry with an unstinting lavishness, even raising the dead with a strangely commanding power to author life where there was no life but only fear, anger, and rejection. Con-versely, Jesus' harshest words and deeds seem to have been directed quite narrowly against those whose self-satisfaction and self-righteousness closed them off from these signs of divine grace.

Why was this divine giving, quite beyond all human expectations, so important to Jesus? Simply put, I think it was because this was the very expression, within the constraints of this world, of the life Jesus desired so intensely to share with his people. It was a life he experienced as flowing to him without reserve from the Father. Thus he came to be understood as the very Incarnation of this life, this Word, from God. And, most significantly, Jesus seems to have felt he could only be the perfect expression, the Word, of this gift by communicating it to others, and by preparing others to partake in it. He does so throughout his earthly ministry by acts of unstinting hospitality, generosity, mercy, and forgiveness which reach their culmination on the cross – and by sending the Spirit of this life upon his followers. Not coincidentally, all the gospels include an account of Jesus' baptism near the beginning of his ministry. In this moment, Jesus enacts his full identification with the people and shares in their longing expectation that God would deliver them. All the gospels describe this moment as a definitive unfolding of Jesus' sense of self and of mission. In the stark simplicity of Mark's Gospel:

> In those days Jesus came from Nazareth of Galilee and was baptized by John in the Jordan. And just as he was coming up out of the water, he saw the heavens torn apart and the Spirit descending like a dove on him. And a voice came from heaven, "You are my Son, the Beloved; with you I am well pleased." (Mark 1: 9–11)

It is precisely as he unites himself with the people in their longing and need that Jesus is depicted as sensing fully his identity as God's beloved. It is then that the gospels describe him as being marked externally by an outpouring and anointing of God's Spirit. In Israel's tradition, God's chosen agent in history was anointed by the Spirit (the Hebrew for anointed one is *messiah* and the same term in Greek is *Christ*). In accepting his mission as the agent of God's loving deliverance for his people, Jesus enters deeply into the sense of his true identity and mission as God's beloved, filled and empowered with Spirit of God. This Spirit is then described in the gospels as leading Jesus into the wilderness. It becomes in him a burning desire, and intense hunger to fulfill and even to be the fulfillment of God's will and word. "I have food to eat that you do not know . . . my food is to do the will of him who sent me" (John 4: 32, 34). This unvanquished generosity, Christ's Spirit, is what in the glory of his resurrection he pours out upon his disciples at Pentecost (see Acts 2).

What I'm suggesting then is that the grace, the loving abundance that Jesus knows as the very root of his being – and which radiates into the world definitively as the resurrection of Jesus from the dead – is the expression within our world of an eternal abundance. It is the expression in our world of an infinite giving, the free self-sharing of the Father to the Son and in the Spirit, or what Christians call the Trinity. As we'll see below, the first questions in this process of reflection revolved around how, exactly, Jesus could be said to be divine. Then came the same questions about the Spirit. And then came the questions regarding how to conceive of Christ as both divine and yet also fully human. We might try to visualize the process of theological development as a cycle of deepening reflection (as set out in the diagram), a process of roughly four steps running (1) from the historical events of Christ and the Spirit, up through reflection on the implications of this (2) for Christian understanding of God (3), and then back again (4) to re-conceive Jesus and the Spirit with their divine aspect in view:

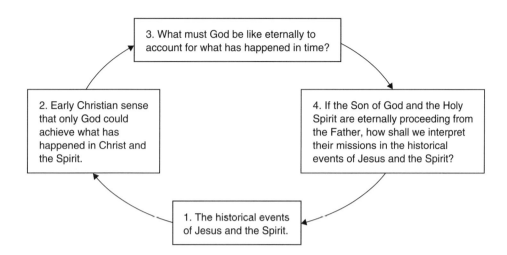

Because these developments in the history of Christian theology are so momentous, it will be helpful to consider them briefly in the following section. Indeed, one might say that it was through the process of these unfolding reflections on salvation – a process in which Christianity was led to perceive the mystery of the Trinity – that Christian theology really came to birth.

The Developing Principles of Trinitarian Theology

Unity and difference in God

The first and most basic principle that early Christian theology adhered to was its conviction inherited directly from Israel's faith: "Hear, O Israel: The LORD our God, the LORD is one" (Deuteronomy 6: 4). Far from being the invasion of Christian thought by some supposedly distorting Greek metaphysical speculation (as one still occasionally hears), theology's concern to guard the oneness and transcendence of God emerged from the most central feature of Christianity's inherited biblical faith. The trinitarian and Christological controversies in the first five centuries of Christianity's existence grew out of the creative tension between this central belief in God's oneness and, on the other hand, the community's ongoing experience of Christ and the Spirit as working the work of God. One of the most misleading pieces of conventional theological wisdom, now disproven over and over, is the misapprehension that eastern trinitarian theology "begins" from the diversity in God, the three divine persons, and that western trinitarian theology "begins" from the unity in God, the divine essence or being.[4] In fact, it has been the universal concern of both eastern and western theologians to safeguard the oneness of God, as the imperishable inheritance of Christianity from Israel. And realizing that this is the case will quite often help us to understand the emphases and the decisions various theologians make in their efforts to think out the doctrine of the Trinity.

Augustine and Aquinas, for example, do not attend to God's oneness in order to confine trinitarian theology within some kind of philosophical preconception about divine essence, but precisely because they want to show that the God whom Christians adore as Father, Son, and Holy Spirit is none other than the one God of Israel, the Creator of heaven and earth.[5] In fact it is this awareness, namely, that Christians are trying to talk about the Creator, that often functions as a critical rule in developing trinitarian theology. We might sketch the line of reasoning as follows:

1 Christian faith and practice assures me (a theologian might say) that Jesus and the Spirit are in some sense divine. But how?
2 The divine life, as the unitary (one) source of all creatures, is not limited or dependent or liable to age and decay as creatures are.
3 So God's life cannot be thought of as somehow analogous to a kind of material "stuff" like a creaturely life. In other words, God's being is not large or small, or multiple, or separable into bits and pieces, or subject to anything else, simply because then it wouldn't be God that I'm talking about.
4 Therefore, however I try to conceive of Jesus as the Son of God (or the Spirit as the Spirit of God), it cannot be in such a way that could imply that God's life is somehow divisible into three "parts" or as changing from a unitary life into a multiple life.

It would be fair to say that not one single theologian of Christianity's first five centuries, of any perspective whatsoever, would take issue with such a line of argument. The dispute was entirely over the question of how, precisely, to understand the generation of the Son of God and the breathing forth of the Spirit of God – within this fundamental adherence to the one God of Israel. There were two opposite extremes, of course, who equally avoided dealing with how the unity of God and the Trinity of Persons could be thought together: one of these tendencies, sometimes referred to as various forms of "modalism" (see the Terminology Survival Guide, p. 132), insisted that the eternal Word or Son was an *aspect* or mode of God's life, in no way a distinct reality, but simply a way in which God might appear at one time or another in the course of history; the opposite extreme, often referred to as various types of "subordinationism," solved the problem by insisting that God the Father is alone the One God, but that there could be other lower levels of being accorded a quasi-divine status and appointed by God, perhaps as the first of all creation, to exercise God's will in the world. Given the affection of the ancient Mediterranean world in general for an abundance of deities and spiritual forces, it is not perhaps surprising at all that the longest-running rival to more middle-of-the-road approaches was this subordinationist bent, enjoying as it did the attractive benefit that it could proclaim Jesus as an accessible quasi-divine savior-figure whose status would have been fairly intelligible to any number of Greeks and Romans.

But most Christian theologians eschewed these two extremes and tried a little harder to see how Jesus and the Spirit might really be said to be divine and how God could still be said, even so, to be one. There were a great variety of schools of thought, and theological histories that tidy them into clearly defined camps set against each other are likely to miss out the central principles they often held in common and which, in time, emerged as the most important aspects of what God seemed to be teaching the Christian community. Certainly it would be fair to say that there were those who tended to emphasize the unity of God's life as the fundamental norm for theological reflection and, by contrast, others who tended more to emphasize that there could be something like diversity in God. Both ranges of thinkers, however, were strongly united in wishing to avoid ascribing to God any sort of material or changeable form of existence, for they believed this would mean they were no longer talking about the Creator at all but simply a very powerful creature.

Clearly a central way of thinking about all this was by trying to understand the relation between the Father and the Son. Lewis Ayres, in his magisterial survey of fourth-century trinitarian theology, very helpfully summarizes the chief emphases of these two basic tendencies. He reminds us that at the beginning of this period theologians "are still grappling with the problem of whether Father and Son are both 'true God,' with the question of whether it is possible to speak of degrees of divinity."[6] Let me try to schematize Ayres's observations by laying them out in parallel columns, and as you consider each point, try to envision the emerging theological imagination that these trinitarian perspectives were calling forth.

Theologies emphasizing sameness between Father and Son . . .	Theologies emphasizing difference between Father and Son . . .
(a) use language naming the same quality in both Father and Son: Father is divine, Son is divine; Father is light, Son is light;	(a) use language highlighting the relationship between Father and Son precisely as marking difference between Father and Son;
(b) adopt metaphors of unbroken derivation of Son from Father: Son is the Wisdom, Power, or Word of the Father;	(b) adopt metaphors of hierarchical order: Father is archetype, Son is image; Father is Creator, Son is first creature;
(c) speak of the Son's "generation" or procession from the Father not simply as mirroring some quality of the Father but as actually sharing in the nature or being of the Father;	(c) criticize those who speak of the Son's generation as implying materiality in God, of conceiving the Son's procession as a division of material substance in God;

(d) use "Word of the Father" imagery
to mean that which is intrinsically
connected to the Father, rather like a
rational capacity that is always present
with the Father.

(d) use "Word of the Father"
imagery to mean that which is a
subordinate and independent being,
not necessarily existing eternally with
the Father.

What do we learn from these points of comparison? First, that reflection on the
relation of the Spirit to God emerges somewhat later in the discussion (although
it will follow many of the same paths). Second, that both ranges of tendencies
were trying to be faithful to the scriptural language and imagery about Jesus and
about God's word and wisdom in the Old Testament; and yet each group of tendencies could coherently interpret these passages as, more or less, opposing the
meaning they had for the other group. This means that far from relying on mere
collections of single verses taken out of context to interpret scripture, early Christian theologians read particular elements of biblical language in terms of their
overarching sense of the scriptural witness to God's saving work and to God's
character. How does a scripturally-shaped theological imagination apprehend what
God is doing in Christ and the Spirit?

Now here is the key, and ultimately definitive difference. Note that those emphasizing the sameness of Father and Son are concerned to show that the Son (in whom
Christians had found salvation) really is divine in the same sense as the Father, the
implication of course being that therefore the Son does indeed have the power to
save, to re-create the human condition from within our dying human existence as
only God could do were God to exist humanly, as none other than Jesus of
Nazareth. By contrast, those emphasizing the difference of Father and Son are
concerned that the Son be truly and savingly available to humanity, something that,
in their view, would not be possible if the Son were God in the same sense as the
Father, for then (as they thought) either the divine life would be subjected to
human suffering and death (which seemed impossible to them) or the Son could
not really be incarnate and present to us in Christ (which would leave us with a
Christ who is not truly able to save). The remarkable achievement of the next
hundred years or so, from the Council of Nicaea in 325 through the Council of
Chalcedon in 451, was the forging of a gradually converging consensus: that God's
unity, God's existence as the one God, is nothing less than the eternal flowing forth
of the three divine Persons. In other words, from seeing unity and difference posed
somehow uneasily against each other, Christian theology began to see the unity of
God as the richly unceasing event of the divine Persons' relations to each other.

Persons in relation

A crucial step in this development was the insistence at the Councils of Nicaea
(325) and Constantinople (381), respectively, that the Son and the Spirit are in

fact divine in the same way that the Father is divine. An enormous variety of views existed about what it could mean to say that the Son is "of the same being" (*homoousios*) as the Father, or "of the being of the Father" (as the Creed of 325 declared), but saying such things clearly ruled out certain possibilities – above all the idea that Jesus was only the historical presence of something or someone other or less than God. So as you examine the text of this Creed, try to sense "between the lines" how the language – even in its apparently positive affirmations – is struggling to articulate what cannot be said, quite literally. In other words, when it uses the term *homoousios* (same being or essence or substance), the divine being or *ousia* is actually not being defined at all; for we literally cannot say what God is, because by definition God's life exceeds all our concepts and language. So the use of terms like this functions as a kind of variable, like x or p in an equation: we have no idea what x or p might be exactly, but they certainly cannot be not-x or not-p. We have no idea what the divine *ousia* is, but if the Son is of the same *ousia* as the Father then this clearly means that the Son cannot be of some other *ousia*, and the only other "type" of *ousia* there can be is a non-divine or creaturely one, therefore the Son is clearly not that. Here's the original text of Nicaea in the translation of Rowan Williams with my commentary on the right.[7]

We believe in one God, the Father, the ruler of all, the maker of all things visible and invisible;

As we've noted all along, the commitment to God's unity is the foundational principle, and here the one God is identified as the Father. So whatever this divine oneness might mean, it would seem to include a relation: God is Father to a Son.

and in one Lord, Jesus Christ the Son of God, begotten as the only Son out of the Father, that is, out of the substance (*ousias*) of the Father,

Jesus is clearly identified as none other than the eternal Son of the Father, this sonship is further specified by a profound sameness with the Father: i.e., the Son is not just in any kind of sense "out of" the Father (as, e.g., an portrait or statue could be an image "out of" the subject and yet be quite other than the subject), so the Son is not "out of" any other kind of essence but the Father's – not out of creaturely essence nor, like all creatures, out of nothing.

God from God, light from light, true God from true God, begotten not made, *homoousios* with the Father,

Here predicates are shared entirely between Father and Son and again the Son's closeness is likened to a child's to a parent not an image to its very different subject. We may not know what divine essence is, but we know that the Father and the Son share the same essence or life; the Son's is not other than the Father's and is not therefore a non-divine or creaturely existence.

the one through whom all things came to be, things in heaven and

This important section identifies this divine Son of the Father as none other than the one through whom the Father's creation of the universe is carried out things in earth; who for the sake of us human beings and our salvation, descended and became flesh, became human, suffered, and rose on the third day, ascended into the heavens and is coming to judge the living and the dead;

(see 1 Cor. 8: 6 and John 1: 3), and specifies that this same Son was able, for the sake of human salvation, to live out his relation of sonship to the Father within the historical constraints of a human life, including its suffering and death, and that this same human form of the Son, Jesus, was raised from death, restored to God's glory and will have ultimate authority over the final disposition of the world's history.

Significantly implicit here is the fact that the human existence of the Son is not left behind in death but that the Son in glory and judgment continues to be none other than Jesus of Nazareth.

and in the Holy Spirit.

This brief mention of the Spirit is fully amplified in the Creed of 381 to affirm that the Spirit also is Lord, proceeds from the Father (i.e., is not a creature), is worshiped and glorified together with the Father and the Son, and is the real speaker through the words of the Hebrew prophets.

As for those who say, "there was when he was not," or "he did not exist before he was begotten," or "he came into being out of non-existence," or who fantasize that the Son of God is [made] from some other *hupostasis* or *ousia*, or that he is created or mutable or changeable, such people the catholic and apostolic Church anathematizes.

Here begins a section very precisely identifying the particular views that the Creed just above intends to rule out. As you can see, the common thread in these opposed views is that the Son is not eternally present with the Father and is not divine – at least not in the same way as the Father. These phrases had to be specified because what is being ruled out was a position viewing the Son as "begotten" not of the Father's essence eternally but of the Father's will (like the external effect of a decision), a first and perfect creature prior to the creation of time itself or of other creatures. The concern of this view was above all to safeguard the pure unchangeability of God, which could not, it was thought, undergo the "change" of coming into relation with an eternal other. As you can see, both sides were equally concerned to avoid ascribing materiality or changeableness to God.

The Council of Nicaea in 325 was a major milestone in early Christian theology, not because it settled debate about the Trinity – which continued for a century or more – but because its particular emphasis on the Son's relation to the Father opened the communal mind to this new way of imagining God: that whatever we mean by the word "God," perhaps that divine reality *includes* relation, the interplay of Father, Son, and Spirit. Williams crystallizes this emerging insight as the view that there is no gap conceivable between God as he acts towards us – as the Father of Jesus Christ – and that activity in and by which God is eternally what he is. . . . What is revealed in the incarnation of the Word is the eternal nature of God, not a moment or aspect of his life.[8]

This would mean that the missions of the Son and the Spirit as we meet them in time are the historical expressions of their eternal relations to the Father; and these relations would be seen not as somehow compromising the purity or oneness of the divine essence, but rather, in an unfathomable sense, as constituting the divine life – a life that would be seen as no less ineffable and unitary than before, but as nonetheless infinitely sharing, giving itself away in an unbounded abundance of mutual, relational joy. It would mean that there is "room" for the other in God's life, room for divine others, and, Christians believe, also for human others in Christ.

We want, then, to get inside early Christian thinking about this developing idea of an eternal differentiation of God's life, about what it means to say that God is three Persons in relation as that develops in the years after Nicaea. To do this without being subtly kidnapped by our own era's perspectives is especially tricky, because we have a variety of strongly ingrained views about personhood and relationships; most of these we really must park at the door before we can honestly venture within the theology of fourth- and fifth-century Christians. When such thinkers speak of the three divine "Persons," they certainly do not mean something like a Cartesian autonomous individual, nor do they mean an isolated psychological self whose very health is seemingly defined by self-interest and sometimes even by an "independence" that verges unpleasantly towards narcissism. But nor, alas, do such important theologians as Basil of Caesarea (*c*.330–79) or his brother Gregory of Nyssa (*c*.330–*c*.395) or their friend Gregory of Nazianzus (329–89),[9] when they speak of divine personhood, mean something like the more recent *overcoming* of the modern individualist ego in a more mutually-affirming, relationally-oriented self (i.e., a self that is still just as psychologically individual but which now understands reality in ways that affirm both other and self as inherently relational, inherently dialogical). There are contemporary theologians, such as Elizabeth Johnson, Miroslav Volf, and John Zizioulas among others, who argue very persuasively, from quite different perspectives, that the doctrine of the Trinity should be developed in ways that do affirm the relational dimensions of all life. As you'll see below when we consider such proposals, I find them wonderfully worthwhile and commendable, but we probably cannot with historical accuracy find anything quite like these views in early Christian theologies of the divine Persons.[10] So with that caveat in mind, what *are* the Three in God? How can we speak of "them" in ways that are true to God and so also are more likely, Christians think, to allow the Three to draw humanity into divine life?

Here's one intriguing clue: as we move from the Council of Nicaea to its aftermath, we find a striking conceptual shift, a new focus on the eternal relations that constitute God's life. As Michel Barnes points out, earlier theologians had spoken

Terminology Survival Guide, part 1

More than any other facet of Christian theology, reflection on the Trinity and Incarnation has a robust crop of jargon and technical terms growing within its fields.

Economic Trinity: the Divine Trinity as known in the "economy" or plan of salvation, especially in the historical work of Jesus and the Spirit in time, as contrasted with the life of the Trinity in itself, eternally (which is called the immanent Trinity).

Essence/nature/*ousia*/*physis*: all terms relating to the unitary being of something, what something is, and, in trinitarian and Christological thought, distinguishable from who someone is (called the person or hypostasis). There is one essence in God, and there are two (divine and human) in Christ.

Person/hypostasis/*prosopon*/subsistence: all terms relating in slightly different ways to the idea of distinct, concrete identity, that which actualizes and makes real an essence or nature. In trinitarian thought, "hypostasis" (which originally was almost interchangeable with *ousia* – see above – was gradually adopted as the technical term signifying what there are three of in God, three Persons in one nature. In Christology, Jesus' divine and human natures are held together and "personalized" in the hypostasis or personal identity of the eternal Son.

Immanent Trinity: the same Divine Trinity as revealed in history (economic Trinity), but considered in terms of its eternal inner trinitarian life of perfect blessedness and communion, without direct reference to the "missions" of the Son and Spirit in time (see Mission).

Mission: technical term for the work in time of the eternal Son and Spirit, a revelation within the terms of historical existence of their eternal "processions" (see Procession).

Procession: technical term for the eternal coming forth of the Son (generation or begetting) from the Father and for the distinct eternal coming forth of the Spirit (spiration or breathing) from the Father and Son.

Relation: technical term for what the eternal processions express and the missions reveal, namely the eternal patterns of interaction or relation or origination of the divine Persons from and with one another.

of the Son's eternal generation from the Father as a way of emphasizing the continuity and sameness of the Father's and Son's essence; but as more Christians came to accept this, to embrace Nicaea's claim that the Son is of the same essence (*homoousios*) with the Father, Gregory of Nyssa among others saw the Son's generation from the Father as theologically significant in an additional way: namely, as pointing to the eternal *difference* or relation between Father and Son – within the very life of God.[11] Perhaps this sounds a bit obscure to start with, but look at it this way. For a long time you've been trying to find some way, some language, by which to express the belief that the Son of God, who has become human as Jesus, is everlastingly the Son of the Father, fully divine as the Father is divine, and not some manner of subordinate deity in a pantheon or some fashion of super-creature. Now suppose you've done this, and there you are, thinking to yourself, "well, this means that *God* is like this, that this Father–Son relation is somehow eternally what it means to *be* God; but, hang on, if God is not a creature, then I can't be imagining God as somehow made up of parts or separate substances, so what in God's name am I to say about Father and Son – for if they are 'different' to each other how is God's essence still one?"

Here's the dilemma: the philosophical commonplace in the ancient Mediterranean world (a notion inherited from Aristotle), was that everything is either an essence (substance, nature) or it is an accident, a qualification of that essence (e.g., a cow is in essence just cow, but its accidents might include the contingent facts that the cow happens to be brown or sleepy or sprawling under a tree). So what are the Father and the Son? Essence or accident? If you say the Father is the essence of God then surely the Son is another essence and now we've got two gods! If you say the Father and the Son are accidents with respect to the divine essence then we've got some weird primordial divine essence that just happens, apparently, to grow fatherish or sonlike from time to time – not good! And if you say, well, the Father is the divine essence and sonship must be accidental to the divine being, then we've got the Son as a super-creature and not divine after all. Here's Gregory of Nazianzus coping with just this dilemma (in this case his opponents pose the distinction as either essence or action, which is a type of accident with respect to the essence doing the acting):

> Father, they say, is a name either of an essence or of an action, thinking to bind us down on both sides. If we say that it is a name of an essence, they will say that we agree with them that the Son is of another essence, since there is but one essence of God, and this, according to them, is pre-occupied by the Father. On the other hand, if we say that it is the name of an action, we shall be supposed to acknowledge plainly that the Son is created and not begotten.[12]

As ever, you can see here that such pro-Nicene theologians as Gregory entirely agree with their interlocutors about one thing: the divine essence is one and, by definition, not subject to the limitations of creaturely existence. So then how can both Father and Son be God? Gregory proposes what will become a crucial next step in trinitarian theology:

> I should myself have been frightened with your distinction, if it had been necessary to accept one or other of the alternatives, and not rather put both aside, and state a

third and truer one, namely, that the Father is not a name either of an essence or of an action, most clever sirs. But it is the name of the relation [the way of being] in which the Father stands to the Son, and the Son to the Father.[13]

Gregory says here that he's ruling out two possibilities: (a) that being the Father is the exclusive essence of being God, or (b) that Father or Son are names of features that are simply accidental, external as it were, to the divine essence. Instead of either of these, he argues that the whole history of salvation simply demands another category of thought – neither essence nor accident but something new – an inherent relation, a vision of existence or being which is constituted by being *with another*. Or again, Gregory is saying, when we look at God through Christ in the Spirit, we seem forced to see that God only is God in relation to the other, that the divine being is not a mere stuff but is itself the everlasting interaction of the Father, the Son, and the Spirit. It is not that there is a primordial, unitary, divine essence that can then be logically differentiated into the divine persons of Father, Son, and Holy Spirit, but rather that being Persons everlastingly to and from and for the other *is* the divine essence without remainder.

As I've said before, whenever we think such things, we have to keep prying our minds loose from any propensity to believe we've now grasped what precisely divinity is, what the divine essence is. The Cappadocians were very far from countenancing any such thought. All we are permitted to say, in their view, is that God is one, unitary, and that this divine life exists as the never-ending communion of the Father, the Son, and the Holy Spirit. We may squabble over the best terminology to employ to for the oneness (*ousia*, essence, substance, etc.) and for the relationality of that divine life (Persons in relation, hypostases, subsistences, *prosopa*, etc.), but we have to recall that we are really just constructing a grammar for talking about the ineffable: for trying to say something about what God alone can say of Godself in Christ and the Spirit. And that means that if we are not simply and tediously to repeat various formulae (one essence, three Persons), we have to allow God to draw us contemplatively into the interplay of divine life. For Gregory of Nyssa, this being overtaken by God might transpire while meditating on the implicitly trinitarian structure of Jesus' baptism or transfiguration in the gospels, or it might come while contemplating the trinitarian structures of the world around us and within us. Consider a passage from Nyssa's extremely significant work, the *Catechetical Oration*; first he reminds us that we are speaking only analogically, and moreover that our terms for the analogy are of course drawn from our own experience of the weak and perishing sorts of things that creatures are, and then he says:

Just as our nature, by being perishable, has a speech which is perishable, so the incorruptible and eternal nature [of God] has a speech which is eternal and substantial. If, accordingly, it is granted that God's spoken word subsists eternally, it is necessary to admit that the subsistence of the Word is endued with life. . . . This Word, however, is different from Him whose it is. For in a way it is a relative term, since "the Word" certainly implies the Father of the Word. For there cannot be a word without its being someone's word. . . . In our own case, we say that a spoken word comes from the mind, and is neither entirely identical with it nor altogether different. For by being derived from something else, it is different and not identical with it. Yet, since it reflects the mind, it can no longer be thought to be different from it, but is one with it in nature, though distinct as a subject. So the Word of God, by having its own subsistence, is distinct from Him from whom it derives its subsistence.[14]

Drawing obviously on the language of John's Gospel, Gregory works here to show both the unity of the Word or Son with the Father, and also the really distinct otherness. And he does this by emphasizing precisely the kind of relation at work in this analogy. Like the Father–Son relation, the analogy of speaker–word invites us to ponder the communicativeness, the expressivity, the revelation of one-in-another quality of the Word's relation to the Father.

But Gregory's analogy is not complete yet, for he goes on to remind us that we could not utter a word without breath or spirit (the Greek is *pnueuma*, which means both), by means of which our word or concept may become communicative and intelligible. And when we apply this analogy to God, we of course have to remember we are groping towards a perfection of this pattern far beyond our imagining.

When we learn that God has a Spirit, which accompanies his Word and manifests his activity, we do not think of it as an emission of breath. For we should degrade the majesty of God's power were we to conceive of his Spirit in the same way as ours. On the contrary, we think of it as a power really existing by itself and in its own special subsistence. It is not able to be separated by God in whom it exists, or from God's Word which it accompanies. It is not dissipated into non-existence; but like God's Word . . . is capable of willing, and is self-moved and active. It ever chooses the good; and to fulfill its every purpose it has the power that answers to its will.[15]

Perhaps the force of Gregory's analogy becomes the more apparent if we recollect the gospels' descriptions of the Spirit at work in Jesus' life and ministry: brooding over Mary as the Word comes to her in the annunciation, descending upon Jesus as he is declared to be God's Beloved in his baptism, and empowering Jesus' resurrection to speak the truth of the Father even beyond death itself. The Spirit is the breathing life, the powerful vivacity, that brings the Word to expression. It is also worth noting that although Gregory uses the technical term "hypostasis" from time to time, he is not much concerned to define what precisely "person" or "subsistence" is, but rather he does two things: (1) he teaches his readers how to employ a kind of logic or grammar for healthy theological reflection on God (one essence, three persons), and, just as importantly, (2) he draws the reader's mind into a trinitarian structure of reflection that might open towards a contemplative encounter with the Trinity "in person" so to speak, drawing the contemplative through the concepts and beyond them into a kind of knowing that inevitably transcends those concepts.

We may now usefully gather the observations of this and the previous section by quoting Ayres's clear summary of the key points in common among all pro-Nicene theologies in this period.

1   a clear version of the person and nature [or essence] distinction, entailing the principle that whatever is predicated of the divine nature is predicated of the three Persons equally and understood to be one;
2   clear expression that the eternal generation of the Son occurs within the unitary and incomprehensible divine being;
3   clear expression of the doctrine that the Persons work inseparably.[16]

This last point was significant because it functioned as evidence of the divine unity, i.e., if the work of the Trinity is one undivided working, then we are not talking of the Son and Spirit as though they are subordinate agents of the Father. The unitary divinity or essence of God also ensures that in speaking of the Trinity we are ruling out any chain of intermediate beings stretching between the realm of the supreme God and the lowest creature. God, in other words, is not closed-off in heaven, and does not need a string of mediators to be present within the life of the creation; the Son and the Spirit *are* the sharing, outreaching life of God, expressed within the web of human relations and transplanting into the heart of creation the perfect and holy, relational life of God.

This emphasis on the full divinity of Son and Spirit did, however, raise a new issue as Christian theology attempted to fathom its implications for the Son's incarnate life as Jesus.

How the Word can be human: the hypostatic union

Imagine yourself reflecting once more on the historical human being Jesus of Nazareth, in light of the fact that you have now concluded that he is also the eternal Word or Son of the Father. How can this be? How can the divine relation between the eternal Son and Father stretch "down" into the bitterly fragmented history of our planet and live itself out in the relation between Jesus and the one he called "Abba"? Jesus' followers felt impelled by the Spirit into this relation that Jesus opened to them, and because of this they grew to sense – as we have just seen – that this relation (between Jesus and Abba) was in fact an eternal pattern of God's own life (the Father–Son relation). But if, with the pro-Nicene theologians, you've concluded that the eternal Son or Word is fully divine in the same sense as the Father, then how, precisely, he can also be human is not an easy question. Let me recall the cycle of theological reflection on the Trinity that I sketched out earlier. We are now at that point in the cycle where the insights of (3) are leading to the questions of (4) and so back again to look more deeply into the mysteries of (1) (see diagram).

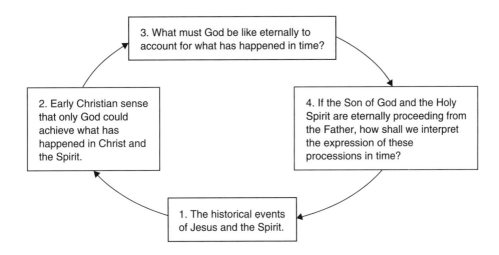

3. What must God be like eternally to account for what has happened in time?

2. Early Christian sense that only God could achieve what has happened in Christ and the Spirit.

4. If the Son of God and the Holy Spirit are eternally proceeding from the Father, how shall we interpret the expression of these processions in time?

1. The historical events of Jesus and the Spirit.

Everyone accepts that Jesus was a fully human historical figure, but how do we imagine a human being actually exists when he or she is united to the eternal Word of God, or better, when this historical human being *is* the very expression or speaking of this Word in human terms? That was the question. How would you answer? What would your priorities be? Let's imagine two fundamentally different perspectives (corresponding roughly to the theological positions of Alexandria and Antioch, the dominant schools of thought in the years before the Council of Chalcedon in 451). If you were an Alexandrian, you might be transfixed by the beauty of humanity's exaltation in Christ. Try to catch a glimpse of what this would mean: the broken, defeated nature of the human race, tenderly embraced in Christ, and caught up into an unfathomably healing unity with the eternal Word of God, blessedly alive with the very life of God, and through Christ's mystical Body, the Church, pouring out this endless resource of divinizing power within the world. For you, the hallmarks of true Christology would be a radical emphasis on divine initiative, and on the most complete and divinizing union of human existence in the Word. Perhaps you might want to say that aspects of Christ's humanity are simply subsumed and even possibly superseded by the activity of the divine Word, for in your view, nothing should be imagined as lessening or attenuating this taking-up-of-humanity-into-God which is the event of the Incarnation.

But if you were an Antiochene you might not be much attracted to these Alexandrian aspirations. In the first place, in terms of your own vision of salvation, you would ask, "What about Jesus' human nature? Does our humanity have no role to play in rescuing us at all? Does God not honor us by strengthening our humanity in Christ to respond, at last, and savingly, to God's call as we were always meant to?" For Antiochenes, the Incarnation means that an existing human being, Jesus, is accompanied so radically by the Word, that the divine goodness and justice and strength are shared with Jesus in ways that enable him to restore humanity's right relationship with God. So the Alexandrian vision of Christ seems problematic in

---

Terminology Survival Guide, part 2

Heresies or heterodox positions (usually named after their "founder" or leading exponent)

Arianism/Eunomianism/subordinationism: a range of differing schools of thought, holding considerable influence within the Church both before and after Nicaea/Constantinople, insisting that God (the Father) is alone God and that the Son is utterly subordinate, "God" by title or honor only, but is in fact the first of the creatures, and so able to enter into human life without jeopardizing the divine unity or immutability.

Docetism: from the Greek, *dokeo*, to seem or appear to be, the view that Jesus only seems to be human but is really only divine, God appearing for a certain time, disguised as a human being.

Modalism/monarchianism/Sabellianism: a range of differing schools, holding considerable influence, insisting that to speak of the Son or the Spirit as truly divine as the Father is divine would be to undermine the divine unity and simplicity; rather, this view holds that the Father is alone God (monarchianism) but at different times permits certain of his attributes to appear in history as Son or Spirit; a variation (modalism) is that Father, Son, and Spirit are simply names humans ascribe to different temporarily expressed modes of the unitary divine life within history, but that they have no eternally existing distinctness or subsistence as Persons in relation within the divine life.

Monophysitism/Apollinarianism/Eutychianism: a range of views, often associated with extreme positions within the Alexandrian school of Christology, holding that the eternal Word or Son simply takes the place of the soul or mind of Christ, such that there is finally only one nature (mono-*physis*) in the Incarnate Word, the divine.

Nestorianism: a range of views, often associated with extreme positions within Antiochene approaches to Christology, holding that the divine Word remains entirely distinct from the historical man Jesus; the Word may fully grace the man's work and share certain divine qualities with him but is entirely unaffected by the man's experiences; an extreme emphasis on the two natures tending towards a less definite incarnate union of God and humanity.

---

terms of the human side of Jesus, but this only betrays another feature that would horrify you about the Alexandrian view: its apparent fixation on God's presence in history and suffering would seem to involve God in change, mingling the pure divine nature with time and creatureliness in an appalling manner.

As you can see from this little exercise, both sides were honestly trying to hold together the two crucial aspects of any Christology: (1) how you conceive the work of salvation as taking place, (2) how you conceive the divine and the human as related in Christ. Trying to work out the implications of these two aspects, their mutual bearing upon each other, would be enormously difficult. Suppose you thought, for example, that divine existence and creaturely existence were mutually exclusive, then how exactly would you imagine God being "present" in Christ? And how, then, would salvation be accomplished through Christ?

Here are brief excerpts from Cyril of Alexandria (d. 444) and Nestorius of Antioch (d. *c.*451).[17] As you read, try to put your finger on the crucial underlying concerns for each writer (to assist you a bit, I've boldfaced the passages in each that directly mirror each other).

The First Letter of Nestorius to Celestine	The Third Letter of Cyril to Nestorius
We also have found no slight corruption of orthodoxy among some of those here [at Constantinople in 428; Nestorius presumably finds it helpful to alert the bishop of Rome, Celestine, that the others he may also hear from are not to be trusted!]. . . . It is no small error . . . **blending together** the Lord's appearance as man into a kind of **confused combination**. . . . They refer the Godhead of the Only-begotten to the same origin [Mary] as the flesh joined [with it], and **kill it with the flesh, and blasphemously say that the flesh joined to the Godhead was turned into deity by the deifying Word, which is nothing more than to corrupt both** [the divine nature of the Word and the human nature of Jesus – by "mingling" them together].	We say that the unique Word of God himself, who was begotten of the very substance of the Father. . . . coming down for the sake of our salvation, and humbling himself even to emptying, was made flesh and became man. That is, taking flesh of the holy Virgin, and making it his own from the womb, **he underwent a birth like ours . . . not throwing off what he was,** but even though he became [human] by the assumption of flesh and blood, yet still remaining what he was, that is, God indeed in nature and truth. **We do not say that the flesh was changed into the nature of the Godhead, nor that the ineffable nature of the Word of God was transformed into the nature of flesh** . . . But when seen as a babe and wrapped in swaddling clothes, even when still in the bosom of the Virgin who bore him, he filled all creation as God, and was enthroned with him who begot him.

Comparing these two passages, we can readily see how concerned Nestorius was to preserve the clear distinction between divine and human in Christ, particularly so as not to "corrupt" the nature of either; and we can also see how concerned

Cyril was to affirm that *God* really did come to dwell among us, even held in Mary's lap. For Cyril everything hinges on this, that it is no corrupting danger to divine or human nature for them to be united at all! Quite the contrary, it means that God is fully capable of expressing the divine life within the constraints of human existence and, crucially for human redemption, that human life can be drawn back into its own true, pure, and God-embraced reality as it is united to God in Christ.[18]

The question remains, however, whether there is some coherent way for Christians to understand this saving union of God and humanity in Christ. It is a deeply beneficent theological principle, perhaps learned through studying the journey to Chalcedon, that theology advances farthest when it is able to hold together what is worthiest and truest in everyone's views. And in some ways, that is what the Chalcedonian Definition really represents: an attempt to hold together what is best in both Antiochene and Alexandrian views. For the former clearly and rightly emphasizes the full and true humanity of Jesus and his human contribution to salvation, and the latter clearly and rightly emphasizes the reality of the divine initiative and presence in Christ, lifting human life into sanctifying union with God. The theologians at Chalcedon were perhaps assisted in their efforts by the voice of Pope Leo (d. 461), whose letter or "Tome" called both sides back from their more metaphysically-hardened positions into the vital rhythms of the gospel narrative. Leo insisted, with Antioch, upon the abiding distinction of the divine and human natures in Christ, and also, with Alexandria, upon the absolute unity of Christ's person, but he preferred to describe the two natures in one person simply in terms of the journey of the divine Son into human life and death for human salvation; that is, who Christ is can only really be known in the story that narrates his action among the peoples of the earth.

Here then is the Chalcedonian Definition with my running commentary. As further assistance, I follow the good example of the revered Orthodox theologian, John Meyendorff, in using different typefaces (boldface and small capitals) for passages more inclined toward the Alexandrian and the Antiochenene positions – thus illustrating the effort to hold them together in the Definition. As you read, try to decide which passages are the more Alexandrian and which the more Antiochene (answers below!).

The Chalcedonian Definition

Following the holy Fathers [of the Councils of Nicaea and Constantinople], we all with one voice confess our Lord Jesus Christ **one and the same Son, the same** perfect in Godhead

The definition begins by assuring us that what is to be declared at Chalcedon is intended to be fully consonant with Nicaea (325) and Constantinople (381) and is merely an attempt to draw out the implications of those councils.

Chalcedon emphasizes throughout a single and very particular person, Jesus Christ, who *is* [divine nature], **the same** consisting in a reasonable soul and a body, of one substance with the Father as touching the Godhead, **the same** OF ONE SUBSTANCE WITH US AS TOUCHING HUMANITY, LIKE US IN ALL THINGS APART FROM SIN; begotten of the Father before the ages as touching the Godhead,

none other than the one eternal Son of God. This was one of the pre-eminent concerns of Alexandria and so the boldface type represents text affirming their view that *who* we are meeting in Christ is none other than the eternal Son.

But this same One is also in no way other than *both* fully and unalteredly divine and fully and unalteredly human – a chief concern of Antioch (as indicated by the small capital type face). Thus, however much Jesus' humanity is taken up into perfect union with God, this must not be thought of as in any way rendering Jesus somehow beyond humanity or lacking any features of human nature (e.g., the Word does not simply replace the human mind or soul in Jesus as some extreme Alexandrian thinkers had seemed to imply).

the same in the last days, for us and for our salvation, born from the Virgin Mary, **the Theotokos** [the God-bearer], as touching humanity, **one and the same** Christ, Son, Lord Only-begotten, to be acknowledged

Calling Jesus' mother Mary the "God-bearer" was a specially cherished feature of Cyril's theology, emphasizing her great honor, but also, and much to the consternation of Nestorius, that in a sense God the Son is born in time from the Virgin Mary as the human being Jesus, just as God the Son is also born eternally from the Father – it is the same Son in both cases.

IN TWO NATURES WITHOUT CONFUSION, WITHOUT CHANGE,

Absolutely central to the Antiochene view: the two natures are both at work in Christ and their union in no way results in any mingling or altering of either, something that it would be blasphemous to imagine of the divine nature in any case.

without division, without separation;

At the same time, Chalcedon very evenhandedly equally insists on the Alexandrian concern that the two natures of Christ not be so distinguished as to be divided or merely operating separately as though Christ were merely somehow accompanied by the Word rather as the prophets of Israel were inspired by the Spirit. Such a view would, Cyril argued successfully, completely undermine the sense in which God genuinely and compassionately enters the human condition in order to redeem it, and would also vitiate the sense in which human existence is truly taken up and divinized in union with God.

THE DISTINCTION OF NATURES BEING IN NO WAY ABOLISHED BECAUSE OF THE UNION, BUT RATHER THE CHARACTERISTIC PROPERTY OF EACH NATURE BEING PRESERVED, and

Some Alexandrian thinkers had suggested that while there was of course a distinct human nature prior to the union of the Incarnation there was merely one, united being after the union; this view was deeply problematic for Antioch, suggesting as it did that the human nature of Christ was lost or mingled as a result of the union. This is clearly ruled out here.

concurring in one person, or hypostasis, not as if Christ were parted or divided into two persons, but one and the same Son and Only-begotten God, Word, Lord, Jesus Christ.

But, and this is a big "but," Chalcedon asserts here that a central feature of Cyril's view should be accepted, namely that the union of God and humanity in Christ is by no means best conceived in the category of natures or essences or substances (as Antioch kept worrying about), but rather in the category developed with such effort in discussion of the Trinity: the category of person or hypostasis. In other words, however one may understand the fact that Jesus is both fully divine and fully human, one must – to speak adequately – realize that these two natures are held together precisely as they are hypostasized or "personalized" by the eternal person of the Son or Word who exists humanly as Jesus.

If you have read through the Definition and considered my effort to elucidate it, I now have a little theological exercise for you. Think back to the discussion of persons in relation in the previous section above and tell me why and how the principles worked out in that discussion come into play in this Christological discussion in Chalcedon. How does the distinction between essence (or nature), on the one hand, and person (or hypostasis) become helpful here? In a sense, we probably have the strongest vindication in this example of why the effort to work out a common theological language or grammar for coherent speech about God is so important. There are some things you just cannot "get at" without the right sort of concept. And here, as ever, we remind ourselves that the concepts in question do not pretend to exhaust the ultimate meaning of divine "essence" or "person." How could they since we have, in fact, almost no idea what we're talking about when we use these terms with respect to God! The point, however, is that there is something (call it essence) that, in the Trinity, can be distinguished from the pattern of relations by which that essence is itself, a pattern of relations with particular centers or foci (call them Persons). So how does this help in understanding what Chalcedon means?

First, it helps simply because it did indeed teach Christian theologians to distinguish between the categories of essence and person, and thus to conceive of divine being or essence as not simply closed-off or complete in itself but as only really constituted by the personal being, the free, choosing Persons who together are that essence. There is not some prior "divine essence" which determines what the Persons of the Trinity may or may not do, for the essence is nothing other than the perfect communion of the Persons. By analogy, you might think of how your own personal identity is not simply determined by your human biology or natural impulses – to be a person is precisely to concretize and realize one's nature with a certain intelligence, freedom, and relation to others. This distinction between essence and person, then, makes it possible to see essence and person as, so to speak, interacting in distinct planes: they do not come together like a triangle and circle such that they must interfere or interrupt each other as elements of the same sort; rather, the person is the quality of distinctness and freedom that, at least in the case of intelligent beings, brings essence to life. Your essence is *what* you are, but this is entirely distinguishable from your personal identity, *who* you turn out to be.

The result of this train of thought is that one can conceive of Jesus' human and divine essences as given their personal actualization, by the *person* who is the eternal Son or Word. Put another way, we could say that the personal identity that distinguishes Jesus from Peter or Paul is the same personhood that distinguishes him from the Father or the Spirit; it is the expression in time of an eternal pattern of relationship, i.e., the very same pattern of relation we might call sonship, the Son's relation to the Father. What Jesus is, is both human and divine; who Jesus is, is the Word. This understanding of the Incarnation, in which the two natures of Christ are brought to expression in the one Person (hypostasis) of the Word or Son, is called the hypostatic union – that is, the union of the two natures in the hypostasis of the Word. This does not mean, Christians believe, that there was a man Jesus who was then somehow taken up by the eternal Son; rather, the theology of the hypostatic union means for Christians that the fully human historical being, Jesus of Nazareth, is the very expression in human terms of the divine Son, the translation into human language of the divine Word. When Jesus humanly hungers or thirsts or weeps or dies, it is God the Son who undergoes these human experiences and bears them into the heart of the divine life. As Meyendorff observes, "The hypostatic union implies also that the Logos made humanity *His own* in its totality; thus the Second Person of the Trinity was indeed the subject, or agent, of the *human* experiences, or acts, of Jesus."[19]

But does that mean, once again, that we are back with a Jesus who is not really human? Not at all. Recall that hypostatic union means Jesus' humanity is actualized according to a certain pattern of relationship we call sonship. But this identity of "being the son" can be carried out both in heaven and on earth, within the beatitude of the trinitarian life or within the fractured existence we have made of human life. By analogy, you might think of some deeply wise and loving person who readily exercises these very personal qualities in different contexts: with her friends, her wisdom and delight take many happy and celebratory forms, but in her professional work with war refugees around the world she finds other ways, profoundly giving and perhaps costly ways, of being the person she is; and yet no one who knows her well would doubt that it is the same one, the same person in both environments. In the case of Jesus, his relation to the One he calls Abba defines and gives meaning to his existence, to be the beloved child of this One is who Jesus is; and this same pattern of relation is the identifying pattern of life, the Person, whom Christians believe is the eternal Son of God.

Few thinkers have expressed this interaction of trinitarian and Christological thought so well as the twentieth-century Anglican theologian and philosopher, Austin Farrer. As you read, cast your mind over the long development of Christian thinking about God we have been surveying, and see if, at least as Farrer puts it, you can see what might be the point of it all.

> We cannot understand Jesus as simply the God-who-was-man. We have left out an essential factor, the sonship. Jesus is not simply God manifest as man; he is the divine Son coming into manhood. What was expressed in human terms here below was not bare deity; it was the divine sonship. God cannot live an identically godlike life in eternity and in a human story. But the divine Son can make an identical response to his Father, whether in the love of the blessed Trinity or in the fulfillment of an earthly ministry. All the conditions of action are different on the two levels; the filial response is one. Above, the appropriate response is a co-operation in sovereignty and an interchange of eternal joys. Then the Son gives back to the Father all that the Father is. Below, in the incarnate life, the appropriate response is an obedience to inspiration, a waiting for direction, an acceptance of suffering, a rectitude of choice, a resistance to temptation, a willingness to die. For such things are the stuff of our existence; and it was in this very stuff that Christ worked out the theme of heavenly sonship, proving himself on earth the very thing he was in heaven . . . a continuous perfect act of filial love.[20]

LANDMARKS

Now you have a good, basic sense of what's at stake in Christian talk of God as Trinity and how it emerged through reflection upon what was happening to the community in Jesus and the Spirit. The next step is to consider two master practitioners of trinitarian reflection, trying not so much to learn everything they had to say about Trinity or Christ or the Spirit, but rather to learn from them about how to engage theologically with these mysteries ourselves.

Augustine on the Mysterious Attraction of the Trinity

Few, if any, merely human authors have had as much influence on the shape of Christian thought as Augustine of Hippo (354–430), especially with respect to trinitarian theology. It was perhaps inevitable, therefore, that when twentieth-century theologians began to announce that something had gone seriously wrong with trinitarian theology, they identified Augustine as the chief culprit.[21] Generally there have been two overriding criticisms of Augustine. The first is that he so privileged discussion of the divine substance and oneness in western theology that the three divine Persons and their relations came almost to be seen as secondary, as emerging from some prior divine reality. The second is that by thinking about the Trinity, in part using analogies drawn from the inner activity of human psychology, he directed the attention of western theology almost exclusively upon the inner (immanent) life of the Trinity; in doing so he severed the connection in trinitarian theology between the immanent Trinity and the economic Trinity (the Trinity as revealed in the economy or historical dispensation of salvation through Christ and the Spirit). Thus, in a very famous call for theological reorientation, the eminent Jesuit theologian Karl Rahner (1904–84) asserted: "The 'economic' Trinity is the 'immanent' Trinity and the 'immanent' Trinity is the 'economic' Trinity."[22]

It is an interesting question whether Augustine might not, in fact, have agreed with "Rahner's axiom" (as it has come to be called), given suitable clarifications of course. What I think is much less debatable is that the consensus castigation of Augustine is in fact erroneous. Whether I can convince you of this in the discussion below remains to be seen, but let me at the outset briefly say why I think neither of the chief criticisms of the Bishop of Hippo holds water.[23] With respect to the first charge, that Augustine's emphasis on the oneness of the divine substance seems to subordinate the divine Persons, the fact is that Augustine was writing in the midst of a defining historical struggle (often overlooked by the critics). In the western regions of the Christian Church of Augustine's day, there was very persistent and politically powerful opposition to the teaching of Nicaea that the Father and the Son are of the same essence and equally divine. It was not inconceivable that this version of Christianity (sometimes referred to as Arianism though actually even more radically subordinationist), with a supreme, absolute God the Father, mediated to creation through two primordial but entirely subordinate creatures (the Son and Spirit), would in fact prevail, possibly isolating western Christianity from the rest of the Mediterranean world in terms of its most central belief. So what we will find Augustine emphasizing again and again is not, contra his critics, a bare divine essence that somehow precedes the divine Persons, but rather that the Persons always act in unity in history – a view that Augustine saw as supporting the pro-Nicene teaching that the Three share the same essence and are co-equal.

With respect to the second critique, that Augustine's "psychological analogy" for the Trinity in our human experience (of memory, understanding, and will, for example) severs the immanent from the economic Trinity (and generally conduces to a merely "theoretical" approach to the Trinity divorced from everyday Christian concerns), here surely Augustine would be mightily puzzled indeed. The entire first half of his great work *The Trinity* is given over to a painstaking analysis of the Trinity as revealed in the economy of salvation, so when the bishop does get round to proposing "analogies" in the second half they are surely better read as journeys of faith in search of understanding, as attempts to inhabit the historical events of salvation spiritually, not as stand-alone efforts to "prove" or "ground" trinitarian faith in an analysis of human memory, understanding, and will. Indeed, as Augustine explores the Trinity's images in human existence, what he emphasizes above all is the historical encounter of the human image of God (now broken and distorted by sin) with its archetype, Jesus; thus Augustine highlights precisely the "economic" restoration of the *imago dei* through the process of salvation. And finally, I would argue, the analogies are not really analogies at all! They are, ultimately, spiritual exercises in which everyday ordinary Christian experience is pried open towards prayer and then confronted with the heartbreaking intimacy of God's loving self-communication; they are not ways of "defining" the Trinity – just the opposite – but of allowing the Trinity to overtake and commune with those whom the Trinity mysteriously attracts quite beyond themselves, into a relationality beyond all limits.

With this important clearing away, at least provisionally, of certain vexing misconceptions, I hope we will be more able to see what Augustine has to teach us about how to reflect on the Trinity. Because he was a teacher of rhetoric and a great lover of textual beauty, it wouldn't do to overlook the delightful structure which he has hidden (just as with the *Confessions*) in plain view: for *The Trinity* is constructed, as Edmund Hill has demonstrated, in a remarkable pattern of descent and ascent.[24]

Before considering some crucial passages, a few observations about Augustine's structure might be helpful (see figure). First, notice that the "descending" books (1–7) and the "ascending" books (9–15) mirror each other in important ways:

Book 1: Equality of the divine Persons shown from scripture

Book 15: Unlikeness of image to divine Persons, but Trinity draws image into God

Book 8: Spiritual exercise: longing to gaze on God

Books 2—4: Missions of Persons in economy of salvation

Books 12—14: How the image falls in Adam and is raised in Christ

Books 5—7: Arguments with opponents over proper "grammar" for speech about the divine relations

Books 9—11: Finding the image of God in human experience

The structure of *The Trinity*

- Books 1 and 15 anchor the entire work, upwards, in the Church's faith and contemplative goal, with Book 1 explicating the basic teaching of Christianity as Augustine has received it and desires to understand it, and Book 15 leading the reader to sense that this journey of faith towards understanding can only be fulfilled if it is overtaken by the gracious presence of the Trinity.
- Books 2–4 and 12–14 work very closely with scripture to discern the Trinity in the history of salvation (2–4) and in the transformation of the Trinity's image in humanity (12–14).
- Then Books 5–7 and 9–11 seek to elucidate this faith in terms of a rational discussion of the logic of trinitarian belief (5–7) and a rational imagining of trinitarian structures in human experience (9–11).
- The turning point or central pivot of the whole work is Book 8, in which Augustine models the theological yearning of trinitarian faith for deeper understanding and direct encounter with God; because of what "happens" in this book, the author is able to take us on the journey of the second half, in which the concerns of faith, received and elucidated, are now set in motion toward the divine object of that faith.

Now let me try to show you what I mean by all this, and why Augustine is such a good teacher, not just of trinitarian theology but a teacher of how to think "trinitarianly." I will do this by considering an important passage or two from each of the several books or groupings of books I've just outlined.

(A) Book 1. Augustine begins by giving us an important principle of his theological interpretation: human reasoners, in our fallen state, are congenitally inclined "to be deceived through an unseasonable and misguided love of reason," and this usually takes one of three forms:

> Some of them try to transfer what they have observed about bodily things to incorporeal and spiritual things, which they would measure by the standard of what they experience through the senses of the body or learn by natural human intelligence, lively application, and technical skill. There are others whose concept of God, such as it is, ascribes to him the nature and moods of the human spirit, a mistake which ties their arguments about God to distorted and misleading rules of interpretation. Again, there is another type: people who indeed strive to climb above the created universe, so ineluctably subject to change, and raise their regard to the unchanging substance which is God. But so top-heavy are they with the load of their mortality, that what they do not know they wish to give the impression of knowing, and what they wish to know they cannot; and so they block their own road to genuine understanding. (I. 1)

In his *Confessions* Augustine had described his own intellectual journey as, at various times, embodying all three of these mistaken approaches to God, so he is well aware of their allure. The first two provide "good" examples of what happens when the creator/creature distinction is not allowed full play as a principle of theological grammar. We saw the Cappadocians employing this principle in their pro-Nicene theology and here Augustine announces its prominence in his very first paragraph. To recall, the idea is this: we don't know what God is, but we know that whatever it means to be God, it means being the source and cause of all the creatures; therefore God is not one of the creatures; therefore when we talk about God we cannot speak as though God were, like the creatures, made up of many parts or passions or subject to time or decay. By raising this point right at the beginning of his reflections on the Trinity, Augustine is setting out a theological tool of great value, for it will help him show that the Son and the Spirit are not subordinate deities, or somehow lesser grades of divine substance as though this could be composed of different parts or divided up.

The third type of theological mistake in Augustine's catalogue is the most refined and therefore most dangerous, for it springs from what in Augustine's view is the primal human debility: the fallen tendency towards a nervous assertion of our own correctness and superiority. When this attitude dominates theology, no matter how clever or intellectually cultured and sophisticated it may be, it is inherently incapable of deeper theological understanding, precisely because this can only be received as an unfolding gift from God that leads human understanding beyond itself by healing and transforming it. "When some people" are brought face to face with their own dependence on God as the real teacher and expositor of theology, says Augustine, "they get angry and think they are being insulted" (I. 3). Once more, we can see Augustine carefully sensitizing us to our own theological mindset or attitude: are we open and expecting the "object" of our study to become the active Subject who in fact teaches us (see Part I of this book), or does this in some way, perhaps without being consciously acknowledged, threaten our sense of self-worth or pride or professional identity?

In a very important section, Augustine draws all these observations together, showing the mutual implication of our status as creatures and our status as learners who, if we would learn about God, can only be taught by God.

> So then it is difficult to contemplate and have full knowledge of God's substance [what God is], which without any change in itself makes things that change, and without any passage of time in itself creates things that exist in time. That is why it is necessary for our minds to be purified before that inexpressible reality can be inexpressibly seen by them; and in order to make us fit and capable of grasping it, we are led along more endurable routes, nurtured on faith as long as we have not yet been endowed with the necessary purification. (I. 3)

In this little passage, Augustine deftly does three things at once: first, he reminds us of the theological grammar needed to talk about God (i.e., the creator/creature distinction); second, he reminds us that theology is inherently also spirituality, for apart from genuine spiritual training and discipline humanity cannot really be available for the vision of God; and third, he gives a thumbnail sketch of his entire book on the Trinity: beginning with the faith of the Christian community, elucidating that faith, and by spiritual exercise making the mind's journey available to the divine teacher and revealer.

The final point I wish to make about Book I is simply to underscore Augustine's starting point and reference point in the faith he has inherited, which, he says, "is also my faith inasmuch as it is the Catholic faith" (I. 7). First he will show that this faith in the Father, the Son, and the Holy Spirit as one God in three co-equal Persons is indeed what the scriptures teach. And then he will endeavor to show those who are perplexed by this faith that it can, in a limited fashion, be shown to be intelligible and not simply a nonsense. Now here's a good test for you: why does Augustine insist on beginning with faith? Why not begin, as we might today, with people's immediate perplexities, with their own ways of looking at things, and then try to show how faith in the Trinity makes sense in terms they can immediately grasp? After all, we might think that it is more usual to travel as far as we can with people on the common ground of reason and then, only when we have come to the ultimate mysteries that transcend reason, turn to faith.

But there are at least three reasons why Augustine does not think this will work. First, as we saw above, the mindset of the human race apart from faith is congenitally disposed to shrink reality to its grasp; so faith, in Augustine's view, is a necessary healing and transforming of human perception and must be present from the beginning. Second, as Augustine will demonstrate repeatedly, the truths of faith, such as the Trinity, can be shown to be amenable to some degree of human understanding (i.e., as I said, they are not nonsensical), but that is very different from thinking that we could ever get to the truths of faith from some supposed common ground marked out by reason alone. We can explore into these beliefs using our minds-in-healing, but they ultimately are truths that have, as it were, "happened to us" in Christ and the Spirit and simply will not be graspable as brilliant achievements of rational invention. And finally, as a foreshadowing to the beautiful and heart-stopping vision of Book 15, we have to work from the beginning with faith, thinks Augustine, because it is the present mode of our apprenticeship to the one teacher who can ever reward our efforts. Faith in this sense is patient trusting in Christ and in what Christ is conducting the believer towards; it is a refusal to stop prematurely at the vision of truth currently within our grasp (not the ultimate truth), precisely because of a loving trust in the one who is preparing believers for the one vision that can ever satisfy them, the vision of the Trinity in true glory. As a figure for this contemplative dynamism inherent in faith, Augustine offers the image of Mary Magdalene, longing to touch the risen Christ and yet urged by him to await his ascension, to live now by faith:

Touching concludes as it were the process of getting acquainted. [Christ] did not want this heart [Mary], so eagerly reaching out to him, to stop at thinking that he was only what could be seen and touched. His ascension to the Father signified his being seen in his equality with the Father, that being the ultimate vision which suffices us. (I. 18)

(B) Books 2–4. After his introductory Book 1, in these books of *The Trinity* Augustine commences his real work by considering the Trinity as revealed in the economy of salvation, witnessed to by scripture. The fact that the Son and the Spirit are spoken of in scripture as having been "sent" into the world has received a divergent interpretation in the long history of the Church's reflections. For those who see the Son and Spirit as merely "like" God or as agents of God (but not divine as the Father is divine), the sending of Son and Spirit in the economy of salvation not only points to their distinction from the Father who sends them, but also proves their subordinate status, or their non-divine status. Like the Cappadocians, then, Augustine seeks to highlight the distinct but united action of the Trinity in history, yet he intends to do so in a way that does not entail subordination but co-equality.

Augustine's solution manifests an important theological principle: when in confusion, re-focus the discussion within the terms of salvation. What Augustine does is to ask, very precisely, "What does it mean that the Son and the Spirit have been sent?" You can only say, he points out to his theological opponents, that the Son or the Spirit are subordinate if you think their sending or mission in the world entails this subordination. For instance, if you thought the Son's saving mission was simply to make a visible sign of the invisible Father, then you might think that this mission was in fact predicated on the Son being subordinate, visible, a graspable pointer to the ungraspable God. But, asks Augustine, is that really what the Son was sent to accomplish? This line of discussion drives to a climax in Book 4, focusing on salvation and on the faith it brings about.

At the risk of considerable oversimplification, we could sketch Augustine's argument this way. The only ultimate fulfillment of human life is the contemplation of God and so it's no surprise that all manner of pagan religions and philosophies have urged humanity in that direction. The fall of humanity into alienation from God has, however, left us with this same divine desire but a diseased and self-inflated manner of reaching it: we think we can do so by our own power and within the constraints of our own rational understanding. As we saw in Book 1, these are seriously misleading assumptions that actually, Augustine thinks, bind humanity within its sinful condition, gratefully stoking the furnace of pride:

> There are some people who think that they can purify themselves for contemplating God and cleaving to him by their own power and strength of character, which means in fact that they are thoroughly defiled by pride. No vice is more vehemently opposed by divine law, no vice gives a greater right of control to that proudest of all spirits, the devil, who mediates our way to the depths and bars our way to the heights. (IV. 20)

Thus humanity's fallen tendency to magnify itself subjects it all the more to the lethal confidence games of the devil, "that proudest of all spirits," who uses humanity's desire to ascend to "mediate" a deadly descent. In such circumstances, says Augustine, the true mediator, Christ, provides the only possible antidote, the authentic humility of absolute love stooping down to reach the depths of the human condition. The proud despise Christ's suffering humanity, his death, and the bodily resurrection, but for Augustine these are the very marks of a true savior's love, tokens of his greatness and humility in descending to accept the very lot of humanity even as humankind scrabbles egotistically to ascend on the wings of pride. Three crucial points emerge from this brief summary of Augustine's excursus into soteriology.

First, the mediator can only provide this healing and purifying of the human condition if he is genuinely and co-equally God with God the Father, for the whole value in his redeeming work lies precisely in the fact that it is fully *divine* life that humbles itself to rescue humanity. An intermediate figure, or a kind of super-creature who merely represents divinity could not perform the same act of self-giving humility. So the Son is shown, by virtue of achieving the work of salvation, to be co-equal with the Father.

Second, this objective, historical act of self-humbling by the Son engenders and nourishes a subjective, personal act of faith in believers. Because our natural drive to ascend to the contemplation of divine life is corrupted by pride, we need something to feed our minds upon that which is earthly, finite, and material but which will not manipulate our desire for God (as the devil does) intoxicating it into idolatry. The incarnation of the Son is precisely this wholesome, iconic, object: "eternal life, truth itself, co-eternal with the Father" entered into our material, temporal condition "when the Son of God came in order to become Son of man and to capture our faith and draw it to himself, and by means of it to lead us on to his truth" (IV. 24). Just as the humility of the eternal Son in becoming human is the antidote to human pride abetted by the devil, so the presence of eternal Truth in our transitory existence (in the Incarnation) is the medicine for our mind's journey: it gives our faith something healthy to believe that inherently leads it onwards to the contemplation of divine life.

Finally, then, we see the crucial implication of all this for Augustine's theology of the Trinity: "there you have what the Son of God has been sent for" (IV. 25). Recall that Augustine's aim has been to re-conceive this "sending" of the Son (and Spirit) by the Father within the economy of salvation in such a way that these historical missions do not necessarily imply subordination of the Son and Spirit to the Father. And both the objective work of Christ and the subjective unfolding of that work (in bringing about human faith) point, as we have seen, to the full co-equal divinity of the Son (and by implication, of the Spirit) with the Father. Indeed apart from this the work of salvation would not be achieved. So what, finally, does this "sending" in time tell us about God? It tells us, not that there are levels of hierarchy or subordination in God, but that there is an eternal relationship. The Son is sent by the Father, says Augustine, "not because one is greater and the other less, but because one is Father and the other Son" (IV. 27). In other words, the sending of the eternal Son into the world of time and history and suffering and death makes visible to us an eternal coming forth of the Son from the Father, an eternal relation of life from life, of infinite life existing precisely by being for another:

> We can now perceive that the Son is not just said to have been sent because the Word became flesh, but that he was sent in order for the Word to become flesh. . . . We should understand that it was not just the man who the Word became that was sent, but that the Word was sent to become man. For he was not sent in virtue of some disparity of power or substance or anything in him that was not equal to the Father, but in virtue of the Son being from the Father, not the Father being from the Son. (IV. 27)

Here we can see Augustine argue against any notion of salvation as simply the work of a subordinate deity or a super-creature who somehow mediates to humanity God's best wishes. Rather, for Augustine, the Word was sent just in order to become human. Not because the Word is somehow lesser than the Father, but because the Word proceeds from and expresses the Father, because the Father sends the Word to embody within the very brokenness of this world nothing less or other than the outgoing love of the Father, and thus to embrace the world within this relation of outgoing love, within the relation, that is, of the Father to the Son. When this relation weaves itself into our world, says Augustine, what you get is the historical human being Jesus crying out from within our existence for the One who sent him. The missions of the Son and the Spirit open the relations of the Trinity to humanity, holding before the eyes of faith a historical icon or sacrament of those relations that can draw faith through healing to contemplation.

> Eternal life is promised us by the truth, from whose transparent clarity our faith is as far removed as mortality is from eternity. So now we accord faith to the things done in time for our sakes [the life, death, and resurrection of Christ], and are purified by it; in order that when we come to sight and truth succeeds to faith, eternity might likewise succeed to mortality. Our faith will then become truth, when we come to what we are promised as believers. (IV. 24)

Thus we see how very far indeed is Augustine from abstracting the Trinity from either the historical economy of salvation or from the everyday life of believers who struggle in hope toward the promises of God.

(C) Books 5–7. In the previous section, as we have seen, Augustine was arguing against those who find the scriptures indicating a subordinationist notion of the Trinity. Now, however, he has to argue in the other direction, so to speak, showing that his reading of the scriptural witness to the Trinity is not unintelligible rationally. In particular he has to argue against those whose concept of divine simplicity and unity is perhaps grounded more in Hellenistic metaphysics than in a basic understanding of the creator/creature distinction. They might say to Augustine: look, you insist on the oneness of Father, Son, and Spirit, and on not thinking of the Three in material terms as different bits of some divine stuff. So far so good; but then you will keep on saying various things about God such as begotten and unbegotten, proceeding and ingenerate, and so on, and these various terms are

all either reducible to the one undivided divine substance (in which case they really mean nothing); or you are really meaning to talk by means of each term about different divine substances, in which case you've finally arrived (as we always said you would) at polytheism! Now as we saw in the case of the Cappadocians, one provisional sort of response to this metaphysical or linguistic wedge is to say that these terms (e.g., begotten and unbegotten) simply do not refer to the divine substance but to the mutual relations. And this is exactly what Augustine works out in careful detail: a whole grammar for speaking about God in which we can say things either about God's essence or about the mutual relations that constitute that essence.

Lewis Ayres emphasizes helpfully that we can best understand Augustine, in these books, if we realize he is fundamentally working to overcome our dominating human experience of material substances. Our underlying, material frame of reference tends to make us think of the divine persons as somehow emerging from a prior divine "stuff" of which they themselves are necessarily "made up" and which is distinguishable from them. In Ayres's summary: "Augustine's insistence that God is not material and that the essence is not prior to the persons should already have enabled us to see that Augustine's God is not one thing or substance with secondary internal divisions."[25] The implication of all this is that the mutual relations of Father, Son, and Spirit simply *are* what it means to be God; in other words, the divine essence is nothing other than the event of an eternal interplay of differentiated life, the communion of the divine Persons.

To my mind, one of the most instructive if unusual passages in these three books on the right way to speak about God is a little passage in which Augustine simply seems to be delighting in the beauty of the trinitarian life, radiating within the very structures of creation. In Book 5, Augustine had clarified that while "Son" is a name that clearly implies relation, "Spirit" does not necessarily do so; how then shall we speak of the Holy Spirit in a way that clearly points to the mutual relations of the Spirit with the Father and the Son? Augustine proposes naming the Spirit as Gift, everlasting bestowal of joy in and to the other in God, from before time – even though we of course are taught to recognize the Spirit as Gift because of our receiving the Spirit as Gift in the economy of salvation. Then in the Book 6, Augustine seems to allow himself to muse somewhat playfully with these relational namings in a way that shows us something often overlooked in Augustine. He is regularly criticized for insisting on the undivided working of the Trinity in creation so categorically as to undermine the distinctions or relations of the divine Persons – or at least to deny their inner-relationality as having any significance for creation. It is true, of course, that Augustine emphasizes the undivided working of the Trinity, but he does not deny their different roles within history; for example, the Son alone becomes incarnate as Christ, although of course the act of the Incarnation is accomplished by the whole and undivided Trinity. Yet there are interesting passages in which Augustine not only emphasizes the mutual relations by which the Father, Son, and Spirit are distinguished with respect to each other, but also the beautiful ways in which that pattern of mutual relationality might become, as it were, translated luminously into the structures of creaturely existence. Here is one of these moments. Augustine is commenting on a brief text of Hilary of Poitiers (*c*.315–67) in which Hilary speaks of "eternity in the Father, form in the image, use in the gift" (VI. 11). This enigmatic little phrase sets Augustine musing: the Father is from eternity, without origin, of course; but more interesting are the references to Son as beautiful image and Spirit as enjoyable gift. The eternal Word is this primordial beauty streaming from the Father, the radiance of perfect expression and understanding

> which is like the art of the almighty and wise God, full of all the living and unchanging ideas [by which the Father expresses himself perfectly], which are all one in it. . . . In this art God knows all things that he has made through it, and so when times come and go, nothing comes and goes for God's knowledge. For all these created things around us are not known by God because they have been made; it is rather, surely, that even changeable things have been made because they are unchangeably known by him. Then that inexpressible embrace, so to say, of the Father and the image is not without enjoyment, without charity, without happiness. So this love, delight, felicity, or blessedness (if any human word can be found that is good enough to express it) he [Hilary] calls very briefly "use" [*usus*, intimate habituation leading to joy], and it is the Holy Spirit in the triad, not begotten, but the sweetness of begetter and begotten pervading all creatures according to their capacity with its vast generosity and fruitfulness, that they might all keep their right order and rest in their right places. (VI. 11)

Let us "enjoy" this remarkable "image" ourselves for a moment, as I suspect Augustine intended us to do, thus evoking for us some faint personal experience of the very thing he was talking about. Note first of all that the Father's art, the eternal Word, pre-contains the truth of all the creatures who exist eternally in the form of this primordial event of expression and knowing. But that's not all, for Augustine points out that these eternal reasons of all things are, in the Word, caught up everlastingly in "that inexpressible embrace, so to say, of the Father and the image"; and this embrace is infinitely flowing joy and love and blessed happiness and this "is the Holy Spirit" in Hilary's triadic phrase.

Now just pause for a moment to recapitulate the theological trajectory implicit in this little musing of Augustine's. With the whole Church, Augustine has been led by his faith to the discipleship of Christ, and having been called and claimed by Christ he enters into Christ's own relation with the Father. Over centuries of theological reflection, this relationship of Jesus and the Father in their Spirit has been opened up to disclose the infinite divine relationality which it manifests. And Augustine has just voyaged within this train of reflection up into the eternal knowing and loving, allowing us a taste of that contemplative vision of trinitarian ecstasy which, as he always points out, is the beatitude that calls us. What Augustine's critics often fail to note is that he doesn't stop there! Caught up in the trinitarian dynamic, the passage continues by imagining the eternal ideas of all beings flowing forth into their creaturely existence in time and space; and thus the beatific joy of the Father in the Son, and in all the creatures in the Son, overflows and radiates within the creatures. For the Holy Spirit is now received as "the sweetness of begetter and begotten pervading all creatures according to their capacity with its vast generosity and fruitfulness." In other words, the trinitarian knowing and rejoicing is, so to speak, translated, mystically radiant, within the structure of creaturely life, urging and fructifying every creature towards the fulfillment of its own unique truth, its identity in the Word, and so onwards towards its "right order and rest." In this way, Augustine suggests, the identity (Word) of every creature (its form or expression), and the yearning joy (Spirit) at the heart of creation's drive towards its consummation in every fiber of its being, reflect the everlasting, relational dynamic of divine life. Thus, Augustine seems to be saying, if we learn to speak rightly about God's life, we may find the key to understand our own life as God's.

(D) Book 8. In Books 1–4, Augustine expressed what he takes to be the Church's inherited trinitarian faith, and showed how it emerges from scripture. Then in Books 5–7, as we have seen, he developed a language for speaking rightly about the Trinity against the backdrop of the theological arguments of his day. But now the bishop remains unsatisfied. He remarks that he has been repeating doctrinal formulae, perhaps rather a lot, precisely so that these sorts of habits of speech would become more familiar and ease confusions in trinitarian discussion, thus permitting Christians to "temper our fondness for controversy" (VIII. 1). Augustine wants more than anything to assist his readers into a living encounter with the truth of God as Trinity, and this means that, having made the preparations of Books 1–7, he wants to discuss the mystery of the Trinity "in a more inward manner than the things that have been discussed above [in Books 1–7], though in fact they are the same things" (VIII. 1). Only God make this encounter possible, as Augustine says: "The God himself we are looking for will help us, I confidently hope, to get some fruit from our labors" (XV. 1).

By discussing the Trinity "in a more inward way," I believe Augustine intends not so much to give his readers more inwardly personal or existential analogies for thinking about their inherited faith, but something far more startling. He intends to swing open a hidden door within the minds of his readers, running ahead of their thoughts and opening up those thoughts into a line of communication: thoughts becoming transparent to a presence just beyond them, thoughts perhaps recognized as being, themselves, whispers of divine life in the depths of the believer's mind. For Augustine does not intend to lead us step by step to arrive at a deeper understanding of God as Trinity, but rather to lead us step by step to the point when we will see, and rejoice, that our concepts for God as Trinity are wonderful but hopelessly inadequate. And in that moment, he hopes, we will be open to the Trinity's own far more direct and inward teaching.

So in Book 8 Augustine teaches us how to sense the mysterious presence, by grace, of what lies entirely beyond our grasp. He does this by asking us to notice two fascinating facts about ourselves. We naturally seek to know the truth of things, their reality, but how is it that we can know when our knowing of them *is* true? There must be some sense in which our minds are illuminated by the light of Truth itself, not the truth of this or that thing which we know, but the Truth by which we judge the truthfulness or rightness in our understanding of things. God is this Truth, the condition for the possibility of our knowing anything at all (VIII. 2–3).[26] In one of his loveliest passages Augustine takes us to the same brink of awareness with respect to our desire for the good:

> Once more come, see if you can. You certainly only love what is good, and the earth is good with its lofty mountains and its folded hills and its level plains, and a farm is good when its situation is pleasant and its land is fertile . . . and the heart of a friend is good with its sweet accord and loving trust, and a just man is good, and riches are good because they are easily put to use, and the sky is good with its sun and moon and stars, and angels are good with their holy obedience, and speech is good . . . Why go on and on? This is good and that is good. Take away this and that and see good itself if you can. In this way you will see God, not good with some other good, but the good of every good.

Now notice the crucial next step Augustine takes:

> For surely among all these good things I have listed and whatever others can be observed or thought of, we would not say that one is better than another when we make a true judgment unless we had impressed on us some notion of good itself by which we both approve of a thing, and prefer one thing to another. This is how we should love God, not this or that good but good itself. (VIII. 4)

Just as with truth, Augustine says, in our every act of loving good things we are guided by Goodness itself, God, and indeed it is God we are really yearning for in all our desiring.

In these two little spiritual-theological exercises, which Augustine will repeat a third time (combining both the true and the good in our pursuit of justice), the bishop has been training us to recognize the absolute transcendence of God to our minds and hearts; God cannot be *one of* the things we know or love because by "God" we simply mean the One by whose radiant truth and sweet goodness we live in a world that has truth and goodness as inherent qualities and structures, and by whose absolute, transcendent Truth and Goodness we are able to sense and recognize the truth and goodness in things. But at the same time, Augustine helps his readers to sense God's intimate presence and agency, for apart from this hidden presence of God to each person, no one could sense the true or the good in the world around them. In effect Augustine is saying, every time you know the truth, or delight in the good, or seek justice, you are always already being addressed by God; your very seeking and finding is the sign within your own life of God's self-communication.

How does all this help us in trinitarian reflection? Again and again throughout Book 8, Augustine practices variations on this pattern of sensing God as the source and agency of our knowing and loving, even when the very One we seek to know and love, God, is beyond our grasp. Augustine has, so to speak, habituated his readers to an awareness: (1) that they are seekers, (2) that there are realities they seek (to know or to love), (3) that there are forms of truth and goodness and justice that animate and give life to their life-quest for truth and goodness and justice; and above all, that God is mystically present through all and in all and as the real goal of all human seeking. Indeed, says Augustine, with regard to all these patterns that so define human life, the more purely they flame up within us, the more they make the sign to us of God's presence: "the more brightly burns our love for God, the more surely and serenely we see him, because it is in God that we observe that unchanging form of justice" by which we sense and yearn for justice upon earth (VIII. 13).

And then Augustine concludes the book with a final telling observation. What, he asks, do we notice about all these cases in which we are animated by God to know or to love? "Love means someone loving and something loved with love. There you are with three, the lover, what is being loved, and love. . . . We have said enough to provide ourselves as it were with the frame of a kind of warp on which we can weave what remains to be said" (VIII. 14). The weaving loom upon which a deeper understanding of the Trinity may be woven is clearly not just an analogy or two, drawn from the structures of human existence, but is rather the whole life, the whole yearning, of human persons being addressed by God.

(C') Books 9–11. In these three books, which parallel the logical/linguistic Books 5–7, Augustine "weaves" a logical analysis of the human experience of knowing and loving. He teaches his readers two things. First, pondering how human beings know and love things can give us some practice in the "grammar" we learned in Books 5–7. Augustine is not simply giving an analysis of human cognition and volition; he is trying to get us to "practice" the basic rules for thinking trinitarianly (e.g., God is one, God's unity consists in a pattern of relations, etc.), and to try out this new kind of trinitarian thinking on the knowing and loving he has awakened us to in Book 8. Second, and all-importantly, Augustine never lets the reader forget that the source and goal of this "practicing" is really God's presence drawing us beyond ourselves. I would liken Augustine's intentions here to those of a master language teacher: first, she states some basic grammar rules for her students to learn, even though, of course, the students have no real sense of what those rules will actually mean or make possible; second, she lets them practice the rules in the form of little conversations about things like going to buy ice cream or meeting a friend at school; third, when the students are ready – or perhaps just before – she throws open the classroom door and lets a real, live native speaker walk into their midst and begin conversing with them; in that magical and terrifying moment, her students will at last realize what it's all been about. Augustine, too, is intending to throw open the door to the Native Speaker of trinitarian language.

So, Augustine says, you've been learning how to speak rightly about God the Trinity. All right, show me how you would use those basic rules to notice the Trinity's image in human life. In suggesting all this, please notice that, contrary to the usual view, I am definitely not saying here that Augustine is using various models of human knowing and loving to "prove" the Trinity (whatever that could mean) or even to construct a "psychological analogy" for the Trinity for instructive purposes. I'm saying, rather, that he encourages his readers to try out different triad analogies, including, yes, personal or "psychological" ones, in order to practice and get clear about what the Church believes is the right way to talk about God. Thus throughout these chapters we will see him, nearly endlessly, trying out different sorts of little trinities. If you thought he was really only trying by means of all these to convince you that this is how to think about God, surely you would have to say that for a master teacher of rhetoric and theology he is mighty inept! Rather, I'm suggesting, the plethora of examples and analogies is meant to give us practice for trinitarian conversation. Looking at these chapters in this way, I hope, makes more sense of them, and not incidentally, allows us to see how we might go with their grain rather than against them by learning from Augustine how to conduct theological exercises.

Space doesn't permit me to highlight the many little "learning moments" when, as he tries out the different trinitarian analogies before us, Augustine helps us to see the various ways in which each one does or does not quite parallel the Church's grammar for trinitarian conversation. At the heart of these books are, however, two central analogies, which Edmund Hill calls a first draft (Book 9: mind, self-knowledge, self-love) and a second draft (Book 10: self-awareness, self-understanding, self-love). Before we look briefly at these two "drafts," here is a reminder not to get too attached to any of these models, especially not to think of them as providing handy one-to-one correspondences with the persons of the Trinity (the Father as memory, etc.). As tempting as that may be, it will distract you from Augustine's real aim, which is to practice thinking trinitarianly so that the Trinity may overtake your thinking and loving and take you into the Trinity's own thinking and loving. Or as he says, we are examining the trinitarian structures in our own more familiar mind so that "after practicing the mind's gaze on the lower image we may be able to shift it [our gaze] from the illuminated creature to the unchangeable illuminating light" (IX. 17).

In Book 9 Augustine wants us to explore the mind and its self-knowing and self-loving. He wants us to grasp how there can be three distinct activities all of one essence or being: "mind is itself loving itself and itself knowing itself, and these three are such by our definition that mind is not being loved or known by any other thing. So these three must be of one and the same being" (IX. 7). As ever, Augustine then brings the basic model to life, so to speak, by reminding us that it all happens by the mysteriously intimate radiance of God's own truth and goodness illuminating our consciousness. Here is his description of how we come to know the truth and to judge the goodness of things through the transcendental communion of our existence with God:

Thus it is that in that eternal truth according to which all temporal things were made we observe with the eye of the mind the form [i.e., God's idea of each reality, eternally known in the Word] according to which we are and according to which we do anything with true and right reason . . . And by this form we conceive true knowledge of things, which we have with us as a kind of word that we beget by uttering inwardly. . . . This word is conceived in love of either the creature or the creator, that is, of changeable nature or unchangeable truth; which means either in covetousness or in charity. (IX. 12–13)

This passage very importantly foreshadows things to come. For as we'll see in Books 12–14, when humanity *does* hold its consciousness open to the divine truth and goodness, it is graced with a fulfilling communion with God and thus enabled to know and love all things as they should be, that is, as they are eternally known and loved in God.

It is precisely the fall away from this communion with God that corrupts and distorts humanity as the image of God. As Augustine already hints in the passage just quoted, our knowledge-event is like the birth of a word; we "conceive" an idea, and we conceive our ideas precisely because we desire the goodness of the reality we are itching to know. The question is whether we are really loving the good of a reality according to its merely creaturely, changeable status as we can grasp it – that is, according to some objectifying or self-gratifying sense *we* have of the reality – or whether we want to know the reality according to God's eternal cherishing of it, according to God's own desire for its reality. When we do the latter, says Augustine, we are led to know things in charity; when the former, we are driven to know things out of covetousness. By analogy, think of how you "know" someone or something when all you really want of them is something for yourself; you may not really care about them at all in themselves but only as they help or hinder your own designs. This kind of knowing can become a demeaning fantasy or a manipulation of creatures for selfish ends. By comparison, Augustine wants us to see, opening ourselves to know things as God knows and loves them means that our knowing is animated by God's charity, God's loving intention for each reality to become the fullest and truest kind of thing it is. This sort of knowledge is what Augustine calls *sapientia*, wisdom.

It is also worth noting how much significance Augustine ascribes to the role of desire in all our acts of knowing. As we saw in the last passage quoted above, it is love that causes our minds to "conceive" or beget a word of truth. It is because we long so much to understand something which we now merely sense intuitively that we struggle mentally to bring to birth the idea that is gestating in our minds:

Parturition [giving birth] by the mind is preceded by a kind of appetite which prompts us to inquire and find out about what we want to know, and as a result knowledge itself is brought forth as an offspring; and hence the appetite itself cannot appropriately itself be called brood or offspring. The same appetite with which one longs open-mouthed to know a thing becomes love of the thing known when it holds and embraces the acceptable offspring, that is knowledge, and joins it to its begetter. And so you have a certain image of the Trinity, the mind itself and its knowledge, which is its offspring and its word about itself, and love as the third element, "and these three are one" (1 John 5: 8). (IX. 18)

In this passage Augustine clearly distinguishes the way the word of knowledge proceeds from the way love proceeds: love is the agency that brings the word to conception and unites it in acceptance with its source; therefore it is quite a different act of mind than the truth being conceived. Even more interestingly, Augustine describes love as having both a generative role and a unitive role: generative because love is the yearning that animates the mind's search for truth, unitive because love is also the joy and delight one feels when the word one has struggled to conceive is clearly right and just, the truth of things.

There are those who criticize Augustine for (as they think) undermining the Holy Spirit's full personhood by means of what they take this analogy of love's role in knowledge to mean, that is, that the Spirit is "merely" the bond of love uniting the Father (mind) with the Son (word). As I have already suggested, I'm not so sure we are justified in making these sorts of one-to-one correspondences between elements of Augustine's various models and the persons of the Trinity. But if we are going to insist on doing so, then in fairness we ought to notice how Augustine emphasizes the significant agency of love. Indeed, love seems, for Augustine, to play a crucial (even prior) role in the word's begetting. And we should notice how well these two roles, the generative and the unitive, correspond to or even account for the strange shifts in the gospel narratives' account of the Spirit: first (generative role) bringing about Jesus' conception and sending him forth into the world and then later (unitive role) resting upon him as the delight and favor of the Father, who proclaims him as indeed the true offspring in his baptism and resurrection.

In Book 10 Augustine revises this triad of mind, self-knowledge, and self-love by means of the trinitarian grammar. He asks us to notice that the first term, "mind," is rather more absolute and not as inherently in relation as are the other two. So throughout Book 10 Augustine works to develop a triadic model that is more intrinsically relational, and not surprisingly it is his concern for humanity's relation to God that motivates his conception. The mind, says the bishop, is never entirely clear to itself; it can be deeply obsessed with the world around it in ways that drive it to distraction and utter lack of self-awareness, but it is also always in motion towards a greater attentiveness, awareness, and clarity, as though there were something drawing it towards the moment when, by beholding Truth itself, the beholding mind would finally be truthful to itself, clear, and self-aware. For this to happen, the mind needs to receive from above the vision of truth and contemplate it in peace, rather than try to nourish itself on what it can more easily grasp and subject to its own designs. Look at how Augustine describes the two directions in which the mind is pulled as it searches for itself, for *memoria* (memory or self-awareness):

It [the mind] sees certain inner beauties in that more excellent nature which is God; but instead of staying still and enjoying them as it ought to, it wants to claim them for itself, and rather than be like him by his gift it wants to be what he is by its own right. So it turns away from him and slithers and slides down into less and less which is imagined to be more and more; it can find satisfaction neither in itself nor in anything else as it gets further away from him who alone can satisfy it. So it is that in its destitution and distress it becomes excessively intent on its own actions and the disturbing pleasures it culls from them; being greedy to acquire knowledge of all sorts from things outside itself, which it loves as known in a general way and feels can easily be lost unless it takes great care to hold onto them, it loses its carefree sense of security, and thinks of itself all the less the more it is in its sense that it cannot lose itself. (X. 7)

Note here the echoes of the serpent's view of things, which he foists upon Adam and Eve in what Christians regard as the Fall (Genesis 3): the beauty of God reduced to an object somehow withheld and needing to be seized, the slithering away into a more and more frantic effort to hang onto what turns out to be less and less satisfying or secure, with the upshot that one is driven entirely away from self-remembrance or self-awareness.

Once more, then, we can see Augustine not only practicing the trinitarian grammar by trying out a new and better analogy within human experience, but just as importantly we see him underscoring within human experience its authentic dynamism towards communion with God – the loss of which will mean the distortion of all analogies and the garbling of all conversation.

(B') Books 12–14. These books parallel Books 2–4: they ascend from the more abstract linguistic and logical approaches back up again into the history of salvation attested in scripture. We can briefly recall the chiastic sequence here.

Augustine
(A) begins with the inherited faith,
(B) sees how it is grounded in scripture,
(C) explores it logically,
(D) holds everything he's come to understand so far up towards the light of God's grace, exposing it to this ultimate presence of God which is his goal,
(C') logically explores this God-oriented dynamism of human life according to several models,
(B') brings the fruit of this exploration back up into its scriptural context for elucidation,
(A') finally holds this faith of the community, now explored and appropriated personally, open to the more direct teaching of the Trinity.

Seeing Augustine's methodological sequence like this emphasizes the bishop's concern for theological formation. The theological journey of faith in search of understanding clearly requires, in his view, a kind of practice, exercise, and prayerful formation, all of which allow the theologian to sense the living presence of his "subject matter" and to engage that presence in ways that allow it freedom and agency to disclose itself.

I raise all this here not simply as a methodological aside but because in these books (12–14) Augustine persistently directs our attention to the kind of thinking or knowing we are employing in life and in theological life in particular. Augustine shared the common ancient Mediterranean view that knowledge (*scientia*) was the mind's proper relationship to items it could fully grasp and master, while wisdom (*sapientia*) was a kind of knowing in which the mind is, as it were, befriended by the great truth beyond its grasp, the truth so fulfilling that its contemplation is the very consummation of human existence. Why is all this of significance in a treatise on the doctrine of the Trinity? Because, Augustine believes, God has created humanity to share, contemplatively, in the communion of the Trinity, to enjoy the vision of one God in three persons. Therefore the fact that, after the Fall, humanity has a good bit of trouble thinking rightly about the Trinity is a symptom of humanity's problem: its fallen approach to perception and understanding now disdains contemplative wisdom and insists on utter absorption with the little self-gratifying items it can possess and manage for itself. As Augustine explains it:

> What happens is that the soul, loving its own power, slides away from the whole which is common to all into the part which is its own private property. By following God's directions and being perfectly governed by his laws it could enjoy the whole universe of creation; but by the apostasy of pride which is called the beginning of sin it strives to grab something more than the whole and to govern it by its own laws; and because there is nothing more than the whole it is thrust back into anxiety over a part, and so by being greedy for more it gets less. (XII. 14)

The "whole which is common to all" and which humanity could have enjoyed is the whole truth and goodness of God and of God's knowing and loving of all creatures. In other words, living according to "God's directions," humanity could have perceived the divine truth of all things, enjoyed them in God, and in the very event of doing so also simultaneously lived in communion with God. The Fall, in Augustine's view, begins with a niggling uncertainty about whether everything is really given by God or whether it would be safer to insist upon having certain knowledge, certain possession, of things for oneself. The tragedy is that, because humanity is created for communion with God, this smaller, possessive kind of knowing of things just as they can be grasped by humanity can never fulfill human longing to know and love infinite truth and infinite good (God).

So humanity descends into ever more anxious forms of knowledge about less and less fulfilling objects; and the more obsessively it attends to these, in its small-minded sort of way, the less able it is any longer to sense the divine presence. The image of the Trinity in humanity, which is actually humanity's dynamic orientation towards God, has shrunk into an anxious, envious state in which it no longer knows or loves anything much beyond its own fantasies. Now the mind "drags the deceptive semblances of bodily things inside, and plays about with them in idle meditation until it cannot even think of anything divine except as being such, and so in its private avarice it is loaded with error and in its private prodigality it is emptied of strength" (XII. 15). Augustine argues that humanity's spiritual decline also, inevitably, undermines its understanding of the faith. The human mind, obsessed with its avaricious sort of knowing, "cannot even think of anything divine except as being such" as the small possessions the mind now hoards within its nervous grasp. And this is precisely why Christians cannot search for deeper understanding of trinitarian doctrine until and unless they also allow the Trinity to encounter and rescue them.

Having shown us this in Book 12, Augustine devotes Book 13 to an account of how the Trinity reaches into history to re-create its image within humanity, and Book 14 to a renewed reflection on the Trinity in the light of its redeemed image in human existence. We've examined Augustine's teaching on salvation in Chapter 5, so here we can simply note the crucial way in which the bishop relates redemption to the healing of humanity's noetic orientation towards God. The problem, as we've just seen, is that instead of a proper longing for the contemplation of divine truth and goodness, humanity focuses on the small, graspable material things that can never satisfy it. Yet by entering this world of material things, the eternal Word incarnate gives himself to humanity as Jesus, a material, sensible creature able to place himself within the small and fragile grasp of human belief, and human knowing. But of course his humanity, as the expression of the Word, draws human attention after him into the mystery of his union with the divine. In this way Christ, as both human and divine, re-creates human knowing and loving by giving humanity both an object to know and a vision of wisdom to contemplate:

> Our knowledge therefore is Christ, and our wisdom is the same Christ. It is he who plants faith in us about temporal things, he who presents us with the truth about eternal things. Through him we go straight toward him, through knowledge toward wisdom, without ever turning aside from one and the same Christ. (XIII. 24)

In this way Christ's redeeming work continues through the transformation it accomplishes in the knowing and loving of those who believe in him. So in Book 14 Augustine finally considers what possible analogy to the Trinity this restored *imago dei* in human existence might bear, always remembering that this is only a very provisional and partial image now, "for only when it comes to the perfect vision of God will this image bear God's perfect likeness" (XIV. 23). As I have indicated all along, Augustine's aim is clearly not simply to teach something about trinitarian theology but to induce his readers to encounter the Trinity for themselves, precisely as they marvel at God's recalling them to communion:

> This trinity of the mind is not really the image of God because the mind remembers and understands and loves itself, but because it is also able to remember and

understand and love him by whom it was made. And when it does this it becomes wise. If it does not do it, then even though it remembers and understands and loves itself, it is foolish. Let it then remember its God to whose image it was made, and understand and love him. To put it in a word, let it worship the uncreated God, by whom it was created with a capacity for him and able to share in him. In this way it will be wise not with its own light but by sharing in that supreme light, and it will reign in happiness where it reigns eternal. (XIV. 15)

The calling to image or reflect the divine life is only momentarily present, in each instant that the self is in motion towards God. And this passage makes clear how utterly relational and mutual is the life with God to which the creature is called, for it "was created with a capacity for him and able to share in him." It is perhaps this dynamic, participation-in-the-other trajectory that has finally emerged for Augustine as the image of the Trinity in humanity, an image, that is, that reflects God's life precisely by being ceaselessly called out of itself and into a joyous sharing in another; thus, of course, it echoes the trinitarian self-sharing which is the creature's own cause.

At last, then, Augustine reveals that the Trinity whom he has been teaching his readers to remember and long for has not only sought them out in the historical economy of salvation but also continuously works within them a crucial freedom from all anxious self-reliance and miserable isolation: "When the mind truly recalls its Lord after receiving his Spirit, it perceives quite simply – for it learns this by a wholly intimate instruction from within – that it cannot rise except by his gracious doing" (XIV. 21). The creature in motion towards God is no longer a solipsistic self but is always already addressed intimately "from within" and learns the truth by the grace of receiving all from another, just as the persons of the Trinity also live by the gracious eternal self-sharing of one to another.

(A') Book 15. This note of receiving from another appropriately brings Augustine full circle. For in the final book of *The Trinity* he reminds his readers that, as in Book 1, faith in the Trinity is a gift that can only be *received* from God. No matter how clever we are, we could never construct such a doctrine nor prove it apart from God's self-disclosure through the economy of salvation attested in scripture. This human limitation – which is also humanity's blessed openness to God's giving – foreshadows, in Augustine's view, the final gift to be received, namely the gift of full participation in trinitarian life, when faith will give way to vision. In reviewing all the books of *The Trinity*, Augustine concludes that all he has said will be of little use unless it prompts those who read it to draw near to the living reality whose life their own creaturely lives now image so fitfully. The images he has tried to uncover may be echoes but remain entirely inadequate and only useful insofar as they prompt those who ponder these analogies to "refer what they see to that of which it is an image" (XV. 44).

Few works of Christian theology can more clearly be distinguished from what we would expect to find in the theology books of our own time, for Augustine seems finally almost to relish his failure, using it as a spur, even a kind of salutary shock, awakening his readers to another kind of work they must undertake in the realms of grace. He concludes by also modeling this journey for them himself. Addressing God directly in the final paragraphs of his great work, Augustine declares:

> Before you lies my knowledge and my ignorance; where you have opened to me, receive me as I come in; where you have shut to me, open to me as I knock. Let me remember you, let me understand you, let me love you. Increase these things in me until you refashion me entirely. (XV. 51)

Karl Barth on the God Who Loves in Freedom

If Augustine unquestionably shaped western reflection on the Trinity for centuries, Karl Barth (1886–1968) might arguably be called the single most significant exponent of trinitarian theology in the modern period. In many ways, his refusal to accommodate theology to the modern critical turn has rendered his thought a continuing object of suspicion in academic theology. Yet it was just this conviction of Barth's that God's meaning in Christ would always be its own truest interpreter, even in the minds of theologians, that makes his massive theological endeavor so intriguing. The doctrine of the Trinity, in Barth's work, no longer stood isolated as in most post-Kantian theology, alone in a question-haunted fog of "mere speculation," nor was it feverishly transformed, as in post-Hegelian thought, into a form of historical or spiritual necessity. The great American theologian Robert Jenson famously observed that Barth perceived the difference between natural theology's quest for God (according to reason and generic experience) "and the gospel's proclamation that Jesus is God's quest for us . . . more rigorously than any before him . . . and uses this insight as the sole motor of trinitarian discourse."[27] God is coming to you and will speak with you; that is the first thing one has to be aware of (or beware of, depending on your perspective!) when trying to understand Karl Barth. God is not shy or unintelligible. God has even figured out, *pace* Kant, how to communicate to humans in ways that make their perceptions valid, even in ordinary common forms of human speech.

The distinctly perplexing thing about this, at least in the view of modern academic theology, is that Barth's approach seems to refuse the dominant criteria-setting of whatever standards of universal reason or of privileged experience we might normally employ to verify the insights of a particular theology. Barth, however, thinks that such standards are never quite as universal as they hope to be, and that every group's experience has to be clarified in the light of the crucified and risen Christ. When he was writing the first volumes of the *Church Dogmatics*, for example, the German Christian movement of the Nazi era was strongly influencing the criteria of both popular and academic theology in Germany, subjecting Christian belief, in Barth's view, to an obviously malignant distortion that influenced many sorts of theological decisions.

Of course human agency and participation are involved in the theological task; this Barth never denies. But his reading of the event of revelation in Christ convinced him that this human effort was most authentic to the Gospel when it attempted to unfold and interpret what God is already doing and saying in Christ, and to do this in the bold confidence that God is really the prime theological Subject, the true initiator and sustainer of all healthy talk about God. What makes all this so interesting from our point of view is that this self-communicating or self-declaring characteristic of God springs directly, in Barth's view, from the fact that God is triune. Indeed Barth first introduces trinitarian doctrine as he is unfolding his theology of revelation.

It is often mistakenly believed, therefore, that Barth's theology of the Trinity is simply a function of his interest in revelation. The reverse would be more accurate: Barth finds revelation so compelling precisely because he thinks it is really God who is speaking in the event of revelation and that God does this – and does it in a way that really makes God known to humanity – *because* God is the Trinity. Also worth bearing in mind is the fact that Barth is the first great modern theologian to think through every corner and fold of Christian theology trinitarianly; that is, he does not treat in isolation the fact of God being the Trinity, but rather, shows the outreach of trinitarian life undergirding every feature of Christian faith. In consequence of this, whether we find ourselves persuaded by Barth's approach to theology or not, we can learn a lot from him about the interaction of Christian doctrines and the remarkable explanatory power and vigor unleashed in theology when the mysteries of faith are considered in terms of their intrinsic interrelatedness.

For example, consider the close connection between the doctrines of the Trinity and of revelation. If you thought that Christ was not really divine in the same sense as God the Father, then you would think that what he reveals in the economy of salvation could not exactly be the divine life itself, expressed humanly, but rather some sort of report *about* God. Or if you thought that the Spirit was not fully divine, but rather the spirit of the community or of human aspiration in general, then, you would think, it could not really be God's own knowing of God that the Spirit makes possible within those in whom the Spirit dwells, but only a heightened form of human perception. To clarify these sorts of doctrinal interactions in theology, you may like to turn back for a moment to Chapter 3 where I outlined the structure of Barth's theology in parallel with that of Origen and of Thomas Aquinas. In what follows I'll consider briefly the trinitarian vision Barth unfolds in different doctrinal contexts: his teaching about revelation, and about election and reconciliation.

Revelation

To begin, here is perhaps the most quoted text from the works of Karl Barth, complete with his very own famous emphases. As you read it, consider why he seems to repeat or echo himself, and what significance the emphases are meant to have.

> *God* reveals Himself. He reveals Himself *through Himself.* He reveals *Himself.* If we really want to understand revelation in terms of its subject, i.e., God, then the first thing we have to realise is that this subject, God, the Revealer, is identical with His act in revelation and also identical with its effect. (I. 1. 296)[28]

Later, Barth will speak of God, as it were, "happening" three times in three different ways of being God. So in the passage just quoted, Barth, who was a master stylist, evokes this repetition, the thrice-active presence of God. Analyzing the event of revelation in Christ, Barth renders revelation transparent to the acting subject, the Trinity, with the distinctive but undivided working of the three persons highlighted by the emphases. We could lay it out like this:

God reveals Godself: the Father is the initiator.

God reveals Godself *through Godself:* the Holy Spirit makes this event happen for creatures, brings it about by the Spirit's own agency that humanity sees and in some sense understands what God is doing in its midst.

God reveals *Godself:* the Son who is revealed, Jesus Christ, is God again, God is the "content" or subject matter of what is revealed.

Two crucial implications emerge right away. First, it is the Holy Spirit who brings it about that humans are gifted with real "hearing" and understanding of what is revealed, and it does not in any way depend upon some innate quality or capacity of humankind, which might limit or control revelation. The event is avowedly always a miracle. Second, because Jesus is God the Son, what humanity encounters in revelation is not something that merely tells the creatures *about* God, something behind and beyond which the "real," perhaps quite different God would inevitably be lurking. It is truly God whom the world encounters in Christ, and, as Michael Ramsey has said, in God there is nothing that is not Christ-like at all.

Barth's approach created a kind of seismic shift in modern theology. For the dominant question that modernity asks has always been, how can we arrive at certain, universally verifiable truth; how can we know what we think we know? But Barth asks, what impact has this turn to the human-knowing-subject had upon theology? Has it not tended to front-load theology with questions whose answers, naturally, are critical analyses of human knowing? These very interesting observations about the capacity and incapacity of the human subject have then become, naturally, the template and the matrix within which any theological question may be asked or judged to be proper and appropriate. Thus emerges what Barth describes as "the common idea that one must follow the far too obvious and illuminating scheme: How do we know God? Does God exist? What is God? and only last of all: Who is our God?" (I. 1. 301). But it is precisely this question which modernity puts last that the Bible always puts first, for which deity it is that one thinks one is talking about makes quite a lot of difference, in Barth's view.

Put it this way: if you thought you were dealing with one of the gods (perhaps Thor?), who though powerful and invisible is still one aspect of the whole of reality, then your knowing of this super-thing among all the other things would indeed be contingent upon how you know things in general. Barth argues that as believers have been confronted by the God made known in the events concerning Jesus of Nazareth they were forced to ask "Who is this God?" The answer they received is that God is the One who makes God known, and who can only be known by bringing believers to share in God's own knowing of God. This is so because this God is not one of the gods, not an aspect of the whole, but the reason why there is a whole at all. In other words, Barth's approach to theology insists on a ceaseless attention to God as the *teacher* of theology, precisely because of who Christians believe God is: the one who can only be known as God makes God known: "The beginning of our knowledge of God – of this God – is not a beginning which we can make with Him. It can only be the beginning which He has made with us" (II. 1. 190). What we are likely to know of the "divine" on our own is quite splendid, perhaps exalted, even philosophically plausible, but nothing more than "idolatrous pictures" and "projections of our own glory" (II. 1. 182). So how, precisely, does God makes Godself known, and why is it an act that particularly manifests the Trinity?

The first thing to say is simply that Barth does not mean that God just "takes over" and substitutes divine acts for our own human processes of perception and conceptualization and understanding. "Although the knowledge of God certainly does not come about without our work, it also does not come about through our work, or as the fruit of our work" (II. 1. 183). So our perceiving and conceiving are necessary but not sufficient conditions for knowing God. This is so because the event of human knowing of God, revelation, is for Barth entirely dependent upon having fellowship with God, a kind of intimate self-sharing that humanity can by no means bring about. The problem, in other words, is not that God is somehow the asymptotic unknown on the other side of all human categories of perception (as Kant would have it). To assume this, in Barth's view, would mean that, like Kant, we had already decided what God is or ought to be as the result of our analysis of the human knowing subject, and had ruled "God" beyond bounds. But this would of course be a human knowing about the divine apart from the gift of friendship with God (faith) and would therefore, in Barth's view, simply be a wonderfully refined idol. "God's hiddenness is not the content of a last word of human self-knowledge" (II. 1. 183).

So how does God create the sort of fellowship or friendship with humanity that Barth thinks is the crucial condition for the possibility of revelation? As always, Barth reminds us that his answer to our question is not a general theory of revelation, much less of human cognition, but a theological reflection on what has happened to humanity in Christ. For Jesus is the "first and proper Subject of the knowledge of God" (II. 1. 252), in other words, the particular human knower who has been drawn into revelatory fellowship with God is, in the first instance, Jesus. As you read Barth's full unfolding of this, consider the trinitarian ground that accounts for it all.

In Him [Jesus] who is true God and true man it is true that in His true revelation
God gives to man a part in the truth of His knowing, and therefore gives to man's
knowing similarity with His own and therefore truth. On the basis of the grace of
the incarnation, on the basis of the acceptance and assumption of man into unity of
being with God as it has taken place in Jesus Christ, all this has become truth in this
man, in the humanity of Jesus Christ. The eternal Father knows the eternal Son, and
the eternal Son knows the eternal Father. But the eternal Son is not only the eternal
God. In the unity fulfilled by the grace of the incarnation, He is also this man Jesus
of Nazareth. It is not our knowledge of God, but the knowledge which is and will
be present in this man Jesus, that we have described. . . . When we appeal to God's
grace, we appeal to the grace of the incarnation and to this man as the One in whom,
because He is the eternal Son of God, knowledge of God was, is and will be present
originally and properly; but again through whom, because He is the eternal Son of
God, there is promised to us our own divine sonship, and therefore our fellowship
in His knowledge of God. (II. 1. 252)

So the eternal ground of all knowing of God is the trinitarian fellowship, the
eternal knowing of Father and Son in the joy of their Spirit. Humanity is welcomed
into this fellowship in Christ, and through him, by the power of the Spirit, adoption into this relationship of personal knowing is offered to everyone. Why is there
any knowing of any kind whatsoever? Because the Trinity knows and loves itself.
From that eternal event of trinitarian life flows God's intention to create others
for the purpose of calling them to share in this fellowship themselves.

Barth offers extended sections on what he means by this triunity or fellowship,
and sections on each of the divine persons. Throughout he reminds his readers
that he is not saying "that revelation is the basis of the Trinity, as though God
were the triune God only in His revelation and for the sake of His revelation" (I.
1. 312). The eternal life of the Trinity is complete, free, and loving in and of itself.
Because of that, God's presence within time and history does reveal God truly
(because the Father and the Son eternally know each other) and make the joy of
this revelation present (because the Holy Spirit eternally rejoices in the other, and
is God-in-communion-with-other). As Barth puts it:

As He is the Father who begets the Son He brings forth the Spirit of love, for as He
begets the Son, God already negates in Himself, from eternity, in His absolute simplicity, all loneliness, self-containment, or self-isolation. Also and precisely in Himself,
from eternity, in His absolute simplicity, God is orientated to the Other, does not
will to be without the Other, will have Himself only as He has Himself with the
Other and in the Other. He is the Father of the Son in such a way that with the Son
He brings forth the Spirit, love, and is in Himself the Spirit, love. (I. 1. 483)

Unlike all notions of deity in Hegelian thought or Process thought, God is already
Other to Godself and lovingly free of "all loneliness, self-containment, or self-
isolation" quite apart from creation, time, or history. The gift of existence to the
creatures and the further gift of their relation to God is entirely that, gift, and in
no way necessary to God.

Yet because God is in Godself already Other, and makes space in joy for communion with the Other, God's presence to creation can indeed include the creature within this eternal othering and fellowship of the trinitarian life – without the loss of the creature's own creatureliness or "otherness" in respect of God. In other words, because of God's own fellowship with God, God the Holy Spirit can cause this fellowship to become an event within humanity: by the Holy Spirit, says Barth, "this being of ours is thus enclosed in the act of God" (I. 1. 462). As this eternal, personal act of communion and joy, the Holy Spirit can effect communion with the creature, "and in virtue of this presence of His, effect the relation of the creature to Himself"; and Barth importantly adds, God's "own presence in the creature" in this way effects within the creature "a relation of Himself to Himself" (I. 1. 450). That is, the creature's relation to God in fellowship is not just the creature's own relationship, so fragile and tenuous, rather it is a real presencing within the creature of God's own fellowship with God. "The Spirit guarantees man what he cannot guarantee himself, his personal participation in revelation. The act of the Holy Ghost in revelation is His Yes to God's Word which is spoken by God Himself for us, yet not just to us, but also in us" (I. 1. 453). The eternal delighting of the Father in the Son, and the Son in the Father, their mutual affirmation is poured out by the Spirit within creation. Just as Jesus transcribes the Son's eternal obedience to the Father into the nexus of human fidelity to God, so too the Spirit pours out the Father's affirmation of Christ and acceptance of his work upon Christ's followers so that they might participate in it and know the Father in and through Christ's knowing of him.

Throughout this account we've seen not simply Barth's emphasis on the initiative of God but also on the communion-making power of God. These are examples of the way Barth thinks "trinitarianly" about everything, for he understands the revelatory initiative of God to spring from the mutual knowing of the divine persons and the communion-making power to spring from the mutual delighting and fellowship of the persons. In this way Barth is able to disclose what we might call the trinitarian radiance at the heart of every aspect of the economy of salvation.

Election and reconciliation

To illustrate this consistently trinitarian vision, it will be helpful to notice briefly the important role trinitarian analysis plays in other parts of the *Church Dogmatics*. The Trinity is the ground of the mystery at the very core of Barth's conception of faith: everything springs from the fact that from all eternity God has freely chosen never to be God without the creatures and to offer fellowship with them through Christ, a fellowship that is not only revelatory but salvific.

"Our starting point must always be that in all His willing and choosing what God ultimately wills is Himself. All God's willing is primarily a determination of the love of the Father and the Son in the fellowship of the Holy Ghost" (II. 2. 169). God's very existence is, Barth says, an event of loving affirmation and relational communion of infinite goodness. This is what the doctrine of the Trinity tells us about divine life – that it is not a static, self-enclosed, absoluteness but inherently a delighting in the other. And for that reason, Barth says, we can begin to fathom that this eternal choosing to be for the other which is the life of the Trinity, was and always will be a decision in which "God does not choose only Himself"; in Christ and the Spirit, the world has met a God who seems to be choosing a partner:

> In this [eternal trinitarian] choice of self He also chooses another, that other which is man. . . . In this movement God has not chosen and willed a second god side by side with Himself, but a being distinct from Himself. And in all its otherness, as His creature and antithesis, this being has been ordained to participation in His own glory, the glory to which it owes its origin. It has been ordained to exist in the brightness of this glory and as the bearer of its image. (II. 2. 169)

Thus the trinitarian pattern of divine life is not simply a making space for the other, but an active and eternal choosing of the other; and for this reason it makes sense that God could do this and be this for humanity. But that God does do this is, in Barth's view, always a stunning and unfathomable miracle of grace. "What a risk God ran when he willed to take up the cause of created man" (II. 2. 163).

The eternal decision of the Trinity, then, is to be for humanity by raising humanity to fellowship with God in Christ, in the very person of Christ. And this is entirely free grace on God's part: "He had no need of a creation. He might well have been satisfied with the inner glory of His threefold being, His freedom, and His Love. The fact that He is not satisfied, but that His inner glory overflows . . . is grace, sovereign grace, a condescension inconceivably tender" (II. 2. 121). So why does God choose to be for the creature? Again, Barth considers the relation of Jesus of Nazareth to the one he called Father in their Spirit, and he reads this so that the trinitarian light illumines its deepest meaning. If anything could be said to reflect the very heart of Barth's understanding of the Gospel, this passage would surely come close:

> In the beginning, before time and space as we know them, before creation, before there was any reality distinct from God which could be the object of the love of God or the setting for His acts of freedom, God anticipated and determined within Himself . . . that the goal and meaning of all His dealings with the as yet non-existent universe should be the fact that in His Son He would be gracious towards man, uniting Himself with him. In the beginning it was the choice of the Father Himself to establish this covenant with man by giving up His Son for him, that He Himself might become man in the fulfilment of His grace. In the beginning it was the choice of the Son to be obedient to grace, and therefore to offer up Himself and to become man in order that this covenant might be made a reality. In the beginning it was the resolve of the Holy Spirit that the unity of God, of Father and Son should not be

disturbed or rent by this covenant with man, but that it should be made the more glorious, the deity of God, the divinity of His love and freedom, being confirmed and demonstrated by this offering of the Father and this self-offering of the Son. This choice was in the beginning. As the subject and object of this choice, Jesus Christ was at the beginning. (II. 2. 101–2)

Here we see not only the making space for and choosing the other of trinitarian life, but more precisely the distinct aspects of each Person's united mutual choosing. The giving away of the Father, the obedience of the Son, the unifying resolve of the Spirit are together the trinitarian ground of all creation and of salvation. The universe and its destiny come into being within the relations that mark out this eternal choosing of God in love and freedom.

And as Barth says, this poses a terrible risk to God. For the decision of the Trinity to be for humanity means that the Trinity also and in the same event of choosing agrees to enter the place of humanity in all its alienation from God and to bear that dereliction on behalf of humanity. "The exchange which took place on Golgotha, when God chose as His throne the malefactor's cross, when the Son of God bore what the son of man [humankind] ought to have borne, took place once and for all in fulfillment of God's eternal will, and it can never be reversed" (II. 2. 167). This is what the eternal Son has chosen to accept in taking humanity to himself, and this is the very basis of Barth's understanding of salvation. We see here in the starkest fashion that reconciliation is utterly a trinitarian event for Barth, a transposition into the world's broken fragments of that eternal choosing and being for the other: the Trinity.

Throughout the massive parts of Volume IV on reconciliation, Barth explores this eternal trinitarian decision to be for humanity, and he discloses the trinitarian sub-structure of Christ's life, death, resurrection, and sending of the Spirit. Space precludes even a cursory view of this remarkable effort unfolding over hundreds of pages.[29] Merely to choose one brief example: Barth renders Christ's death and resurrection transparent to its trinitarian ground, in part, by highlighting the role of the Spirit in confirming the eternal choosing of the three divine persons that underlies the whole earthly sequence. "It was in the power of the Spirit that He went to His death; and it was also in the power of the Spirit that He was raised again from the dead in order that what happened in His death should not be hidden but revealed" (IV. 2. 323). For Barth to say that these things take place by the power of the Spirit is not, as we've now seen, just pious talk. It means that at the root and basis of these earthly events in time lies the loving eternal decision of the trinitarian Persons, and, in particular, the yearning resolve of the Spirit that the Son's entrance into human alienation should not be the undoing of the divine life and communion, but its glorious unfolding within the life of the creation. In this way, the self-sharing and being for the other of the divine Persons becomes for creatures, as Barth put it, "a condescension of inconceivable tenderness."

PATHFINDING

Having a good sense of the major issues in trinitarian theology, and now also the examples of Augustine and Barth before you, you are ready to venture forward into the directions and questions of trinitarian theology today. You are equipped to make your own way through this landscape, but I'll offer some last assistance and even go along part way. For those who are eager to be off, the first section below gives a short briefing on some major issues in contemporary trinitarian thought today, and in some cases particular questions you may like to begin with in exploring any of these issues. For those who would like a little more companionship on the way, the final section offers a path through one significant issue that might be explored today by means of trinitarian thought: mystical participation in the God.

Questions in Trinitarian Theology Today

The Holy Spirit

Perhaps the single most persistent and disputed question in trinitarian theology concerns the proper understanding of the Holy Spirit. Western Christianity has introduced into the Nicene Creed the belief that the Spirit proceeds from the Father *and* the Son (*filioque*), much to the consternation of the Eastern Church. And this remains at issue to this day. Much common ground has been found, however, affirming that the Spirit's relations to Christ in the economy of salvation do express an eternal relation of Spirit and Son. More significantly, a growing sense of disquiet in contemporary theology has developed regarding the adequacy of western accounts of the Spirit as the "bond" of love between the Father and the Son. At the heart of this question lies a concern over the fullness and eternal reality of the Spirit's distinctness from the Father and the Son: those who intend to argue in favor of this emphasize the distinct agency of the Spirit in the biblical accounts and the important role of the Spirit in the continuing growth of the community of disciples through time.[30]

If you were to pursue this question, after appropriate preparations in scripture and the unfolding developments of Christian thought, what paths would you want to explore? Here are a few possibilities:

1 What was Augustine noticing in his depiction of the Spirit as the Father's sheer joy and delight in the Son, and the Son's yearning to do the will of the Father? Does this formulation indeed diminish the Spirit? By what criteria would you go about deciding such a question?

2   Is the Spirit's role in the economy limited to any particular sphere, such as the domain of the people of God, for example? What about Bonaventure's sense of the Spirit as the divine ecstasy, at work throughout the universe bringing *all* things to their consummate form of expression as mirrors of the divine goodness?

3   Or could it be that we only recognize the role of the Spirit throughout creation more broadly as we notice the Spirit's work re-creating the community of Jesus' followers in his likeness? Here you might consider Rowan Williams's intriguing suggestion that the Holy Spirit does not simply make believers present to the Father or the Son but, rather, interprets the relation of the Father and Son "re-creating, *translating* it, in the medium of human existence."[31]

4   As a first theological exercise in pneumatology, what might you say about the role of the divine "breath" in Genesis 1 and the significance of the Gospel of John's "commentary" on this passage in Genesis 1 at John 20: 22 when the crucified and risen Word "breathed" on the disciples and said to them, "Receive the Holy Spirit"?

The problem of "persons"

Probably the next most fundamental issue in contemporary trinitarian theology remains the question of how best to conceive of the Three in God. As we have seen above, the gradual development of a technical terminology in the ancient Christian community permitted believers to affirm their confidence in the eternal distinctness and relationality of the Father, the Son, and the Holy Spirit. But the terms in which these "Three" might be referred to were never sensed as being fully adequate, let along non-negotiable. The essential goal was always to have some commonly accepted term by which to distinguish (like a grammatical rule) the distinct and eternally existing realities of the Source, the Word, and the Spirit. Theologians consistently expressed the conviction that, whatever terminology was used, it should never be understood as referring to the Three in a way that might imply either tri-theism on the one hand or a unitarian modalism (in which the three are only temporary emanations of a prior divine One) on the other hand. So where's the problem?

The difficulty is that, as Catherine LaCugna clearly puts it, "since the Enlightenment 'person' has been understood psychologically rather than ontologically, as 'individual conscious subject.' If God is three persons, God is three centers of consciousness, or three gods."[32] And this obviously is not what the early councils meant to say. In fact, historically speaking, one might even argue (though it would be difficult) that our notions of human personhood and subjectivity originally emerged from the use of this language with respect to the *divine*, the most supremely personal. But the modern Cartesian subject, not to mention its Romantic era dramatization, suggests a self-enclosed ego fundamentally at odds with the Christian understanding of God's primordial self-sharing life. So beyond a careful review of the terminological history and etymological misunderstandings, how would you proceed? Perhaps the most basic question to start with is simply this: what is at stake in having a category or term for speaking about what the Father, Son, and Spirit are? If we were to abandon such a term as person or hypostasis altogether, would theology be in danger of collapsing the Three into a dominating divine substance?

Gender and society

Another contemporary question that gets at the intertwining of our theological language and our cultural self-understanding has to do with the gender and social implications of trinitarian thought. While Christian theology has emphatically highlighted the analogical nature of language for God, it remains the case that exclusively masculine language for God functions in many ways to constrict human reflection on God and to enforce structures of subordination and dominance in human communities.[33] Few have stated both the ethical and the theological problems so well as Elizabeth Johnson:

> Feminist theological analysis makes clear that exclusive, literal, patriarchal speech about God has a twofold negative effect. It fails both human beings and divine mystery. In stereotyping and then banning female reality as suitable metaphor for God, such speech justifies the dominance of men while denigrating the human dignity of women. Simultaneously this discourse so reduces divine mystery to the single, reified metaphor of the ruling man that the symbol itself loses its religious significance and ability to point to ultimate truth. It becomes, in a word, an idol. These two effects are inseparable, for damage to the *imago Dei* in the creature inevitably shortchanges knowledge of the Creator in whose image she is made. Inauthentic ways of treating other human beings go hand-in-glove with falsifications of the idea of God.[34]

The important point to grasp here is not simply that narrowly masculine language for God can be mistakenly taken literally, as though God were a male being, but something a good bit more complex: the fact that feminine imagery for God has had so little voice reflects the social subordination and denigration of women's agency, therefore when narrowly or exclusively masculine language and conceptualities are employed they are never merely neutral but carry within them this social denigration and are, for that very reason, all the more unfit as terms for the divine source of all mutuality, freedom, and flourishing.

A second level of reflection on these questions raises the interesting observation that gender differences and reversals often provide significant analogical bridges to trinitarian differences and relations. A constructive engagement with gender identities might offer a creative way forward in trinitarian thought today. Jesus' motherhood in bringing the Church to birth through the labor of the cross, for example, might point to the Father's motherhood in an eternal bearing of the child Jesus.[35] Besides recovering the variety of gender imagery for God in scripture, how might you bring specifically trinitarian features into this discussion? What new or emancipatory social and gender possibilities might be articulated, for example, by reflection on the co-equality and mutuality of the divine persons of the Trinity as the archetype in whose image humankind is created?

Trinitarian self-abandon and divine suffering

Modern theology has been led by these gender reflections to wonder with some suspicion about the classical conceptions of a self-contained and impassible God; and in light of modernity's overwhelming encounters with massive human suffering, theology has felt compelled to argue that God is not aloof from this pain but in some sense suffers it also, bears it with and in the creatures. Although she argues for God's profound connectedness with creaturely travail, Elizabeth Johnson cautions that "when spoken to women, stress on the powerless suffering of God is particularly dangerous":

> Predicating suffering of God in such a way that suffering becomes a value in itself, or that God becomes essentially weak or powerless, and then holding up this model for emulation is a trap that ensnares women's struggle for equality and full humanity. . . . Structurally subordinated within patriarchy, women are maintained in this position, not liberated, by the image of the God who suffers in utter powerlessness because of love. The ideal of the helpless divine victim serves only to strengthen women's dependency and potential for victimization.[36]

Equally counterproductive, in my view, are those forms of post-Hegelian thought (sometimes called "Process theology") that insist on God's involvement in human suffering so entirely that divinity is in fact only "achieved" as the sum outcome of the process and struggle of history. One should ask whether a god who by definition can only come to godself through the suffering of every innocent victim, whose goodness is only emergent in dialectical response to historical brutalities of unimaginable horror is really coherent with a God of grace and mercy – or whether such a god is, rather, a covert outbreak of ancient pagan divinity, requiring the endless, costly sacrifice of its "fellow sufferers" in order that the ultimate solution to history will be final tranquility.[37] Moreover, the old canard that Christian notions of divine impassibility represent the triumph of Hellenistic metaphysics over the Gospel is truly an irresponsible assertion in light of the historical evidence.[38]

Again, you might want to make your way through these matters by making use of trinitarian theology: rather than conceiving of divine presence in human suffering as the abstract metaphysical either/or of an impassible divine essence or a victimized and ultimately victimizing divinity emergent in the suffering world-process, why not bring the trinitarian relations to bear? Consider, by way of a hint, this text found in notes made by Gerard Manley Hopkins during a retreat in 1881:

> Why did the Son of God go thus forth from the Father not only in the external and intrinsic procession of the Trinity but also by an extrinsic and less than eternal . . . one? To give God glory and that by sacrifice, sacrifice offered in the barren wilderness outside of God, as the children of Israel were led into the wilderness to offer sacrifice. This sacrifice and this outward procession is a consequence and shadow of the procession of the Trinity, from which mystery sacrifice takes its rise. . . . It is as if the blissful agony or stress of selving in God had forced out drops of sweat or blood, which drops were the world, or as if the lights lit at the festival of the "peaceful Trinity" through some little cranny striking out lit up into being one "cleave" out of the world of possible creatures.[39]

Perhaps the poetic imagination of Hopkins allows him to catch sight of a crucial analogy. In this passage he considers the world's creation and, by extension, its fulfillment through the Incarnation and self-offering of Christ; but he sees these temporal realities as radiant with passion, as though he glimpses burning within them the primordial fire of an eternal act of self-offering, self-sharing: the very life of the Persons of the Trinity.[40] In other words, when confronted with a stark reality like the suffering of the world, trinitarian theology invites the theologian not simply to pose Creator and creatures against each other (such that God or creatures become assimilated to each other in some historical process), but rather to consider whether there is not something "going on" eternally in the trinitarian life – quite apart from creation – that has in Christ and the Spirit been translated into earthly history.

So if you were going to strike a path through this range of issues, here are some leading questions that might guide you:

1 When in doubt, start with the historical events of Christ and the Spirit. If the question arises, "How is God present to human suffering?" then what response does the story of Jesus suggest?
2 If you accept the idea that God is present to human suffering and alienation in Jesus, what happens when you re-imagine Jesus' story in terms of the fullness of its trinitarian dimensions?
3 If Jesus offers himself in love and freedom to humanity and humanity rejects and destroys him, but the Father raises Jesus in the power of the Spirit, what does this suggest about God's presence and response to human suffering?
4 Now consider what goes on between Jesus and the Father in their Spirit, on the cross and in the resurrection and at Pentecost. What does this pattern of sending, self-giving, and radical affirmation suggest about the eternal patterns of relation within the Trinity? What "takes place" eternally within the life of

the Trinity that could be the condition for the possibility (a) of Jesus' presence to humanity in its suffering and (b) of his life beyond the grip of death?

5   Feminist theologians have cautioned against ascribing to Jesus or to God a merely passive victimization that would seem to legitimate the "value" of suffering in and of itself. How would re-conceiving the Jesus' participation in suffering *in terms of trinitarian theology* draw insight from this feminist concern? Could one conceive Jesus' earthly suffering not as passive victimization but as the active expression in historical terms of that eternal freedom-for-the-other which is the ground of his identity in relation to the Father and Spirit?

Relationality: being and human being

Perhaps the most far-reaching issue in contemporary trinitarian thought is the question of relationality. The doctrine of the Trinity teaches that God, at the heart of all reality, is an endlessly abundant event of communion, of relational self-sharing in love and freedom. What are the implications of this for our concepts of existence (or being) per se and particularly for the human being whom Christians believe is created in the image of the Trinity? These questions arise presently against a very dynamic background of discussion about the lineaments of post-modernity. In particular, questions have been raised (usually associated with the German philosopher Martin Heidegger, 1889–1976)[41] about the nature of "being" and what we might mean philosophically and theologically when we say that something "is," and also about the nature of human personhood and whether the post-Cartesian and post-Kantian conception of the self is at all lifelike or life-giving. Before considering the "relationality" question in contemporary trinitarian theology, it will be helpful to say more about these current discussions of being (ontology) and personhood.

First the question of being. Suppose you thought, as most Christians throughout history have, that the finite existence of creatures depends upon a more radical kind of existing – an infinite, endlessly resourceful, inexhaustibly beautiful act of existing, whom we might call "God" – and that the creatures come to exist just because God shares with them, in a finite, reflected way, this divine act of existing. This would mean that the sheer fact that creatures exist, moment by moment, is a sign in finite terms of the *infinite* act of existing – who is God. Thus we might even say that, in a dependent sort of way, the being of creatures is analogous, even sacramental or symbolic in various ways, of the being of God from which the creatures spring every millisecond of their existence.[42]

Two corollaries immediately arise: (1) As Thomas Aquinas remarks over and over, the fact that the universe exists tells us *that* there must be One who is the sheer act of existence itself, but this tells us absolutely nothing about *what* the existence or being of this One is like; we know nothing of the "essence" or "substance" of God. As the sheer act of existing itself, God's existence is not just more plentiful or more powerful than our existence but otherwise the same sort of "stuff." (2) We are dealing with, if you like, Existence and "existence," real divine Existence and a kind of fragile, finite *sign* of this divine Existence, the fragile, finite sign being what we call creaturely "existence." The point is that we go around talking about existence as *we* know it, but of course our kind of existence only exists at all as a sort of finite reflection of something altogether beyond ourselves. God, in other words, is not in competition with us for being and has somehow managed to get more of it than we have. Let me try to clarify this with a parallel: imagine a novelist and the characters in her novel. The novelist has a very real existence of course, and, in a way, so do her characters. Yet we recognize that their "existence," their "being," is really only *analogous* to the actual existence of their author: they "exist" in a novel that she holds in being through her artistry and invention, and so their "being" is entirely dependent upon, and echoes, the very real being of their author. Christians believe that the "existence" of creatures is similarly analogous to the real existence of their divine Author, parallel to the way the "existence" of characters in a novel is analogous to the real existence of the novelist. Certainly the "being" of creatures is in no way a lesser *amount* of the *same* being as God's. Interestingly, this analogical or symbolic quality of finite creaturely existence, pointing in its fashion to its Creator's divine existence, bestows upon creaturely existence great beauty. The creatures, in their sheer existence precisely as creatures, luminously evoke the mysterious ground from which they spring, so resonant are they with the echoes of that divine Word by which they are at every moment called into existence. It is for this reason that the creatures can, simply by the wonderfully particular events of existence they are, reflect each in their own way the glory of God.

Now various forms of postmodern thought have pointed out that at some point in the history of western thought (when is a matter of debate), the notion of creaturely being and of divine being came to be thought of within the same category, simply as, so to speak, finite and infinite extensions of the same substance. Thus our analogical way of thinking about "being" shifted, without our realizing it, into a *univocal* understanding of being – and at the very same time, inevitably, into a reified notion of being as some sort of stuff or substance, rather than as an act or event.[43] In this view, there is simply some kind of basic stuff that God has infinitely more of and we have less of. Devout theologians worked frantically throughout early modernity to preserve a hallowed precinct, "supernatural" being, where God could still be thought of as existing without interfering with, or coming under the critical eye of, finite natural being. This entirely extrinsic supernatural deity sets the creation going in good order but politely remains beyond it. And by the late Romantic era, this aloof imperturbable deity was felt to be either a pernicious fantasy and projection of humanity's own frustrated ambitions, or else a being who ought now to be re-conceived as immanent within the suffering process of history. The upshot of this story of being in modernity is that many of us, theologians and philosophers alike, feel that somewhere what is actually meant by "existence" has been lost to view.

Some thinkers such as Jacques Derrida would say that the whole story of being has been illusory, the grasping of human minds for manipulative control of reality in conceptual terms. Several theological schemes of "deconstructive" theology have been developed along these lines, soberly eschewing any talk of being, ontology, metaphysics, or presence beyond the sheer void of unsaying, erasure, and deferral of meaning. But other thinkers such as Jean-Luc Marion or, in a somewhat different way, John Milbank, Catherine Pickstock, Graham Ward, and others would say that the being which Heidegger decried (as a mere substance masquerading as infinite reality) was never, in fact, what the classic traditions of Christian theology were talking about when speaking of God.[44] Therefore, in this view (and I would judge it to be largely correct), it would make sense for theology today to advance by a fresh discussion of analogy, of the mysterious giving to creatures of their existence, and of the transcendence of divine life by which God – as the infinitely giving source of every creature – is more intimately present to each creature than they could be to themselves.

And one crucial way forward in this direction could be to re-frame the discussion within a trinitarian framework. For if the infinite act of existence, who is God, were an act of free self-bestowal, a generous and loving eternal decision of the three divine Persons to be-for-the-other – if this is what constitutes the divine act of existence, rather than some necessary outcome of the divine "nature" – then we have a whole new context for considering being. An outspoken exponent of this view, John Zizioulas, proposes that ontology (the discussion about being) be re-framed in terms of the free act of relating to the other that constitutes God's life. While some might feel he overstates his case, he nonetheless raises the issue very clearly:

> The ground of God's ontological freedom lies not in His nature but in His personal existence. . . . The manner in which God exercises His ontological freedom, that precisely which makes Him ontologically free, is the way in which He transcends and abolishes the ontological necessity of the substance by being God as *Father*, that is, as He who "begets" the Son and "brings forth" the Spirit. This ecstatic character of God, the fact that His being is identical with an act of communion, ensures the transcendence of the ontological necessity which His substance would have demanded – if the substance were the primary ontological predicate of God – and replaces this necessity with the free self-affirmation of divine existence. For this communion is a product of freedom as a result not of the substance of God but of a person, the Father – observe why this doctrinal detail is so important – who is Trinity not because the divine *nature* is ecstatic but because the Father as a *person* freely wills this communion.[45]

Here Zizioulas clearly proposes the mystery of the Trinity as the ground of an entirely non-objectifiable act of existence, whose freedom and love are concomitant with existence. This would also mean that ontology could get beyond any notion of being conceived of as a sort of stuff or substance – for we would be talking of being or, better, the act of existence, as always and only a free act of relation with the other, an event of communion. And this would of course prevent us from conceiving of the divine existence as somehow simply more of our own, but would open up once more the space for analogical perception and imagination to flourish.

This has direct implications for Christian anthropology. If the ground of every creature's existence is an eternal event of being-for-the-other, then all creatures might bear an analogical impulse towards interaction and mutual involvement. However, feminist theology points out quite rightly that it would be ironic if trinitarian relationality were deployed in questions of theological anthropology in ways that perpetuated the effacing of women's selfhood instead of re-conceiving agency as relational for all creatures.[46] Also in apparent congruity with trinitarian developments, modern science has shown more and more awareness of the profound interrelatedness of every dimension of the environment and, at the most basic level of reality we can study, the quantum level, of something remarkably analogous to relationality. For creatures with noticeable levels of freedom and intelligence, this being-for-the-other comes yet more to image the trinitarian life, for intelligent creatures have the freedom to choose loving the other.[47] In such ways, contemporary trinitarian reflection might well turn out to be a central shaping factor in theology's approach to metaphysics, the understanding of the environment, and of the human person. To offer you a little further company on your own pathfinding in these areas, I'll conclude this chapter on the Trinity with an example of how trinitarian theology might inform our understanding of human persons in relation to God.

The Trinity and Mystical Participation in God

Now here is one last pathfinding expedition, a way to see how trinitarian thinking might open outwards. Few acts could be more central to Christianity than what believers think of as sharing in Christ's dying and rising. This is understood as the reality identified sacramentally in baptism and it extends ever more profoundly, Christians believe, towards a mutual indwelling of the believer in Christ and of the Trinity in the life of the believer (see, e.g., John 14: 23). What light can trinitarian reflection shed on this fundamental companionship with Christ?[48]

In the remarkable closing lines of his *Journey of the Mind to God*, the great Franciscan theologian Bonaventure (*c*.1217–74) radically transforms the classical contemplative ascent of the mind by re-contextualizing it within the paschal mystery. Elucidating the experiences of Francis of Assisi, Bonaventure showed that the ultimate goal of the mind's journey is not simply a silent beholding of truth but a passing over from this life to a wholly other existence by way of the cross. It would, unfortunately, be easy enough to find examples in the history of Christian spirituality of passion mysticism gone awry, either grown self-involved, mesmerized by covert dramas of self-despising, or on the other hand, grown into a manipulative tool of the powerful over the marginalized, endlessly legitimizing their suffering and enforcing their oppression. Bonaventure, by contrast, sees the passion as deliverance and transition into the unimaginable reality of God, into the liberating truth of endless goodness endlessly bestowed. In the spiritual journey, says Bonaventure, the mind can advance through many degrees, but its final stage is not simply a yet more costly moment of "advance" by suffering, a self-annihilation which somehow wins a more refined vision of truth. No, the mind must "transcend and pass over, not only this visible world, but even itself" (VII. 1).[49] Bonaventure does not admonish the soul to attempt a more rigorous suffering in imitation of the suffering Jesus; rather, he advocates that we gaze upon the mystery of the Father's love hidden in Jesus on the cross, and beholding this unutterable mercy, be set free; "such a one celebrates the Pasch, that is, the Passover, with Him. Thus, using the rod of the Cross, he may pass over the Red Sea, going from Egypt into the desert, where it is given to him to taste the hidden manna" (VII. 2). What is the goal of this journey from slavery into new life? "With Christ crucified, let us pass out of this world to the Father, so that, when the Father is shown to us, we may say with Philip: It is enough for us" (VII. 6).

Bonaventure's trinitarian vision of the passion allows him to hold Christ's suffering open to the mystery of the Father. In so doing he restores to Christian spirituality the deep relational grammar of Christ's passion, and sets spirituality free from temptations to solipsistic self-absorption. Also because he emphasizes this trinitarian dimension, he undercuts a toxic counter-spirituality of self-denigration or oppression; the cross is not a brutal constraint, forever immuring suffering persons or groups into their status, for it is the rod and staff of the free pilgrim who is called to journey on into immeasurable bounty, to the hidden manna of true life and the liberty of the ever greater Father.

Bonaventure also emphasized the role of the Holy Spirit in passion mysticism. Indeed the Seraphic Doctor ascribes to the Holy Spirit that intense stirring of love that he so prizes in contemplating the passion. The Spirit is the true agent who effects within the believer the passover to the Source which Christ accomplishes on the cross. No one receives this "mystical and most secret" transformation into divine life "except him who desires it, and no one desires it except he who is penetrated to the marrow by the fire of the Holy Spirit" (VII. 4). Later, Bonaventure remarks that God *is* this fire and that "Christ enkindles it in the white flame of His most burning Passion" (VII. 6). Christ's passionate desire to do the will of the one who sent him bursts into full flame on the cross, and Bonaventure reveals the secret name of this fire to be the Holy Spirit. In making this identification, I suggest, the Franciscan again brings to light the fully trinitarian nature of the passion and its consequent capacity to enkindle the same fire within the believing community. This trinitarian ground for passion mysticism delivers it from any tendency toward a privatizing individualism or emotionalism, for the yearning of those who contemplate the cross is never simply their own feeling, their own possession, but rather the communal, relational passion of the Holy Spirit at work throughout time and space.

Not only, I'm suggesting, does the Holy Spirit open a spirituality of the passion to an ever fuller relational and communal depth; the Spirit also awakens new voice and agency within those drawn into the mystery of Christ's incarnation and passion. In other words, this trinitarian dimension within spirituality preserves it from collapsing inward either into a divine monism in which the soul is simply annihilated (with all the dangerous potentials for quietism, passivity, or even the legitimizing of an abusive condition) or into a peculiar form of idealism in which the "divine" metamorphoses into a mere cipher for the most exalted forms of human narcissism. Recovering the agency of the Holy Spirit in passion mysticism reveals in a gracious light the "space," the room for alterity and authentic human agency, even in that most intimate union of self-giving marked by sharing in the cross. The Carmelite mystical doctor, John of the Cross (1542–91) explores this theme most keenly, perhaps especially in the *Spiritual Canticle*.[50] After observing how Christ communicates to the soul the "sweet mysteries of his Incarnation and of the ways of the redemption" (23. 1), John says that from this "espousal made on the cross" (23. 6) the soul's relationship with Christ the bridegroom grows gradually onward towards an unimaginable depth.[51]

As John unfolds the mysteriousness of this growing union, he brings to light the important sense in which the soul is gifted with the desire of the Spirit, not so as to take the place of the soul but rather to strengthen it for real agency of its own within the infinite self-sharing of divine existence. "The soul's aim is a love equal to God's. She always desired this equality, naturally and supernaturally, for a lover cannot be satisfied if he fails to feel that he loves as much as he is loved" (38. 3). Significantly, John envisions a new identity and voice for the soul, an identity no longer conceivable in terms of either subordination or rivalry but of equality, a relational identity whose selfhood and agency is constituted by receiving all and giving all freely from the other. And of course, for John, this developing identity of the soul springs directly from the trinitarian pattern of life in which it is increasingly participating. This means that the soul will know and love God by sharing in God's knowing and loving of God, and yet, precisely because of the trinitarian space for genuine otherness in God, this knowing and loving in which the soul participates will also be truly the soul's own.

> As her intellect will be the intellect of God, her will then will be God's will, and thus her love will be God's love. The soul's will is not destroyed there, but it is so firmly united with the strength of God's will, with which He loves her, that her love for Him is as strong and perfect as His love for her. . . . This strength lies in the Holy Spirit, in Whom the soul is there transformed. (38. 3)

John interestingly highlights both the soul's own desire and the need for the soul to have a strength of its own so as to love God as much as the soul desires. We might think here of the role ascribed to the Spirit in the gospels, sending Jesus into the wilderness to discover yet more deeply the authenticity and truth of his desire to do the will of the one who sent him.

Interpreting passion spirituality in this trinitarian light points to a healthy form of spiritual self-surrender, a self-sharing enacted out of a growing freedom and authority to love with a strength (given by the Spirit) that is both beyond oneself and yet increasingly one's own. John emphasizes that God does not simply give the soul the divine love, but that "He will show her how to love Him as perfectly as she desires. . . . As if he were to put an instrument in her hands and show her how it works by operating it jointly with her, He shows her how to love and gives her the ability to do so" (38. 4). The soul's apprenticeship does not infantilize but empowers a voice fully enfranchised by the trinitarian making space for the other. Discerning the relational-trinitarian role of the Holy Spirit holds spirituality open to this paradoxical freedom.

This section should have given you a sense of how I, at least, would think the theology of the Trinity might be advanced in new ways, precisely by bringing it to bear on questions whose deep trinitarian substructure has not always been made apparent. Before you turn to the next and final chapter, you may like to make a provisional list for yourself of questions and topics in which trinitarian "pathfinding" might be of considerable help in finding a way forward: e.g., the meaning of freedom? theology of culture? theology and poetics?

————— Chapter 7 —————

Creaturely Life: A Journey towards Beatitude

ORIENTATION

Throughout this book, we have been trying to think about theology by taking seriously the idea that only God can really teach theology – at least "theology" in the deepest sense of sharing in God's own triune understanding of God. In the first part of the book we considered what that would mean for theologians themselves, and how God's teaching might happen to them. Then turning to the particular teachings that Christians have come to believe, we began with the mystery of salvation because that is the most definitive form (Christians believe) of God's teaching. As we then saw in Chapter 6, this divine teaching (in the form of salvation) has over the centuries led believers deeper and deeper into its wellspring in God's own life: what they take to be the eternally blessed and ecstatic life of the Trinity.

Now in *this* chapter we conclude the theological journey by trying to catch sight of God's creatures as they themselves fare forth on "pilgrimage": from their eternal state of being known and loved in the Trinity through their finite creaturely existence in time. Christians believe that the same love which has eternally cherished the creatures also draws the human family into the death and resurrection of Christ, and so into Jesus' own human participation in God's joy: the beatitude of trinitarian life. So from humanity's saving encounter with God in Christ, we have followed a theological trajectory "up" into God's trinitarian life, and now we follow the creatures' flowing forth and return to God through Christ and the Spirit.

Because we are trying to consider all this in terms of how God teaches it, we are holding together a number of elements that often get treated quite separately in academic theology: creation, revelation, human existence, the Church and the life of grace, eschatology, to name only some of the most central issues. By way of analogy, in our own lives we sometimes experience the various times and seasons of life, when we're in the midst of them, as a confusing welter of discrete, seemingly unrelated, and often contradictory moments; so too theology can tend to isolate various "moments" of creaturely life and thus grow a little deaf to the divine themes that harmonize them into one great diverse music. Yet the goal of theological wisdom is to see things not just in themselves but in the full context of their source and goal in God. The mysteries of salvation and of trinitarian life teach theologians to understand creatures this way, as springing from the joy of the trinitarian communion and created to enter into that joy.

Death No Longer Has Dominion:
Creation's Path in the Light of Easter

As ever, we begin where Christians believe God teaches most definitively by speaking the Word in the life of Christ, and consummating that speaking by raising Jesus from the dead through the power of the Spirit. In other words, what can we learn about the creatures by considering the one creature whom God has united to divine life? Suppose we took John's portrait of Jesus and worked out the correlation between what's going on in Jesus and what might be true for creatures more generally. Thus, we notice that Jesus sensed his human destiny to be entirely fulfilled in coming from the One he called Father and in returning to the Father; and, likewise, to be a creature is to come from God and to return to God. For Jesus, teaching and doing the will of the One who sent him was not in conflict with his humanity but his very food and life; analogously, creatures are most themselves in being true signs of their source, revelatory of divine meaning and purpose. Jesus could not have been who he was without Mary and Joseph to love him, and, later, the disciples to teach, the hungry to feed, and the broken-hearted to console; in a similar way, creatures are never themselves alone but in relation, particularly in relation with a community of others who summon the greatest and deepest truths of their being into actuality.

Yet you might say, "But all these things about Jesus are true in virtue of his being the incarnate Word, God the Son existing humanly." Fair enough, I'd reply, but don't forget that being the *incarnate* Word is exactly the point. Jesus incarnates the truth of the One who loves him precisely by being fully the human being he is, being fully a creature. And it is from his fully realized creatureliness, Christians believe, that we can learn the truth about creatures. The problem is that some of the creatures, at least those with freedom and intelligence, seem very often not to want to risk the full calling of their creaturely life. Mountains and roses, water beetles and bears all carry on with being their remarkable creaturely selves. But humans (and some angels) seem haunted by the knowledge of their own finitude. The fact of limitation and death mesmerizes and stunts their creaturely flourishing into a distorted, self-aggrandizing, and fearful rivalry with each other and even with God; death does indeed seem to have and to be the last word about them, for everything they do is calculated in terms of death – the death they fear and the death they mete out to others.

That's exactly why it is so crucial to reflect theologically about the whole sweep of creaturely existence through the lens of Christ and the Spirit; for the general story that creation wants to tell itself about itself is far too often a lying, lethal spell of tragic but supposedly unavoidable outcomes. Among these mendacious accounts of created existence we might name the following. (1) Material reality, and the body and sexuality in particular, are evil and to be escaped, or are without final meaning and are thus to be used indifferently or possessively; or else, materiality and the body are all there is to reality and are therefore the fitting objects of our most desperate obsessions. (2) Or again, the only "truth" about things and about persons is finally determined by the powerful and the violent, who seem to hold the power of death and its minion, fear, over others. (3) Evil is somehow inevitable or an inescapable and necessary part of the divine order of creation. (4) Death is the worst thing that could ever happen to us but we can somehow stave off its menace to us or those whom we love if we have enough money or control over things. (5) The future is ultimately fearful and without hope, an annihilation that mocks every relationship or achievement as futile.[1] Just analyzing the world and nature as they now appear could easily suggest the validity of any or all of these perspectives. Their hypnotic power derives from many fears, shadows of death made the more seductively ominous by the power that persons and whole civilizations have wielded in their witting or unwitting enslavement to the power of violence and death.

Because of this lying and deceitful dominion of death over humanity, it is not really possible to understand creation or its destiny truthfully apart from Jesus' passion and death, or apart from his resurrection by the Father in the power of the Spirit. Thus the Letter to the Hebrews insists that the eternal Word became incarnate in human existence precisely "so that through death he might destroy the one who has the power of death, that is, the devil, and free those who all their lives were held in slavery by the fear of death" (2: 14–15). How, exactly, Jesus' death and resurrection frees humanity, and what it teaches us about the journey of the creatures – this is where we must begin. First, then, a word about the paschal mystery as the liberation of creation, and then an overview of the truth this makes known (a) about the act of creation, (b) about the creatures' calling to share in trinitarian beatitude, and (c) about the journey of the creatures in this world towards their consummation in God.

The contemporary theologian James Alison, in his innovative development of Girardian thought (see Chapter 5), portrays Jesus' self-giving in death as a setting of creation into labor, so that the truth and fullness of creation might finally come to birth.

> When in John 16: 20–21, Jesus uses the language of a woman in labor to describe his going to his death, John places in his mouth the same metaphor which Paul uses to describe the whole of creation in travail, through the persecutions which bring to

light the children of God (Rom. 8: 18–23). Jesus' self-giving up to death *is* the fulfillment of creation, the putting of creation into a state of labor, so that we also, by our creative imitation of him in the midst of the order of death can come to be the fully created creatures which God always wanted us to be, and with us, the whole of creation. It is because of this that Jesus' last word before his death in John's Gospel is *tetelestai*: it is accomplished, it has been brought to fulfillment. This means *that creation itself has been brought to fulfillment by his self-giving up to death in order to open up for us a creative way by which we may come to participate fully in creation*. It can be understood, then, why the resurrection happens on the first day of the week, in the garden. Creation has started again, a creation in which the tomb is empty.[2]

Alison argues here that Jesus' refusal to be cowed and dominated by the fear of death is the consummate expression (in the sort of world we have made) of his abundant life, his willingness to become fully the human creature God sent him to be. By doing so, Jesus breaks open a cleft in the prison that death has made of life, a way for others also not to be dominated by the fear of death. Throughout his life, Jesus has received his being entirely as a gift from the One whom he calls Father, and his creaturely humanity expresses this divine generosity by means of an analogous self-bestowal and lavishness throughout his ministry: as seen for example in the miraculous abundance of the feedings and fish-catchings, the prodigal vivacity of the healings (and raisings from death), the mysterious expansiveness of the parables about growth beyond all expectations. All these aspects of Jesus' life and work bear witness to the freedom from death-driven fear that animates his existence. Jesus' work and teaching are far too wonderfully alive and generously life-giving to be crippled or dominated by mortality and its shadows of deprivation and envy. This contending between life and death reaches its climax in Jesus' death and resurrection.

In John's Gospel Jesus speaks of this conflict in terms of the false and the true shepherds of creaturely existence: "The thief comes only to steal and kill and destroy. I came that they may have life, and have it abundantly. I am the good shepherd. The good shepherd lays down his life for the sheep" (10: 10–11). The power of death, which terrorizes the creatures, is undone by Jesus who pours out life so abundantly and seems to command and authorize its overflowing availability so freely, that death simply has no more dominion over him:

> For this reason the Father loves me, because I lay down my life in order to take it up again. No one takes it from me, but I lay it down of my own accord. I have power to lay it down, and I have power to take it up again. I have received this command from my Father. (John 10: 17–18)

In this remarkable passage, Jesus' authority is truly that of one who authors, one who has the creative source of life at his command: no one takes life from him but he lays it down in generous love and trust and he takes it up again. And yet even as Jesus is portrayed as authoring life, we also see that he does so as an expression of the Father's own creative authority as the very source of life.

This is quite important, for were it thought that Jesus' suffering and death were primarily a punishment that the Father required of him in order to forgive us, then, once again, death would have insinuated itself into the creative work of God as somehow necessary and inevitable. But Jesus in John calls death a thief and the devil a liar; they have no genuine authority, no rightful dominion, over creation. I am arguing, then, that the Father's "command" to Jesus is to fulfill creation by being completely and fearlessly human, to do so not by the aggression and anxious rivalry with which death has infected life, but by a love so alive to God's endless resource that it is truly stronger than death. In this way, following Alison, we can see how the risen Jesus, pouring out this Spirit of generous love, sets in motion a movement unleashing creation's completion and fullness, its liberation from death's dreadful perversion of life. John points directly to this fulfilling, consummating, role of Jesus' death: at 13: 1–2 he writes that "before the festival of the Passover, Jesus knew that his hour had come to depart from this world and go to the Father. Having loved his own who were in the world, he loved them to the end (*telos*)"; and this same *telos*-language, as Alison notes, is used at the climactic moment of the passion (John 19: 30), when Jesus at the moment of death says, "It is finished (*tetelestai*)." The *tel-* root in both passages points to idea of Jesus' loving self-giving as fulfilling and bringing to completion the work of creation. It is no coincidence, I think, that John has Mary Magdalene mistake the risen Jesus for "the gardener" on the first day of the week, when she rushes to the garden where she thought him bound by death (John 20: 15). Jesus is indeed the primordial "gardener," the creative Word of the Garden of Eden, who is Life himself and gives life and through whom all life has come into being (John 1: 3–4).

But why does God not seem to have been satisfied with teaching only through the life and death of the incarnate Word? What does the resurrection add? It might be that, apart from the resurrection, Jesus' life and death would always remain in the past, an example for each generation to imitate as well as it can. Nonetheless, Jesus would have made, simply by his life and death, the consummate expression of self-giving, and creation could not have hoped for more than such an example of loving freedom. Therefore I think we have to understand the resurrection of Jesus as being utterly gratuitous, a sign within earthly terms of that mysteriously ecstatic goodness which is God's own life, and which we can only call "grace." So what God teaches by raising Christ from the dead is the sheer gratuity of the act of creation, its unboundedness by death, and its freedom from the constraints or necessities of any pre-existing conditions. What I'm suggesting here is that the resurrection of Christ from the dead is the definitive framework for thinking about the mystery of creation.

Just as the resurrection of Jesus is not simply a resuscitation of a corpse but the beginning of an utterly new form of creaturely sharing in God's life, so also the creation is not simply a re-arranging of matter but its bringing into existence out of nothing (*ex nihilo*). The crucified but risen Jesus is not simply a reversal of death for a time, or a re-ordering of things; the resurrection is, rather, the revelation to creatures of the Creator's authority to bring into existence that which is not. After all, none of us were present at the beginning of creation; so in raising Christ God reveals a glimpse of what the act of creation is like; and as it appears within the time and space of our world, it looks like the startling and heartbreaking appearance of one whom you love, alive, overflowingly alive, quite beyond all the power of death to contain him.

It is for this reason, I think, that Paul found himself pondering the conjunction of creation out of nothing and resurrection from the dead. In a moving consideration of Abraham and Sarah, whose lives seemed to have been running down to death, Paul is drawn to wonder about the authority and freedom that could bestow upon them an utterly unexpected life, a bestowal consummated in the resurrection of Christ. What happens to Abraham, says Paul, happens as a sheer act of grace, an act that Abraham and Sarah can only receive in faith; it is not the natural development or outcome or modification in any way of their own lives or efforts; it is out of nowhere, it is a life beyond death. And that is who God really is: the one "who gives life to the dead and calls into existence the things that do not exist" (Romans 4: 17). For the early followers of Jesus, the resurrection seemed to have been a revelation of God's gracious freedom to bring life into being. In this way, as they encountered the risen Jesus through the outpouring of the Spirit, they began to understand the truth about creation: that creation is something God brings about freely and as a bestowal of grace. This would mean that God's freedom, grace, and love for each creature are the deepest truth about *every* creature no matter what lies or distortions may overtake it in this world. Thus the whole creation is purely good and springs directly and immediately from God's own existence and not from any prior conditions or material that God merely re-orders; rather, God's loving authority over creation extends far more deeply and imperishably than death would like us think.

Again, James Alison draws these themes together in an especially clarifying way:

> Here is the central point: we understand creation starting from and through Jesus. God's graciousness, which brings what is not into existence from nothing, is exactly the same thing as Jesus' death-less self-giving out of love which enables him to break the human culture of death and is a self-giving entirely fixed on bringing into being a radiantly living and exuberant culture. It is not as if creation were a different act, something which happened alongside the salvation worked by Jesus, but rather that the salvation which Jesus was working was, at the same time, the fulfillment of creation. This was the power and authority in Jesus' works and words and signs. Through him the Creator was bringing his work to completion. The act of creation was revealed for what it really is: the bringing into existence and making possible of a human living together which does not know death.[3]

Alison already points us here toward the implications of understanding creation through the lens of Christ's dying and rising: (1) how creation comes from God, (2) what is its true destiny, and (3) how we are meant to live in this world so as to participate in bringing it to fulfillment in the new creation. We can gather the full fruit if this consideration of Jesus' death and resurrection if we look briefly at each of these three.

First, creation has its ground in the processions or forth-faring of the Word and the Spirit from the Father. The resurrection gives us an image in time of this, for there Jesus' humanity is caught up radiantly in the eternal Sonship and in the eternal rejoicing of the Spirit which are the very ground of his being. Paul writes that Jesus "was declared to be Son of God with power according to the Spirit of holiness by resurrection from the dead" (Romans 1: 4). As one biblical scholar remarks: "The Resurrection brought Christ wholly to birth in the life of the Son, extending to his whole being the glory of his eternal generation."[4] We might say that the resurrection makes the sign, within the constraints of this world, of that eternal flowing forth of the Persons of the Trinity, showing us that this is the very wellspring of unbounded life, of grace, and so, of creaturely existence. The revelation of this trinitarian ground is crucial to understanding creation rightly, for it discloses the true status of each creature and its fundamental orientation towards God. In a very intriguing passage from the *Summa Theologiae* on the Persons of the Trinity (I. 32. 1), Thomas Aquinas shows the difference it makes when we see the creatures, so to speak, as transparent to their trinitarian ground; in fact he says that the revelation of the Trinity was "necessary for the right idea of creation."[5] Here is Thomas on the left and my commentary in the right hand column.

The fact of saying that God made all things by His Word excludes the error of those who say that God produced things by necessity.

The coming to be of all things in and through the eternal Word, suggests Thomas, means that all creatures exist through an infinite act of freedom and intelligence. God does not emanate creatures the way a boiling pot emanates steam, because it cannot help it! Rather at the heart of every creature is an eternal flowing of wisdom and rationality. This is the very reason why creation is itself "reason-able," intelligible and full of meaning rather than merely chaotic or random, and why intelligent creatures can think about things and find that they make sense.

When we say that in Him there is a procession of love [the breathing forth of the Holy Spirit], we show that God produced creatures not because He needed them, nor because of any extrinsic reason, but on account of the love of His own goodness.

The eternal procession of the Holy Spirit, which Thomas, following Augustine, likens to the flowing of love that animates and rejoices in the event of knowing (which is the procession of the Son) also crucially marks each creature. In this case the fact that each creature flows from the procession of love or Holy Spirit means that it is grounded in an eternal event of loving desire and free giving. Creatures don't just happen spontaneously, nor are they in any way necessary to God, but rather God delights to call them into being, as Thomas puts it, "on account of the love of His own goodness." Each creature exists because it flows from God's eternal delight, and as such it exists gratuitously, freely, as an act of grace that expresses God's own goodness.

So Moses, when he had said "In the beginning God created heaven and earth," subjoined, "God said, 'Let there be light,'" to manifest the divine Word; and then said, "God saw the light that it was good," to show the proof of the divine love. The same is also found in the other works of creation.

Thomas upholds the traditional view that all the works of the Trinity in the economy of time and space are works of all the divine persons acting in concert; nonetheless, as we can see here, he also emphasizes that the creatures are each grounded in the eternal processions of the divine Persons. We see the intelligibility and formal pattern (or rational structure) of each creature as an echo of the procession of the Word and the goodness and gratuity of each creature as a reflection in time of the procession of the Spirit. By adding at the end that "the same is also found in the other works of creation," we might see Thomas as pointing us to certain ineradicable features of every creature's existence: it exists not because God was constrained in some way by pre-existing matter but rather as a free act, created *ex nihilo*; it exists with a deep meaning and truth given it by God; it exists as cherished and delighted in by God.

Jesus' death and resurrection also points "forward," to the beatific destiny of creation. We have just been looking through the resurrection of Christ "backwards," so to speak, in order to catch a glimpse of the origin of the creatures in God's processions of knowing and loving; but we can also look from the resurrection towards the goal of creation. In his resurrection, Jesus no longer lives by means of the mortal, biological life that flows in creatures through their finite existence. Instead he lives directly from the infinite giving life of God, over which death has no dominion, and, as we've just been seeing, that gives us a kind of sacrament or glimpse of the infinite giving at work in creation. But the very same resurrection life also gives us a glimpse of what it is like for creatures as they are taken up forever into that infinite abundance of trinitarian joy or beatitude. Jesus' own human sense of God's ultimate faithfulness and gracious love sustained him in the face of death's terrors and threatenings, and it is the final vision of this blessedness of God, this beatitude, that brings creation to its consummate state.

The Letter to the Hebrews focuses our attention on this vision of God's glory that animated Christ so entirely: "who for the sake of the joy that was set before him endured the cross, disregarding its shame, and has taken his seat at the right hand of the throne of God" (12: 2). Our trinitarian reflections suggest to us that we might fruitfully interpret the joy Hebrews speaks of as the joy who is the Holy Spirit, the Father's delighted response to the goodness and truthfulness of the Word incarnate. The resurrection of Jesus does by no means depend upon his humanity being somehow left behind, but upon God's authority as the Creator to bring creaturely existence to live directly from and with the life of God. Therefore by showing (in the resurrection) the victory of Christ which he accomplished in his self-giving, the Father intends to teach about the destiny of creatures as they are united to Christ, and so come to share in his glory, his life lived directly in the presence of God.

Third, and finally, in his dying and rising Jesus not only reveals the truth about creation's origin and about its destiny but also about its transforming life in this world. James Alison draws on Jesus' sense of being from and for the Father, so central to John's vision of Jesus, as a crucial clue. Alison considers how Jesus' relation to the Father might be seen as the basis of the creation's becoming, but also how this relation might become woven, transformingly, into the relations of this world, in order to re-create them as an image of the triune communion:

> Jesus is aware of having been sent by the Father. That is, his condition as a human being is the creative making present of the eternal generation of the Son. His self-giving up to death is the exact image of the creative self-giving between Father and Son which eternally brings forth the Holy Spirit. So he is aware that his living out his life toward death in obedience to the Father is exactly his sending of the Holy Spirit: the making present in the conditions of humanity of the creative love between Father and Son in such a way that it can be participated in by human beings. It is therefore his whole life, going to his death, which brings about the concrete praxis by which humans will be enabled to participate in the Holy Spirit. This means our breaking out of the negative, destructive mimesis (in its violently structured forms) in which we live and our beginning to enter into the creative construction of diversity that is a dynamic reflection of God.[6]

Cross and resurrection create a new pattern of relations that can be filled and made fruitful by the Spirit of divine abundance and life, a way of handing over the community of this world to the creative power of God. In this sense, the Day of Pentecost, when the Spirit pours out within the life of the early followers of Jesus, may be seen as the sign of Christ's self-giving – from and for the Father – beginning to animate a communal personhood, gathering people of enormous diversity, and yet filling each with the story of Christ in ways that rejoice and re-create them. The life of the Christian community, as a life of grace, is intended to be a sign of this possibility of new creation in the midst of the present creation, a continuing Pentecost-event. It is, so to speak, a sacrament, a divine speaking within the world, using the language of this world, which is really a speaking to this world from its future, from its life in God. And as such, it is a kind of provisional sharing even now in the life of the world to come, a sharing in those perfect relations of the Trinity which are the eternal joy of everlasting life.

In this section I have attempted to show how we might see the death and resurrection of Jesus, and their outpouring within the world through the continuing Pentecost of the Church, as the lens for pondering the whole sweep of creaturely existence – from creation to beatitude. I have done this because, as ever, I am trying to get us to think about how we learn and do theology. And my argument has been that Jesus' dying and rising and sending of the Spirit are the definitive form of God's teaching about creatures. Proceeding this way has, thus, at least three advantages. First, if Jesus' death and resurrection really are the definitive form of what God is saying to us about everything, and the continuing Pentecost of the Church's life is the world's way of appropriating and being drawn into this divine teaching, then this approach would seem to have considerable authority and aptness (and, as I showed above, creation considered apart from God does not necessarily tell the truth about itself). Second, by grounding our understanding of such massive doctrinal complexes as creation, Church, or eschatology in the experience of Jesus, we reach up into rather lofty ontological mysteries while always remaining respectful of the existential cost by which, Christians believe, Jesus made these ultimate truths about reality available for the world's salvation. And third, rooting these doctrinal complexes within the paschal mystery assists theology in seeing them in their integrity, their interrelationship; for after all, they are all about one great journey from creation to consummation.

Creation – Revelation – Sacrament

Here's a quick sense of what I'm proposing in this section: Jesus of Nazareth is fully human, a creature in the truest sense; he is also, during the whole course of his life, death, resurrection, ascension, and sending of the Spirit, an event of revelation: a disclosing by God of the truth about God and about creation; and Christ is also the primal sacrament, the strange visibility within this world of the life of the world to come. How can all three of these features of Christ be true at once, and what does that tell us of the meaning of creation, revelation, and sacrament?

Jesus comes to exist, Christians believe, precisely because the Father infinitely knows the truth about himself and about all things, and loving that truth infinitely, he desires to speak it resoundingly and to the fullest extent. Jesus is what happens in our world when this divine Word is expressed, that is, a creature comes into existence. Every creature is the echoing in its own way of the eternal Word; and Christians believe that one particular creature, Jesus, is not only the result of that creative speaking that calls everything into being from nothing, but is also the personal expression, indeed the very Person of that Word living *within* the world it has called into being. When that happens, what you get is the historical human being Jesus.

So Jesus is a creature who, like all others, is called into being by the Word and so, as we saw in the first section, he gives us a glimpse into the eternal divine freedom and delight which are the ground of every creature. But in his case that intelligence, freedom, and delight express themselves very personally to us; for they show themselves as a human being captivated by the love of the One who sent him, who hungers to make that Father known to his fellow creatures and indeed to bring them into his relation with the Father, to pour out the Spirit of their life together within the relations of the world. And so, in this way, because Jesus' creatureliness is lived out in transparency to the divine life, Jesus is also revelation. Moreover, because the Father raises Jesus from the dead, and by the Spirit presents him to us in the fullness of his everlasting life, Jesus is also a sacrament: his crucified body, bearing all the marks of this world and our betrayal of him, is given back to us in radiant glory, communicating to us a life that is unimaginably more wonderful and more living than the world can presently bear. That is why such everlasting life can only appear to us within the terms of *this* life, sacramentally, bearing the wounds of this world even as those wounds are now radiant with vindication and divine embrace. Now let's see how we might elucidate these matters.

Trinitarian self-giving as the ground of creaturely freedom

We have already seen above how the Father's raising of Christ by the power of the Spirit points us to creation's source in the loving self-giving of the Persons of the Trinity. The creatures have this joyful trinitarian life, this "giving space" one-to-another-in-love-and-freedom, as their deep structure and dynamic rhythm: they are called out of nothing as sheer gift and this very calling by which they exist inherently orients them towards a full and freely-chosen sharing in this trinitarian communion from which they spring. In John's Gospel, early Christians heard something of this trinitarian joy and communion expressed in the language of this world, when Jesus, speaking about the disciples and all who will come after them, prays to the Father: "All mine are yours and yours are mine. . . . But now I am coming to you, and I speak these things in the world so that they may have my joy made complete in themselves" (John 17: 10, 13). Jesus is portrayed here as having, in his life and work, gathered up the "gifts" that the Father has given him, the creatures who have been perishing and heading toward death; on the eve of offering himself (and, in himself, the gifts mutually given and received) entirely to the Father in his passion, Jesus reveals the meaning of this offering as a way of drawing the disciples (and those who come after) into the full joy of this consummate sharing in the trinitarian life (a trinitarian self-sharing that, in this broken world, takes the form of sacrifice).

Perhaps thinking of passages such as these, the great medieval Franciscan theologian Bonaventure (*c.*1217–74) often wrote of the Father's ideas of all things coming to birth eternally within the eternal begetting of the Word and then, in creation, of how these ideas come to have their own finite forms of existence. Yet for Bonaventure their very creaturely existence is consummated as they are taken up again in the incarnate Word, Jesus, and through his self-offering to the Father the creatures are brought to their deep truth, most fully realized as themselves, in being offered back to God in freedom, and in the joy of the Spirit.[7] In a particularly intriguing passage in his vast "commentary" on the six days of creation, Bonaventure speaks of the Father's ideas of all the creatures as "conceived from all eternity in the womb or uterus of eternal wisdom. . . . and as it [wisdom] conceived them from all eternity, so also it produced [them] or bore [them] in time, and later, gave birth [to them] by suffering in the flesh."[8] Bonaventure conceives of Christ's "suffering in the flesh" as nothing less than the bringing to birth, through the labor pains of the cross, of the creatures' consummate state of being. But how can this be?

To understand Bonaventure we have to realize that it is not the bloody suffering that consummates creation in his view, but rather Jesus' loving freedom to make of himself and all he loved a perfect and complete gift to the Father, a return to him of all that he had received. In a similar way, the twentieth-century Swiss Catholic theologian Hans Urs von Balthasar speaks of the creatures as a series of gifts that the divine Persons of the Trinity give to one another as sheer expressions of their infinitely joyful freedom to give themselves away to one another eternally; the creatures, in other words, exist as finite signs of this infinite trinitarian self-sharing.[9] Creatures are not necessary to God, but they are, precisely in all their creaturely fullness, delightful to God and created to share in God's delight, God's beatitude. As gifts of the divine Persons, God's intentions for all creatures are for each and every creature's utter fulfillment and realization and joy.

The crucial point in all this, for our present purpose, is that the ground of the creatures is clearly nothing *necessary* but rather the delight of communion. The Persons of the Trinity do not create in order to acquire or possess something – as though the Father wanted to have something that he did not eternally share with the Son! – but precisely as a sign of their free giving, and in order to share that free giving. The divine Persons do not act as possessive rivals to one another, and thus the ground of creation is not rivalry but sheer gratuity, not a competition between God and creatures for scarce resources but abundance and infinitely ecstatic joy. This matters so hugely because the most pervasive and invasive misconception about the relation of creatures to the Creator is the insidious suggestion that God is somehow a threat to creaturely freedom, a rival to the creatures' share of existence and fulfillment. In Chapter 6 on the Trinity, we have already discussed the difference between finite creaturely "existence" and the infinite divine Existence upon which it depends. They are not two rival forms of sharing in existence. It would be better to say that God does not exist at all, if we are insistent upon speaking from the creaturely point of view; God is not, that is, one of the things that exist alongside all the other things only somehow top dog of all the beings; rather, God is the sheer, inexhaustible act of existing itself and the immediate and direct giver of existence to each creature in the unique way that each creature partakes of existence.

So we could say that, like the author of everything in a novel, God is not any sort of rival to the figures in the novel. The author could in no sense be imagined as interfering with elements in the novel, but as continually the source of each thing's or character's existence. What God wants, contrary to the serpent's view in Genesis 3, is not to withhold anything from the creatures but to think and love them into the fullest possible realization of what they each can be. Once this is clear, there should be no difficulty in overcoming the other common misconception: namely, that every action in the universe must be either the action of God or the action of creatures. As the author of every creature's existence, instant by instant, we could and should say that everything that takes place is in some sense an action of God, an action causing the creaturely agent to exist and upholding its identity and drawing it forward to its fullest realization. But this divine acting is precisely what makes it possible for creatures to act at all, so it could hardly be in conflict with it or a rival power. In fact, we could add that the more fully attuned a creature is to its particular divine calling into existence, the more fully it can be and act out of the deepest truth of itself. Among creatures, who are on the same plane of existence, there is of course a sense that the more an action is one creature's action, the less it is the action of some other creature. By analogy, within the world of Shakespeare's *Hamlet*, it is true that Hamlet may do something instead of Laertes doing it. But God is in no sense on the same plane of existence: if Hamlet does something, anything, this is not *instead* of Shakespeare doing it but rather because Shakespeare is thinking Hamlet into his very Hamletness moment by moment. Every action of Hamlet's is, in a deep sense, also the action of Shakespeare; and Shakespeare's "doing" of Hamlet is the very fulfilling of Hamlet, not his setting aside. In an analogous way, God's action is present in and through every creaturely action, as the source and ground of that creature's very existence.

Here's a good test of this idea: place it back into the context of how we learn the truth about creation in the events concerning Jesus and then see what you notice. For example, does the divine in Christ act "instead of" his humanity? Not at all; in fact the Christological heresies are all various examples of the inability to conceive of the Word speaking in history precisely as the ground and source of everything Jesus humanly is and does and achieves. The fact that Jesus expresses so perfectly the divine source of his existence does not make him less than human but all the more freely and robustly human. His humanity, living so unhinderedly from its divine source, is less subject to the stultifying fears or distortions that often reduce human existence to a painfully tentative version of what it might be. Indeed, we can learn something important about creaturely freedom when we notice that Jesus' humanity seems all the more vibrant and commandingly alive for the very reason that he is so utterly attuned to the divine speaking, the Word, that calls him into existence.

Most of us, I would venture to say from my own experience, have times and seasons of relatively low availability, low attentiveness, to the divine calling which is the very ground of our existence. And as a result we are sometimes the more easily misled into a false sense of the particular way in which we are called into the truth of our being; we may, for example, have been raised in a dysfunctional family where we learned a lie about ourselves (e.g., that your parent's addiction is really your fault), or we have grown up in a region of war and conflict in which human aspirations beyond mere survival are inconceivable. In such cases, or during certain times of our lives, it may be very difficult to know how to live out the truth of ourselves, the fullness of our humanity to which God is calling us by creating us. And for that very reason, Christians believe, joining oneself to Christ in his dying and rising leads to the death of these old, false forms of existence that entrap and diminish humanity, and to a new creation in which our identity, in Christ, is given a fresh beginning, made alive in Christ to the Father's creative love and the truthful and liberating teaching of the Spirit.

Sometimes the question may arise, however, does this mean that God's "will" somehow determines my life? Is my freedom to be myself somehow constricted by obedience to God? Again, this is a good test of this fundamental Christian teaching that God is the source of the creature's full life, not a competitor to creaturely life. I believe there are two aspects to these sorts of questions, usefully treated separately. First, what about God's creative will, God's idea for each creature by which God calls everything into being and towards the fullest and truest expression of itself? Does this limit creaturely freedom or subject creatures to determinism? Recall that God is not a pushy someone up there with occasional power over one's life; God's will or desire for each creature is nothing less than that it should be able to become the full and undistorted realization of who it really is. Does this limit my freedom? Well, yes, if you think of freedom as meaning just anything: in this sense it's true that I, as a human being am not "free" to become, say, perhaps by an intensive series of lessons, an alligator. But if you mean by freedom the unhindered pursuit of what is my consummation, my fulfillment as who I am, then this is precisely what God is giving me moment by moment, and, in Christ, liberating me to understand and embrace more deeply.

But while this might be notionally the case, there is, second, the more existential side of the problem; for the fact is that many people do experience their lives as in some sense obstructed by God, as though they cannot be fully who they want to be because they sense this is opposed by God. There is of course the sort of case where, say, I want to be a bank robber; here we would obviously say that my sense of the truth of myself is simply askew, i.e., that my idea of the truth of myself is just not right, and that God, by seeming to stand in my way (perhaps by the command, thou shalt not steal), is really helping to *preserve* my freedom by directing me away from what will be the undoing or diminishment of my full existence.

Chances are, however, that the matter is a bit more ambiguous: perhaps I sense that God is nudging me towards a way of life that I anticipate as dreadful or oppressive, or perhaps I just feel that trying to be "religious" is somehow getting in the way of being authentic and true to myself. In these sorts of cases, what Christians call spiritual discernment may be of great assistance; this would consist of attending to the truth of what God is saying in one's life with the help of a practiced listener who is somewhat attuned to the sorts of ways in which God may be at work in someone's life. The basic principle, grounded in Christ, will always be simply that God longs for you to have the freedom to be most completely yourself. The caveat is, of course, that we may not always understand very clearly what the truth of ourselves is, and so at various points in life our belief about who we are, or what our calling is, can be seriously tone deaf. And, unsurprisingly, in those times we may well experience God's call into the fullness of our existence as in conflict with our own sense of self or in some vague way as a threat to our freedom. The doctrine of creation insists, however, that the true God always calls each creature to its most authentic fulfillment; only idols insist on having slaves as their worshipers.

Revelation and sacrament: creation on the way to communion

But what if you really did think, perhaps unconsciously, that God is a secret rival throughout life, withholding the best of everything so that reality was in fact a vast economy of scarcity, a Hobbesian state of nature? Few biblical scenes evoke so uncomfortably our deep sense of deprivation, of dissatisfaction with things, as the Genesis 3 story of the Fall. There the serpent evokes within Eve this very sense that God is not so beneficent as she had naively thought, that perhaps her innocent enjoyment of Eden is merely a clever infantilizing ploy of God, and that a much greater sort of life could be hers if only she asserted her autonomy against God, broke with the divine word not to eat of a certain tree, and seized for herself what she desired for herself.

Notice the bitter intersection of outcomes in this remarkable story: Eden, the paradigm of all gardens of fruitful beauty, the earthly image of Paradise, is drained of abundance and made a scene of encroaching fraudulence and suspicion, grasping anxiety, and an almost brute rapacity; the primal word of God is no longer experienced as creative and loving communication but as subtly manipulative and untrustworthy; and as the story goes on to suggest, the original inhabitants rapidly descend to finger-pointing, mutual hostility, and a newly utilitarian struggle for mere survival. The scene clashes so miserably with what had gone before, not simply because of the terrible loss and debasement of Adam and Eve but because it seems to entail a bewildering loss of intimacy and divine presence in general. In Eden every leaf, every fruit, every moment of radiant light beheld by fellow creatures, every touch, every act of eating – all, all was effectively an intimacy between creatures and Creator. Nothing was merely a thing but all were events of converse and friendship and communion, because all was received directly as cherishable gift from the Creator, an act of sharing in God's giving life. The Fall stands for the muting, even the distortion, of creation's flamboyant echoing of the divine speaking from which it springs. This Edenic state is closed to the first humans and they can no longer sense the truth of God in everything.

I emphasize all this because it helps us to see Christ as restoring creation to this revelatory, sacramental quality: in him, creaturely existence is taken up again into communion with God and so becomes once more an event of communication, the Word made flesh, and the means – even in the stuff of this world – of communing with the life of the world to come. Let me try to spell this out in four steps.

(1) We've seen that Christians regard all creatures as grounded in the eternal processions of the Word and the Spirit: their deep structure as creatures is precisely this eternal event of endlessly abundant communion among the Persons of the Trinity. And this is the source of their freedom, their beautiful form or particularity, and their yearning to share, according to their ability, in the divine dialogue of the Trinity that means their consummation. Created in and through the *Logos* or Word of God, the creatures are themselves intelligible, *logikos*, for they are embodied expressions (*logoi*) of the primal Speaking that creates them.

(2) The creatures therefore have intrinsic meaningfulness and inner rationality which are beautiful to perceive and to understand: the shining visible form of their truth in the mind of the knower. Creatures with self-moved freedom and intelligence, such as humans and angels, are themselves actualized and fulfilled as they are enabled to quench their thirst for truth by beholding and understanding their fellow creatures. And in doing this, humanity was intended to assist the whole creation in achieving the recognition of its inner meaning, its resonance as an element in the great "conversation" of God and the creatures which is the universe.

(3) Sin distorts the perception of everything: from being cherishable gifts and moments of encounter or dialogue, creatures become mere objects to each other. Now the creatures are either potential threats or possessions whose meanings are constricted to the shrinking and distorted aim of intelligent creatures. Humanity is no longer free to fulfill its existence through communion with God, and having lost touch with the language of loving self-sharing in which God speaks, it can no longer hear the divine Word in creatures but subjects the creation ever more desperately to its self-serving and depleting ends.

(4) But the eternal Word, in whom and through whom the Father knows and speaks all creatures into being, becomes, by the power of the Spirit, definitively resonant within creaturely existence once more. In the Incarnation, human existence is re-created as the unhindered speaking of the One who calls into communion; at Pentecost, the Spirit of Christ's lavish self-sharing is poured out; a fire of hearing and speaking the true meaning, the true *Logos*, of everything, and an unquenchable yearning for the divine, are poured out upon creatures. The possibility of creaturely communion with the divine, made actual in Christ, begins to be made available to all.

Sometimes Christian theology has sought to clarify matters by distinguishing between natural revelation (e.g., in the order of the universe or the moral conscience) and supernatural or "positive" revelation (in the divine encounters with Moses, the Word spoken through the prophets, and above all in the Word made flesh). The point I have been making, however, is that the creatures are all, per se, revelatory, in that they spring from and are called towards the eternal communion of God's life. They are, as Eastern Orthodox theology puts it, *logoi* of the *Logos*, meanings of the Word.[10] The problem is simply that this shining meaningfulness and intelligibility of creation as, in effect, divine speech, is distorted and muted and obscured by sin. This comes about through mistrust of the divine Speaker, and of God's intentions in "addressing" the creatures by creating and calling them to Godself. So we might say that what we think of as "revelation" – whether it be in the form of a spoken word, a historical event, or a community pondering a sacred text – takes place in that moment when God lifts creatures into the resounding joy of the triune life and makes their existence ring once more with such abundance and goodness and truth that freedom and salvation break out into the world.

In this sense, revelation is always salvific, it liberates creation from the dim and dismal false identity it has been degenerating into through mistrust of God, and it also initiates the creatures into a new moment of encounter with God. Athanasius of Alexandria (*c*.296–373) highlights this context of fall and redemption in which revelation occurs:

> Men, having turned from the contemplation of God to evil of their own devising, had come inevitably under the law of death. Instead of remaining in the state in which God had created them, they were in process of becoming corrupted entirely, and death had them completely under its dominion. For the transgression of the commandment was making them turn back again according to their nature; and as they had at the beginning come into being out of non-existence, so were they now on the way to returning, through corruption, to non-existence again. The presence and love of the Word had called them into being; inevitably, therefore, when they lost the knowledge of God, they lost existence with it.[11]

Crucially here Athanasius shows the inextricable link between creation and the Word: the creatures exist in and through the Word, thus to turn away from the Word diminishes their ability to listen for him in everything. And this diminishing of the creatures' perception sets loose their downward spiral towards non-existence. We could put it in shorthand: the speaking of God means existence for the creatures; refusal to hear and commune, to share in the divine dialogue, means loss of existence.

David Bentley Hart, commenting on this theme in Gregory of Nyssa, observes that for Gregory, the Son eternally mirrors the Father in the delight of the Spirit; and therefore the creation of the universe through the Son means that all creatures bear an analogous "mirroring" function. As the Son mirrors the Father, so the creatures reflect the glory of the Creator: but much more than this, they *are* this mirroring, they are constituted by the reflection of this glory, as *logoi* echoing the *Logos*. As Hart puts it:

> Apart from that reflex of light that lies at creation's heart, there is no world to speak of at all; Gregory, like Basil before him, in various places denies that the world possesses any material substrate apart from the intelligible act that constitute its

perceptible qualities: the world of bodies is a confluence of "thoughts," "bare concepts," "words," noetic "potentialities," proceeding from the divine nature.[12]

This intelligible-expressive-communicative character of creaturely existence means
that its full realization depends on being engaged in a form of communication
with God, of conversation such as the Garden of Eden story depicted. Apart
from that, neither the human creature is able to realize its vocation nor are the
creatures able to actualize their communicativeness. After the Fall, in other words,
the divine speaking can only take place as a distinct act of revelation, of revelation
that must also be the setting free and the saving of the creatures: their restoration
(as in the Incarnation and at Pentecost) to being hearers, bearers, and speakers
of the Word.

Needless to say, this view of revelation has an inescapably paschal character to it:
God communicates God's saving presence and truth among creatures, precisely by
drawing creaturely existence, in Christ, back into that loving self-giving of the trinitarian life from which it springs; and in the world we have made, this infinite act of
self-giving love took the form of Christ's self-giving life, even to death. Jesus accomplishes creation's trusting self-abandonment into the hands of the Father. Why is
this revelatory of God? For the very reason that Jesus' freedom and loving trust in
doing this are themselves the actual self-disclosing, the revelation, of God. In other
words, God does not reveal God to the world by imparting some extremely recondite data otherwise unavailable; rather, God reveals God by setting creation free to
share in God's way of being, to share in communion once more.

God's revelation to creatures, I am arguing, can never take the form of anything
other or less than the taking up of creatures into communion with God. God has
nothing less than God to communicate, and to share or understand this in any
way would mean, ultimately to share in God's own knowing and loving of God.
Therefore if revelation is to unfold within the lives of the creatures, the creatures
will have – one way or another – to be drawn into that continuing conversion and
transfiguration, that death and resurrection, which Christ shares with them. The
resurrection of Jesus attests that this is the case: for it shows that the most intense
and consummate form of revelation is nothing less than the creation living, directly
and irreversibly, inexhaustibly and immediately, from the life of divine joy. The
life, death, and resurrection of Jesus are thus the fulfillment of creation and its re-
creation as revelation, its restoration towards full communicativeness: the communion of trinitarian life. As Olivier Clément puts it:

> The book of the cosmos . . . and that of the Scriptures match each other, since they
> have the same author. Both of them find their full revelation in Christ who, after
> writing them, made them his body and his face. The incarnate Logos frees the speech-
> less tongue of creation and unites it with the world as *logos alogos*. Christ has become
> the direct divine-human subject of the cosmic *logoi*. He confers on them their deepest
> meaning, their paschal nature, the power of the resurrection to work in them. He
> reveals their roots in the abyss of the three-Personed God.[13]

But how can this revelation, this dying-and-rising, become genuinely available for creaturely participation? In the sacraments, Christians believe, Christ the incarnate Word gives himself not only to *disclose* the divine encounter, but to *be* the very means of renewed communion among the creatures and between them and God. Here it is crucial to note the role of the Spirit: the One who burns within Christ as a great yearning to do the will of the Father, as the One who pours out this infinite self-communication of Christ within the community of his followers (thus calling the Church into being), and as the One who draws creaturely existence into Christ's self-sharing by releasing creatures (water, bread and wine, oil, human lives) to express this radical self-sharing as sacraments. For it is the Spirit whose unstinting joy and givingness becomes, in Christ, an absolute yearning within a creaturely heart to do the will of the Father once more. In yielding himself, and therefore creaturely life, back again into the hands of the Father, Jesus transfigures the creation, renders it translucent once more to the divine communication from which it springs. Jesus' self-offering in his life and death, and the Father's response in raising him from death, are what the Holy Spirit pours out within creation as the sacramental life, the life of the Church.

For Thomas Aquinas, the worship of the Church is in fact a sharing in the prayer of Jesus accomplished on the cross (*ST* III. 62. 5). And, as I've been suggesting, this prayer, this complete self-giving of Jesus is really the visibility in our world of that primordial "prayer" at the heart of all reality: the self-giving of the Father to the Son (shown in the Incarnation), the Son's responding self-offering (shown on the cross), and the Father's joyful affirmation of the Son in the loving superabundance of the Spirit (shown in the resurrection). In these events, Christians believe, we find the warrant for thinking that creation can indeed become conversant once more with God. Thus we've been considering creation, revelation, and sacrament all as various expressions of this fundamental, trinitarian source and goal of creaturely existence. So creation itself is symbolic, a shining into finite form of the infinite mirroring (as Gregory of Nyssa put it) of the Trinity's own life; and for that reason, when God takes up creatures more particularly, in revelation, into the act of divine self-communication, this is their fulfillment, their salvation, and not their undoing. Furthermore, it is because of this expressivity, this potentially revelatory quality, that creatures can become – as is Jesus himself – sacramental, symbolic participations of earth in the life of heaven, of this world in the world to come, of the creature in the Creator. We could say that the sacraments are simply – to begin with – human events and acts of meaning (such as meals, washings, anointings, weddings, and so on), and yet they are symbolic acts whose meaningfulness Christ sets loose, sets free, fills to overflowing by his employment of them as elements in his own communication of the Father's love. The twentieth-century Eastern Orthodox theologian Alexander Schmemann puts it this way:

> The world is symbolical . . . in virtue of being created by God; to be "symbolical" belongs thus to its ontology, the symbol being not only the way to perceive and understand reality, a means of cognition, but also a means of *participation*. It is then

the "natural" symbolism of the world – one can almost say its "sacramentality" – that makes the sacrament *possible* and constitutes the key to its understanding and apprehension.... Therefore, the institution of sacraments by Christ ... is not the creation *ex nihilo* of the "sacramentality" itself, of the sacrament as a means of cognition and participation. In the words of Christ, "do *this* in remembrance of me," the *this* (meal, thanksgiving, breaking of bread) is already "sacramental." The institution means that by being referred to Christ, "filled" with Christ, the symbol is fulfilled and becomes *sacrament*.[14]

Or, as I've been putting it, the symbol becomes taken up, in the hands of Jesus, into God's own human form of self-communication.

In an oversimplifying scheme, we might think of an ascending trajectory: at the base there are the good things of creation, inherently expressive as mirroring the divine self-sharing, but often muted or distorted by sinful human misuse of the creation. In wholesome and healthy human life, however, there is a sense in which the creatures are taken up (or "realized") as elements within our normal everyday acts of conversation and communion with one another. For example, a dish of chemicals becomes recognized as a plate of food and is furthermore realized, perhaps, as a meal between friends and so imbued with the significance of their desire to communicate with each other. Christ takes these good things, now already given a kind of linguistic significance through human communication, and makes of them a yet more intense and fulfilling event of communion; by his life and death, he offers himself through these communicative elements to become the superabundant event of communication which is life with God. In the process of doing this, Jesus brings about a new pattern of relations among his friends, a sacramental pattern by which they discover themselves anew – precisely through the relations with each other that Jesus makes possible in his outpouring of life in the sacraments.

Jesus, therefore, is the primal sacrament, human life existing in and through and as the self-sharing of God. Herbert McCabe puts this most clearly:

> The Father, then, summons man to real communication, but it is more than a summons from outside, a call from the unattained future. The Father offers us this real communication in the present. This offer is Jesus Christ. He is the Father's giving of himself. ... [Jesus] offered himself as a new medium of communication between men. This we must be clear about. Jesus did not offer a new social theory, or a new religion, he did not offer even a full analysis of the contradictions of his society, he did not provide an ideal for a new kind of human community. He offered himself. The new kind of community was to be founded upon him, upon the new relationships he was able to establish with his friends, which released them from themselves, freed them from sin and made them open and able to risk becoming human. Jesus offered not a doctrine about what friendship of this kind might be, but the friendship itself.[15]

McCabe goes on to say that as humankind lives all the more fully into this sacramental life, Jesus is the more clearly apparent as the "medium in which we finally meet each other, in which we are finally able to communicate ourselves to each other," and as we communicate and share ourselves fully in that way we are taking part "in the life of the Father." In this sense Christ, the primal sacrament, by sharing a way of life with his friends on earth which is really the life of heaven, unfolds the fully communal quality of his being, drawing them into his divine freedom to be-for-the-other. As we'll see just below: on earth this looks like human existence being drawn towards fulfillment as ecclesial existence, and ecclesial life being illuminated as an sign of the life to come, life in that infinite self-sharing of the Trinity.

Human Life – Ecclesial Life – Beatitude

By now the basic principles I've been proposing as a theological path are, I hope, fairly clear: start with the events of Jesus and the Spirit, then allow God's teaching there to transform the understanding of God, and so seek to think according to the patterns of trinitarian self-giving as they bring a universe of creatures into existence. So far this has led us to consider creaturely life, revelation, and sacrament as, so to speak, the structural elements of the universe. That is, we've been talking about the inherently expressive dynamic or trajectory of creation. As the mirror of the trinitarian self-sharing, the creatures are most themselves in reflecting (as creatures per se) or revealing (as events of revelation) or sharing in (as sacramental moments) this eternal event of communion. But into this milieu the Word and Spirit come, as it were, from behind the scenes to play certain roles as actors within the very drama they have been authoring. As McCabe puts it just above, Jesus gives himself to be the mode of communication, the new language among the creatures, by which humanity is finally able to communicate with the true depth within each other, that depth which is really the Spirit's yearning to fulfill communion. And this brings about a disclosure of what human life might really be, what it might be capable of becoming. Christians believe that the Church is meant to be the sign of this communion in the present world, and that beatitude is the consummation of it in the world to come, for the life that creatures are learning to communicate and commune with is simply the eternal communion of God.

So we could say that from the structure of creation as communicative and sacramental, we are now turning to the emergence of a certain form of creaturely life within this resonant environment: humanity in motion towards God. I'm suggesting that we see human life as a particular form of creaturely existence, a form in which creation's communicable, linguistic orientation reaches up into ever more blessed fulfillment, or else falls back into ever more pernicious anti-communication and antagonism. As an example of this, think of how Jesus, as assumed into the personal mission of the Word, was not stunted in his humanity thereby, but lived all the more vibrantly as passionate communication. By offering himself as the ground of this new communication, Jesus calls humanity out of isolation and antagonism and towards the true source of unity in God. This is what life in the Church is meant to be: life in transition from subjection to merely biological necessities (in which one group is often pitted against another) to life open toward an abundance and communicativeness that carries humankind into communion with God. The Church's life is called ecclesial from the Greek roots, *ek-kaleo*, to be called out, called out from the present world's version of life and towards the life of God in Christ. We might also say that ecclesial life means life in motion away from fearfully antagonistic, individualistic life and towards life that shares in communion.

With this in mind, we might want to test our theological skills by a little exercise: humanity is often classically described as created in the image and likeness of God (from Genesis 1: 26); how should we interpret this understanding? For the priestly editors of Genesis, probably at work during exile in Babylon, the fact that their God's image should be living human beings was probably meant as a bitter jest at the expense of their Babylonian captors, whose own deities apparently preferred images of the massively sculpted-in-stone variety. Still, this has raised a terrific theological question down the centuries: in what does the image of God consist? Is it simply the fact, as the contrast with hulking Babylonian statues suggests, that humanity is *alive* and so reflects the inexhaustible life of God? Let's try to put our basic line of thought so far to work on this question. For example, it has sometimes been argued that the image of God consists in some particular element of the human person: perhaps intelligence or the mind and its free judgment. In a sense, we could make a pretty good argument for this: the mind is that element of humanity that allows us to recognize the inherent communicability of the creatures and to respond, to converse with the divine intentions in all of them, lifting them up in right use and understanding and praise.

And yet, if we return to basic principles, wouldn't we want to think about this question by looking at how God teaches in Christ and the Spirit? Jesus' individual human intelligence, per se, does not perhaps seem at the very heart of his mission. But what about the theme we've just been emphasizing: his giving of himself to be the means of communication, of communion, among humans and with God? This seems central to his identity as the Word incarnate; we say that it is consummated in his self-giving on the cross, and that its meaning is vindicated and universalized at Easter and Pentecost. So would this argue for the image of God being simply our linguisticality? I think that's part of it, but could we push this deeper and say it is precisely humankind's orientation towards communion, towards relation with the other?

This view in fact receives some confirmation from Thomas Aquinas, for example, who argues that what constitutes humanity as image of God is not really something solely interior to the human being, so much as humanity's common existence in freedom for the other, both the creaturely other and the divine other. For Thomas, the whole of human life is best understood by thinking about it in terms of human consummation, which is nothing less than life in God, the blessed-making or beatifying vision of God. This means that being created as the image of God is better thought of, as Thomas's Latin translation of Genesis 1: 26 has it, as creation "for" or "towards" the image: humanity bears a deep impulse or dynamic that is ever tugging it towards the other, ultimately towards the divine Other. To be in the image of the Trinity is, thus, to be in motion, as the divine Persons are, towards another. So, for example, Thomas speaks of how Jesus' motion from and towards the Father, his "filial" relation of sonship, becomes available through Jesus for other persons to be adopted into (following Ephesians 1: 5); human beings may be adopted as beloved children of the Father by sharing in Jesus' trinitarian relation with the Father. Why does God create and fulfill humans like this, asks Thomas? Because

> God is infinitely good: for which reason He admits His creatures to a participation of good things; especially rational creatures, who forasmuch as they are made to the image of God, are capable of Divine beatitude. And this consists in the enjoyment of God, by which also God Himself is happy and rich in Himself – that is in the enjoyment of Himself. (*ST* III. 23. 1)

Two crucial features of this little passage must be noted: (1) The *imago Dei* is clearly not for Thomas some static inherent feature of human nature, but is perhaps more like a drive or magnetic pull that God is always exerting upon humans, calling them towards the delight of the triune communion; and (2) this orientation or calling of humans is itself nothing less than the joy or happiness, the beatitude, that the divine Persons have in each other and have created a universe in order to share. And this gives us a very helpful clue, thinks Thomas, about how we might notice this image-of-God-dynamic at work in humans. The divine joy that attracts us is one with the divine relations of the trinitarian Persons. For God, as Thomas said just above, is One who is eternally "happy and rich in himself," and this is because of the eternal event by which God knows and loves Godself. In theological jargon, as we have seen in previous chapters, we speak of God's eternal knowing and loving as the eternal procession of the Word or Son and the eternal breathing of the Spirit.

The upshot of all this is that God's beatitude is what "happens" as the Father knows the whole divine life, and all that it will create, in the Son, and loves this Word in the Spirit. God's beatitude is simply God being God. And that would mean, Thomas argues, that to be created "towards" the image of God would mean that humanity's own acts of knowing and loving are capable, in some unimaginable way, of being drawn by God to share in *God's* own acts of knowing and loving. This does not mean only that the human person comes to have God, per se, as the object of his or her knowing and loving; that's just a start! The fully realized image of God in humanity comes about as this divine "object," so to speak, comes to life as the knowing and loving Subject, in whose knowing and loving the human person is participating. This is what Thomas thinks of as the journey from nature to grace to glory: by *nature*, God has created humanity with "a natural aptitude of understanding and loving God" and this is the preliminary or natural state of the *imago Dei*; by *grace* God inspires humanity actually but imperfectly to know and love God in this life; but in *glory* humanity is taken up actually to know and love God "perfectly"; this, of course, could only be perfect knowing and loving of an infinite life if it is a sharing, a living into, that life itself, i.e., beatitude (*ST* III. 93. 4). As the foremost scholar of this theme in Thomas puts it, by the work of the Spirit and Son in the soul,

> the soul truly comes to participate in their divine processions so that the soul knows and loves God *by the very acts of God in which the Son and the Spirit proceed*. It is as if the divine Word were proceeding in the mind of man, and from thence the Person of Love [the Spirit] were proceeding in the human act of loving God.[16]

The calling of Jesus to human beings, and the breathing through their lives of the Spirit, is the calling into being of ecclesial life. The Church, in other words, is meant to be the locus of this event in which Jesus' knowing of the Father and the Spirit's delight in their knowing can take hold in a little community on earth, and so transform the patterns of human knowing and loving more generally. The sacramental or worshiping life of the community, as we saw above, is the pattern by which this transformation of knowing and loving takes place. Here we might want simply to pause a moment and try to imagine what this could be like. What is it like to share a practice of life with others in which Jesus' life in the Spirit is the deepest rhythm and theme? The contemporary Greek Orthodox theologians John Zizioulas and Christos Yannaras both describe it as the transformation, even the realization, of humanity.[17] Coming to share in a pattern of life that springs from the Trinity means coming to share in the free bestowal of life of the divine Persons. The life of God is not governed by some primal divine nature whose necessities the Persons merely obey; rather, God's life is above all the life which is constituted by the free and loving decision of the divine Persons to be-for-each-other. Using the Greek term for the Persons in God, *hypostasis*, Zizioulas and Yannaras speak of the divine Persons as "hypostasizing" the divine nature, bringing it to be by their personal communion with one another. And then applying this analogically to human being, we could say that it is one's personal identity that hypostasizes, "personalizes," one's humanity and brings it toward its full state of actualization. The crucial point both theologians make is this: what most deeply and authentically characterizes personal identity is not the fallen subjection to mere biological necessities, but the free decision to be for and with others, to love and be loved. And the Church is meant to be the place where this actualization of one's humanity can occur, where humankind can be drawn from merely biological to ecclesial forms of identity in communion with God who is personal communion itself.

We could also imagine this sharing together in Jesus' knowing of the Father in the Spirit as a kind of "waking up" into the risen life of Christ. After all, this is what Christians believe is going on in the sacrament of baptism, an initiation in Jesus' dying and rising, so that Jesus' "yes" to the Father is achieved by the Spirit more and more transformingly within the lives of communicants. In a sense, their life together as Christians is one long procession from this initiation into Christ's death and resurrection (in baptism) towards the fulfillment of his self-offering in the heavenly banquet that the Father makes of that offering, a fulfillment signified sacramentally (in the Eucharist). Christ and the Spirit thus call Christians to make a place, a network within the world's life, within which this baptismal and eucharistic journey towards the last things (Greek: *eschata*) can take place. "Eschatology" as a sub-field of theology is simply our fragmentary human talk about these last or fulfillment-making things, but whatever we can say or imagine is always governed by the showing forth into our world of these last things already in Christ.

As Karl Barth never tired of reminding his readers, the destiny of all creation is made secure and hopeful because in Christ God has already taken the creation up into its fulfillment as a beloved partner and friend, eternally alive from the life of God, which we call resurrection life. In Jesus, says Barth, humankind "has already been put in the place and kingdom of peace with God," and therefore the life of Christians is already headed in this direction and always subject to this calling; but, as Barth explains, this divine attraction "is not a loud and stern and foreign thing, but the quiet and gentle and intimate awakening of children in the Father's house to life in that house" (*Church Dogmatics* IV. 1. 100). This waking up in the "Father's house" and realizing that one has been long expected and is invited to share "life in that house" – this is already happening to humanity through its fellowship with Jesus. He has already awoken in his Father's house and has assured his followers that "if I go and prepare a place for you, I will come again and will take you to myself, so that where I am, there you may be also" (John 14: 3). The life to come is thus, as Barth puts it, "an echoing and mirroring of the divine Yes which God Himself spoke . . . when He raised Jesus Christ from the dead" (*Church Dogmatics* III. 1. 385). The life to come is already visible to us, for the life to come is already begun in the risen Jesus Christ; his "Eastering" is, so to speak, a brief glimpse of coming attractions. The Father's raising of Jesus in the joy of the Spirit is the sign made to humanity of creation's calling into the life to come, says Barth, for it is humanity which is "envisaged in this event"; thus Barth goes on to imagine how each human person should think of herself or himself when they see Jesus crucified yet risen:

> He is the creature whom God has taken to Himself, whose peril and hope, death and life, woe and weal, God has made His own, and in whose interests He has conducted this strange warfare and gained this victory. . . . [The human person] is the one whom God in His own Son has eternally taken to His heart of love. His cause is pleaded in the heart of God. He is defended against the menace of nothingness. Eternal life is won for him. He has been clothed with the glory of God. Christian

faith does not merely contemplate what God has done; it receives it as done for us. It is our own participation in this divine event, even as the latter is God's participation in our own being and nature. (*Church Dogmatics* III. 1. 387)

We might even say, thus, that the life of the world to come is best understood by a practice of faith, a practice of living ever more fully into the dying and rising of Christ.

Olivier Clément describes this practice of theological understanding as eucharistic life, a life in which the world to come is made known now through the work of the sacramental life of the Church, and perhaps even realized, finally, in the Eucharist that Christ makes more and more fully of the world through his Body the Church. The work of humankind with the creation is brought to a new level in the sacramental work of ecclesial life so that

> in the end we shall have food bringing us nothing but life, that in the end the flesh of the earth may become, through our work, a chalice offered to the Spirit. And the effect is also the cause; for from this luminous centre, from this dot of matter brought into the incandescence of the glorious Body, the fire spreads even to the rocks and the stars whose substance is present in the bread and wine; the Eucharist guards and sanctifies the world, gradually pervading with eternity the heart of things, and making ready the transformation of the world into Eucharist. So the Church appears as the spiritual place where we are apprenticed to the eucharistic life . . . through the liturgy the world is revealed as transfigured in Christ, henceforth cooperating in its final metamorphosis.[18]

LANDMARKS

Thomas Aquinas on Creation: "A Representation of the Divine Wisdom"

In his commentary on the Gospel of John, Thomas comes to the first moment of John's characteristic irony: "He [the Word] was in the world, and the world came into being through him; yet the world did not know him" (1: 10). Thomas notes dryly that the creatures indeed fail to recognize the presence of their Creator: first, because such knowledge is too far beyond them, but second, because being guilty sinners hardly helps human beings to look beyond themselves. Yet, undaunted by either human finitude or blindness, Thomas insists that "as a work of art manifests the art of the artisan, so the whole world is nothing else than a certain representation of the divine wisdom conceived within the mind of the Father."[19] As recent Aquinas scholarship has noted, Thomas envisions a creation entirely reflective of the Creator's giving life and mystical presence.[20] In this section then, I want to display Thomas's thought, a massive landmark in the theology of creation, by emphasizing the Angelic Doctor's consistent teaching about the mysterious intimacy of God to the creatures.

Why God creates

As we saw in the earlier sections of this chapter, the fullest possible happiness of the creatures lies in their coming to share God's infinite happiness, or beatitude. And this end or goal of things is really Thomas's answer to the question, "Why does God create?" Not because God *has* to create in order to fulfill the divine life, nor because divinity simply *cannot help* overflowing into finite beings, does God create – but only because the Trinity's knowledge and delight is infinitely complete does God choose freely to extend existence and the possibility of beatitude to what does not exist. The Father freely knows and intends the fullness of the divine life in the Son, and the Spirit rejoices in and communicates this knowing, this truth, as goodness itself. And it is because of these processions of the Word and Spirit, constituting the eternal life of God, that the procession of the creatures takes place externally to God in time. God, as Thomas says, is the pure act of existing itself (e.g., *ST* I. 3. 4), but this act should not be conceived as either ontologically or logically prior to the processions of the trinitarian Persons. And that means that the sharing of existence with the creatures has its reason or rationale not in any need or compulsion in God, but in the delighted communion of the divine Persons; their self-sharing processions *are* the eternal act of existence from which created existence proceeds.[21] As Gilles Emery puts it:

> Just as the generation of the Son is the reason (*ratio*) for the entire production of the creatures, the procession of the Holy Spirit as the Love of the Father and of the Son is the *ratio* in which God accords to the creatures the effects of his love.[22]

This should tell us something of why God creates. For everything, says Thomas, acts for some end or goal, in order to achieve something lacking or fulfill some need or desire; "but it does not belong to the First Agent, Who is agent only, to act for the acquisition of some end" (*ST* I. 44. 4). In other words, God is "agent only," the only reality that is purely and wholly act and not acted upon by anything or by any need or lack. So whatever we mean by "creation" (which Thomas defines as the giving of a share in God's existence to what does not exist, e.g., *ST* I. 45. 1), it cannot be an act that God in any way is required to do. And therefore it must be something God does freely; but why does God freely do this? Because, says Thomas, God "intends only to communicate His perfection, which is His goodness" (*ST* I. 44. 4). Thus, at the heart of every creature's existence, according to Thomas, is divine freedom, divine intention, and divine liberality or good-givingness. The creature is not "just there," a meaningless or bizarre happenstance in the cosmic scheme of things. Rather every creature exists as an event of divine self-communication, an epiphany of goodness-sharing. This also means that every creature is itself free, the plaything of no cosmic forces or determinisms, but a gift to itself from God that it might come to share in the life of God.

How God creates

Thomas believes that, unlike the many gods well known to the human race through history, the God of Abraham and Sarah, and of Jesus Christ, does not simply move pre-existing matter around nor produce a kind of descending cascade of lesser and lesser creatures at further and further removes from divine life, each dependent upon a higher intermediary for some access to being. In Thomas's view, God is present to each and every creature immediately and directly and entirely, giving it its particular share in the act of existing. So what God does in creating is to "cause" *everything* to exist, absolutely and without any mediation (*ST* I. 45. 1). I put "cause" in scare quotes because we find it, naturally, quite tricky to imagine a kind of causing that doesn't depend on there being something already there to work on or change or bring to a new condition. This is precisely what Thomas says is ruled out by the doctrine of creation; rather, God brings existence out of nothing, and this is because God is the very act of existing itself. Every existing thing in the universe, unlike God, is not sheer existence per se but rather existence "contracted," bundled into the particular form of a horse or a human; Thomas thinks each creature exists as the particular "contraction" of existence it is because God thinks and loves it into existence according to the eternal idea or model of it which the Father knows eternally in the Word and which the Spirit cherishes.

I confess that this is one of my favorite aspects of Thomas's teaching on creation, namely that everything gets to exist in the Word of God, and will always exist – in its fullness and beauty and unhindered truth – even before it comes to exist in time and space, in its creaturely form. Of course, it is not the creatures per se that exist in God's mind, but rather God, knowing and loving the creatures, and this divine knowing Thomas calls the divine ideas, models, or exemplars of all creatures. Even so, as we'll see, there's a sense in which God's infinite understanding and delight in the creatures-to-be is really the truth of them, the absolute potential of what they each have it in them to be or to become in this world. After all, who could better understanding and rejoice in the reality of each creature than the author from whose creative mind and love it springs? Thomas insists that God doesn't know things because they are or have been or will be, but rather they are or have been or will be just because God knows them, "for the knowledge of God is to all creatures what the knowledge of the artificer is to things made by his art" (*ST* I. 14. 8).

This is not some piece of recondite arcana for Thomas. Rather, he is vindicating the biblical witness to God's creative wisdom, by which the unfolding of the universe of heaven and earth, with all its vast particularity and diversity, is directly according to the divine plan and approval, the divine knowing and approbation (i.e., the processions in God of Word and Spirit). This rules out, in Thomas's view, the idea that the universe is merely

> the accidental result of a succession of agents, as has been supposed by those who have taught that God created only the first creature, and that this creature created a second creature, and so on, until this great multitude of beings was produced. According to this opinion God would have the idea of the first created thing alone; whereas, if the order itself of the universe was created by Him immediately, and intended by Him, He must have the idea of the order of the universe. Now there cannot be an idea of any whole, unless particular ideas are had of those parts of which the whole is made. . . . So, then, it must needs be that in the divine mind there are the proper ideas of all things. (*ST* I. 15. 2)

God's ordering wisdom sees the whole pattern of the universe and brings it into intelligent and integral existence in time. Thus God knows the truth, the real identity, and *telos* of each creature, in the very act of knowing Godself. And although these divine thoughts, these eternal models or exemplars of each creature, are of course many with respect to the many individual creatures they come to be in time, yet "in reality [they] are not apart from the divine essence, according as the likeness to that essence can be shared diversely by different things" (*ST* I. 44. 3). In God's eternal life, all the creatures-to-be are united and unified, diverse patterns of potential sharing in the one pure act of existence, the self-sharing of the divine Persons.

Because God gives creatures their own finite form of existence, God is in no sense in competition or rivalry with creatures. The existing of creatures does not mean there is less existing for God to do or be! That would be as if there were somehow a finite amount of existing that both Shakespeare and the characters in *Hamlet* had to share, and that if Shakespeare gives some of it to his characters then he himself has less; but there is no such common or general existence, for the existence of the characters in the play is of a quite different, analogous kind to the existence of Shakespeare. And the more fully a character shares in the creative genius of the playwright, the more she or he comes to be – in an analogous fashion. Creatures exist because God calls them into a kind of likeness or analogy to the divine act of existence.

A leading scholar of this theme in Thomas, Rudi te Velde, puts it very clearly:

> The notion of participation enables Thomas to conceive of the relationship between the divine agent (the transcendental causality of being) and the proper action of nature itself (the categorical causality) in a non-excluding and non-competitive manner. God is everything and does everything in the precise sense that He is the universal cause sustaining every other thing in its proper being and in its proper action. God is "everything," but not in the sense of excluding or repressing the

existence of something else, since this would mean that God is conceived of in the manner of a creature. God is not a partner in the existence and activities of the world, cooperating with creatures on the same level. The causality of creation is situated at the transcendent level: as such it transcends and encompasses the whole domain of nature and its categorical causality (secondary causes) by letting nature free in its own substantial existence and proper activity.[23]

By using the language of transcendental and categorical causality, te Velde is clarifying for us what we mean by saying that the creatures' ways of being and of causing is an analogy to God's way of being and causing. God's causing is transcendent, it is the condition for the possibility of any causing in the categorical sense of particular causes. By way of an example, we might think of a woman writing at her desk. To one side of her are a pleasing assortment of pens and markers and pencils; each of these writing utensils does some writing, but only because the woman is writing with them. Her writing is transcendent with respect to the various categories of pens and markers, each of which, when employed by her, becomes a secondary cause of writing on the paper. So, as te Velde puts it in the quotation above, "God *is* 'everything', but not in the sense of excluding or repressing the existence of something else." God is the existing at the heart of every creature's ability to exist on its plane of existing, just as the woman's writing is at the heart of every pen's and pencil's ability to write on its plane, in its category of writing. In both cases, the transcendent cause in no way diminishes the categorical cause, but is instead its very ground and its source.

How God is present to creatures

Now you might think, at first glance, that God being transcendent to the creatures puts divine life at quite a distance. By now, however, the concept of the creature's participation in God's existence, its analogical sharing in God's life, should overcome this sense of distance. Indeed, it is only because God is not one thing among all the others, but at the heart of everything, that God can actually be closer to each creature than anything else. As Thomas puts it, God is in fact "innermost" in everything:

> Other agents act as existing externally: since they do not act except by moving and altering a thing. . . . But God acts in all things from within, because he acts by creating. Now to create is to give existence (*esse*) to the thing created. So, since *esse* is innermost in each thing, God, who by acting gives *esse*, acts in things from within.[24]

So everything that is and acts does so because of God's "innermost" presence to it, giving it its own way of existing and acting precisely so that it can really be and do what it is and does. God does not act instead of creatures, but is the source of all their acting.

Let me also, once more, underscore the significance of the primordial presence of the creatures to God in the divine mind, for this also points to a special way in which God is present to creatures on earth. Because of God's primordial knowing of it, the truth of the creature is not ultimately at the whim of whatever forces happen to confront it during its earthly existence; for in Thomas's view its truth is revealed "in so far as it fulfills the end to which it was ordained by the divine intellect"; nor is the truth of things willy-nilly whatever humans might like things to be, for "even if there were no human intellects, things could be said to be true because of their relation to the divine intellect."[25] There is a very real way in which God's knowing and cherishing of God's idea of each creature is what safeguards each creature's freedom and its true identity. No matter what befalls it, no matter what lies about itself it may be told or come to believe about itself, its authentic goodness and identity are still alive in God, and may by grace (and ultimately by resurrection) be restored to the creature. Perhaps this is what Paul means when he says that "if anyone is in Christ, there is a new creation" (2 Corinthians 5: 17): not that a different creature has come to birth but rather that "everything old has passed away; see, everything has become new!" (ibid.). The truth of the creature has been renewed, brought to life again. For Christ is the Word incarnate, the one in whom the Father has eternally spoken and known the truth of every creature, so as the creatures affiliate with Christ and pass into his death and resurrection, the Spirit who raised Jesus from the dead also raises into life the true and primal reality of the creature.

For Thomas, the exemplars or ideas of all creatures as they are known by the Father in the Word "are the measures of the truth of all things, because a thing is said to be true in so far as it imitates that upon which it was modeled, and this archetype exists in the Word. Therefore, things exist more truly in the Word than in themselves."[26] In Thomas's view, the creatures-to-be are, as we've seen, eternally known in the Word and loved in the Spirit; from this it follows that the indwelling of the Trinity in the human person as she or he struggles through the life of this world may become a rekindling of that original truth and goodness of the creature in the eternal life of God. Discussing the indwelling of the divine Persons in the soul, Thomas writes:

> For God is in all things by His essence, power, and presence, according to His one common mode, as the cause existing in the effects which participate in His goodness. Above and beyond this common mode [of being present to all creatures], however, there is one special mode belonging to the rational nature wherein God is said to be present as the object known is in the knower, and the beloved in the lover. And since the rational creature by its operation of knowledge and love attains to God Himself, according to this special mode God is said not only to exist in the rational creature, but also to dwell therein as in His own temple. (*ST* I. 43. 3)

We could say that the primordial existence of the creature, in God's knowing (the procession of the Word) and loving (breathing of the Spirit), comes by grace to indwell the creature in time, re-creating it as it comes to sense the deep truth of itself in sensing God's loving and transforming presence. Creatures are, for Thomas, utterly permeable to God's life, and they are all the more fully themselves the more fully attuned to God they can become.

Blaise Pascal on Human Existence

For quite a different perspective on the theology of the creatures, we might turn to the remarkable French Catholic Blaise Pascal. A mathematical genius who laid the foundations of calculus, statistics, and the science of probability, Pascal (1623–62) developed into an astonishing theological interpreter of the human condition.[27] Like his fellow early moderns Machiavelli, Descartes, and Hobbes, Pascal was certain that only now, with the advent of new modes of thought and the development of modern experimental science, was humanity poised to advance in huge strides beyond the infancy of ancient thought. Pascal himself led the way, inventing the calculator, the barometer, and the modern public transportation system. Yet the very successes of modern mechanical science seemed to Pascal – precisely *because* of its blinding successes – to obscure in a most dangerous way the true heights and depths and orientation of human existence. In many ways, Pascal is among the first moderns to critique modernity. The more that human yearning is harnessed by modern technology to improving the bodily machine (as Descartes seemed to have proposed), the more humanity is taught to find its only repose in the satisfaction of the machine. Soon, thought Pascal, it will seem as if the truly great and high aspects of human existence have only ever really been there for the sake of the lower necessities and biological needs – rather than the other way round, as the ancients thought.

Pascal seems to have become uneasy about all this as he considered the theoretical claims of the new modern thought. As a result of his discovery of probability calculus, Pascal was able to show that there *can* be truth of a reliable sort even when the mind cannot be certain of it beyond all probability; thus to go on insisting upon indubitable certainty in everything leads the mind into a kind of craziness and alienation from the world.[28] In his own treatise on method in the sciences, *De l'esprit géometrique* (The Mathematical Mind), Pascal had agreed with Descartes and Hobbes that mathematical reasoning could serve as the very model for every intellectual activity. But he goes on to note that some people (he has in mind Descartes) think that they can go "farther" than this: that they can actually arrive by reason at a proof of the first principles of reason. Here is where Pascal fears that the great possibilities of humanity betray themselves into pretension and the mad belief that humankind can have absolutely certain knowledge at its own disposal, within the terms of its own epistemic life. The ever more unyielding pursuit of this, he fears, will blind humanity to the real truth about where it is being led; suddenly, without warning, the new science will confront its own supposed master, absolute rationalism, with the annihilating immensity of the universe, and the human mind will either reel into nausea or hide behind ever more refined technological advances from the truth of its own mortality: "The eternal silence of these infinite spaces fills me with dread."[29]

> When I survey the blind and wretched state of man, when I survey the whole universe in its dumbness and man left to himself with no light, as though lost in this corner of the universe, without knowing who put him there, what he has come to do, what will become of him when he dies, incapable of knowing anything, I am moved to terror, like a man transported in his sleep to some terrifying desert island, who wakes up quite lost and with no means of escape. Then I marvel that so wretched a state does not drive people to despair. . . . Then these lost and wretched creatures look around and find some attractive objects to which they become addicted and attached. (198)

To be marooned in infinite space, no longer able to recall one's own sense of purpose or destiny, and then to anaesthetize oneself to this reality – this is what modernity was doing, Pascal feared, to the human race.

Pascal was influenced by a contemporary Catholic reform movement (named after a bishop who espoused it) called Jansenism, emphasizing the absolute priority of divine grace. It has been customary, ever since Pascal's own time, to wink knowingly at Pascal's more lugubrious thoughts as nothing more than the inevitably pessimistic outpourings of one influenced by Jansenism. This would, I think, be a naive, even foolish, evasion of Pascal's concerns. In fact, while Pascal's theology does indeed emphasize humanity's need for God (hardly a novel view in the Christian tradition), his insights as a mathematician and scientist are what led him, I would argue, to his sense that humanity is increasingly lost in the cosmos – and hiding from the fact; and his growth as a theologian is what allowed him to see why this might be happening. The great twentieth-century French Jesuit Henri de Lubac astutely remarks:

> If we want to understand the anguish of Pascal, let us make an effort to recall the critical situation created at that time for the Christian faith by the new orientation of the human mind. Many, within the Church, suspected nothing of it . . . Pascal himself realized this situation. He saw the tragedy of it in his own soul. . . . He carries within himself, in reality, the solicitude for so many Christian souls, surprised, frightened, abandoned before the vision of the universe that has been ascending to the horizon for a century. . . . It is all human hope that is weakened. Man starts doubting his own dignity, or rather, he looks at it, a frail stem, broken by this newly looming giant, the enormous and brutal Universe. Such is the crisis that, already, in thousands of consciences, is obscurely knotted. Pascal foresees the outcome of it. . . . Extending his gaze, he forms an evaluation of this new civilization, built upon science, having lost the sense of its eternal destinies, having repudiated its greatness. He sees it, unhappy and no longer even understanding its unhappiness.[30]

So, while Pascal will develop a theological vision of the human condition, he does so in ways calculated to get beneath the jaded cynicism masking modernity's despair, and he chiefly sets about his project by surfacing the hidden role of our likes and dislikes, the magnetic pull of our will; he wants us to see what really shapes our thinking, often without our realizing it. At first this unmasking of the will's role is merely somewhat piquant and tantalizing, but gradually Pascal trains us to notice the very real influence and role of what he calls "the heart," the deep desire and practical deftness that in fact governs much of our life. There, he thinks, we might be made aware again of a vista that our minds had closed off from us. For, as he most famously remarks, "the heart has its reasons of which reason knows nothing: we know this in countless ways. I say that it is natural for the heart to love the universal being or itself, according to its allegiance, and it hardens itself against either as it chooses" (423). In what follows then, we can trace Pascal's argument under three headings: what it really means to be human, what gets in our own way, what would be the fulfillment of human existence.

The human condition

If human beings were angels (in which case, of course, they would no longer be human) *or* if they were utterly beasts (from which, in part, they are emerging), then it would be much easier, thinks Pascal, to cope with the human condition. As it is, we seem to be torn in both directions at once, and are always in danger of trying to evade the facts of one pole or the other of our existence. The real clue to the truth about us, however, lies precisely in the fact that both extremes harry us so persistently.

> This internal war of reason against the passions has made those who wanted peace split into two sects. Some wanted to renounce passions and become gods, others wanted to renounce reason and become brute beasts. . . . But neither side has succeeded, and reason always remains to denounce the baseness and injustice of the passions and to disturb the peace of those who surrender to them. And the passions are always alive in those who want to renounce them. (410)

Pascal puts his finger on the instability of early modern perceptions of humanity. Ancient teachers such as Plato and Aristotle had argued that the base drives are not what define humanity and are meant to serve the higher aims of the mind. Modern thinkers such as Machiavelli and Hobbes had, in strong contrast to this, taught their contemporaries to think of the mind's higher aspirations as nothing more than useful tools serving the overruling human urge to survive and to prosper. Early moderns, hearing both voices, were, and for the most part still are, perplexed. Pascal proposed that instead of simply accepting one side or the other of this quarrel between the ancients and the moderns, humankind would be better off asking itself why, in fact, this is what it is to be human: "It is dangerous to explain too clearly to man how like he is to the animals without pointing out his greatness. It is also dangerous to make too much of his greatness without his vileness" (121).

The ancient view of human greatness can, it's true, lead to hubris. But the modern view is, Pascal fears, likely to prove the more insidious; for if you teach me to focus all my attention on my most basic needs and drives and then also teach me to hope only for a "good" that is but the continual and uninterrupted satisfaction of those animal needs, you will in time cease to have an authentic human being on your hands. "Man's greatness comes from knowing he is wretched: a tree does not know it is wretched" (114). The very greatness of humanity, its capacity to reach out in thought beyond itself toward the infinite – and thereby to realize the truth that it is sometimes unhappy – is denied the tree or the trout. But if humanity, through its very basic need to find happiness, silences its self-awareness, it will become less and less. So Pascal thinks the truest dimension of humanity is its ability to awaken to a "beyond" against which we can see both our greatness and our wretchedness.

> I should therefore like to arouse in man the desire to find truth, to be ready, free from passion, to follow it wherever he may find it, realizing how far this knowledge is clouded by passions. I should like him to hate his concupiscence which automatically makes his decisions for him, so that it should not blind him when he makes his choice, nor hinder him once he has chosen. (119)

So Pascal makes us learn what we are precisely by asking us to adhere to something (truth) beyond the measuring, labeling, grasping apparatus of the self and its own interest. And if we commit ourselves to this truth-beyond-the-self we will, of course, be subverting the pretensions of the Cartesian ego. But the results will not, at first, be pretty: "What sort of freak then is man! How novel, how monstrous, how chaotic, how paradoxical, how prodigious! Judge of all things, feeble earthworm, repository of truth, sink of doubt and error, glory and refuse of the universe!" (131).

If we really look at the *whole* of ourselves, honestly, we are dumbstruck. Good, says Pascal, now you're getting somewhere: "Who will unravel such a tangle? . . . Man transcends man" and so we are driven to see that the only voice of real clarity "is no earthly denizen, but at home in heaven. . . . Let us learn our true nature from the uncreated and incarnate truth" (131). "Listen to God," (131) advises Pascal, and what he thinks we hear when we do is the answer to the riddle of our duality: "You are no longer in the state in which I made you," says Wisdom (149), "I created man holy, innocent, perfect. I filled him with light and understanding, I showed him my glory and my wondrous works" (149). In other words, the greatness, and the best aspirations of humankind are not aberrations nor were they created to serve low ends but rather to permit the contemplation of the absolute beauty of God; but they are now only vestiges, rather distorted and easily misdirected capacities for truth. In the Fall, says Wisdom, humanity wanted to make himself his own centre and do without my help. He withdrew from my rule, setting himself up as my equal in his desire to find happiness in himself. . . . The senses, independent of reason and often its masters, have carried him off in pursuit of pleasure. All creatures either distress or tempt him, and dominate him either by forcibly subduing him or charming him with sweetness, which is a far more terrible and harmful yoke. (149)

Notice here that humanity is, as created, eccentric; that is, we are really created to have our center in God rather than in our own mind or will or needs; and that this is what is most natural to us, fulfilling us as relational-communion creatures, designed to live in dialogue and friendship with God. All the human faculties and senses are now chaotic and misleading precisely because they are no longer attuned to God who was their light and glory, and so no longer serve us but rule over us.

What Pascal shows, then, is that human existence is only really intelligible if we think of ourselves as having been created to dwell continually in friendship with God, but as having wandered away into a wilderness where we have grown lost, and lost also to ourselves. "Man does not know the place he should occupy. He has obviously gone astray; he has fallen from his true place and cannot find it again. He searches everywhere, anxiously but in vain, in the midst of impenetrable darkness" (400). The gates of paradise are closed and we have even taught ourselves to forget why we keep heading in their direction. The first step out of this miasmic condition is, avers Pascal, to stop obscuring our own vision, hiding from ourselves the truth about ourselves.

Human aversion to truth

"We run heedlessly into the abyss after putting something in front of us to stop us from seeing it" (166). Our restless modern quest for certainty and security is only hiding from us the mortality that inevitably awaits us, and that, apart from living with God, is now an unbearable truth to us. So Pascal recommends a good scrutiny of our various practices of self-deception. Probably the deepest and most pervasive result of the Fall, thinks Pascal, is that our love and our intelligence, created for communion with God, having been withdrawn from God are primarily directed at ourselves (and by this Pascal doesn't mean "self-love" only in the sense of self-approval but also self-despising; it is a more general sense of self-obsession). "The mind naturally believes and the will naturally loves, so that when there are no true objects for them they necessarily become attached to false ones" (661). The problem with this self-idolatry is that, in our more honest moments, we have to admit that we are in various ways deeply flawed. If we were still worshiping God that would not be such a problem, but humanity having turned to an obsession with itself becomes enraged at being a merely third-rate or even fifth-rate deity. This self-idolatry is thus forced to "conceive a deadly hatred for the truth which rebukes it and convinces it of its faults. It would like to do away with this truth, and not being able to destroy it as such, it destroys it, as best it can, in the consciousness of itself and others" (978). So this is the first way in which "this aversion for the truth exists" (978), leading both the self and others into an endless spiral of deception, flattery, self-delusion, and hypocrisy, in which reality is ever more completely obscured from sight. Only God can make "the soul aware of this underlying self-love which is destroying it, and which he alone can cure" (460).

As a result of self-love, a number of avoidance patterns develop, by means of which humanity is alienated from real life, and shunted off into a simulated world of its own making. The chief of these are a negative use of imagination (mostly as a way propping up our self-interest and vindicating our rightness in every situation), a self-important zeal for human absolutes, then a more serious souring of interests leading to an instability that Pascal calls "diversion," and finally a descent into morose "indifference" bordering lethally on a vicious nihilism. Consider what Pascal calls "diversion." Before the human person falls into the deadly negligence of nihilism in which nothing really matters any more, there is, says Pascal, a stage when we are consciously or unconsciously trying, with increasing desperation, to avoid sitting still and facing the truth about our lives. "I have often said that the sole cause of man's unhappiness is that he does not know how to stay quietly in his own room" (136). You might just pause for a moment and consider how well this describes so many features of modern life in our own day; why do we divert ourselves so much unless there is some deep disquiet we do not know how to face? In fact, Pascal argues, our wild gyrations between frantic overextension on the one hand, and, on the other hand, a desperate hunger for quietude (which we then immediately flee from) are themselves lingering symptoms of our withdrawal from communion with God.

> They have a secret instinct driving them to seek external diversion and occupation, and this is the result of their constant sense of wretchedness. They have another secret instinct, left over from the greatness of our original nature, telling them that the only true happiness lies in rest and not in excitement. These two contrary instincts give rise to a confused plan buried out of sight in the depths of their soul, which leads them to seek rest by way of activity and always to imagine that the satisfaction they miss will come to them once they have overcome certain obvious difficulties and can open the door to welcome rest. All our life passes in this way: we seek rest by struggling against certain obstacles, and once they are overcome, rest proves intolerable because of the boredom it produces. We must get away from it and crave excitement. (136)

The exhaustion and self-bewilderment that so characterize modern human existence are features that Pascal foresaw and related directly to the truth about human being, namely that we are never quite comfortable with ourselves, never quite able to look reality in the eye, unless we can accept the silent, unbearably vulnerable presence of the God who enters humanity's own suffering and depletion in order to re-create humanity from within.

Humanity in relation to God

In one of his simplest and most poignant observations, Pascal uncovers a secret beauty and goodness that might yet be claimed back from humanity's restlessness – at least if that restlessness can genuinely be converted into a more self-aware pursuit of truth beyond the self: "It is good to be tired and weary from fruitlessly seeking the true good, so that one can stretch out one's arms to the Redeemer" (631). Here Pascal performs a double act of magic: first, he unveils the secret within humanity's endless pursuit of happiness, for if this searching has been converted, its true goal is revealed as, in fact, God; but there is another side of the magic, for the stance of the human seeker (aching, spent, arms outstretched toward the longed-for-good) is also unveiled as echoing and imitating the Redeemer. God-become-human has entered entirely into humanity's plight, and converting the heart to a pure love of God, the Redeemer transforms from within the noxious restless craving of the human condition into a pure and holy act of availability to God and others. The naked, vulnerable truthfulness of Jesus on the cross penetrates and strips away all the layers of human fantasy and escapism and cynical despair. This, says Pascal, is the real truth of humankind, and by revealing the hidden humanity which had been lost, Jesus also reveals the hidden God who had seemed so absent. The crucified Jesus reveals both the true humanity and the true God, and necessarily at the same time: "it is equally dangerous for man to know God without knowing his own wretchedness as to know his wretchedness without knowing God" (446), but "knowing Jesus Christ strikes the balance because he shows us both God and our own wretchedness" (192).

So humanity finds itself only when it forgets itself and seeks again for the truth beyond the self, beyond the measure of the mind. This patient, clear-eyed search for the true good may not always yield the certainty and security we might wish; it may only fit us for the company of another exhausted failure who cannot run away from himself because he is nailed in place. And at that moment, says Pascal, we may realize that our humble longing for the true good turns out to be the reciprocal motion engendered in us by God's longing for the true humanity. It is Christ, the Word incarnate, who makes sense of human greatness and wretchedness, for he shares them both and unlocks the secret of them both: "Take comfort; you would not seek me if you had not found me. I thought of you in my agony: I shed these drops of blood for you" (919). I think we could say that in a very real sense Pascal reads the truth of humanity from the humanity of Christ. In some of his most famous passages, Pascal declared that he had been forced to abandon the god of the philosophers for the God of Abraham and of Jesus; he did so because he thought that, in his day, the most refined conceptual analysis of God had become, unconsciously, the idolatrous glare thrown up by the fallen self-obsession of humanity. In order for humanity to find the true God, God would have to find, indeed re-create, true humanity and reveal afresh how to be truly human. "Consider Jesus Christ in every person, and in ourselves. . . . That is why he took on this unhappy condition, so that he could be in every person and a model for every condition of men" (940).

It is from here, I believe, that Pascal thinks humanity might rediscover itself. Learning through the practice of fidelity to Christ, humankind might recover the balance between its reason and its heart, might find the passions and drives and longings mended and harmonious because reoriented towards God who alone fulfills them. Pascal suggests that there will only be a subtle and perhaps barely perceptible confirmation for us that we are on the right path – at least if we are still inclined to search for certainty within ourselves. But the ground of certainty in the subject is really the very impulse that points the subject *away* from oneself: "Take comfort; you would not seek me if you had not found me." This mystical presence of Christ, says Pascal, is the eccentric recentering of humanity, the yearning that purifies all yearning and sets humanity free from all indifference and despair. First one must hear that such a one has been seeking oneself; and then one must consider if it is not he whom one has, oneself, been seeking. One's center is beyond oneself in another.

PATHFINDING

Two Disputed Questions

As in the previous chapter, I now provide you with some "test cases" in which to see how your theological skills are developing. In the sections below, I offer some guided questions as a way of helping you find your own path through the possibilities before you.

Thinking "trinitarianly" about the Church

In the previous chapter we saw how and why Christian conceptions of God as Trinity and of human personhood are deeply interrelated. But there we had, temporarily, to leave out of account the crucial matrix within which Christian reflection on God and on the human person have both developed, namely, within the community itself. Many Christians believe that the Church is the sacramental environment within which divine teaching is most definitively heard and appropriated – teaching both about God's own life and the life of humankind. In this view, the sign-making ritual life of the Christian community is rather like a living icon in which one can see – in a figural (iconic) way – the world's patterns of life being "brooded over" creatively by the Spirit (see Genesis 1: 2 and Luke 1: 35), converted and re-woven into the all-embracing pattern of the relation between Christ and the One he called Father.

I'm proposing, then, that you might like to practice your theological skills here by pondering the rituals that shape Christian existence most profoundly, baptism and Eucharist. How might these patterns of ecclesial life illumine human life with the life of the Trinity? Just to get you started, you may like to consider the views of John Zizioulas, a significant voice in recent discussions of these questions. Zizioulas conceives of baptism as marking the transformation of the human individual into an ecclesial person: the old biologically-determined identity dies in Christ and, united to him, one is raised up into Jesus' personal identity grounded by his relation to the Father. Describing early Christian understandings of baptismal identity, Zizioulas comments:

> The new identity given "in the Spirit" was constituted through incorporation into the body of Christ, the church, through a new set of relationships. These relationships were identical to the relationship of Christ to the Father, and for this reason baptism amounted to sonship (Rom. 8: 15), to acquiring the privilege of calling God "Father" as Christ himself in a unique and eternal way does. In the same way this identity involved social relationships, which were acquired in and through the community of the church and not through the biological family or the state.[31]

Moreover, the eucharistic community becomes the place, the milieu, in which this new ecclesial identity is practiced and definitively expressed. The patterns of relation within the eucharistic assembly "are identical with the Father–Son relationship of the Holy Trinity."[32] In other words, the ritual action of the Eucharist, and all its extensions into time and space beyond the time of the actual liturgy, calls the human family into a new way of being with one another – a way of being marked by the self-sharing peacefulness and loving generosity of the Trinity's own pattern of being with one another in love and freedom. As the assembly lives into the reality of this way of being, their relationships become the living icon, indeed the real presence in this world, of Christ's relation to the Father upon which the Spirit pours out the gifts of the new creation.

You now might try finding a pathway forward in ecclesiological reflection by responding to this perspective held out by Zizioulas.

(1) Zizioulas's view would seem to imply that the Church comes into being as it lives out the baptismal and eucharistic patterns of existence. If the Church thus flows from this ritual sharing in Christ's dying and rising, how is this ritual event related to the historical event of Christ's death and resurrection?

(2) Is there a parallel between the theology of creation in general (as flowing from the eternal trinitarian knowing and loving) and this theology of the Church

(as flowing from the death and resurrection of Christ)? For example, Jesus offers himself in love and freedom, even in his death, and this perfect offering is, Christians believe, the definitive expression in our world of the Father's giving life; and the resurrection of Christ by the power of the Spirit is the definitive outpouring in our world of the infinite joy and resource of the trinitarian unity. In other words, Jesus' death and resurrection would seem to be the expression in our world of the same pattern of trinitarian life from which the whole universe is given existence. So what does this mean for how the Church is given existence?

(3) Taking this even further, how could this help to understand the Pauline idea that whoever is in Christ is a new creation (2 Corinthians 5: 17)? How might the Church's life of receiving and bestowing the gifts of grace be understood as the "first fruits" of the Spirit in the bringing to birth of a new creation?

(4) If the Church were conceived of as an ever-fresh "event," continually coming into being as the human family is drawn into the pattern of Christ's relation to the Father, how might this shape theological reflection on the patterns by which the ecclesial community lives out its life in the world? What would the "para-liturgical" extensions of baptismal and eucharistic practices look like in everyday life? How does the life of the world get baptized and offered eucharistically in the lives of Christians?

Theology and science: how to enter the conversation

Few domains of theological reflection seem as rapidly expanding as the theology and science discussion. The sheer quantity of published material and the necessary levels of technical or scientific background knowledge in this conversation can tend to inhibit theological participants. It would be easy to embrace scientific theories that turn out to mean something quite different than their new religious champions had expected, or to be quickly superseded by yet newer scientific theories. And yet the theology and science discussion, like the theology and spirituality discussion, shows signs of fruitfully nudging the academic discipline of theology into a very healthy interdisciplinary mode of reflection.

Suppose you begin by recalling our frequent aim throughout this book: thinking about theology as a practice and way of knowing that ultimately have God not only as their "subject matter" but as their acting subject, their teacher. What difference does this make? Well, we've seen that within the discipline of theology itself, it means something rather uncomfortable. It means recalling that theology per se is not simply and purely something *we* do by carefully observing the world and correctly representing it in theoretical fashion; rather, we've been saying that theology seems to emerge out of an encounter between human communities and the reality they take to be divine. So theology has to recall that it is always emerging from this conversation, that it is itself an element in what Christians believe to be God's addressing and teaching and transforming of the world.

And if theology can venture to recollect this, can venture, that is, to recollect that God is not a passive datum waiting for theology to come helpfully along and say something humanly meaningful about God, then theology might have something important to discuss with science today. For as theology wakes up from its long methodological slumber, it will see how enchanted it has been by the early modern approach to knowledge as the purely precise observations of a disinterested, objective self, the sole agent in the process of knowing – an approach to knowledge that theology learned to accept as normative from none other than that method's remarkable pioneer: modern science. But as Nicholas Lash has observed, this kind of spectator's knowledge does indeed seem "to be qualified by the fact of our sole agency," in other words, the knowledge "happens" because I, the observer, attend to a passive object out there. But not all realities in fact *are* such passive objects, for "there is a difference between listening to a waterfall and listening to another person, and in the natural scientist's world there are only waterfalls."[33] What about in the theologian's world: are there only waterfalls, or does theology listen to God as to a person? So theology might want to converse with science about how we do in fact know things (and persons), and about the kinds of realities there are to know, and about the respective roles and agencies and languages of these realities in communicating with us.

After all, science might itself be having some doubts about the efficacy of this empirical observation model, grounded in the sole agency of the spectating self. For early modern confidence in the sole agency of the observing self sprang up from the great success of reductionist, anatomizing approaches to the "objects" of knowledge: the objects are reduced to bits and pieces in order for us to arrive at their irreducible elements. Thus they have no role to play, no agency, so that the sole agency is that of the observing experimenter who stands apart from them. Yet this mutually implicating bond between the observing self and the reduction of reality to passive objects may well be starting to unravel. Philip Clayton, a leading analyst in the religion and science field, argues that theology should no longer assume that reductionist approaches to knowing are unchallenged within science:

> It is widely agreed that by the end of the twentieth century the reductionistic program had suffered a major, and possibly fatal, setback. What is crucial is that theologians should understand this change, lest they go on battling the windmills of reductionism – or worse, assume that the windmills have won and retreat from the field.
>
> What are the causes of this surprising shift? First and foremost, physics encountered what appeared to be permanent limits on the dream of a single explanatory system from which all the world's phenomena could be derived. The setbacks were multiple and diverse. . . . [for example] the Copenhagen theorists came to the startling conclusion that quantum mechanical indeterminacy was not merely a temporary epistemic problem but reflected an *inherent* indeterminacy of the physical world itself. . . . The *methods* of reduction – that is, the attempt to understand natural phenomena in terms of their constituent parts, their causes, and the laws that determine their behavior – still characterize the daily practice of science and will continue to do so into the

future. But the *philosophy* of reductionism has started to lose its hold among students of science, allowing for a new awareness of the interrelationships between the natural sciences and other disciplines.[34]

So now would be a good time for theology to propose some interdisciplinary conversations about how we know, across a range of different realities, and a further discussion of the underlying metaphors and metaphysics by which we conceive what counts as "knowing" in each instance.

As you explore into this territory, here are some leading questions for reflection:

(1) In considering issues relating to the beginnings or origins of beings, are we being asked to reflect solely in chronological terms? Christian teaching about creation is often assumed to be about the beginnings of things at the beginning of time, and even, therefore, to be contingent upon a congenial report from the latest physics about the origins of the universe. This presupposes that if there is any "object" like God out there, the divine role or agency must somehow be fitted into whatever little gap may be left (probably temporarily) in the cosmic processes by which the universe began. But would a theology that takes divine agency deeply seriously want to approach things this way? Christian theology has always considered that this chronological question is itself distinct from a more transcendental question about the ground of reality per se, about God's abiding creative agency across all times and spaces and not simply at the beginning of time. In other words, the doctrine of creation is concerned with the source of reality in every moment, instant by instant, even supposedly self-sustaining or self-generating realities. Why are there realities at all, rather than simply nothing?

(2) As science begins to reconsider the philosophy of reductionism (understanding everything solely in terms of its most basic elements), can theology be helpful in fostering dialogue about the emergent whole and about the openness of beings to realities beyond themselves, about reading reality "upwards" rather than solely "downwards"? Theology is good at this sort of reflection and ought to show how to do it. For example, as bread and wine are conceived, purely in themselves, they are entirely reducible to their chemical constituents and then down to their molecular structures, and so on. But it is equally the case that, when taken up into a particular community's life and history, they become elements of a larger communal reality, a sacred or ritual meal, which is itself open toward a yet larger reality (divine self-sharing in the life and death of Christ). Reality can be understood reductively but also holistically and relationally. No reality is entirely explicable apart from the larger communion in which it participates.

(3) Science is very aware of this phenomenon with respect to human consciousness, which seems to open beyond itself into larger structures, and yet human life can also be read by science in an implacably downward and reductionistic manner, as a meat-machine entirely determined by the organic drive of the genes. Here is where theology would want to engage science conversationally about the sort of reality it is seeking to know. If you thought that theology could not really do its

job properly unless it attended to the personal agency of the one it seeks to know (God), how might that insight prompt you to converse with science about the analogues in knowing human persons?

For example, what if you thought that the "data" were not only passive objects but were communicating with you, drawing you into a language and encounter that shapes the very conceptualities by which you know anything at all? Science itself is a human language, drawn into being by the communal interactions of chemicals and cells and human persons and research communities. The investigations and analyses and interpretations of science, as of theology, are all part of language, part of an open-ended communication-event. Who are the partners of this language or communication-event in which science or theology can take place? And how do we best understand them, given that our very means of understanding (language) is itself only apprehensible as we approach them in wholes, opening out towards communication with the other, existing as those to whom a Word has been spoken?

The Human Calling in Creation

As a final theological exercise, let me take these questions yet a step further and consider a theme that cuts across many of the topics we have considered in this chapter: what might it mean for the whole creation that there are humans in its midst – indeed, humans capable of drawing elements of the creation up into language, conversation, and communion? Of course this question makes us think, rather painfully, about the devastating impact of humanity on the fragile earth and its creatures, but in a real sense we wouldn't even know how to conceive the full implications of humanity's misuse of creation if theology did not also provide a peaceful and holistic vision of what the human calling might authentically be. As we've seen, Christians believe that God creates and saves the creatures so that they may come to share in the communion of trinitarian life. Given this, how might we interpret the mysterious possibilities inherent in the fact that among the creatures there are some who seem capable of choosing how they act and what they make of their lives, creatures who can respond to the beauty and wonder of the cosmos with both song and theory, both praise and understanding?[35] How, in other words, might we respond to the Christian belief that the creation is radiant with intelligibility and truth, and that humanity is called to serve and facilitate the creation's consummation in glory? Why, theologically speaking, *is* the cosmos intelligible, recognizable, and appreciable? What does it mean that some of the creatures can sense this and that their understanding of their fellow creatures gives them such tremendous power, for good or evil, over other creatures? For example, we find one important sign of the creation's intelligibility in the fact that humanity is now mapping the genetic code in many forms of life, i.e., there is a genetic "code" that the human mind can perceive and "crack" in the creatures. But what is, or should be, our calling with regard to this powerful perception? What is this knowledge really for?

One way of beginning to approach these questions in Christian thought might recall the origins of all creatures in the divine knowing and loving. Thus, one might say, the intelligibility of the cosmos arises from the fact that the creatures are themselves nothing less than the flowing forth of an infinite act of wisdom. Indeed, a fairly central thread in Christian theology has been the idea that all the creatures have been known and loved eternally within the knowing and loving that is God's trinitarian life. In Origen's *On First Principles* (I. 2–3), Augustine's *Lectures on the Gospel according to St John* (I. 17), and the *Chapters on Knowledge* (I. 42ff.) by Maximus the Confessor, to name only three particular instances, we can find various expressions of this theme. The idea is that the fullness and joy of the eternal trinitarian processions include, as a dimension of their relational self-sharing, the ideas of all the ways in which God can share this giving life with the other, not only the divine Others (i.e., the three divine Persons) but with completely *other* others (i.e., the creatures). Indeed it is part of the divine delight and freedom that God's life can choose to give itself in the creation and consummation of these others. The remarkable seventeenth-century theologian and poet Thomas Traherne could even go so far as to say that this love for the creatures is entirely one with the loving yearning of the Spirit who animates Father and Son, and with the conceiving by which God knows the Other in God, namely the eternal begetting of the Son. This Person, says Traherne, "as He is the Wisdom of the Father, so is He the Love of the Father. . . . And this Person did God by loving us, beget, that He might be the means of all our glory."[36] On this view, the secret depth of every creature radiates the divine self-knowing, called forth by love, and this deep structure of every creature is the reason why it *is* itself, and *as* itself is knowable, intelligible. Thus every creature has the quality of a word, and not just any word but a word expressing infinite love.

We find the same view in Thomas Aquinas. In his *Commentary on the Gospel of St John* (2. 91), Thomas says that all the creatures-to-be exist as eternal archetypes in the mind of God, as the plan of an artisan has an intellectual existence apart from the actual chest or table that comes to be made of wood. It is important for Thomas that the creatures come forth from this knowing of the Father in the Son. Why? Because this trinitarian relationality is the "truthing" that is Truth itself, the eternal and infinite correspondence in joy of the divine Persons one to another (i.e., the Son perfectly expresses the truth of the Father). And because creatures spring from this eternal event of truth-making they are "veritable" themselves, they have a truth that is intelligible to other creatures capable of apprehending and delighting in it, as an earthly echoing of the trinitarian celebration from which all things flow. As Thomas observes in his *Summa Contra Gentiles*, "Since God by understanding Himself understands all other things . . . the Word conceived in God by His understanding of Himself must also be the Word of all things."[37] Noteworthy here is the fact that all things are produced within and from this eternal act of divine self-knowing and loving; the Word who is this self-knowing is therefore, as Thomas puts it, "the perfect existing intelligibility" (IV. 13. 6). So knowing the creatures in their full significance is going to entail an encounter with the Word who speaks them all; and the desire to understand them and rejoice in them properly, according to their own truth, is kindled by the Holy Spirit who inspires the production of their eternal archetypal form in the mutual loving of the Trinity.

So Christians believe that, in and of themselves, all creatures are miracles of divine delight; they exist as events of pure gratuity and freely self-giving love between the divine Persons. Whatever biological constraints each creature may be under, whatever cultural constructions may come to shape creaturely meaning, all creatures have, as it were, a true voice and beauty that only become radiantly apparent as the creatures are heard and seen in their divine truthfulness. But how are the creatures to be appreciated in this way, discovered in their true giftedness and freedom, recognized and cherished for what they are, namely, expressions of eternal joy and desire to be with and for one another eternally? For this alone is to perceive their true sign-fullness, their echoing of the trinitarian life which originates them. In the deepest sense, the truth of the creation is only accomplished through the historical missions of the Word and Holy Spirit, reaching consummation in Christ's death and resurrection and the sending of the Spirit at Pentecost.

As Maximus the Confessor (c.580–662) argues, the incarnation of the Word means the taking up of various dimensions of the creation into their proper speaking.[38] This is not simply a matter of the *logoi* (the rationale and truth) of human bone, blood, muscle, and hair being freed into their true resonance in expressing (as Jesus) the *Logos* in whom and through whom they exist. That certainly is the case, but Jesus also extends more widely this same incorporation of the creation into the life of the Word: the earth itself becomes fruitful with a mysterious abundance and hidden treasure in his parables; the broken relations among humankind become exposed in their sterility and drawn into the healing relationship he creates among his followers. The Incarnation extends to include more and more of creation, restoring to it a true voice as it shares again in the speaking of the Word. At Pentecost the secret work of the Spirit is revealed, moving the creation through a burning desire; the heart of creation is set free to know and its mouth to speak the truth in a manner that surpasses all earthly divisions of nature or culture.

The risen Christ, according to Maximus, "in rising on a pure mind manifests both [himself] and the principles (*logoi*) which have been and will be brought to existence by [the Word]."[39] The power of the resurrection working within humanity through the Holy Spirit continues to accomplish this liberation and "truthfaring" of all the creatures. But, in keeping with the incarnational momentum, this is an activity in which the creatures themselves take part. Intelligent creatures especially have a role to play, for they not only can be taken up into a more radiant earthly sign of the trinitarian joy which is their source (as in the elements of the Eucharist), but they can also freely choose to draw the other creatures into this offering. In the hands of the human community, says Maximus in the *Mystagogia*, the bare stuff of creation (usually subjected to bitter division, quarreling, and manipulable possession) can be made into bread and wine, and offered again into the loving hands of the Creator, and so be received back again all glorious in its true light, become not just biologically nutritious but Life itself.

None of this theology would be possible apart from a deeply trinitarian grammar, a deep structure of the creation that echoes and resounds with the joy of the divine Persons. Indeed, one might even argue that whenever humanity has grown deaf to this deep trinitarian resonance, the living gratuity and freedom of the creatures have been trampled; creation itself is rendered into a silent mute object, an essence, a bare nature to be investigated and if possible exploited, rather than an expression of trinitarian personal freedom and relationality. Humankind is one element within creation, Christians believe, along with the angels, capable through grace of expressing this journey from bare natural and biological necessity up into personal relationship, freedom, and love. And along with other intelligent creatures, humans have the capacity, as empowered by the Holy Spirit, to participate in the Word's restoration of voice and communal, flowing life to all creatures.

Few theologians or spiritual teachers, in my judgment, have equalled Thomas Traherne in exploring this intrinsic giftedness of creation – God's desire to give life to all through all – and humanity's vocation to share in this celebration. Humanity is called to discern this deeper truth of all things, to hear and respond to the divine giving in them all. The question is whether humanity will operate more like visionary angels or more like greedy pigs in this regard:

> The services of things and their excellencies are spiritual: being objects not of the eye, but of the mind: and you are more spiritual by how much you esteem them. Pigs eat acorns, but neither consider the sun that gave them life, nor the influences of the heavens by which they were nourished, nor the very root of the tree from whence they came. This being the work of Angels, who in a wide and clear light see even the sea that gave them moisture: And feed upon that acorn spiritually while they know the ends for which it was created, and feast upon all these as upon a World of Joys within it: while to the ignorant swine that eat the shell, it is an empty husk of no taste nor delightful savour. (I. 26)

Angelic knowledge here opens onto a vision of sublime charity and abundance of limitless extent, and, more importantly, includes a real sense of the joy intrinsic to each creature as a sign of the trinitarian delight that gave being to it. Swinish perception, by contrast (and I would venture Traherne has human grubbing more in mind than any of the more literally porcine variety) is dimmed down to a dull snuffling up of whatever lies immediately at hand, grabbing it for oneself before anyone else can consume it.

In Traherne's view, the trinitarian vision of creation leads to a serious critique of social wrongs. Instead of being freed into the limitless bounty of divine giving, humankind has developed a distinctly swinish appetite for the quickly grasped and consumed; and this translates into human relations, so that people want to possess each other and invent schemes of false self-presentation and a whole simulated realm of appearances designed to get the better of each other:

> You would not think how these barbarous inventions spoil your knowledge. They put grubs and worms into men's heads that are enemies to all pure and true apprehensions, and eat out all their happiness. They make it impossible for them, in whom they reign, to believe there is any excellency in the Works of God, or to taste any sweetness in the nobility of Nature, or to prize any common, though never so great a blessing. They alienate men from the Life of God, and at last make them to live without God in the World. (III. 13)

For humanity to fulfill its potential as the generous knowers and celebrants of creation's truth, a very different eye will be needed. What Traherne seeks to awaken is a new vision of the trinitarian generosity that grounds all creation, a recognition that this is "the highest reason in all things" (III. 18).

In one of his most famous passages, Traherne imagines this revolution in human perception of creation:

> You never enjoy the world aright, till you see how a sand exhibiteth the wisdom and power of God: And prize in everything the service which they do you, by manifesting His glory and goodness to your Soul, far more than the visible beauty on their surface, or the material services they can do your body. Wine by its moisture quencheth my thirst, whether I consider it or no: but to see flowing from His love who gave it unto man, quencheth the thirst even of the Holy Angels. To consider it is to drink it spiritually. To rejoice in its diffusion is to be of a public mind. And to take pleasure in all the benefits it doth to all is Heavenly, for so they do in Heaven. To do so, is to be divine and good, and to imitate our Infinite and Eternal Father. (I. 27)

Traherne signals a trajectory inherent within this deeper seeing and appreciating of all creatures: it leads not just to an enjoyment of God's generosity per se, but to an awareness of the very roots of that generosity in the "public mind" of heaven itself, the self-diffusive bounty of the Trinity.

As humanity comes to participate more deeply in this trinitarian knowing and loving of all things, it becomes more able to see the divine purpose in all things: a desire to delight the other, to give joy, and to share together in the happiness of mutual life. Because all creatures are in fact expressions of this divine intent, they are only brought to their consummate state as they are themselves appreciated and offered in thanksgiving to the giver, thus echoing within the created order the trinitarian giving and receiving. "What are the cattle upon a thousand hills," asks Traherne, "but carcases, without creatures that can rejoice in God and enjoy them?" (III. 82). In a crucial sense, Traherne argues, intelligent creatures who are capable of knowing the full truth of creation by receiving it in gratitude and thanking God for it may help each creature into its consummate state, precisely as an event of sharing:

Praises are the breathings of interior love, the marks and symptoms of a happy life, overflowing gratitude, returning benefits, an oblation of the soul, and the heart ascending upon the wings of divine affection to the Throne of God. God is a Spirit and cannot feed upon carcases: but He can be delighted with thanksgivings, and is infinitely pleased with the emanations of our joy. (III. 82)

We should note here that in calling on humanity to bear creation into the trinitarian life, Traherne is not somehow denigrating the material creation: spirit, in his theology, is not so much set in opposition to matter as to isolation and bare essence, the muting of creatures' inherent intelligibility and relationality so that they become mere "nature." Thus when Traherne speaks of the human vocation to think the creatures back into a state of thankfulness and praise, he is not intending (I would argue) to extricate them from matter; he is suggesting that their "matter" is inherently far more relational, an event of communication, than our usual treatment of creation suggests.[40]

In this trinitarian perspective on creation, then, we recover not only a new and blessed generosity in every creature, but rediscover also a role for humankind more conducive to creation's praise and consummation than its exploitation. Traherne envisages humanity not as reducing creation to useful consumable form but in fact extending creation into its intended fullness and resonance, precisely by appreciating it in praise:

The world within you [i.e., as intelligible, as thought] is an offering returned, which is infinitely more acceptable to God Almighty, since it came from Him, that it might return unto Him. Wherein the mystery is great. For God hath made you able to create worlds in your own mind which are more precious to Him than those which He created; and to give and offer up the world unto Him, which is very delightful in flowing from Him, but much more in returning to Him. (II. 90)

The greater delight and enhancement of creation, as taken into the celebration of praise, does not imply a denigration of its sheer createdness per se. It is precisely so that the creatures may have the freedom and opportunity to choose in love a responsive friendship with the Creator that they receive created existence. Not all the creatures are, perhaps, capable of making this free act of oblation, this willing sharing in the trinitarian communion, but God has given some of the creatures the capacity to accomplish this (appropriately enough) through a communal relationship among themselves. As the intelligent creatures unite together to lift up their fellow creatures in the act of praise, they "translate" them, as it were, back into their native heavenly tongue; they facilitate their expressivity in the language of eternal giving and receiving love. Perhaps as this takes place, the creation is already, in part, at rest from its cosmic pilgrimage, and already, in part, beholding the mystery from which it springs even as it lives the very life it seeks.

The consummate "end" of all things in the endless joy of their Creator seems a good place to end this book. My aims throughout have been two: to help you

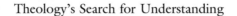
move towards a deeper understanding of what Christians have believed and taught over the centuries, but also, and perhaps more importantly, to give you a taste for the sort of theological teaching and inquiry that have their perfect form not simply in classrooms but in that life of communion with God that Christians think is heaven itself.

Notes

Chapter 1   How God Makes Theologians

1   Karl Barth, *Evangelical Theology: An Introduction* (Grand Rapids, MI: Eerdmans, 1963), pp. 63–4.
2   Thomas Aquinas, *Summa Theologiae* I–II, question 62, article 1, reply to first objection, trans. Fathers of the English Dominican Province (1911; reprinted Westminster, MD: Christian Classics, 1981). Most references to the *Summa Theologiae* are from this edition and will be cited parenthetically according to the usual custom (i.e., by part [I, I–II, II–II, III], question, and article). In the main body of this article Thomas explains that human beings have certain natural capacities and strengths that assist them to their natural goals (e.g., good sense or prudence assisting one toward the goal of successful decision-making). But in Thomas's view, humankind is invited by God toward a goal quite beyond our natural capacities, namely a share in God's eternal life. To assist us toward this end, God bestows these God-faring habits within human beings. And these "are called *theological virtues*: first because their object is God, inasmuch as they direct us aright to God: secondly, because they are infused in us by God alone: thirdly, because these virtues are not made known to us, save by Divine revelation" (I–II. 62. 1).
3   For a landmark discussion of this sea change in theology see Michael J. Buckley, *At the Origins of Modern Atheism* (New Haven: Yale University Press, 1987), especially chs. 1 and 3.
4   John Polkinghorne, *Faith, Science, and Understanding* (New Haven, CT: Yale University Press, 2000), p. 5.

Chapter 2   Strange Calling

1   Simone Weil, "Forms of the implicit love of God," in *Waiting for God*, trans. Emma Craufurd (1951; reprinted New York: HarperCollins, 2001), p. 100.
2   Augustine of Hippo, *The Trinity* XII. 3. 14, trans. Edmund Hill (Brooklyn, NY: New City Press, 1991), p. 330.

3 Weil, "Forms of the implicit love of God," p. 103.

4 Herbert McCabe, *God Matters* (London: Geoffrey Chapman, 1987), p. 177.

5 William of St Thierry, *The Golden Epistle: A Letter to the Brethren at Mont Dieu* II. xiv. 249, trans. Theodore Berkeley (Kalamazoo, MI: Cistercian Publications, 1980), p. 92.

6 For more on the theological significance of this passage from William and more generally on the themes of the following section, see Mark A. McIntosh, *Mystical Theology: The Integrity of Spirituality and Theology*, Challenges in Contemporary Theology series (Oxford: Blackwell, 1998).

7 See the illuminating works of Pierre Hadot, *Philosophy as a Way of Life: Spiritual Exercises from Socrates to Foucault*, ed. Arnold Davidson, trans. Michael Chase (Oxford: Blackwell, 1995) and *What is Ancient Philosophy?*, trans. Michael Chase (Cambridge, MA: Harvard University Press, 2002).

8 Origen of Alexandria, *Commentary on the Song of Songs* in *The Song of Songs: Commentary and Homilies*, trans. R. P. Lawson. Ancient Christian Writers series (New York: Paulist Press, n.d.), p. 22.

9 Andrew Louth, *The Origins of the Christian Mystical Tradition: From Plato to Denys* (Oxford: Clarendon Press, 1981), p. 108.

10 Origen, *Commentary on the Song of Songs*, pp. 29–30.

11 Evagrius Ponticus, *Chapters on Prayer* §61, in *'The Praktikos' and 'Chapters on Prayer'*, trans. John Eudes Bamberger, Cistercian Studies series (Kalamazoo, MI: Cistercian Publications, 1981), p. 65.

12 Herbert McCabe, Appendix 1 ("Knowledge") in *Thomas Aquinas*, Summa Theologiae I. 12–13, trans. Herbert McCabe (London: Blackfriars/Eyre & Spottiswoode, 1964), p. 100. My emphasis.

13 William of St Thierry, *Golden Epistle* II. xviii. 268, p. 97.

14 For a fine summary of this perspective on theology in Thomas Aquinas see a growing number of important studies, particularly: John I. Jenkins, *Knowledge and Faith in Thomas Aquinas* (Cambridge: Cambridge University Press, 1997); Mark F. Johnson, "God's knowledge in our frail mind: the Thomistic model of theology," *Angelicum* 76 (1999): 25–45; Mark Jordan, *Ordering Wisdom: The Hierarchy of Philosophical Discourses in Aquinas* (Notre Dame, IN: University of Notre Dame Press, 1986).

Chapter 3   Divine Teaching and Christian Beliefs

1 Karl Barth, *Church Dogmatics*, vol. IV/2: *The Doctrine of Reconciliation*, trans. G. W. Bromiley (Edinburgh: T. & T. Clark, 1958), pp. 38–9.

2 Thomas Aquinas, *Summa Theologiae* I. 32, 1, reply to third objection, trans. Fathers of the English Dominican Province (1911; reprinted Westminster, MD: Christian Classics, 1981).

3 Thomas Aquinas, *Faith, Reason and Theology*, questions I–IV of the "Commentary on the *De Trinitate* of Boethius," 2. 2, trans. Armand Maurer (Toronto: Pontifical Institute of Medieval Studies, 1987), p. 42.

4 Aquinas, *Summa Theologiae* I. 12. 13.

5 Ibid.

6 As should be expected, the literature on these great thinkers is enormous. To get your bearings, the following will be deeply helpful. John Anthony McGuckin (ed.) *The Westminster Handbook to Origen* (Louisville, KY and London: Westminster John Knox Press, 2004); Joseph W. Trigg, *Origen*, The Early Church Fathers series (London and New York: Routledge, 1998); Brian Davies, *The Thought of Thomas Aquinas* (Oxford: Clarendon Press, 1992); Thomas F. O'Meara, *Thomas Aquinas: Theologian* (Notre Dame and London: University of Notre Dame Press, 1997); Jean-Pierre Torrell, *Saint Thomas Aquinas*, vol. 2: *Spiritual Master*, trans. Robert Royal (Washington, DC: Catholic University of America Press, 2003); Joseph L. Mangina, *Karl Barth: Theologian of Christian Witness* (Louisville, KY and London: Westminster John Knox Press, 2004); John Webster (ed.) *The Cambridge Companion to Karl Barth* (Cambridge: Cambridge University Press, 2000).

7 Aquinas, *Summa Theologiae* II–II. 1. 2. My emphasis.

8 Ibid. II–II. 2. 3.

9 John Locke, *An Essay Concerning Human Understanding* IV. 19. 11, ed. Roger Woolhouse (Harmondsworth: Penguin, 1997), p. 620.

10 Ibid. IV. 19. 14, p. 621.

11 Ibid. IV. 18. 5, p. 611.

12 For more on Locke and the difficulties of religious belief in modernity, see Paul J. Griffiths, *Problems of Religious Diversity* (Oxford: Blackwell, 2001); Eric O. Springsted, *The Act of Faith: Christian Faith and the Moral Self* (Grand Rapids, MI: Eerdmans, 2002); and Nicholas Wolterstorff, *John Locke and the Ethics of Belief* (Cambridge: Cambridge University Press, 1996). For more generally on these questions see the essays edited by Paul J. Griffiths and Reinhard Hütter, *Reason and the Reasons of Faith* (New York and London: T. & T. Clark International, 2005).

13 Rowan Williams, *On Christian Theology*, Challenges in Contemporary Theology series (Oxford: Blackwell, 2000), p. 8.

14 Pierre Hadot, *What is Ancient Philosophy?*, trans. Michael Chase (Cambridge, MA: Belknap Press of Harvard University Press, 2002), p. 274. Emphasis in original.

15 John Henry Newman, *Fifteen Sermons Preached before the University of Oxford (University Sermons)*, 3rd edn., Sermon V. 12 (Notre Dame, IN: University of Notre Dame Press, 1997), pp. 83–4.

16 Ibid., Sermon XII. 29, p. 242.

17 Ibid., Sermon XII. 17, p. 234.

18 Ibid., Sermon XII. 25, p. 238.

19 Ibid., Sermon XII. 27, pp. 240–1.

20 Ibid., Sermon XIV. 41, pp. 305–6.

21 Ibid., Sermon XIV. 42, p. 307.

Chapter 4 Salvation: The Foundation of Christian Theology

1 For good accounts of how the influence of Descartes and Kant led to this sort of misreading of Thomas, and of the alternative readings, see Michel Corbin, *Le Chemin de la théologie chez Thomas d'Aquinas* (Paris: Beauchesne, 1972); John I. Jenkins, *Knowledge and Faith in Thomas Aquinas* (Cambridge: Cambridge University Press, 1997); Fergus Kerr, *After Aquinas: Versions of Thomism* (Oxford: Blackwell, 2002); John

Milbank and Catherine Pickstock, *Truth in Aquinas* (London and New York: Routledge, 2001).

2   A more detailed analysis of this passage can be found in "Discernment and the Paschal mystery," ch. 5 in Mark A. McIntosh, *Discernment and Truth: The Spirituality and Theology of Knowledge* (New York: Crossroad/Herder, 2004).

3   Martin Hengel, *The Atonement: A Study of the Origins of the Doctrine in the New Testament*, trans. John Bowden (London: SCM Press, 1981), p. 31.

4   For a trenchant elucidation of this problem of how we know (or fail to know!) what we think we know, see Alan J. Torrance, "*Auditus fidei*: Where and how does God speak? Faith, reason, and the question of criteria," ch. 1 in Paul J. Griffiths and Reinhard Hütter (eds.) *Reason and the Reasons of Faith* (New York and London: T. & T. Clark International, 2005).

5   Joel B. Green, *Salvation*. Understanding Biblical Themes series (St Louis, MO: Chalice Press, 2003), p. 36.

Chapter 5   Salvation: Meeting Heaven Face to Face

1   For good recent introductions to Irenaeus, see Robert M. Grant, *Irenaeus of Lyons* (New York: Routledge, 1997) and ch. 5 in John Behr, *The Formation of Christian Theology*, vol. 1: *The Way to Nicaea* (Crestwood, NY: St Vladimir's Seminary Press, 2001).

2   Irenaeus, *Against Heresies*, IV, preface, §4, ed. A. Roberts and J. Donaldson. The Ante-Nicene Fathers series, vol. 1 (reprint, Grand Rapids, MI: Eerdmans, 1981), p. 463. Subsequent references to this edition will be noted parenthetically by book, chapter, and section number.

3   Augustine of Hippo, *The Trinity* XIII. 4. 15, trans. Edmund Hill (Brooklyn, NY: New City Press, 1991), pp. 354–5. Subsequent references to this edition will be noted parenthetically by book, chapter, and section number.

4   Anselm of Canterbury, *Why God Became Man* I. 11, trans. Eugene Fairweather, Library of Christian Classics series (Philadelphia: Westminster Press, 1956), p. 119. Subsequent references to this edition will be noted parenthetically by book and chapter number.

5   For an excellent discussion of the cultural background to Anselm's thought see R. W. Southern, *Saint Anselm: A Portrait in a Landscape* (Cambridge: Cambridge University Press, 1991).

6   Vladimir Lossky, "Redemption and deification," ch. 5 in the same author's volume of essays, *In the Image and Likeness of God*, ed. John H. Erickson (Crestwood, NY: St Vladimir's Seminary Press, 1985), p. 99. For a recent Orthodox reconsideration of Anselm, in the light of critiques, see the illuminating work of David Bentley Hart, *The Beauty of the Infinite: The Aesthetics of Christian Truth* (Grand Rapids, MI and Cambridge: Eerdmans, 2003), especially pp. 360–72. More severe are the words of Christos Yannaras, *Elements of Faith: An Introduction to Orthodox Theology*, trans. Keith Schram (Edinburgh: T. & T. Clark, 1991), especially pp. 111–14.

7   Elizabeth Johnson, *She Who Is: The Mystery of God in Feminist Theological Discourse* (New York: Crossroad, 1992), pp. 158–9. For a womanist theological discussion of salvation, see Delores Williams, "Black women's surrogate experience and the Christian

notion of redemption," in *After Patriarchy*, ed. P. Cooey, W. Eakin, and J. McDaniel (Maryknoll, NY: Orbis Books, 1991).

8 Darby Kathleen Ray, *Deceiving the Devil: Atonement, Abuse, and Ransom* (Cleveland, OH: Pilgrim Press, 1998), pp. 3, 58.

9 Kathryn Tanner, *Jesus, Humanity and the Trinity: A Brief Systematic Theology* (Edinburgh: T. & T. Clark, 2001), p. 29.

10 Ray, *Deceiving the Devil*, p. 123.

11 See René Girard, *Things Hidden since the Foundation of the World*, trans. Stephen Bann and Michael Metteer (Stanford, CA: Stanford University Press, 1987) among many other works. Of particular value, in my judgment, are the several books by two theologians who have developed mimetic theory's theological implications most creatively: James Alison and Raymund Schwager.

12 James Alison, *Raising Abel: The Recovery of the Eschatological Imagination* (New York: Crossroad/Herder, 1996), p. 27.

13 Raymund Schwager, SJ, *Must There be Scapegoats? Violence and Redemption in the Bible*, trans. Maria Assad (New York: Crossroad/Herder, 2000), pp. 206–7.

14 Thomas J. Talley, *The Origins of the Liturgical Year* (New York: Pueblo, 1986), p. 3.

15 Alison, *Raising Abel*, p. 26.

16 Herbert McCabe, *God Matters* (London: Geoffrey Chapman, 1987), p. 93.

17 Athanasius, *On the Incarnation* §4, trans. by a religious of the Community of St Mary the Virgin (Crestwood, NY: St Vladimir's Seminary Press, 1996), pp. 29–30. Subsequent references to this edition will be noted parenthetically by paragraph number.

18 F. X. Durrwell, *In the Redeeming Christ*, trans. Rosemary Sheed (New York: Sheed and Ward, 1963), pp. 261–2.

19 Daniel Day Williams, *The Spirit and the Forms of Love* (New York: Harper & Row, 1968), p. 207.

20 McCabe, *God Matters*, pp. 99–100.

21 Ibid., p. 100.

Chapter 6   Divine Life

1 Arthur Michael Ramsey, *The Glory of God and the Transfiguration of Christ* (1947; London: Darton, Longman & Todd, 1967), p. 75.

2 Herbert McCabe, *God Matters* (London: Geoffrey Chapman, 1987), pp. 219–20.

3 Nicholas Lash, *Believing Three Ways in One God: A Reading of the Apostles' Creed* (Notre Dame, IN: University of Notre Dame Press, 1993), p. 32.

4 Amid the growing chorus of those who have cleared away this misconception, see the fine arguments of Lewis Ayres, *Nicaea and its Legacy: An Approach to Fourth-Century Trinitarian Theology* (Oxford: Oxford University Press, 2004); Michel Barnes, "De Régnon reconsidered," *Augustinian Studies* 26 (1995): 51–79; Gilles Emery, "Essentialism or personalism in the Treatise on God in St Thomas Aquinas?," *The Thomist* 64/4 (2000): 521–63; and Matthew Levering, *Scripture and Metaphysics: Aquinas and the Renewal of Trinitarian Theology* (Oxford: Blackwell, 2004).

5 Among many important studies emphasizing this, see Lewis Ayres, " 'Remember that you are Catholic' (*Sermon* 52.2): Augustine on the unity of the triune God," *Journal*

of Early Christian Studies 8 (2000): 39–82; Michel René Barnes, "Re-reading Augustine's theology of the trinity," in S. T. Davis, D. Kendall, and G. O'Collins (eds.) *The Trinity: An Interdisciplinary Symposium on the Doctrine of the Trinity* (Oxford: Oxford University Press, 1999); and Rudi te Velde, *Aquinas on God: The "Divine Science" of the* Summa Theologiae (Aldershot: Ashgate Publishing, 2006), esp. ch. 3, "The heart of the matter: What God is (not)."

6 Ayres, *Nicaea and its Legacy*, pp. 41–3.

7 Rowan Williams, *Arius: Heresy and Tradition*, rev. edn. (Grand Rapids, MI: Eerdmans, 2002), p. 278.

8 Ibid., pp. 238–9.

9 For a helpful summary of the historical evidence regarding the real achievement of these three figures, often referred to collectively as the Cappadocian Fathers, see Joseph T. Lienhard, SJ, "*Ousia* and *hypostasis*: the Cappadocian settlement and the theology of the 'One *Hypostasis*'," in Davis et al., *The Trinity*.

10 See Michel René Barnes, "Divine unity and the divided self: Gregory of Nyssa's trinitarian theology in its psychological context," in Sarah Coakley (ed.) *Re-Thinking Gregory of Nyssa* (Oxford: Blackwell, 2003); and Sarah Coakley, "'Persons' in the 'social' doctrine of the Trinity: a critique of the current analytic discussion," in Davis et al., *The Trinity*.

11 Barnes, "Divine unity and divided self," p. 53.

12 Gregory of Nazianzus, *The Theological Orations* (*Orations* 27–31) III. 16, trans. C. G. Browne and J. E. Swallow, in E. Hardy (ed.) *Christology of the Later Fathers* (Philadelphia: Westminster Press, 1954), p. 171.

13 Ibid.

14 Gregory of Nyssa, *An Address on Religious Instruction* (*Catechetical Oration*) §1, trans. C. C. Richardson, in E. Hardy (ed.) *Christology of the Later Fathers* (Philadelphia: Westminster Press, 1954), pp. 271–2.

15 Ibid. §2, p. 273.

16 Ayres, *Nicaea and its Legacy*, p. 236.

17 Both texts printed in "Documents illustrating the Christology of the Ecumenical Councils," in Hardy, *Christology of the Later Fathers*, pp. 347–8, 350.

18 For a very fine account of Cyril's theology see Daniel A. Keating, *The Appropriation of Divine Life in Cyril of Alexandria* (Oxford: Oxford University Press, 2004).

19 John Meyendorff, *Byzantine Theology: Historical Trends and Doctrinal Themes*, 2nd edn. (New York: Fordham University Press, 1979), p. 155.

20 Austin Farrer, "Incarnation," a sermon in the same author's collection, *The Brink of Mystery*, ed. Charles C. Conti (London: SPCK, 1976), p. 20.

21 For a brisk, bracing, and illuminating survey of recent trinitarian theology and its self-understanding or lack thereof, see Bruce D. Marshall, "Trinity," ch. 12 in Gareth Jones (ed.) *The Blackwell Companion to Modern Theology* (Oxford: Blackwell, 2004).

22 Karl Rahner, *The Trinity*, trans. J. Donceel (London: Burns and Oates, 1970), p. 22.

23 For the serious historical research that genuinely makes the case, see the many definitive works of Michel René Barnes, especially "Re-reading Augustine's theology of the Trinity," in Davis et al., *The Trinity*, and of Lewis Ayres, especially "The grammar of Augustine's trinitarian theology," ch. 15 in the same author's *Nicaea and its Legacy*. Also of seminal significance in the ongoing rereading of Augustine is the rather difficult

but deeply thought-provoking essay by Rowan Williams, "*Sapientia* and the Trinity: reflections on the *De Trinitate*," in B. Bruning (ed.) *Collectanea Augustiniana: Mélanges T. J. Van Bavel* (Leuven: Leuven University Press, 1990).

24 We are all indebted, and I with particular gratitude, to Edmund Hill, OP, for his felicitous translation and penetrating introduction and notes to Augustine: *Augustine, The Trinity*, introduction, translation, and notes by Edmund Hill, OP (Brooklyn, NY: New City Press, 1991). For the structural scheme, see Hill's introduction, p. 27. All references to *The Trinity* will be by book and paragraph, and will be given parenthetically in the text. See also the very helpful Edmund Hill, OP, *The Mystery of the Trinity*, Introducing Catholic Theology series (London: Geoffrey Chapman, 1985).

25 Ayres, *Nicaea and its Legacy*, p. 377.

26 For more on what has come to be known as Augustine's illumination theory of knowledge (which is in my view really a form of mystagogy, that is, a form of spiritual reflection intended to conduct one deeper into the presence of the mystery one seeks to understand), see "Illumination and truth," ch. 9 in Mark McIntosh, *Discernment and Truth: The Spirituality and Theology of Knowledge* (New York: Crossroad/Herder, 2004).

27 Robert W. Jenson, *The Triune Identity: God According to the Gospel* (Philadelphia: Fortress Press, 1982), p. 137. Quoted also by Alan J. Torrance in his very fine work, *Persons in Communion: An Essay on Trinitarian Description and Human Participation, with Special Reference to Volume One of Karl Barth's* Church Dogmatics (Edinburgh: T. & T. Clark, 1996). Jenson's observations are always worth the price of admission, but I do wish to note that in the pages just previous to the one I've quoted he interprets Augustine in a fashion entirely opposed to my own. Regretfully I must confess that I believe his account suffers from the common tendency to discuss Books 8–15 of *The Trinity* as though they were meant to be read separately, quite against Augustine's intentions, and without the basis of the first seven books.

28 Karl Barth, *Church Dogmatics* I. 1: *The Doctrine of the Word of God*, 2nd English edn., trans. G. W. Bromiley (Edinburgh: T. & T. Clark, 1975), p. 296. All quotations from this and the other volumes of the *Church Dogmatics* (all published by T. & T. Clark) will be cited parenthetically in the text by volume number, then part number, and then page number.

29 Barth offers a very valuable experiment at one point in his survey, briefly reframing the whole of his treatment of soteriology in terms of the high priestly ministry of Christ as the one who offers himself as perfect sacrifice for the sake of the covenant. For this concisely encapsulated vision of the trinitarian structure of salvation see *Church Dogmatics*, IV. 1., pp. 273–83.

30 For two quite different but significant accounts of pneumatology, theology of the Holy Spirit, see Yves Congar, *I Believe in the Holy Spirit*, 3 vols., trans. David Smith (New York: Seabury, 1983) and Sergius Bulgakov, *The Comforter*, trans. Boris Jakim (Grand Rapids, MI: Eerdmans, 2004). For a next step, see the thought-provoking essays on the Spirit by John Milbank, chs. 7 and 8 of his work, *The Word Made Strange: Theology, Language, Culture* (Oxford: Blackwell, 1997).

31 Rowan Williams, "Word and Spirit," ch. 8 in his *On Christian Theology*, Challenges in Contemporary Theology series (Oxford: Blackwell, 2000), p. 120.

32 Catherine Mowry LaCugna, "The trinitarian mystery of God," ch. 3.2 in F. S. Fiorenza and J. P. Galvin (eds.) *Systematic Theology: Roman Catholic Perspectives*, vol. 1

(Minneapolis: Fortress Press, 1991), p. 179. For an extended rethinking of how we might conceive of the Three who are God, see David S. Cunningham, *These Three are One*, Challenges in Contemporary Theology series (Oxford: Blackwell, 1997).

33 For what are now classic accounts of these concerns, see Sallie McFague, *Metaphorical Theology: Models of God in Religious Language* (Philadelphia: Fortress Press, 1982) and Rosemary Radford Ruether, *Sexism and God-Talk* (Boston: Beacon, 1983).

34 Elizabeth A. Johnson, *She Who Is: The Mystery of God in Feminist Theological Discourse* (New York: Crossroad, 1992), p. 36. For more recent constructive work on these questions, see Susan Ross, *Extravagant Affections: A Feminist Sacramental Theology* (New York: Continuum, 2001).

35 Crucial work of quite different kinds has been done here by Grace M. Jantzen, *Power, Gender and Christian Mysticism* (Cambridge: Cambridge University Press, 1995), Gavin D'Costa, *Sexing the Trinity: Gender, Culture and the Divine* (London: SCM Press, 2000), and Sarah Coakley, *Powers and Submissions: Spirituality, Philosophy and Gender* (Oxford: Blackwell, 2002). See also the historical studies of Caroline Walker Bynum, e.g., *Jesus as Mother: Studies in the Spirituality of the High Middle Ages* (Berkeley: University of California Press, 1984).

36 Johnson, *She Who Is*, pp. 253–4.

37 On this point see the painfully perceptive comments of David Bentley Hart, *The Beauty of the Infinite: The Aesthetics of Christian Truth* (Grand Rapids, MI and Cambridge, UK: Eerdmans, 2003), pp. 155–67.

38 See the definitive work of Paul L. Gavrilyuk, *The Suffering of the Impassible God: The Dialectics of Patristic Thought* (Oxford: Oxford University Press, 2006).

39 Gerard Manley Hopkins, "Creation and redemption: the great sacrifice – Nov. 8, 1881, Long Retreat," in *Mortal Beauty, God's Grace: Major Poems and Spiritual Writings of Gerard Manley Hopkins*, ed. J. F. Thornton and S. B. Varenne (New York: Vintage, 2003), pp. 175–6.

40 See Hans Urs von Balthasar, *Mysterium Paschale*, trans. Aidan Nichols, OP (Edinburgh: T. & T. Clark, 1990), pp. viii–ix: "We shall never know how to express the abyss-like depths of the Father's self-giving, that Father who, in an eternal 'super-Kenosis', makes himself 'destitute' of all that he is and can be so as to bring forth a consubstantial divinity, the Son. Everything that can be thought and imagined where God is concerned is, in advance, included and transcended in this self-destitution which constitutes the person of the Father, and, at the same time, those of the Son and the Spirit. God as the 'gulf' (Eckhart: *Un-Grund*) of absolute Love contains in advance, eternally, all the modalities of love, of compassion, and even of a 'separation' motivated by love and founded on the infinite distinction between the hypostases – modalities which may manifest themselves in the course of a history of salvation involving sinful humankind."

41 A very helpful introduction is provided by the premier translator of Heidegger and venerable theologian, John Macquarrie, in *Heidegger and Christianity*, The Hensley Henson Lectures, 1993–1994 (New York: Continuum, 1999).

42 I can never recommend too often the delightful essays and talks on these matters by Herbert McCabe, *God Matters* and the same author's *God Still Matters* (London: Continuum, 2002). Only very slightly less entertaining, and enormously helpful, is Fergus Kerr's masterly survey and analysis, *After Aquinas: Versions of Thomism* (Oxford: Blackwell, 2002).

43 For an excellent introduction to this very odd period of transition, see Louis Dupré, *Passage to Modernity: An Essay in the Hermeneutics of Nature and Culture* (New Haven, CT: Yale University Press, 1993).

44 A very helpful survey and anthology of the full range of these thinkers is provided by Graham Ward (ed.) *The Postmodern God: A Theology Reader* (Oxford: Blackwell, 1997). For a clarifying introduction, see also James K. A. Smith, *Introducing Radical Orthodoxy: Mapping a Post-Secular Theology* (Grand Rapids, MI: Baker, 2004).

45 John D. Zizioulas, *Being as Communion: Studies in Personhood and the Church*. Contemporary Greek Theologians series, no. 4 (Crestwood, NY: St Vladimir's Seminary Press, 1985), p. 44. For very helpful analyses on Zizioulas and constructive views on this theme more broadly, see Paul McPartlan, *The Eucharist Makes the Church: Henri de Lubac and John Zizioulas in Dialogue* (Edinburgh: T. & T. Clark, 1993); Alan J. Torrance, *Persons in Communion*; and Miroslav Volf, *After Our Likeness: The Church as Image of the Trinity* (Grand Rapids, MI: Eerdmans, 1998).

46 For an introduction to feminist concerns in anthropology see Ann O'Hara Graff (ed.) *In the Embrace of God: Feminist Approaches to Theological Anthropology* (Maryknoll, NY: Orbis, 1995); also Ruth L. Smith, "Relationality and the ordering of differences in feminist ethics," *Journal of Feminist Studies in Religion* 9 (Spring–Fall, 1993): 199–214.

47 For a good survey of the theology and science discussion, see Philip Clayton, "Theology and the physical sciences," ch. 20 in David Ford with Rachel Muers (eds.) *The Modern Theologians*, 3rd edn. (Oxford: Blackwell, 2005); and more particularly on the question of relationality in theology and science, see Robert J. Russell, Philip Clayton, Kirk Wegter-McNelly, and John Polkinghorne (eds.) *Quantum Mechanics: Scientific Perspectives on Divine Action* (Vatican City: Vatican Observatory Press, 2002).

48 A slightly different version of this section appeared as part of Mark A. McIntosh, "Knowing and loving God: trinitarian perspectives on Christian spirituality," in Arthur G. Holder (ed.) *The Blackwell Companion to Christian Spirituality* (Oxford: Blackwell, 2005).

49 Bonaventure, *The Journey of the Mind to God* VII. 1, trans. P. Boehner, ed. S. F. Brown (Indianapolis: Hackett, 1993), p. 37. All references will be given parenthetically by chapter and paragraph number.

50 For excellent considerations on human agency in John see Edward Howells, *John of the Cross and Teresa of Avila: Mystical Knowing and Selfhood* (New York: Crossroad, 2002), and Rowan Williams, "The deflections of divine desire: negative theology in trinitarian disclosure," in O. Davies and D. Turner (eds.) *Silence and the Word: Negative Theology and the Incarnation* (Cambridge: Cambridge University Press, 2002).

51 John of the Cross, *The Spiritual Canticle* in *The Collected Works of St John of the Cross*, trans. K. Kavanaugh and O. Rodriguez (Washington, DC: Institute of Carmelite Studies Publications, 1979). All references given parenthetically by chapter and paragraph number.

Chapter 7   Creaturely Life

1 For some uncommonly thoughtful analysis of these sorts of misconceptions and many others, see Christopher Morse, *Not Every Spirit: A Dogmatics of Christian Disbelief* (Valley Forge, PA: Trinity Press International, 1994).

2 James Alison, *Raising Abel: The Recovery of the Eschatological Imagination* (New York: Crossroad Herder, 1996), p. 74.
3 Ibid., p. 55.
4 F. X. Durrwell, *The Resurrection: A Biblical Study* (New York: Sheed and Ward, 1960), p. 131.
5 Further on the important idea that the creatures are grounded in the trinitarian processions, see Gilles Emery, OP, *Trinity in Aquinas* (Ypsilanti, MI: Sapientia, 2003).
6 James Alison, *The Joy of Being Wrong: Original Sin through Easter Eyes* (New York: Crossroad/Herder, 1998), pp. 201–2.
7 See, e.g., *The Breviloquium* II. 1. 4, where Bonaventure envisions the structures of creaturely existence as bearing the traces of their trinitarian causation through the working of the divine Persons (each creature comes to exist, it exists according to a particular form, it exists for some consummating good). For an excellent introduction, especially to Bonaventure's idea of the Incarnation as bringing creation to its fulfillment, see Zachary Hayes, *The Hidden Center: Spirituality and Speculative Christology in St Bonaventure* (New York: Paulist Press, 1981).
8 Bonaventure, *Collations on the Six Days* 20. 5, trans. J. de Vinck (Paterson, NJ: St Anthony Guild Press, 1970), pp. 301–2.
9 E.g., Hans Urs von Balthasar, *Theo-Drama: Theological Dramatic Theory*, vol. V: *The Last Act*, trans. G. Harrison (San Francisco: Ignatius, 1998), pp. 506ff.
10 See, e.g., Dumitru Staniloae, *The Experience of God: Orthodox Dogmatic Theology*, vol. 2: *The World: Creation and Deification*, trans. Ioan Ionita and Robert Barringer (Brookline, MA: Holy Cross Orthodox Press, 2000); also very interesting in this respect are the newly translated texts of Maximus the Confessor in *On the Cosmic Mystery of Jesus Christ: Selected Writings from St Maximus the Confessor*, trans. Paul M. Blowers and Robert Louis Wilken (Crestwood, NY: St Vladimir's Seminary Press, 2003).
11 Athanasius, *On the Incarnation* §4, trans. and ed. by a religious of the Community of St Mary the Virgin (Crestwood, NY: St Vladimir's Seminary Press, 1996), pp. 29–30.
12 David Bentley Hart, "The mirror of the infinite: Gregory of Nyssa on the *Vestigia Trinitatis*," in *Re-Thinking Gregory of Nyssa*, ed. Sarah Coakley (Oxford: Blackwell, 2003), p. 118. Hart cites Gregory, *In Hexaemeron, Patrologia Graeca*, vol. 44, pp. 68–72; *De Anima et Resurrectione*, p. 124; *De Hominis Opificio*, pp. xxiv, 212–13.
13 Olivier Clément, *The Roots of Christian Mysticism* (New York: New City Press, 1995), p. 216.
14 Alexander Schmemann, *For the Life of the World: Sacraments and Orthodoxy* (Crestwood, NY: St Vladimir's Seminary Press, 1973), pp. 139–40. Emphases original.
15 Herbert McCabe, *God Matters* (London: Geoffrey Chapman, 1987), pp. 123–4.
16 D. Juvenal Merriell, "Trinitarian anthropology," ch. 6 in Rik Van Nieuwenhove and Joseph Wawrykow (eds.) *The Theology of Thomas Aquinas* (Notre Dame, IN: University of Notre Dame Press, 2005), pp. 137–8; my emphasis. See also Merriell's magisterial work, *To the Image of the Trinity: A Study of the Development of Aquinas' Teaching* (Toronto: Pontifical Institute of Mediaeval Studies, 1990).
17 See John D. Zizioulas, *Being as Communion: Studies in Personhood and the Church* (Crestwood, NY: St Vladimir's Seminary Press, 1985) and Christos Yannaras, *Elements of Faith: An Introduction to Orthodox Theology* (Edinburgh: T. & T. Clark, 1991).
18 Olivier Clément, *On Human Being: A Spiritual Anthropology*, trans. J. Hummerstone (London: New City Press, 2000), p. 116.

19 Thomas Aquinas, *Commentary on the Gospel of St John*, Lecture 5, para. 136, trans. J. A. Weisheipl with F. R. Larcher (Albany, NY: Magi, 1980), p. 75.

20 For an extremely helpful survey of the developments and trends in how Thomas has been interpreted, see Fergus Kerr, *After Aquinas: Versions of Thomism* (Oxford: Blackwell, 2002). And more specifically on the often disputed question of what Thomas was up to in the *Summa Theologiae*, see John I. Jenkins, *Knowledge and Faith in Thomas Aquinas* (Cambridge: Cambridge University Press, 1997).

21 Attentive readers will immediately wonder if I have forgotten that, in the *Summa Theologiae*, Thomas first discusses God's existence and unity before he discusses the Trinity; indeed this fact is usually taken by Thomas's critics as definitive evidence of his relegation of the doctrine of the Trinity to a secondary role in theology. Obviously this is a massive and continuing debate, and a footnote is not the place to introduce all the evidence that would be necessary to confirm my view. Let me just say that, in my judgment, the order of Thomas's discussion in no way reflects any belief on his part that whatever one might think about the Trinity is somehow secondary to what might be known about God from reason or the natural existence of things. Rather, I would argue, Thomas has two sequences in mind in devising the order of the *Summa Theologiae*: the order of salvation history, in which the people of God do actually find themselves encountered by God before they realize, through Christ and the Spirit, that God is the Trinity, and secondly, the order of learning that Thomas intends, in which, gradually, the learner is enabled to apprehend the higher, or more nearly the first principles of divine life by which the learner's knowledge of truth must be caused in the mind. So learning about God as actually existing and as good and so forth is a kind of training or theological formation, fitting the learner for the ascent to the ultimate principles of divine life, the Trinity and its processions and relations, which will be seen not only as the *ratio* of all existence, but also become the *ratio* of the learner's own thinking and understanding.

22 Gilles Emery, *Trinity in Aquinas* (Ypsilanti, MI: Sapientia, 2003), p. 61.

23 Rudi te Velde, *Aquinas on God: The "Divine Science" of the* Summa Theologiae (Aldershot: Ashgate Publishing, 2006), p. 141. See also the very fine work by the same author: *Participation and Substantiality in Thomas Aquinas* (Leiden: Brill, 1995).

24 Thomas Aquinas, *Commentary on John*, Lecture 5, para. 133, pp. 73–4.

25 Thomas Aquinas, *Truth* I. 2, trans. R. W. Mulligan, SJ (Indianapolis: Hackett, 1995), vol. 1, p. 11.

26 Ibid. IV. 6.

27 For a good introduction to Pascal and his anthropological thinking see Nicholas Hammond, *Playing with Truth: Language and the Human Condition in Pascal's Pensées* (Oxford: Oxford University Press, 1994); on the peculiarly non-religious interpretations of Pascal, see Jacob Meskin, "Secular self-confidence, postmodernism, and beyond: recovering the religious dimension of Pascal's *Pensées*," *Journal of Religion* 75/4 (1995): 487–508.

28 See the very helpful analysis of what was at stake in the argument between Descartes and Pascal in Louis Dupré, *Passage to Modernity: An Essay in the Hermeneutics of Nature and Culture* (New Haven, CT: Yale University Press, 1993), pp. 80–90.

29 Blaise Pascal, *Pensées*, 201, trans. A. J. Krailsheimer (Harmondsworth: Penguin, 1966, rev. edn. 1995). Pascal's "Thoughts" were found, after he died, in little bundles of many separate strips of paper, without entirely clear indications of how he had intended

to organize and edit them all for his projected final work on the truth of Christian faith. This has given rise, currently, to four quite different editions – Lafuma, Brunschvicg, Sellier, and Mesnard – each, unfortunately, with some highly significant differences in the ordering and numbering of the individual "thoughts." Readers wishing to read further in Pascal are advised to make friends quickly with the various concordances of edition numberings usually found in most texts of the *Pensées*. I will quote from the most widely used translation in English, by Krailsheimer in the Penguin Classics series; Krailsheimer uses the Lafuma edition and numbering. All references, as just above to 201, refer to the thought or *pensée* number in Lafuma, and will hereafter be given parenthetically.

30 Henri de Lubac, "On a thought by Pascal," in the same author's collection, *Theology in History* (San Francisco: Ignatius Press, 1996), pp. 50–4.

31 John D. Zizioulas, "The early Christian community," in *World Spirituality: An Encyclopedic History of the Religious Quest*, vol. 16: *Christian Spirituality: Origins to the Twelfth Century*, ed. Bernard McGinn and John Meyendorff (New York: Crossroad, 1987), p. 28.

32 Ibid., p. 29. See also the analyses and critiques of Zizioulas in Paul McPartlan, *The Eucharist Makes the Church: Henri de Lubac and John Zizioulas in Dialogue* (Edinburgh: T. & T. Clark, 1993) and Miroslav Volf, *After Our Likeness: The Church as the Image of the Trinity* (Grand Rapids, MI: Eerdmans, 1998).

33 Nicholas Lash, *The Beginning and the End of 'Religion'* (Cambridge: Cambridge University Press, 1996), p. 85.

34 Philip Clayton, "Theology and the physical sciences," ch. 20 in David Ford and Rachel Muers (eds.) *The Modern Theologians*, 3rd edn. (Oxford: Blackwell, 2005), pp. 344–5.

35 Few subjects have witnessed a greater renaissance (and more ambiguity) in recent decades than the question of spirituality and creation. For a creative and incisive analysis of the intersection of creation life-centered theology, spirituality, and pneumatology, see Mark I. Wallace, *Fragments of the Spirit: Nature, Violence, and the Renewal of Creation* (New York: Continuum, 1976).

36 Thomas Traherne, *Centuries* II. 43 (Oxford: A. R. Mowbray, 1985), p. 77; for an excellent brief introduction to Traherne, see Denise Inge (ed.) *Thomas Traherne: Poetry and Prose* (London: SPCK, 2002). References to the *Centuries* will be given by century and paragraph number parenthetically.

37 Thomas Aquinas, *Summa Contra Gentiles* IV. 13. 6: *Salvation*, trans. Charles J. O'Neill (Notre Dame, IN: University of Notre Dame Press, 1975). References to this translation will be given parenthetically by book, question, and paragraph.

38 For a perceptive analysis see Andrew Louth, *Maximus the Confessor* (London: Routledge, 1996).

39 Maximus the Confessor: *The Four Hundred Chapters on Love* I. 95, trans. George C. Berthold, in *Maximus Confessor: Selected Writings* (New York: Paulist Press, 1985), p. 45.

40 Perhaps Traherne is in this sense saying something not far from recent thought in quantum physics; on the relational energy of sub-atomic reality, see John Polkinghorne, *The Faith of a Physicist: Reflections of a Bottom-Up Thinker*, The Gifford Lectures, 1993–4 (Minneapolis: Fortress Press, 1996).

Bibliography

Primary Sources

Alison, James. *Raising Abel: The Recovery of the Eschatological Imagination*. New York: Crossroad/Herder, 1996.

—— *The Joy of Being Wrong: Original Sin through Easter Eyes*. New York: Crossroad/ Herder, 1998.

Anselm of Canterbury. *Why God Became Man*. Translated by Eugene Fairweather. Library of Christian Classics. Philadelphia: Westminster Press, 1956.

Aquinas, Thomas. *Summa Theologiae* (I. 12–13 translated by Herbert McCabe). London: Blackfriars/Eyre & Spottiswoode, 1964.

—— *Summa Contra Gentiles*. Translated by Charles J. O'Neill. Notre Dame, IN: University of Notre Dame Press, 1975.

—— *Commentary on the Gospel of St John*. Translated by J. A. Weisheipl and F. R. Larcher. Albany, NY: Magi, 1980.

—— *Summa Theologiae*. Translated by Fathers of the English Dominican Province, 1911. Reprint, Westminster, MD: Christian Classics, 1981.

—— *Faith, Reason and Theology*. Translated by Armand Maurer. Toronto: Pontifical Institute of Medieval Studies, 1987.

—— *Truth*, vol. 1. Translated by R. W. Mulligan, SJ. Indianapolis: Hackett, 1995.

Athanasius. *On the Incarnation*. Translated by a religious of the Community of St Mary the Virgin. Crestwood, NY: St Vladimir's Seminary Press, 1996.

Augustine of Hippo. *The Trinity*. Translated by Edmund Hill. Brooklyn, NY: New City Press, 1991.

Balthasar, Hans Urs von. *Explorations in Theology*, vol. 1: *The Word Made Flesh*. San Francisco: Ignatius Press, 1989.

—— *Mysterium Paschale*. Translated by Aidan Nichols, OP. Edinburgh: T. & T. Clark, 1990.

—— *Theo-Drama: Theological Dramatic Theory*, vol. 5: *The Last Act*. Translated by G. Harrison. San Francisco: Ignatius Press, 1998.

Barth, Karl. *Church Dogmatics*, 4 vols. Translated by G. W. Bromiley and T. F. Torrance. Edinburgh: T. & T. Clark, 1936–69.

——*Evangelical Theology: An Introduction*. Translated by Grover Foley. Grand Rapids, MI: Eerdmans, 1963.

Bonaventure. *The Breviloquium*. Translated by José de Vinck. In *The Works of Bonaventure*, vol. II. Paterson, NJ: St Anthony Guild Press, 1963.

——*Collations on the Six Days*. Translated by José de Vinck. Paterson, NJ: St Anthony Guild Press, 1970.

——*The Journey of the Mind to God*. Edited by S. F. Brown. Translated by P. Boehner. Indianapolis: Hackett, 1993.

Bulgakov, Sergius. *The Comforter*. Translated by Boris Jakim. Grand Rapids, MI: Eerdmans, 2004.

Clément, Olivier. *The Roots of Christian Mysticism*. New York: New City Press, 1995.

——*On Human Being: A Spiritual Anthropology*. Translated by J. Hummerstone. London: New City Press, 2000.

Coakley, Sarah. *Powers and Submissions: Spirituality, Philosophy and Gender*. Challenges in Contemporary Theology series. Oxford: Blackwell, 2002.

Cunningham, David S. *These Three are One*. Challenges in Contemporary Theology series. Oxford: Blackwell, 1997.

D'Costa, Gavin. *Sexing the Trinity: Gender, Culture and the Divine*. London: SCM Press, 2000.

Durrwell, F. X. *The Resurrection: A Biblical Study*. New York: Sheed and Ward, 1960.

——*In the Redeeming Christ*. Translated by Rosemary Sheed. New York: Sheed and Ward, 1963.

Evagrius Ponticus. *'The Praktikos' and 'Chapters on Prayer'*. Translated by John Eudes Bamberger. Cistercian Studies series. Kalamazoo, MI: Cistercian Publications, 1981.

Farrer, Austin. "Incarnation." In *The Brink of Mystery*. Edited by Charles C. Conti. London: SPCK, 1976.

Girard, René. *Things Hidden since the Foundation of the World*. Translated by Stephen Bann and Michael Metteer. Stanford, CA: Stanford University Press, 1987.

Gregory of Nazianzus. *The Theological Orations*. Translated by C. G. Browne and J. E. Swallow. In E. Hardy (ed.) *Christology of the Later Fathers*. Philadelphia: Westminster Press, 1954.

Gregory of Nyssa. *An Address on Religious Instruction (Catechetical Oration)*. Translated by C. C. Richardson. In E. Hardy (ed.) *Christology of the Later Fathers*. Philadelphia: Westminster Press, 1954.

Griffiths, Paul J. *Problems of Religious Diversity*. Oxford: Blackwell, 2001.

Hart, David Bentley. *The Beauty of the Infinite: The Aesthetics of Christian Truth*. Grand Rapids, MI and Cambridge, UK: Eerdmans, 2003.

Hopkins, Gerard Manley. "Creation and redemption: the great sacrifice – Nov. 8, 1881, Long Retreat." In *Mortal Beauty, God's Grace: Major Poems and Spiritual Writings of Gerard Manley Hopkins*. Edited by J. F. Thornton and S. B. Varenne. New York: Vintage, 2003.

Irenaeus. *Against Heresies*. Edited by A. Roberts and J. Donaldson. The Ante-Nicene Fathers series, vol. 1. Reprint, Grand Rapids, MI: Eerdmans, 1981.

Jantzen, Grace M. *Power, Gender and Christian Mysticism*. Cambridge: Cambridge University Press, 1995.

Jenson, Robert W. *The Triune Identity: God According to the Gospel*. Philadelphia: Fortress Press, 1982.

John of the Cross. *The Spiritual Canticle*. In *The Collected Works of St John of the Cross*. Translated by K. Kavanaugh and O. Rodriguez. Washington, DC.: Institute of Carmelite Studies Publications, 1979.

Johnson, Elizabeth. *She Who Is: The Mystery of God in Feminist Theological Discourse*. New York: Crossroad, 1992.

Lash, Nicholas. *The Beginning and the End of 'Religion'*. Cambridge: Cambridge University Press, 1996.

Locke, John. *An Essay Concerning Human Understanding*. Edited by Roger Woolhouse. Harmondsworth: Penguin, 1997.

Lossky, Vladimir. "Redemption and deification." In John H. Erickson (ed.) *In the Image and Likeness of God*. Crestwood, NY: St Vladimir's Seminary Press, 1985.

Maximus the Confessor. *Maximus Confessor: Selected Writings*. Translated by George C. Berthold. New York: Paulist Press, 1985.

——— *On the Cosmic Mystery of Jesus Christ: Selected Writings from St Maximus the Confessor*. Translated by Paul M. Blowers and Robert Louis Wilken. Crestwood, NY: St Vladimir's Seminary Press, 2003.

McCabe, Herbert. *God Matters*. London: Geoffrey Chapman, 1987.

——— *God Still Matters*. London: Continuum, 2002.

McFague, Sallie. *Metaphorical Theology: Models of God in Religious Language*. Philadelphia: Fortress Press, 1982.

Milbank, John. *The Word Made Strange: Theology, Language, Culture*. Oxford: Blackwell, 1997.

Morse, Christopher. *Not Every Spirit: A Dogmatics of Christian Disbelief*. Valley Forge, PA: Trinity Press International, 1994.

Newman, John Henry. *Fifteen Sermons Preached before the University of Oxford (University Sermons)*, 3rd edn. Notre Dame, IN: University of Notre Dame Press, 1997.

Origen of Alexandria. *Commentary on the Song of Songs*. In *The Song of Songs: Commentary and Homilies*. Translated by R. P. Lawson. Ancient Christian Writers series. New York: Paulist Press, n.d.

——— *On First Principles*. Translated by G. W. Butterworth. Reprint, Gloucester, MA: Peter Smith, 1973.

Pascal, Blaise. *Pensées*. Translated by A. J. Krailsheimer. Harmondsworth: Penguin, 1966. Revised edn., 1995.

Polkinghorne, John. *The Faith of a Physicist: Reflections of a Bottom-Up Thinker*. The Gifford Lectures, 1993–4. Minneapolis: Fortress Press, 1996.

Rahner, Karl. *The Trinity*. Translated by J. Donceel. London: Burns and Oates, 1970.

Ray, Darby Kathleen. *Deceiving the Devil: Atonement, Abuse, and Ransom*. Cleveland, OH: Pilgrim Press, 1998.

Ross, Susan. *Extravagant Affections: A Feminist Sacramental Theology*. New York: Continuum, 2001.

Ruether, Rosemary Radford. *Sexism and God-Talk*. Boston: Beacon, 1983.

Schmemann, Alexander. *For the Life of the World: Sacraments and Orthodoxy*. Crestwood, NY: St Vladimir's Seminary Press, 1973.

Schwager, Raymund. *Must There be Scapegoats? Violence and Redemption in the Bible*. Translated by Maria Assad. New York: Crossroad/Herder, 2000.

Staniloae, Dumitru. *The Experience of God: Orthodox Dogmatic Theology*, vol. 2: *The World: Creation and Deification*. Translated by Ioan Ionita and Robert Barringer. Brookline, MA: Holy Cross Orthodox Press, 2000.

Tanner, Kathryn. *Jesus, Humanity and the Trinity: A Brief Systematic Theology*. Edinburgh: T. & T. Clark, 2001.

Thucydides. *The Peloponnesian War*. Edited by R. B. Strassler. Translated by R. Crawley. New York: Free Press, 1996.

Traherne, Thomas. *Centuries*. Oxford: A. R. Mowbray, 1985.

Wallace, Mark I. *Fragments of the Spirit: Nature, Violence, and the Renewal of Creation*. New York: Continuum, 1976.

Weil, Simone. *Waiting for God*. Translated by Emma Craufurd. 1951. Reprint, New York: HarperCollins, 2001.

Williams, Daniel Day. *The Spirit and the Forms of Love*. New York: Harper & Row, 1968.

Williams, Delores. "Black women's surrogate experience and the Christian notion of redemption." In P. Cooey, W. Eakin, and J. McDaniel (eds.) *After Patriarchy*. Maryknoll, NY: Orbis Books, 1991.

Williams, Rowan. *On Christian Theology*. Challenges in Contemporary Theology series. Oxford: Blackwell, 2000.

William of St Thierry. *The Golden Epistle: A Letter to the Brethren at Mont Dieu*. Translated by Theodore Berkeley. Kalamazoo, MI: Cistercian Publications, 1980.

Yannaras, Christos. *Elements of Faith: An Introduction to Orthodox Theology*. Translated by Keith Schram. Edinburgh: T. & T. Clark, 1991.

Zizioulas, John D. *Being as Communion: Studies in Personhood and the Church*. Contemporary Greek Theologians series, no. 4. Crestwood, NY: St Vladimir's Seminary Press, 1985.

——"The early Christian community." In *World Spirituality: An Encyclopedic History of the Religious Quest*, vol. 16: *Christian Spirituality: Origins to the Twelfth Century*. Edited by Bernard McGinn and John Meyendorff. New York: Crossroad, 1987.

Secondary Sources

Ayres, Lewis. "'Remember that you are Catholic' (*Sermon* 52.2): Augustine on the unity of the triune God." *Journal of Early Christian Studies* 8 (2000): 39–82.

—— *Nicaea and its Legacy: An Approach to Fourth-Century Trinitarian Theology*. Oxford: Oxford University Press, 2004.

Barnes, Michel René. "De Régnon reconsidered." *Augustinian Studies* 26 (1995): 51–79.

——"Re-reading Augustine's theology of the Trinity." In S. T. Davis, D. Kendall, and G. O'Collins (eds.) *The Trinity: An Interdisciplinary Symposium on the Doctrine of the Trinity*. Oxford: Oxford University Press, 1999.

——"Divine unity and the divided self: Gregory of Nyssa's trinitarian theology in its psychological context." In Sarah Coakley (ed.) *Re-Thinking Gregory of Nyssa*. Oxford: Blackwell, 2003.

Behr, John. *The Formation of Christian Theology*, vol. 1: *The Way to Nicaea*. Crestwood, NY: St Vladimir's Seminary Press, 2001.

Buckley, Michael J. *At the Origins of Modern Atheism*. New Haven, CT: Yale University Press, 1987.

Bynum, Caroline Walker. *Jesus as Mother: Studies in the Spirituality of the High Middle Ages.* Berkeley: University of California Press, 1984.

Clayton, Philip. "Theology and the physical sciences." In David Ford and Rachel Muers (eds.) *The Modern Theologians*, 3rd edn. Oxford: Blackwell, 2005.

Coakley, Sarah. "'Persons' in the 'social' doctrine of the Trinity: a critique of the current analytic discussion." In S. T. Davis, D. Kendall, and G. O'Collins (eds.) *The Trinity: An Interdisciplinary Symposium on the Doctrine of the Trinity.* Oxford: Oxford University Press, 1999.

Congar, Yves. *I Believe in the Holy Spirit*, 3 vols. Translated by David Smith. New York: Seabury, 1983.

Corbin, Michel. *Le Chemin de la theologie chez Thomas d'Aquinas.* Paris: Beauchesne, 1972.

Davies, Brian. *The Thought of Thomas Aquinas.* Oxford: Clarendon Press, 1992.

Dupré, Louis. *Passage to Modernity: An Essay in the Hermeneutics of Nature and Culture.* New Haven, CT: Yale University Press, 1993.

Emery, Gilles. "Essentialism or personalism in the treatise on God in St Thomas Aquinas?" *The Thomist* 64/4 (2000): 521–63.

—— *Trinity in Aquinas.* Ypsilanti, MI: Sapientia, 2003.

Gavrilyuk, Paul L. *The Suffering of the Impassible God: The Dialectics of Patristic Thought.* Oxford: Oxford University Press, 2006.

Grant, Robert M. *Irenaeus of Lyons.* The Early Church Fathers series. New York and London: Routledge, 1997.

Green, Joel B. *Salvation.* Understanding Biblical Themes series. St Louis, MO: Chalice Press, 2003.

Griffiths, Paul J. and Reinhard Hütter. *Reason and the Reasons of Faith.* New York and London: T. & T. Clark International, 2005.

Hadot, Pierre. *Philosophy as a Way of Life: Spiritual Exercises from Socrates to Foucault.* Edited by Arnold Davidson. Translated by Michael Chase. Oxford: Blackwell, 1995.

—— *What is Ancient Philosophy?* Translated by Michael Chase. Cambridge, MA: Harvard University Press, 2002.

Hammond, Nicholas. *Playing with Truth: Language and the Human Condition in Pascal's Pensées.* Oxford: Oxford University Press, 1994.

Hart, David Bentley. "The mirror of the infinite: Gregory of Nyssa on the *Vestigia Trinitatis.*" In Sarah Coakley (ed.) *Re-Thinking Gregory of Nyssa.* Oxford: Blackwell, 2003.

Hayes, Zachary. *The Hidden Center: Spirituality and Speculative Christology in St Bonaventure.* New York: Paulist Press, 1981.

Hengel, Martin. *The Atonement: A Study of the Origins of the Doctrine in the New Testament.* Translated by John Bowden. London: SCM Press, 1981.

Hill, Edmund. *The Mystery of the Trinity.* Introducing Catholic Theology series. London: Geoffrey Chapman, 1985.

Holder, Arthur G. (ed.) *The Blackwell Companion to Christian Spirituality.* Oxford: Blackwell, 2005.

Howells, Edward. *John of the Cross and Teresa of Avila: Mystical Knowing and Selfhood.* New York: Crossroad, 2002.

Inge, Denise (ed.) *Thomas Traherne: Poetry and Prose.* London: SPCK, 2002.

Jenkins, John I. *Knowledge and Faith in Thomas Aquinas.* Cambridge: Cambridge University Press, 1997.

Johnson, Mark F. "God's knowledge in our frail mind: the Thomistic model of theology." *Angelicum* 76 (1999): 25–45.

Jordan, Mark. *Ordering Wisdom: The Hierarchy of Philosophical Discourses in Aquinas.* Notre Dame, IN: University of Notre Dame Press, 1986.

Keating, Daniel A. *The Appropriation of Divine Life in Cyril of Alexandria.* Oxford: Oxford University Press, 2004.

Kerr, Fergus. *After Aquinas: Versions of Thomism.* Oxford: Blackwell, 2002.

LaCugna, Catherine Mowry. "The trinitarian mystery of God." In F. S. Fiorenza and J. P. Galvin (eds.) *Systematic Theology: Roman Catholic Perspectives,* vol. 1. Minneapolis: Fortress Press, 1991.

Lash, Nicholas. *Believing Three Ways in One God: A Reading of the Apostles' Creed.* Notre Dame, IN: University of Notre Dame Press, 1993.

Levering, Matthew. *Scripture and Metaphysics: Aquinas and the Renewal of Trinitarian Theology.* Oxford: Blackwell, 2004.

Lienhard, Joseph T. "*Ousia* and *hypostasis*: the Cappadocian settlement and the theology of the 'One Hypostasis'." In S. T. Davis, D. Kendall, and G. O'Collins (eds.) *The Trinity: An Interdisciplinary Symposium on the Doctrine of the Trinity.* Oxford: Oxford University Press, 1999.

Louth, Andrew. *The Origins of the Christian Mystical Tradition: From Plato to Denys.* Oxford: Clarendon Press, 1981.

—— *Maximus the Confessor.* London: Routledge, 1996.

Lubac, Henri de. "On a thought by Pascal." In *Theology in History.* San Francisco: Ignatius Press, 1996.

McGuckin, John Anthony (ed.) *The Westminster Handbook to Origen.* Louisville, KY and London: Westminster John Knox Press, 2004.

McIntosh, Mark A. *Mystical Theology: The Integrity of Spirituality and Theology.* Challenges in Contemporary Theology series. Oxford: Blackwell, 1998.

—— *Discernment and Truth: The Spirituality and Theology of Knowledge.* New York: Crossroad/Herder, 2004.

McPartlan, Paul. *The Eucharist Makes the Church: Henri de Lubac and John Zizioulas in Dialogue.* Edinburgh: T. & T. Clark, 1993.

Macquarrie, John. *Heidegger and Christianity.* The Hensley Henson Lectures, 1993–4. New York: Continuum, 1999.

Mangina, Joseph L. *Karl Barth: Theologian of Christian Witness.* Louisville, KY and London: Westminster John Knox Press, 2004.

Marshall, Bruce D. "Trinity." In Gareth Jones (ed.) *The Blackwell Companion to Modern Theology.* Oxford: Blackwell, 2004.

Merriell, D. Juvenal. *To the Image of the Trinity: A Study of the Development of Aquinas' Teaching.* Toronto: Pontifical Institute of Mediaeval Studies, 1990.

—— "Trinitarian anthropology." In Rik Van Nieuwenhove and Joseph Wawrykow (eds.) *The Theology of Thomas Aquinas.* Notre Dame, IN: University of Notre Dame Press, 2005.

Meskin, Jacob. "Secular self-confidence, postmodernism, and beyond: recovering the religious dimension of Pascal's *Pensées*." *Journal of Religion* 75/4 (1995): 487–508.

Meyendorff, John. *Byzantine Theology: Historical Trends and Doctrinal Themes,* 2nd edn. New York: Fordham University Press, 1979.

Milbank, John and Catherine Pickstock. *Truth in Aquinas*. London and New York: Routledge, 2001.

O'Hara Graff, Ann (ed.) *In the Embrace of God: Feminist Approaches to Theological Anthropology*. Maryknoll, NY: Orbis, 1995.

O'Meara, Thomas F. *Thomas Aquinas: Theologian*. Notre Dame, IN and London: University of Notre Dame Press, 1997.

Polkinghorne, John. *Faith, Science, and Understanding*. New Haven, CT: Yale University Press, 2000.

Ramsey, Arthur Michael. *The Glory of God and the Transfiguration of Christ*. 1947. London: Darton, Longman & Todd, 1967.

Russell, Robert J., Philip Clayton, Kirk Wegter-McNelly, and John Polkinghorne (eds.) *Quantum Mechanics: Scientific Perspectives on Divine Action*. Vatican City: Vatican Observatory Press, 2002.

Smith, James K. A. *Introducing Radical Orthodoxy: Mapping a Post-Secular Theology*. Grand Rapids, MI: Baker, 2004.

Smith, Ruth L. "Relationality and the ordering of differences in feminist ethics." *Journal of Feminist Studies in Religion* 9 (Spring–Fall, 1993): 199–214.

Southern, R. W. *Saint Anselm: A Portrait in a Landscape*. Cambridge: Cambridge University Press, 1991.

Springsted, Eric O. *The Act of Faith: Christian Faith and the Moral Self*. Grand Rapids, MI: Eerdmans, 2002.

Talley, Thomas J. *The Origins of the Liturgical Year*. New York: Pueblo, 1986.

Torrance, Alan J. *Persons in Communion: An Essay on Trinitarian Description and Human Participation, with Special Reference to Volume One of Karl Barth's* Church Dogmatics. Edinburgh: T. & T. Clark, 1996.

Torrell, Jean-Pierre. *Saint Thomas Aquinas*, vol. 2: *Spiritual Master*. Translated by Robert Royal. Washington, DC: Catholic University of America Press, 2003.

Trigg, Joseph W. *Origen*. The Early Church Fathers series. London and New York: Routledge, 1998.

te Velde, Rudi. *Participation and Substantiality in Thomas Aquinas*. Leiden: Brill, 1995.

——*Aquinas on God: The "Divine Science" of the* Summa Theologiae. Aldershot: Ashgate Publishing, 2006.

Volf, Miroslav. *After Our Likeness: The Church as Image of the Trinity*. Grand Rapids, MI: Eerdmans, 1998.

Ward, Graham (ed.) *The Postmodern God: A Theology Reader*. Oxford: Blackwell, 1997.

Webster, John (ed.) *The Cambridge Companion to Karl Barth*. Cambridge: Cambridge University Press, 2000.

Williams, Rowan. "*Sapientia* and the Trinity: reflections on the *De Trinitate*." In B. Bruning (ed.) *Collectanea Augustiniana: Mélanges T. J. Van Bavel*. Leuven: Leuven University Press, 1990.

——*Arius: Heresy and Tradition*, rev. edn. Grand Rapids, MI: Eerdmans, 2002.

——"The deflections of divine desire: negative theology in trinitarian disclosure." In O. Davies and D. Turner (eds.) *Silence and the Word: Negative Theology and the Incarnation*. Cambridge: Cambridge University Press, 2002.

Wolterstorff, Nicholas. *John Locke and the Ethics of Belief*. Cambridge: Cambridge University Press, 1996.

Index